LABOR
and the
AMERICAN COMMUNITY

By DEREK C. BOK *and* JOHN T. DUNLOP

A TOUCHSTONE BOOK
PUBLISHED BY SIMON AND SCHUSTER

ISBN 0-671-20366-5
ISBN 0-671-20415-7 Pbk.
Library of Congress Catalog Card Number: 78–92184
Designed by Andor Braun
Manufactured in the United States of America

7   8   9   10

Contents

Preface

IN EARLY 1966, under the auspices of the Special Studies Project of the Rockefeller Brothers Fund, we agreed to undertake this study of labor and the American community. It would have been more consonant with the traditions of the Special Studies Project to have worked toward a report to be signed by a distinguished panel of labor, management, and public representatives. After consultation with interested parties, however, we strongly recommended against such a procedure because the divergent views of so many participants and observers in the labor field would have made it difficult to reach agreement on any but the most general propositions. Therefore, the following book is entirely our own. In writing it, however, we have benefited, particularly in the formative period of our ideas, from the advice of a small advisory committee headed by David Rockefeller, under whose initiative the project was started. For several years, Mr. Rockefeller had been disturbed by what he saw on the labor-management scene, and it was his thought that an analysis of the internal, community, and employer relationships of the labor movement would be a valuable and timely contribution to the general understanding of the field. Other members of the advisory committee were Victor Borella, Arthur F. Burns, William F. Butler, Louis W. Cabot, Dana S. Creel, Nancy Hanks, David A. Morse, A. H. Raskin, Donald B. Straus, David Sullivan, and Frazar B. Wilde. We are deeply grateful for their interest, suggestions, and critical comments. They

7

should be absolved from any responsibility for our judgments and suggestions.

This study afforded us a rare opportunity to explore individually, or in small groups, a broad range of relevant issues with chief executive officers of businesses, local and national political leaders, professional politicians, public relations staffs in business, labor leaders and their staffs, government agency staffs, and research specialists. It was rewarding, for instance, not only to examine the experience of labor and business leaders on political action and community activity of unions, but also to discuss these programs with elected officials, professional politicians, and community leaders.

A number of research projects, organized and supported by this study to supplement and fill gaps in published materials, enriched our understanding of particular facets of our undertaking. Professor Leo Troy of Rutgers University developed special union membership and union financial data not previously available from the records of the Bureau of Labor-Management Reports of the U.S. Department of Labor. A monograph reporting these rich data in detail is to be published separately. Survey research data have been made available to us from the Survey Research Center of the University of Michigan, and we have had access to the unpublished results of public opinion polls. Several special studies were made concerning the community and political activities of labor organizations in Los Angeles, St. Louis, New York, Texas, and Louisiana. We are also grateful for reports prepared with help from Michael Schwartz and Gordon Davis on community unions in Watts, Newark, and Chicago. Professor Malcolm Salter of the Harvard Business School helped to collect and analyze material that enhanced our understanding of the problems of union administration and of the opportunities to apply more modern methods of management to internal decisions of labor organizations.

One of the very considerable advantages of our relations with the Special Studies Project of the Rockefeller Brothers Fund has been the superb quality of the staff associations. Miss Nancy Hanks, executive secretary, maintained a lively interest in the study and helped to plan and give direction to numerous sessions essential to our work. Miss Jane Dustan worked with us in the New York offices of the Fund over the past three years and gave invaluable help by providing research assistance, undertaking a large number of inter-

views, checking notes and references, working with the publisher, and at every turn greatly facilitating our work.

Special thanks are also due to the staff of the Special Studies Project, particularly to Mrs. Celeste Sismilich, who served as Miss Dustan's very able assistant during much of the study.

Mr. Richard Kluger of Simon and Schuster edited the manuscript with both stern regard for the interests of the reader and sympathetic attention to our views. He has very materially improved the manuscript.

We take this opportunity to express our appreciation to the many officers and representatives of labor organizations, managements, and state and federal agencies, as well as elected public officials, who spent hours answering our questions, sharing their experience and insights, providing detailed information, and permitting us to review internal reports and records. Their cooperation contributed greatly to our effort to undertake a broad review of the major issues involving labor unions in contemporary society and to take a fresh approach to a number of stubborn problems.

DEREK C. BOK
JOHN T. DUNLOP
July 1969

Trade Unions and Public Opinion:

How Fares Labor's Ark?

IT MAY seem curious to begin a book about labor unions with a discussion of public opinion. The more conventional approach would have called for a broad introductory sketch of the American labor movement—its history and structure, its organization and dominant characteristics. But an examination of the attitudes toward the labor movement that are held by the public, the business community, workers (especially union members), and intellectual critics may do more to lay a groundwork for the remainder of the study by exposing the issues involving labor unions that most concern and divide the American community.

The attitudes of these different groups also represent an important force affecting the process of labor relations and the activities of labor organizations. The actions of employers toward unions are conditioned by the views which businessmen share with respect to the strength of unions, the sentiments of their members, and the motives and objectives of their officers. The sentiments of union members can have a decisive influence on the goals and tactics of labor organizations, since the leaders must periodically run for office. Finally, the opinions of the public at large, and of certain influential groups in particular, often can have a marked effect upon the behavior of the union leader. In some cases, community opinions may be influential simply because many union leaders value public esteem. In other instances, the pressure of opinion stems from the latent threat that if the public is too long ignored, its views may be translated into regulatory legislation.

More often still, public opinion will have an influence simply because a hostile climate can weaken the loyalty of the members, harm the union in its political activities, or prejudice its efforts to organize new groups of employees.*

The General Public

Opinion polls have long made clear that a large majority of the American public approves of unions, *in principle*, and of the right of employees to join the union of their choice. The degree of support tends to vary from one segment of the population to another; it is higher in the North than in the South, and substantially higher among manual workers than among farmers. Nevertheless, a clear majority of every major group approves the existence of unions—whether the group is defined by region, occupation, age, income, or political party. The most frequently cited evidence for these beliefs is the question asked over a period of years by the American Institute of Public Opinion (Gallup): "Do you approve or disapprove of trade unions?" The answers, recorded below, provide a fever chart of public opinion toward unionism. Despite several declines—notably after World War II and the postwar strikes, the McClellan Committee revelations of 1957, and the strikes that occurred at many missile sites in 1961—approval of unionism has never dipped below 60 percent.

---

* The discussion that follows is based upon polls conducted by the American Institute of Public Opinion, Louis Harris Associates, Elmo Roper, and the Opinion Research Corporation (O.R.C.). It should be recognized, of course, that opinion polls have definite limitations.[1] Even if adequate samples have been selected and interviews have been properly carried out, any single poll may be heavily influenced by some recent event of only temporary significance. The impressions that the polls convey, moreover, often will be affected considerably by the choice of issues and the phrasing of the questions. Finally, however accurately the public's opinions are represented, most polls do not reflect the intensity with which these views are held. These limitations caution against any effort to attach too great a significance to opinion polls or to draw ambitious conclusions from modest fluctuations in the views they record. But the fact remains that these polls still provide the best approximation of public sentiment on a number of issues relevant to this study. And many of their weaknesses can be mitigated by taking care to compare a given poll either with the results of similar polls in other years or with similar questionnaires prepared by other agencies on the same subject matter.

Apart from opinion polls, the discussion draws upon various published works prepared by intellectual critics and representatives of business. This source of information is indispensable in exploring the attitudes of intellectuals, whose views are not specifically identified in opinion polls. In addition, speeches and other public statements are helpful in giving greater texture and depth to the views recorded in opinion polls for executives and businessmen.

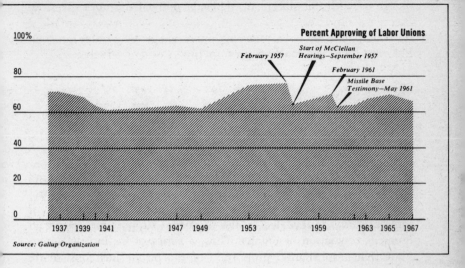

100%   **Percent Approving of Labor Unions**

February 1957   Start of McClellan
Hearings—September 1957

80   *February 1961*

*Missile Base
Testimony—May 1961*

60

40

20

0

     1937   1939   1941   1947   1949   1953   1959   1963   1965   1967

Source: Gallup Organization

Even higher proportions, ranging above 80–85 percent, have affirmed the worker's right to join a union of his choice in order to bargain collectively with his employer. The sole exception to this principle has involved the rights of public employees. As late as 1941, 79 percent of the public believed that government workers should not even be allowed to join a union. In the intervening years, however, attitudes on this question have shifted to conform more closely with the prevailing views on employees in the private sector. A clear majority now seems to concede that teachers, firemen and policemen should be permitted to join a union, with one crucial qualification: that they should not necessarily be allowed to strike.*

The wide support that the public gives to unions seems to be rooted in a conviction that they are necessary to enable workers to receive improvements in wages and working conditions. In an Opinion Research Corporation poll conducted in 1960, 60 percent of the public expressed the view that the gains workers had made

---

* Thus, a Harris poll in October 1967 revealed that 52 percent of the public disapproved of the right of teachers to strike, 41 percent approved, and 7 percent were not sure. As for policemen, 56 percent were opposed to their right to strike, 36 percent were in favor, and 8 percent were not sure. With respect to firemen, 57 percent approved, 35 percent disapproved, and 8 percent were unsure. A Gallup survey reported in August 1969 that 59 percent rejected giving teachers the right to strike.

in this country were chiefly due to labor unions; only 17 percent
disagreed with this statement, while 17 percent did not express an
opinion. Conversely, other O.R.C. polls reflect a prevailing belief
that companies do not try to pay higher wages when they prosper,
but must be forced to do so, presumably by organized labor.

	1946	1950	1954	1957	1962	1966
Have to be forced	56%	55%	43%	42%	47%	52%
Pay as prosper	34	35	37	34	36	36
Don't know	10	10	20	24	17	12

Whatever the public's opinion on the *principle* of unions and
union membership, very different sentiments are expressed regarding the *practices* of these organizations. One indication of
these attitudes is revealed by the persistent support for strict government regulation of unions. Thus, a series of Gallup polls suggests that a substantial proportion of the public has consistently
favored tighter regulation of labor unions, and this proportion has
remained largely the same, even after the federal government
enacted sweeping regulatory provisions in 1959.

	1950	1959	1962	1966
Present laws not strict enough	44%	49%	48%	40%
Present laws are adequate	24	20	25	25
Present laws are too strict	17	6	10	11
Don't know	15	25	17	24

Some readers may regard these figures as merely another illustration of the traditional distrust of Americans for large and
powerful organizations. Yet it is reasonably clear that the public is
especially concerned over the power of labor unions. For example,
a 1966 O.R.C. poll reveals much more permissive attitudes toward
government regulation of business.

	Should regulate closely	*Little or no regulation needed*	*No opinion*
Labor union	58%	24%	18%
Business	33	49	18

Equally revealing are the attitudes of the public toward the future growth of trade unions. According to a series of O.R.C. polls, it has long been evident that only a small minority of the public would "like to see labor unions grow larger and stronger."

	1946	1950	1954	1958	1962	1966
Unions should grow larger	26%	23%	26%	27%	26%	21%
Unions have grown enough	46	52	45	45	51	56
Unions are too large now	22	16	11	6	9	10
No opinion	6	9	18	22	14	13

Once again, the public appears to be more concerned over the power of unions than over that of other institutions in the society. For example, according to a Gallup poll in 1941, 75 percent of the public believed that union leaders had accumulated "too much power," while only 59 percent expressed the same view of the power held by a "few rich men and large corporations," and only 32 percent considered the federal government too powerful. A decade later, the proportions had shifted markedly, but the power of organized labor still aroused particular concern. Thus, a Gallup poll in 1950 revealed that 62 percent of the public believed that unions had too much power over the country, whereas 50 percent took the same view of "politicians" and only 38 percent had the same opinion with respect to "big business."

Many factors have contributed to the uneasiness of the public toward unions. Many people have disapproved of union efforts to sign contracts requiring employees to join and pay dues against their will.* Featherbedding and restrictive work practices have also been resented. (In fact, Gallup polls reveal that 77 percent of the public favored legislation to forbid featherbedding in 1943, although the proportion has since dwindled to less than 50 percent.) A substantial segment of the public also holds labor mainly responsible for inflation and doubtless disapproves of unions on that score. But none of these factors seems to have ranked particu-

---

* Responses to the union-shop issue are particularly likely to fluctuate according to the form in which the question is put. Perhaps the fairest phraseology is that of a 1966 Gallup poll: "Do you think that a person should or should not be required to join a union if he works in a unionized factory or business?" In answer to this question, 49 percent replied in the negative, 42 percent responded affirmatively, and 9 percent did not venture an opinion.

larly high on the public's list of grievances against the labor
movement. Instead, the major sources of discontent have been
three in number: corruption and graft, unnecessary strikes, and a
broad skepticism regarding the competence and integrity of union
leaders.

No consistent series of polls exists with which to chart the ebb
and flow of public opinion on the subject of corruption within
trade unions. Nevertheless, it is clear that there was wide suspicion
concerning the honesty of union leaders long before the McClellan
Committee's revelations in 1957. Gallup polls in 1941 revealed that
74 percent of the public believed that "many" union leaders were
racketeers. A Roper poll in the same year found that only 14.9
percent considered "all" or "most" union leaders to be honest,
while 28.5 percent felt that "half," "less than half" or "none" of the
union leaders were honest. In the wake of the McClellan hearings,
a Gallup poll reported late in 1957 that 43 percent believed "corruption and graft" to be "pretty widespread" in labor unions while
34 percent indicated that these shortcomings were "limited to just
a few unions," and 21 percent expressed no opinion.

A number of polls have revealed a widespread belief that
union leaders often help to cause unnecessary and inconvenient
strikes. A Harris poll in 1967 disclosed the following opinions on
the major causes of strikes:

Cost of living keeps going up	67%
Union leaders encourage strikes	62
Management refuses to understand labor's problems	37
Rank and file are more militant than leaders	26
Workers don't do better unless they strike	24

Although these findings may not come as a surprise, there are
other attitudes about strikes that are not so commonly appreciated. Despite the fears of many labor leaders, there is little evidence that the public blames the unions for every major strike. For
example, a succession of polls conducted just after World War II
revealed that a majority of the public sided with the workers
rather than the management in all but one of a series of major
work stoppages.[2] And a 1968 Harris poll showed that in the matter
of strikes the public sympathized almost equally with unions and
with management; although it was much more likely to sympathize

with neither.* While the evidence is fragmentary, there is also little support for the view, expressed by several government officials in recent years, that the public has become progressively disenchanted with strikes. In 1966, only 27 percent of the public favored a law outlawing all strikes, while 33 percent had indicated in 1949 that the right to strike should be denied. Moreover, a series of Gallup polls suggests that the intensity of public feeling about strikes appears to have declined since the rash of major strikes after World War II. From 1946 to 1949, the public rated "strikes and labor-management problems" as "the most important problem" facing the nation. By the 1960's, despite highly publicized strikes or threatened strikes in the airline, railroad, local transit and publishing industries, the strike problem received negligible recognition by the public, since it had been eclipsed by such issues as unemployment, space, peace, race and national defense.

Some of the clearest insights into the attitudes of the public toward unions can be found in polls about labor leaders. When people are asked about unions as such, their responses may be colored by the general attitude affirming the legitimacy of unions in our society. When asked about labor leaders, however, they can express themselves more freely on the actual behavior of unions. The resulting opinions are highly critical. Perhaps the most revealing evidence can be found in a series of Roper polls contrasting the confidence of the public in union leaders as compared with its confidence in other influential persons in the society.

Which one of these groups do you feel is doing the most good for the country at the present time?

	1942	1948	1957	1965*
Labor leaders	6%	12%	4%	7%
Business leaders	19	20	12	12
Religious leaders	18	34	46	26
Government leaders	28	11	17	31
Congress	6	4	8	12
Don't know	23	19	13	18

* Percentages add to more than 100 because some respondents gave more than one answer.

---

* Only 20 percent sympathized with unions, 22 percent with management, and 40 percent with neither; 18 percent expressed no opinion.

Which one of these groups is doing the least *good for the country?*

	1942	1948	1957	1965
Labor leaders	36%	30%	44%	29%
Business leaders	6	6	12	13
Religious leaders	7	4	6	10
Government leaders	3	12	6	8
Congress	12	27	7	5
Don't know	36	21	25	35

Here is a list of people who frequently make speeches and write articles on how to improve the nation's economic welfare. In general which one *group's thinking would you believe in* most? *Which* one *group's thinking would you believe in* least?

	1965*
Believe most	
Labor leaders	8%
Business leaders	34
Government officials	34
College professors	16
Don't know	11
Believe least	
Labor leaders	42%
Business leaders	13
Government officials	9
College professors	19
Don't know	20

* Percentages add to more than 100 because some respondents gave more than one answer.

In sum, a rather clear set of opinions emerges on the subject of labor unions. The principle of unionism and the right to join a union are heavily supported, apparently on the ground that organization is needed to make sure that adequate wages and working conditions will be secured from management. On the other hand, large proportions of the public are highly critical of the actual behavior and leadership of organized labor. In particular, opinion polls have consistently shown a widely shared belief that unions help cause unnecessary strikes, that corruption is widespread, and that union leaders are more unreliable, self-interested, and insensitive to the general welfare than other highly influential figures in the society.

Workers and Union Members

It is often said that working people have very little class consciousness in the United States. This impression is confirmed by the views that manual workers have expressed in public-opinion polls on the subject of unions. No large differences separate the views of these workers from those of the public as a whole. In fact, there is no significant divergence between the attitudes of the public and those of unorganized manual workers. Where moderate differences of opinion exist, they reflect not a special class sentiment, but a somewhat different set of attitudes held by union *members.*

Union members are more likely than is the general public to have formed an opinion, one way or the other, about unions; as one might expect, they are also consistently more favorable to unions, though only moderately so. The following polls are illustrative.

Should workers be allowed to join labor unions? (*Opinion Research, 1966*)

	Yes	No	No opinion
Union members	92%	4%	4%
Public	74	12	14

Do you agree that the gains that workers have made in this country are chiefly due to labor unions? (*Opinion Research, 1960*)

	Agree	Disagree	No opinion
Union households	82%	9%	9%
Public	66	17	17

Although union members are also more disposed than is the general public to have unions grow larger, an O.R.C. survey in 1966 reveals that even a clear majority of the members believe that labor unions are either large enough already or too large.

	Unions should grow larger	Unions have grown enough	Unions are too large now	No opinion
Union members	38%	47%	5%	10%
Public	21	56	10	13

Unlike the other poll responses presented here, there is in the
answers to this question a steady trend over the years. In 1945, 62
percent of the union members desired that labor organizations
grow larger. By 1950, the proportion had fallen to 50 percent. In
1962, it sank to 46 percent, and it fell still further to 38 percent in
1966.

It is also significant that members are almost as disposed as
the general public to favor close government regulation of unions.

*Should the government regulate unions closely or should there
be little or no regulation?* (*Opinion Research, 1966*)

	Regulate closely	Little or no regulation	No opinion
Union members	55%	34%	11%
Public	58	24	18

Much the same pattern is reflected in the attitude of union members toward strikes and their regulation by the government. Although members are somewhat more inclined than the general
public to reject government intervention, surprisingly high proportions of union members are prepared to have the government step
in when serious stoppages occur. A 1967 Gallup poll provides an
illustration.

*It has been suggested that no strike be permitted to go on for
more than twenty-one days. If after twenty-one days the union
and the employer cannot reach an agreement, the courts would
appoint a committee that would decide the issue and both
would be compelled to accept the terms. Would you favor or
oppose this idea?*

	Favor	Oppose	No opinion
Union members	55%	41%	4%
Public	68	22	10

The desire for government regulation suggests that many
members are suspicious of unions. In general, their criticisms are

the same as those put forward by the general public: corruption, autocratic behavior and strikes. Although union members are less inclined to find fault on these grounds than the public as a whole, two fifths or more of the rank and file seem highly critical of their leaders for these reasons.* Still more revealing is the attitude of union families toward the ability and reliability of the labor leader in treating public economic issues. As the following table reveals, even this audience places less confidence in union leaders than in any of the other specified groups.

In general, which one group's thinking (on questions of economic welfare) would you believe in most? Which one group's thinking on economic welfare would you believe in least? (Roper, 1965)

Believe most	Govt. officials	Business leaders	Union leaders	Professors	No opinion
Union member in family	34%	24%	19%	17%	12%
Public	34	34	8	16	11

Believe least					
Union member in family	11	20	27	21	20
Public	9	13	42	19	20

One significant point about these polls is that they ask the union member to evaluate unions in general rather than his own union in particular. There are no comprehensive surveys on the latter question, but more specialized studies exist that are worthy of comment.

---

* The following polls are illustrative:

Do unions represent the wishes of the members or the wishes of a few leaders? (Harris, 1968)

	The members	A few leaders	Not sure
Union members	50%	40%	10%
Public	30	50	20

Are corruption and racketeering pretty widespread in unions, limited to just a few local unions, or isn't there any corruption or racketeering? (Gallup, 1957)

	Pretty widespread	Limited	None	No opinion
Union member families	40%	44%	3%	13%
Public	43	34	2	21

At the request of the Central Labor Council of Alameda County, a research team from the University of California surveyed over seven hundred members from a representative sample of sixteen local unions in the area.[3] In response to the survey, 70 percent or more of the respondents were either "satisfied" or "highly satisfied" with the job their unions were doing in the field of wages, fringe benefits, grievances, working conditions, political action, and social and recreational activities; 63 percent of the members indicated that none or only a few of the decisions of their officers were based on self-interest; 81 percent declared that the officers took the opinions of the members into consideration in making all or most of their decisions. And 77 percent believed that every member of the union had at least a reasonable chance of being elected to office, while 68 percent were pleased all or most of the time with the way in which their local meetings were run.

Similar findings were reported in a confidential independent survey of the members of one large, predominantly craft union. Although commentators have never included this union among the most progressive, democratic labor organizations, a nationwide sample of its members rated it highly in every one of a number of respects. Once again, 70 percent or more of the respondents considered the union "good" or "very good" in collective bargaining and protecting the economic interest of its members. In addition, 83 percent considered the union "very good" or "good" with respect to honesty in handling funds; 79 percent gave similar ratings to the quality of its leaders; and 77 percent considered it "good" or "very good" in the extent to which the rank and file had a voice in union management.

These studies suggest that when members are asked to evaluate unions in general, they may be influenced by the rather unfavorable image of labor organizations that is shared by the general public and is often reflected in communications media. On the other hand, when members are merely asked to comment on the union with which they are directly familiar, the responses are much more favorable. These conclusions are supported by additional surveys revealing that active members, who regularly attend meetings, take a more positive view of their union and its government than inactive members of the same organization.[4]

Beyond these attitudes on specific problems, it would be extremely interesting to discover how union members envisage the role that the labor movement should play in American society.

Unfortunately, so little work has been done along these lines that it is impossible to know how members as a whole feel toward union efforts to take an active part in such matters as community welfare and the pursuit of economic and social reform. Nonetheless, there are a few scattered polls on individual locals that confirm the general impression that members conceive of their union primarily as an instrument for achieving better wages and working conditions and that community and reform activities play a distinctly secondary role. A typical study of this kind, involving five union locals in Columbus, Ohio, revealed that substantial majorities in each local believed that their union should seek "higher wages, better working conditions, protection of workers from management, better health, pension, and insurance benefits, more job security, better seniority plan, equal rights for all workers," while only one third to one half of the members believed that their union should strive for ". . . more social and recreational activities for workers, a better life for all people in the community . . . and more political action from members."[5]

Organized labor could hardly work seriously toward broad economic and social reforms without becoming heavily involved in political and legislative affairs. Yet most union members are also cool to the idea of large-scale political participation.* Roughly 90

---

* The following polls of union members were conducted by the Opinion Research Corporation. (Figures in parentheses denote the opinions of the public as a whole.)

Is it proper for unions to urge their members to vote?

	1956	1964
Proper	91% (85)	89% (83)
Improper	8 (11)	9 (9)
Don't know	1 (4)	2 (8)

Should unions take up collections among their members for political campaigns?

	1950	1956	1964
Should	37% (25)	21% (15)	17% (11)
Should not	55 (63)	72 (78)	79 (80)
Don't know	8 (12)	7 (7)	4 (9)

Is it proper for unions to campaign for political candidates and campaign to get them elected?

	1950	1956	1964
Proper	53% (37)	40% (28)	33% (25)
Improper	36 (48)	54 (60)	57 (58)
Don't know	11 (15)	6 (12)	10 (17)

[continued]

percent do approve of unions asking their members to vote, and more than two thirds support union efforts to campaign for public housing, minimum-wage laws and similar issues. But less than one third of the members approve of forming a labor party or taking up collections among the rank and file for political campaigns or even working to defeat candidates with unfavorable political records.

It is interesting that there should be such a contrast between the support given to working for new legislation and the seeming disapproval of active involvement in political campaigns. This disparity is hard to reconcile, since unions can hardly lobby effectively for new laws without making efforts to elect sympathetic candidates. In the minds of some union members, the disapproval of campaigning may simply reflect a broad suspicion against politics and politicians. Other members may feel that campaigning for the election of sympathetic candidates can yield only remote and uncertain results, whereas efforts in behalf of specific legislation can bring immediate and calculable benefits.

It is also interesting to note that membership support for political action of all kinds has apparently declined over the past fifteen years. This trend is quite striking in view of the fact that many labor organizations have greatly increased their efforts to interest the membership in politics through broader education programs and greater emphasis on political editorials and columns in their newspapers and communications media. In general, therefore, the evidence suggests a rather tenacious preference for a union movement heavily directed toward collective-bargaining and job-oriented goals, with less political involvement than has been traditional among the labor movements of other industrial democracies.

Is it proper for unions to campaign for public housing, minimum wage laws, et cetera?

	1950	1956	1964
Proper	76% (66)	70% (67)	69% (55)
Improper	11 (19)	19 (22)	24 (25)
Don't know	13 (15)	11 (11)	7 (20)

Would you be for or against workers forming their own political party?

	1950	1956
For	22% (20)	28% (20)
Against	50 (56)	67 (66)
No opinion	28 (24)	5 (14)

Employers and Executives

Despite the determined campaigns by many managements to keep labor unions out of their plants, businessmen do not proclaim hostility toward the principle of unionism. Quite the contrary. If anything, executives are slightly more inclined than is the public as a whole to accept the legitimacy of unions and the employee's right to join the organization of his choice. This tendency has been uniformly revealed in opinion polls extending back over the past thirty years. In fact, the right to join a union has been explicitly recognized as a part of management ideology for more than half a century.* As early as 1909, the president of the National Association of Manufacturers could declare: "I freely accord to wage earners the same right to unite in lawful organization for the advancement of their mutual interests as is accorded to all classes of citizens."[6]

In part this attitude may reflect the strong belief among businessmen in individual freedom and the right to associate for lawful purposes. But many executives now concede, as they rarely did several decades ago, that unions can play a valuable role in protecting employees against abuses. To quote Lemuel Boulware, of General Electric, a management representative renowned for developing a "hard line" toward unions:

> We believe in the union idea. We think unions are here to stay. We think some among even the best of employers might occasionally fall into short-sighted or careless employee practices if it were not for the presence or distant threat of unions.[7]

On the other hand, there are also important qualifications to management's acceptance of unionism. In contrast to many labor spokesmen and social scientists, employers do not normally regard the union as a valuable means for providing greater "democracy in the workplace" or for achieving the psychological benefits of a more active participation by workers in decisions affecting their jobs and their welfare. Nor have most businessmen been inclined to modify their strong, traditional belief in the autonomy of the

---

* This attitude, however, has not prevented many employers from trying to defeat organizing drives by blacklisting union sympathizers or firing employees who have joined the union.

firm and the need for a unity of command and an ultimate control by management over the operation of the company. Thus, the great majority of executives oppose industrywide unions and bargaining, in part because it sacrifices the autonomy of the individual firm.* Management is also firmly opposed to the unionization of foremen, since this would detract from the unity of command and control.† Most important of all, businessmen have fought hard to avoid having to bargain over issues of "management prerogative," issues that they feel would dilute the employer's authority over matters he deems essential to the running of the enterprise.

Within these limits, executives are prepared to accept the principle of unionism. But they are also more inclined than is the general public to distrust and deprecate the actual conduct of unions. Although the differences are not always great, larger proportions of executives believe that unions have grown too powerful, that they are undemocratic, that corruption and graft are widespread, and that union leaders are ineffective and unreasonable.

These observations merely suggest the views of management on a few isolated points. But it is possible to discover a much more tightly integrated philosophy toward trade unions and labor relations by looking to a number of management publications, notably those of the Chamber of Commerce and the National Association of Manufacturers.[8] To be sure, these organizations do not speak for all of American management. They do not necessarily reflect the views of the most sophisticated executives, just as the polls set forth earlier do not always represent the views of the most sophisticated union members. Nor do they accurately reflect the views of labor-relations officers, for these management officials have more continuous, professional contact with unions and often are more tolerant of unions than the top executive whose views are set forth

---

* There are many businessmen who take a different view, especially employers in highly fragmented, competitive industries who have long bargained with a single union on a multi-employer basis. Employers, for example, in the garment or the local hotel industry, find such bargaining arrangements more economical and favor the stability they derive from knowing that a single uniform schedule of wages and terms of employment has been set for them and their competitors.

† This opposition is notably absent in several industries, such as construction and printing, where foremen have been union members for many years. In the maritime industry, supervisors on vessels have long been organized into unions.

below. Nevertheless, after comparing the views expressed in these publications with public-opinion polls and a wide assortment of other evidence, one may safely say that the following complaints against unions would be shared by a majority of high business executives in this country:

1) Unions often insist upon restrictive practices and work rules that hamper efficiency.

2) Union negotiators constantly try to enlarge their share of control in the plant, thus narrowing the employer's freedom of action and curtailing his ability to manage the enterprise effectively.

3) Unions fail to comprehend fully the effect of market forces on the firm and, in particular, the effect of mounting costs upon the firm's ability to compete, to prosper, and therefore to continue to provide employment for the members of the union.

4) Union leaders often disturb the basic harmony of interests between the employer and his employees by seeking to discredit management in the eyes of the workers and by generating needless frictions and misunderstandings.

These criticisms and anxieties have given rise to a clearly defined set of arguments against organized labor, elaborated not only by the N.A.M. and the Chamber of Commerce but by many leading industrialists as well. A basic tenet of this philosophy is that unions have been allowed to grow too powerful. Even by 1946, the president of the Chamber of Commerce could assert that ". . . the American labor movement is the most aggressive and most powerful in the world."[9] In 1960, a Chamber of Commerce publication emphasized: "The problem we are facing is the tremendous economic and political power which union officials can and do use both legally and illegally."[10] These views are further reflected in public-opinion polls, which reveal that "proprietors and managers" are more inclined than any other occupational group to assert that "labor unions have become too big and powerful for the good of the country."*

---

* In 1960, toward the end of the Eisenhower administration and only one year after the passage of the Landrum-Griffin Act, "business and professional" remained the only occupational category wherein a larger proportion considered labor to have more influence over Congress than business. The following responses were recorded in a 1960 Gallup poll asking whether business or labor had more influence. [*continued*]

One may well ask how unions can be considered "too power-ful" if businessmen are prepared to concede the right of every worker to join a union. But businessmen would find no inconsistency here, for they believe that unions have become too powerful, not because of their genuine appeal to the workingman, but because society has allowed them to enjoy certain powers and tactics that have been denied to business and to other groups in the society. Among these are the following:

1) The right (within legal limits) to boycott the products of employers with whom the union has a dispute.

2) The right to picket customers and, on a limited basis, to picket deliveries of an employer whose workers do not wish to join a union.

3) The right (in most states) to execute a union-shop contract compelling workers to join a union and pay dues, even against their will.°

4) The *de facto* power in many communities to utilize force and intimidation, laws to the contrary notwithstanding.

5) The right to combine the local unions of several competing employers into industrywide unions and to engage in industry-wide bargaining.†

Since these practices not only enhance union power but often are injurious to the interests of third parties, one might ask why the unions have been allowed to retain these special privileges. According to management spokesmen, this has occurred because many people believe that strong unions play a vital role in promoting the economic welfare of the wage earner. But businessmen feel that careful analysis will show that unions are not really making such a contribution. Although many unions seem to win substan-

	Business	Labor	No difference	No opinion
All adults	43%	34%	10%	13%
Business and professional	38	41	9	12
White collar	43	37	11	9
Farmers	42	23	17	18
Laborers	48	29	10	13

° According to an Opinion Research Corporation study of February 1966, 72 percent of small businessmen and 68 percent of managers favor a legal prohibition of such contracts, whereas 58 percent of the general public and 35 percent of union members take this position.

† According to one source, 69 percent of a random sampling of businessmen opposed industrywide bargaining and favored a law prohibiting it.[11]

tial wage increases and other benefits, the *real income* of the worker cannot rise faster than increases in productivity. As a result, it is argued, the additional wage gains are illusory, since they are counteracted by the price increases brought about by rising labor costs. Indeed, many businessmen would assert that unions may actually diminish the welfare of workers, and of society as a whole, by pursuing policies which result in wasteful strikes or limit productivity through restrictive work practices.

In view of these arguments, why has the government allowed unions to retain such privileges? Management spokesmen have advanced three reasons. First, labor has become so powerful politically, and so important a source of money and support for the Democrats in particular, that public officials are unwilling to face the facts and take corrective action. Second, union leaders have succeeded, with the help of inertia on the part of many employers, in persuading their members that the union's privileges are necessary to maintain the worker's welfare. Finally, such dissent as may be forthcoming from the ranks of the union is generally ignored or, worse yet, "choked by dictatorship."*

According to many executives, the results of excessive union power are ominous for the economic health of the country. In exercising their power, union leaders too often ignore what these businessmen regard as economic principles of fundamental importance. Labor leaders do not sufficiently appreciate the role of profits in calling forth investment and thereby encouraging economic growth. They often fail to realize what executives often take for granted—namely, that higher wages cannot be financed out of profits and that prices must inevitably rise if wage increases surpass improvements in productivity. They are not sensitive enough to the inequities produced by inflation or the dangers it poses to economic growth, full employment and the achievement of a healthy balance of payments. Many businessmen are also troubled about effects of labor's political power and the political aims they attribute to union leaders. What particularly concerns these executives is the prospect of a "welfare state" involving larger redistribu-

---

* Managers and proprietors seem more inclined to consider unions autocratic than does the public as a whole or union members generally. In response to a 1957 O.R.C. poll, only 15 percent of managers believed that members "have enough to say" about the running of their union, while 57 percent felt that union leaders "usually run things to suit themselves." The general public divided 21 percent and 50 percent on the same question, while union members were evenly split.

tions of income, incursions upon private property, freedom and individual initiative, and, ultimately, a weakening of the social forces that businessmen consider vital to continued growth and progress. The president of the Kimberly-Clark Corporation was typical of many in this group when he warned in 1957 that organized labor ". . . now openly proclaims its intention to dominate our political life to the end that its own basically socialistic aims . . . may be fastened more firmly on the nation."[12]

Intellectual Critics

Over the past thirty years, a constant critique of the labor movement has been carried on by writers of a liberal or left persuasion.* Much of this work has taken the form of articles appearing in such magazines as *Progressive, Commonweal, The Nation,* and *The New Republic,* as well as in such books as B. J. Widick's *Labor Today,* C. Wright Mills' *New Men of Power,* and Sidney Lens' *The Crisis of American Labor,* to cite a few well-known examples. These writers have not been professors specializing in labor relations, although a few, like Mills, have been academic scholars. Nor have they held influential posts in a union, although several, like Lens, have had some connection with the labor movement. Yet they doubtless speak for a large segment of the liberal intellectual community, and their criticisms are already being echoed repeatedly by students associated with the "New Left."†

Although these critics display many differences in emphasis and detail, the main outlines of their thought are markedly similar. Almost all seem to agree that the root problem of American labor lies in the inadequacy of its leadership. They have not always held this opinion. In the thirties, many CIO leaders were thought to be well endowed with initiative, ability and daring. According to

---

* Once again, the opinions that follow are not shared by all liberal intellectuals. Michael Harrington, for example, takes a more sympathetic view of unions.

† The following editorial in the *Harvard Crimson* (November 6, 1968) sounds all the traditional themes in speculating on the effects of repealing the National Labor Relations Act in a Republican administration:

It is possible of course that without its comfortable berth in trades and the Democratic Party and harassed by an anti-labor law, the labor movement might regain the urgency it lost in the 30's. Labor might then become a suitably militant ally for blacks, students, and the poor. But more likely, with growth stifled and membership yielding to automation, an already tired labor movement will simply wither.

liberal critics, however, much of this imagination and energy has now given way to bureaucratic routine: "The young radicals of yesterday are middle-aged pork-choppers today." This alleged deterioration is often linked to the growing affluence of labor unions, an affluence that is repeatedly emphasized by these writers through vivid descriptions of union buildings ("the luxurious headquarters of trade unions, each the capitol of a labor sa- trapy"), union automobiles ("sleek air-conditioned Cadillacs"), and union conventions (replete with "eight-dollar steaks" and "heated swimming pools").* In such an atmosphere, the critics charge, "there has been a corrosion of labor's evangelism," and "the social dynamism that once attracted idealistic men and women to union service has dribbled away." As Daniel Bell describes it, "The real sickness lies in the decline of unionism as a moral vocation, the fact that so many union leaders have become money-hungry, taking on the grossest features of business society."[13]

These quotations are biting indeed, and many of the writers involved would doubtless concede that the language they employ is a shade too flamboyant and probably unfair to important segments of the labor movement. Nevertheless, the terms that are used reveal the indignation that is felt toward the style of life and the attitudes displayed by many labor leaders, especially in an era when many workers and union members are still at the edge of poverty.

Criticism of this kind has pained many of the more sensitive and reflective union leaders. After all, are they not doing a job demanding a degree of skill and effort comparable to highly paid people in other walks of life? And why are they singled out for criticism when the same life style seems to flourish even more abundantly in the ranks of business and the professions? To this reaction, the intellectual critics have a clear answer that is well worth noting as an indication of the criteria used by these writers in judging the labor movement. In the words of James O'Gara of *Commonweal* magazine:

> I suspect that the ethics of the labor movement are at least as high as those in the business or professional community. But that is not enough. The labor leader whose vision is not loftier than that of the average businessman or doctor or lawyer ought to get out of the movement. Organized labor should

---

* It is a curious fact that similar characterizations are seldom, if ever, used in connection with other institutions, notably foundations, that are devoted in large part to aiding the poor and the disadvantaged.

function as the conscience of an industrial society, speaking
for those who would otherwise have no voice and holding aloft
for all to see a vision of a society animated by justice. Some
unions still do exactly that. But a union which ignores this duty
has lost its vocation. It has become just another business,
better than some, perhaps, and worse than others, and entitled
to exactly that amount of respect, neither less nor more.[14]

This lack of dedication, in the eyes of intellectual critics, goes
far toward explaining the drab performance of the union in dis-
charging its traditional functions. Thus, it is not surprising to them
that union membership has declined as a percentage of the labor
force, that unions have had little success in organizing white-collar
workers in most sectors, that Congressional investigations have
disclosed many cases of corruption, and that union leaders seem
less and less in touch with the rank and file.

These are not the only problems—nor indeed the most important ones—that have led such writers to accuse the labor movement
of "sleepwalking along the corridors of history." In the long run,
even greater damage may result from labor's failure to construct a
more powerful political arm to promote the interests of working
people. According to this reasoning, the role of private bargaining
is constantly being restricted. Government policies to contain inflation and to avoid critical strikes will progressively limit labor's
freedom of action at the negotiating table. At the same time, it is
increasingly clear that some of the gravest threats to the worker,
notably automation and unemployment, cannot be attacked effectively through negotiations, but must be met by government
action. Thus, a labor movement that cannot develop imaginative
political programs and press them effectively upon the government
will not adequately represent the interests of its members.

But political action—like other union programs—should not
be devoted simply to the interests of the membership. Intellectual
critics have always emphasized that the labor movement should
take up the defense of all the underprivileged and strive to introduce reforms to bring about a greater measure of social justice.
Indeed, such critics have often gone so far as to try to infiltrate the
movement itself in order to induce the unions to assume this role.
Socialists like Daniel DeLeon advocated this course of action before the turn of the century, and supporters of Eugene McCarthy,
such as Professor David Hoeh and Reverend Channing Phillips,
began speaking of the need "to liberalize organized labor" and "to

move into positions of power within organized labor" immediately after the defeat of Hubert Humphrey in 1968.[15] This call for political action is perhaps the most vital part of the liberal intellectual position on the unions. An editorial in *The Nation* captured the sentiment most vividly in 1936:

> Gradually the way is being cleared for a campaign to organize industrial labor which will, within a very few years, *shift the whole emphasis of political and social life in this country*. . . . For the unorganized millions of workers, as well as for those who welcome the advent of a great revivifying force in American life, there are stirring days ahead.[16] [Emphasis supplied.]

By the 1960's, prediction had given way to prescription, but the basic premises were largely the same. As A. H. Raskin observed in 1963:

> Labor has no more urgent job in the 60's than the focusing of its political energies on the conquest of want, illiteracy, intolerance; the building up of both health and decent housing; the realization of limitless promise of the scientific Golden Age. And apart from their general social necessity, these undertakings would be vastly more inspiriting, to union membership and leadership alike, than the present ever more routine function in the policing of day-to-day plant grievances and the writing of mechanized contracts.[17]

Measured with this yardstick, the performance of the unions seems inevitably disappointing. It is true, as many of the critics recognize, that the AFL–CIO has adopted resolutions on a steadily widening range of social problems. And it is likewise conceded that unions have lobbied hard for antipoverty, Medicare, and civil-rights legislation, and that a few labor organizations have done much to overcome racial discrimination within their own ranks. To union leaders who consider activities of this sort as incidental to the task of bargaining and administering contracts, such achievements constitute a creditable enough record. To the intellectual, who feels that these functions are the most important contributions that unions can make, labor's efforts seem halfhearted.

It is worth noting how sharply the views of these writers contrast with the opinions commonly expressed in business circles. The two groups unite in criticizing the labor movement, especially its leaders. But the substance of these criticisms—and the assump-

tions on which they rest—could not be further apart. To most
executives, organized labor appears extremely powerful, both at
the bargaining table and in the political arena. To the intellectual
critics, unions are unable to deal effectively with the most pressing
economic issues confronting their members and wield even less
influence in political matters.

Public Opinion in Perspective

The views recorded in this chapter are highly critical of the
actions of unions and their leaders. But one must be cautious in
evaluating these opinions. For varying reasons, different groups in
the society have found unions to be a source of irritation, and this
may color their views of the labor movement.

Consider the social reformer, the liberal intellectual, the radical critic. Such men are separated from the labor leader and the
union member by widely differing educational and social backgrounds, and this fact alone can easily produce serious misunderstandings. To social critics, moreover, unions have seemed to be
the only large political force that could conceivably play a major
part in pushing persistently for broad social and economic
changes. As a result, the failure of unions to take a more active,
radical stance has caused these critics to feel a keener disappointment than they might have felt in other industrial democracies
where unions have been flanked by additional forces of reform such
as labor and radical political parties and cooperative movements.

The disappointments of liberal critics have been reinforced by
the events of the thirties, when the CIO seemed to give promise of
becoming the moving force for a liberal reconstruction of society.
Much of this hope was sheer illusion, arising from the fact that
labor's traditional aim of organizing workers happened to coincide
—under depression conditions—with the liberals' concern for helping the poor and disadvantaged. As economic conditions improved, these objectives no longer coincided. Unions were now the
spokesmen for workers who had become more and more prosperous. The inevitable result was to foster widespread disillusion
about unions in liberal circles and to engender much talk about a
decline in the social vision of the labor movement. In retrospect,
the comparisons with the thirties seem seriously distorted. Much

of the radical ethos surrounding the unions in the Depression was supplied by outsiders who joined the movement temporarily, either to help the underdog or to engineer a social revolution. The mainstream of the movement did not depart fundamentally from its traditional goals of winning new members and bargaining for better wages and working conditions. If anything, it was less concerned then than it is now over social and economic issues outside the range of its own immediate interests. Today, more manpower is being used to lobby for these causes, more space is devoted to them in union periodicals, and more money is being spent to support candidates who favor social reforms than ever was true during the thirties.*

The hostility of business toward unions is even easier to understand. In the short run, at least, unions are a natural adversary to the business community both at the bargaining table and as political spokesmen for the less affluent segments of society. The labor leader is inclined to favor lower profits and higher wages, more progressive taxes, and larger social-security and unemployment benefits. Many businessmen are bound to disagree and regard the unions as something of a menace. These tensions are common to most capitalist countries. But they are much enhanced in the United States by the peculiar structure of the collective-bargaining system. In Europe, a company normally joins with all of its competitors in multi-employer associations to bargain over *minimum* wages and conditions for the industry, and the terms that are set are often far below the levels actually observed in the employer's plant. Under these circumstances, collective bargaining is often relatively painless; it may even help employers by preventing competition from low-wage, marginal firms. In the United States, however, most employers bargain individually with

---

* In 1936, organized labor contributed the unprecedented sum of $750,000 for political purposes; in 1968, labor expended what is conservatively estimated to be $6 to $7 million to aid Democratic candidates. As for lobbying, union representatives took very little part in working for the passage of the labor and social legislation of the thirties.[18] This record contrasts sharply with the present situation, wherein more than a hundred lobbyists represent labor in Washington and spend large portions of their time on such issues as Medicare and civil-rights legislation.[19] With respect to union publications, Martin Perline offers the following comparisons of the percentage of space devoted to social reform in Federation periodicals.[20]

American Federationist (1938)	20.3%
CIO News (1939)	14.4
American Federationist, AFL–CIO (1963–64)	40.8
AFL–CIO News (1964)	28.3

the union, so that negotiations set the actual wages to be paid and establish, often in minute detail, the conditions under which the employees will work. The employer often finds this process inconvenient and irritating; it restricts his prerogatives and deprives him of flexibility in running his business. He also suffers from the added danger that the union may require wages and conditions that will cause him to be undercut and undersold by foreign or nonunion competitors. These pressures are bound to color the views of many executives toward the labor movement.

To the public as a whole, the communications media tend to project an unfavorable image of organized labor. The point is not that newspapers and television networks are dominated by the views of antilabor owners. Such a view would doubtless be naïve. Nevertheless, when *both* businessmen *and* intellectuals are often unfavorably disposed toward the labor movement, the picture of unions that is conveyed by the public media can easily suffer. If nothing else, the public perception of unions must be affected somewhat by the natural tendency, human tastes being what they are, for most of the arresting news stories about unions to involve strikes, corruption, and other unfavorable events.

The sources of public disaffection with the unions probably go much deeper than the media. Among established institutions, labor organizations are unique in the degree to which they rely on compulsion and overt force to gain their objectives. Although unions are not necessarily at fault for any particular strike, it is because unions exist that strikes have become a familiar feature of industrial life. Labor organizations have likewise succeeded in making union membership compulsory for millions of employees. Whether or not these practices are desirable, the fact remains that unions gain their ends through the use of compulsion, and institutions that do this will inevitably arouse resentment.

The Relevance of Public Opinion to the Study

The forces just described could easily distort some of the views of various groups about how unions and their leaders operate. To seek out such errors and correct them when they occur will represent a major aim of this study, not only because it is important to promote truth for its own sake but also because such faulty impressions can easily give rise to misguided government policies and shortsighted reactions on the part of all those who must deal with unions.

The views of the different groups toward organized labor are also relevant because of the common premises they share concerning the behavior of unions. All groups are heavily committed to the legitimacy of unions and to the workers' right to join a union and bargain collectively with their employer. There is an equally clear understanding that labor organizations should not be given absolute rights and prerogatives. Even union members agree that such basic union activities as the strike should be subject to regulation where necessary to protect overriding interests of other groups in the society. In addition, there is a strong belief that unions should be attentive and responsive to the wishes of their members. And one can also discern—for example, in the strong sentiments in every group against the union shop—a pervasive feeling that unions should not pursue their objectives at the expense of individual interests, unless it can be clearly shown that such action is necessary to achieve an important interest of the group as a whole. These judgments about unions form a useful framework for evaluating unions in this study, since the very fact that the premises are shared by such different groups gives them greater weight than the personal preferences of a particular author.

In addition to identifying common value premises, this survey of opinion also helps to shape and confirm the issues to be taken up in the study. For example, it is clear that a careful examination must be made of the internal operation and administration of unions. Problems such as corruption and autocratic behavior weigh far too heavily on the minds of every interested group to be overlooked. In addition, public opinion discloses a much more fundamental issue concerning the internal life and behavior of trade unions. One of the most arresting facts to emerge from opinion surveys is the tendency of every group to assume that the union member, on the whole, represents a rather passive and potentially constructive force and that the union leader must be blamed for all the shortcomings of the labor movement. Although businessmen and intellectuals could not disagree more on the role they would like to have the labor movement play, both groups conceive of the employee as a natural ally who has simply been led astray by the union leader. The businessman is inclined to feel that the employee is basically satisfied and that his interests are fundamentally compatible with those of management; it is merely that the labor leader forever tries to rupture this harmony for his own private ends. The intellectual, on the other hand, asserts that employees are not genuinely satisfied and would readily take up the banner of social and economic reform if only their leaders could supply them with the necessary spark and vision.

There are great dangers in assuming too quickly that the faults of unions lie mainly with their leaders. If the assumption proves inadequate or incorrect, not only will a great disservice be done to many union officials but society may also go badly astray in trying to construct a viable labor policy. During the forties, for example, employers successfully petitioned for laws requiring elections to authorize strikes or union-shop provisions. In each case, management forces were confident that once employees were left with a free choice in the matter, they would normally vote to reject the union shop and to accept management's terms without striking. Yet in each case the voting resulted in such heavy and regular majorities for the union that the laws were eventually discarded. Similar dangers could arise in the future if one assumes too readily that wage restraint can be accomplished by publicly exhorting union leaders or that more responsible union behavior will result through legislating greater union democracy. In short, to think realistically about unions and issues of labor policy requires an adequate grasp of the role of union leaders and the forces that determine their behavior. And in particular, it is necessary to have a clear view of the part played by the union member—what he demands of his union, how effectively these demands can be pressed, and, in the last analysis, how much discretion remains with the union leader to determine the policies of his organization.

Public opinion also underscores the importance of several issues of collective bargaining that make up the second part of this study:

1) Inflation is clearly a problem of major importance. It can undermine the economic position of persons with relatively fixed incomes, jeopardize the balance of payments, and provoke the government into taking corrective measures that often result in unemployment. Although the public is divided on who is responsible for rising prices, roughly one third believe that unions are primarily to blame, and a majority of employers seem to share this view. Hence, the evidence will be examined to discover how much unions and collective bargaining have actually contributed to inflation. Moreover, in view of the interest that has been shown both here and abroad in constructing wages and incomes policies, it will be useful to consider the methods by which the government may influence collective bargaining in order to minimize its inflationary tendencies.

2) Strikes, particularly those affecting vital industries or inconveniencing large numbers of people, have agitated the public more than any other issue in the labor-relations field. Many union leaders and businessmen regard the disruption caused by a strike as a small and necessary price to pay for free collective bargaining. But it is clear that the weight of public opinion does not subscribe to this position. Instead, a majority appears to believe that the government should impose a settlement on disputes in major industries, at least where a strike has already gone on for a substantial period. As a result, it seems appropriate not only to consider the evidence bearing on the extent and gravity of strikes but to examine the various ways in which the government might help to protect the public against serious work stoppages.

3) Featherbedding and restrictive work practices have likewise aroused great controversy and interest in years past. Although public concern has diminished in the last decade, large majorities have favored laws to outlaw such behavior. Many businessmen still believe that restrictive practices represent one of the most serious problems in industrial relations, and many more would agree that the issue may become more important in the future as a result of growing automation and mounting competition from abroad. At the same time, the general knowledge about these practices is meager. The entire subject is permeated with colorfully loaded words, yet few would be able to provide even a working definition of featherbedding, let alone make a decent estimate of its extent in American industry.

4) The shift in public opinion over the past thirty years on the right of government employees to join unions and bargain collectively has been accompanied by important changes in public policy, notably in President Kennedy's Executive Order 10988 and in the laws of several industrial states, which have extended and protected the right of public employees to organize and bargain. These recent initiatives have exposed a number of problems. Can a sovereign body bind itself by the terms of a collective-bargaining agreement? On what matters shall a government negotiate with a union? Above all, can government employees be allowed to strike,

and if not, what alternatives can be offered these workers to
guarantee them equitable wages and working conditions? Although these regulatory problems have dominated the discussion
thus far, there are other equally important problems having to do
with the significance of widespread organization among public
employees. What will happen when the trade unions bargain with
an employer (the state) who does not face the market pressures
that restrain unions and employers when they negotiate in the
private sector? Will wages rise inordinately? Will inefficient work
practices become widespread? What changes will occur in labor's
political behavior if large, public-employee unions arise that have
a much more vital stake in the government than the traditional
union in private industry?

    5) One of the most controversial viewpoints disclosed in this
survey is the claim of many intellectual critics that collective
bargaining is losing much of its importance to society and to union
members as well. If this charge is correct, unions will presumably
grow less important to their members and to society unless they
can develop some new and vital functions to perform. But one
should be cautious before accepting such dour predictions. In this
country above all others, collective bargaining has shown a remarkable creativity in providing pension plans, health and welfare
programs, profit-sharing arrangements, cost-sharing plans, automation funds, and a host of other innovations. In light of this history,
the current state of collective bargaining must be examined to
determine whether there are new needs that it can fill.

    Beyond the concrete problems of collective bargaining lie
other areas of union activity, to be considered in the concluding
portion of this study. Over the past thirty years, unions have become increasingly involved in activities beyond collective bargaining: political action, community-service projects, and in a wide
range of welfare activities for their members. Underlying these
efforts is an issue of fundamental importance: How broad a role
should the labor movement play in this country? This issue has
divided businessmen and liberal intellectuals. Within the labor
movement itself, the issue has set important unions in the
AFL–CIO at odds and has recently helped to bring about the
departure of the United Auto Workers from the Federation.

    Closer examination of the subject shows that there are a
number of disagreements of fact concerning labor's activities in the

field of economic and political reform. Intellectual critics and business executives have quite different views about the political influence of the labor movement and the ultimate objectives it is pursuing. Moreover, despite the charges by intellectuals that unions are doing too little outside the domain of collective bargaining, almost no effort has been made to determine systematically just what the unions *are* doing—in political action, in welfare activities for their members and dependents, in antipoverty campaigns, and community programs of all kinds. Thus, a major effort in the third part of this study will be devoted to trying to fill these important gaps in our knowledge. Beyond the search for facts, of course, lies the ultimate question of how much emphasis organized labor *should* place on activities not closely connected to bargaining, activities that may indeed be designed to help the poor and disadvantaged rather than the members who pay dues and elect the officers of the union.

A Profile of the Labor Movement:

Its Membership and Leadership[1]

IN 1966, 18.3 million men and women in the United States were paying dues to labor unions.* By 1968, the figure is estimated to have exceeded 19 million. The number of employees subject to collective-bargaining agreements is still larger by three quarters of a million, since not all employees covered by collective-bargaining agreements are required to be union members. The past five years have been a period of marked expansion in the total number of union members, reversing a decline which set in with the recession of 1958. Nevertheless, the labor force has grown so rapidly that union membership in 1968, as a percentage of employment in nonagricultural enterprises, was little more than 28 percent compared to the level of 33–34 percent achieved in the middle 1950's.†

Union members are organized into more than 70,000 local unions, which are in turn affiliated with 190 national or international unions (except for fewer than a thousand locals, with an aggregate of little more than a half million members, that are directly affiliated with the AFL–CIO or in single-firm and local unaffiliated unions). Two thirds of these national unions with

---

* This Bureau of Labor Statistics figure excludes approximately 1.4 million members of national and international unions with headquarters in the United States who were in Canada and other areas outside the United States. This figure also excludes many members, who may number over 900,000, exempt from dues payments in whole or in part as provided in union constitutions, by virtue of being unemployed, on strike, retired, apprentices prior to being eligible to membership, or in military service.[2]

† Appendix A of this chapter presents the data on union membership, and union membership as a percentage of nonagricultural employees, for the years 1930–68 in chart form.

more than three quarters of the membership are affiliated with the AFL–CIO, even after the disaffiliation of Walter Reuther and the Auto Workers in 1968.

The Union Member[3]

Union members do not represent a mirror image of the entire adult population, or even the work force, of this country. Instead they are rather heavily concentrated in certain income ranges, educational levels, industries, occupations and regions.

Income. Unionists fall mainly in the middle-income group, with relatively few members numbered among the very rich or the very poor. In 1965, 69.1 percent of union heads of households had incomes ranging from $5,000 to $10,000. Among households headed by nonmembers, only 43.4 percent fell within this income range. Conversely, only 3.9 percent of union household heads received less than $3,000 during the same year, while 14.2 percent earned more than $10,000. For nonunion households, the corresponding figures were substantially larger; 14.3 percent fell below $3,000, while 21.6 percent earned over $10,000.

Education. Much the same pattern carries over to the area of education. In 1965, 44 percent of all union heads of households had an education that extended through all or part of high school (but not beyond). Only 32 percent of nonunion household heads fell within these categories. At the upper end of the scale, however, the figures were sharply reversed. Only 1.4 percent of all union family heads had received a college diploma and .4 percent had received an advanced degree. Among family heads who were not members of unions, over eight times as many (11.4 percent) had graduated from college, while almost twenty times as many (7.8 percent) had obtained an advanced degree.

Sex. It is well known that women workers are underrepresented in labor unions. Among employees outside the agricultural sector, only one woman in seven belongs to a union, while one man in every three is a member. To some extent, the difference is explained by the heavy employment of women in clerical and sales occupations and in service industries, where unions have traditionally made little headway. But other causes are probably more important. Women can be among the most loyal, determined union members when their sense of injustice is aroused. In general, however, women outside the professions appear not to place the importance that men do on matters connected with employment; they frequently do not conceive of themselves as remaining in a job for a working lifetime. Thus, even in operative and semiskilled occupations, which are quite highly organized, women seem to be less inclined to join unions than men.

Industry and Occupation. Union members are distributed most unevenly among different industries, as the following table reveals:

Industry	Percentage organized
Transportation, communications, public utilities	74.7%
Construction	70.9
Manufacturing	50.0
Mining	47.2
Government	14.1
Services	10.5
Trade	9.3
Finance, real estate	2.0
Agriculture	.8

These differences are the result of many factors. The variations in the occupational mix of different industries are significant, for unions seem to have much greater appeal in some occupational groups than others. The prevalence of women in certain occupations helps to explain the low rate of unionization in the trade and service sectors. With a few notable exceptions, white-collar workers have traditionally been cool to unions, especially professional and technical employees. On the other hand, blue-collar employees in the skilled and semiskilled categories seem to be the most promising target for unionization.* Unskilled laborers tend to fall

---

* Selig Perlman, writing in the late 1920's, contended that ". . . manual groups, whether peasants in Russia, modern wage earners, or medieval master workmen, have had their economic attitudes basically determined by a consciousness of a scarcity of opportunity, which is characteristic of these groups and stands out in contrast with the businessmen's 'abundance consciousness,' or consciousness of unlimited opportunity. Starting with this consciousness of

between these poles. They are usually more susceptible than white-collar workers, but they are also more apt to be foreign-born, easily replaceable, quickly intimidated by hostile employers, subject to considerable turnover and thus often frustrating to union organizers seeking to attract continuing affiliation. These differences reveal themselves dramatically in figures comparing the rates of unionization among occupations.

Occupations	Percentage organized
Operatives (semiskilled)	63%
Craftsmen and foremen	50
Laborers (excluding agriculture)	38
Clerical	26
Service	20
Sales	
Managers	5–10
Professional and technical	

Geography. Union membership is not distributed throughout the United States in proportion to population or employment. In general terms, the extent of union organization—measured as a fraction of nonagricultural employment—is greatest in the east-northcentral and eastern industrial states and on the West Coast. The extent of organization is least in the South, the Southwest and the Middle West plain states. There are, of course, important variations within these groupings.[5] For example, there appears to be some tendency for employees in metropolitan areas to be slightly more highly organized than employees in smaller communities.[6]

The five states with the largest employment—New York, California, Pennsylvania, Illinois, and Ohio—contain 48 percent of the union members while they employ 38 percent of the nonagricultural work force. These five states have 8.7 million union members.

Many more characteristics of union members could be cited. For example, it is interesting to note that the union movement

scarcity, the 'manualist' groups have been led to practicing solidarity, to an insistence upon an 'ownership' by the group as a whole of the totality of economic-opportunity extent, to a 'rationing' by the group of such opportunity among the individuals constituting it, to a control by the group over its members in relation to the conditions on which they as individuals are permitted to occupy a portion of that opportunity—in brief, to a 'communism of opportunity.' "[4]

includes about the same proportion of nonwhites as in the non-agricultural work force and that unions contain a disproportionate number of war veterans and Catholics.* But even more important than these demographic factors are the attitudes of union employees on social, political and economic questions. For, in the last analysis, these sentiments will probably have the most direct effects upon the course of union behavior.

As suggested in the first chapter, the opinions of union members are particularly striking in their lack of any special class bias. This remarkable state of affairs has been commented upon by a number of European critics.

> In the experience of the European, industrial strife was a conflict between two classes, almost two distinct orders of mankind, separated from each other by a wide and impossible gulf of habits, attitudes and material conditions. The European was fascinated (in the United States) by the general air of prosperity, the free-and-easy relations between persons on different social levels, the lack of social distinctions, class hostilities, class jealousies, class political issues.[7]

Today, the same pattern still reveals itself in opinion surveys on a wide variety of questions.† Whether the issue is Vietnam, admission of Red China to the U.N., civil-rights legislation, aid to education, the poverty program, a labor party, or government ownership of essential industries, the opinions of union members come within a very few percentage points of those held by the public at large. The same is true of questions touching on attitudes toward society and government. Union members are no more likely than the general public is to feel, in the language of the interview question, that "the people running the country don't really care what happens to people like yourself." Nor are they more likely to feel that what they think "doesn't count very much" or to fear that they "don't have as good a chance to get ahead as most people." And they are as overwhelmingly disposed as the rest of society is to reject the notion that "nobody understands our problems" or that they are "left out of the things going on around us."

---

* In 1959, 48 percent of union family heads were war veterans, as compared with 37 percent for nonunion heads. The respective proportions of Catholics are 30 percent and 18 percent. (From the 1959 Survey of Consumers, Survey Research Center, University of Michigan.)

† The results of these surveys are set forth in Appendix B to this chapter.

It is well to compare these findings with the standard theories that popular writers have expressed about the political sentiments of union members. One view, less prevalent now than two decades ago, maintains that union members are, more than the rest of the population, willing to support sweeping social and economic programs.* Another theory has flowered more recently in the wake of repeated claims of "white backlash" in heavily blue-collar areas. According to this opinion, union members were more "progressive" in earlier decades but have become strongly conservative as their wages and conditions have risen to more comfortable middle-class levels.†

Neither of these theories is well supported by the facts. According to recent opinion surveys, union members as a group do not exhibit any special desire for drastic social and economic change. They reject, by about the same margin as the general public, such current proposals as a negative income tax and a multibillion-dollar program for the cities. And they are much more anxious that the government finance the war in Vietnam and combat crime in the streets than that it maintain welfare programs and campaign against poverty. Nevertheless, union members are not more conservative about these matters than the rest of the population. If anything, they tend to stand two or three percentage points to the liberal side on matters of race, the United Nations, the poverty program, and most other public issues. These tendencies also seem to be remarkably durable. There has been no apparent shift to the right over the past two or three decades. On racial matters, for example, the attitudes of union members have grown steadily *more* tolerant, not less (along with those of most other segments of the society).

Various forces have contributed to this peculiar lack of class sentiment among union members (and other manual workers). One important factor was the extreme heterogeneity of the Ameri-

---

* According to C. Wright Mills, "This is where labor stands: there are labor leaders who are running labor unions, most of them along the main drift; there are left intellectuals who are not running labor unions, but who think they know how to run them against the main drift; and there are wage workers who are disgruntled and ready to do what must be done."[8]

† This view was exemplified by the oft-repeated suggestion during the 1968 Presidential campaign that union members were a leading stronghold of support for Governor George Wallace. In fact, only 15 percent of union members voted for Wallace compared with 13 percent of the total number casting ballots. The 2-percent difference could be ascribed to a variety of factors— e.g., the fact that union members are predominantly male, and males throughout the country were significantly more favorable to Wallace than females.

can labor force in the formative years of industrialization. During this period, a network of language, racial and religious barriers was thrown up by repeated waves of immigration. Particular ethnic groups gained control over different jobs, while recent immigrants and Negro laborers were excluded from the better jobs and later used as strikebreakers by employers. These experiences produced cleavages that kept the labor movement from achieving the degree of unity reached in Great Britain and Scandinavia.

Labor organizations in America also grew up in a society that stressed the ideals of classlessness, individual initiative, and abundant opportunity, a society in which workers enjoyed the right of suffrage and the opportunity for a free public education. In this atmosphere, employees were less inclined than workers in Europe to submerge their sense of individuality and identify with a working class. Many of them, moreover, were constantly presented with opportunities to leave the ranks of labor for management jobs or opportunities in the West. In contrast to Europe, real wages were high and rose rapidly, and the spread between skilled and unskilled wage rates was especially large. As a result, class solidarity was slow to develop and potential leadership was constantly siphoned off into other pursuits.

In Europe, on the other hand, labor movements arose against the backdrop of a feudal tradition that denied workers access to economic opportunity or political power. Under these conditions, European workers were driven together to make common cause to advance their interests. In the political sphere, for example, workers often had to struggle for a decade or more into the twentieth century to achieve such elementary rights as public education and, more important, universal male suffrage. As public issues, these questions were important enough to arouse the working classes for a sustained political effort. In contrast to the experience of America, where such rights were granted much earlier, in Europe ". . . the arising awareness of the working classes expressed above all an experience of *political alienation*—that is, a sense of not having a recognized position in the civic community or of not having a civic community in which to participate."[9]

The sense of working-class solidarity, of separateness from the rest of society, still remains strong in countries like France and Italy. Elsewhere in Europe, notably in Scandinavia, manual workers seem gradually to have been integrated more closely into the entire population. Yet, traditions of working-class sentiment have left their mark upon the shape of the labor movement throughout the entire continent.[10]

The Unions

The American union movement has certain characteristics that give it a special flavor and set it somewhat apart from most of its counterparts abroad.

Size. Despite all of the concern expressed over labor's power, union membership in America is a smaller proportion of the work force than in any of the other major industrial democracies.* While this fact is arresting in itself, its significance grows even larger when one realizes that higher levels of unionization have been achieved throughout Western Europe without benefit of the union shop, without elaborate legal safeguards to protect the workers' right to organize, and without expensive campaigns or professional staffs to organize nonunion employers.

The low levels of unionization in America can be explained largely by two factors. One important factor is the widespread opposition of employers—an attitude no longer prevalent in Europe save in Italy and France. Although American labor leaders

---

* Union Membership as Percentage of Nonagricultural Employed Labor Force

	Union membership (thousands)	Total number employed (thousands)	Percentage of organization
Austria	1,540	2,247	68.5%
Sweden	2,165	3,302	65.6
Belgium	1,700	3,407	49.9
Italy	6,320	14,242	44.4
Australia	1,475	3,448	42.8
England	8,757	22,621	38.7
Netherlands	1,430	3,978	35.9
Germany	7,996	23,733	33.7
France	3,071	10,243	29.0
United States	17,299	60,770	28.5

(Australian data are for 1963; data relating to other countries are for 1965.)[11]

Statistical comparisons of union membership among countries should be used with considerable caution, since the meaning of membership varies greatly. In the United States membership is measured by dues payments, but in Europe not only are dues levels much lower, but membership is not reported according to regular dues payments. In addition, it should be emphasized that the political and economic power of the union movement does not bear any simple relation to the proportion of the labor force that is organized; such power depends on several other factors such as the financial strength of the unions, the nature of the party system, etcetera.

often exaggerate the significance of this opposition, its importance can be seen in the ease with which unions can usually organize blue-collar workers once management has been persuaded to remain neutral. Employer opposition, however, does not wholly explain the stunted growth of the American labor movement. Unionization is proportionately much greater in Italy than in the United States despite widespread hostility from employers, and this has been true even though Italian unions have had to cope with severe internal divisions, less impressive achievements at the bargaining table, and an almost total lack of formal organizing efforts. In other countries, moreover, employers were often openly hostile toward unions in the early stages of organization, but their policies eventually changed because they could not overcome the determination of the unions.[12]

A second factor has been the lack of solidarity among workers in the United States. Perhaps opportunities for advancement and geographic movement were greater in this country, thus strengthening the hold on individualism; perhaps employees were influenced by higher wages and rising living standards derived from a chronic scarcity of labor and rapidly increasing productivity. Whatever the explanation, the small size of the United States union movement must probably be attributed in part to the lack of a strongly felt need on the part of many employees to band together for mutual protection. In Europe, on the other hand, feelings of worker solidarity were much stronger. They were typically buttressed by a network of mutually reinforcing institutions based on working-class support—political parties, cooperatives, youth groups, educational programs, and even banks, newspapers and other commercial undertakings. In short, though there is evidence in several countries that class lines may be weakening, the European labor leader has been able to capitalize on a cultural milieu in which union membership has been the natural response of the working man.

Unions and Politics.   The lack of a distinctive ideology among the working people of this country has also had a marked influence on the political activity of American unions. The labor movement in the United States is unique in failing to produce a political party based explicitly on working-class support. Nor have American unions followed the example of many European countries by splitting into rival organizations based upon party lines. In

France and in Italy, there are three large national organizations of workers representing Communist, Socialist, and Christian Democrat ideologies. In Belgium, Socialist and Christian Democrat federations coexist. In the Netherlands separate Catholic, Protestant, and Socialist labor organizations have been established. Cleavages have also developed in the United States, most notably during the thirties, when John L. Lewis and the Congress of Industrial Organizations defied the American Federation of Labor. But characteristically this division took place over pragmatic questions of tactics and jurisdiction in organizing the mass-production industries and not because of any deep-seated differences in religion or political philosophy. In keeping with the nature of the conflict, the differences between the AFL and CIO were submerged twenty years later in the formation of the AFL–CIO.

Strong Local Unions. Unions in this country were generally forced to achieve recognition and establish bargaining relationships on a plant-by-plant basis rather than by agreement with a strong national or regional association of employers. This process encouraged the growth of active local unions in the plant, with important functions to perform. In some industries, of course, control over collective bargaining has gravitated to the national or regional level. But even in these sectors, local unions still retain considerable influence over the administration of the contract and over political and community activities.

The importance of local unions is reflected in the financial holdings of labor organizations in the United States. At the end of 1966, all union bodies had combined assets of $1,839,000,000, and the combined assets of local unions and intermediate bodies* exceeded those of the international unions. In the same year, local unions had receipts of $1,256,000,000; intermediate bodies net receipts of $14,000,000 and international unions net receipts of $560,000,000.[13]

This pattern is not encountered abroad. Viable plant locals do exist in Scandinavia, but even there the grievance process is less developed than in this country, and local bodies have little or no control over political matters, organizing other plants, community

---

* Locals of the same international union in a metropolitan area or state often form a district council or state council for purposes of bargaining or organizing. Such bodies typically maintain their own financial status. Intermediate bodies may also be composed of a number of locals in the same industry from different international unions.

activities, and similar matters that occupy the attention of many local unions in this country. In Britain and Australia, plant organizations may have a strong influence over local disputes and working conditions, but these bodies often behave quite independently of the national unions, to the frequent embarrassment of their parent organizations. On the continent of Europe, the contrast is even more marked. Local unions rarely exist at all and union representatives in the plant share whatever power they have over grievances and local problems with other institutions, such as the elected workers' councils, over which they have little direct control.[14]

A Loose Federation. At higher levels in the union structure, the labor movement in America has remained markedly decentralized in the sense that the central federation has had relatively little authority over its member unions. In part, this is the result of the lack of a class sentiment strong enough to transcend the attachments of workers to their own separate crafts and occupations. In part, the absence of a strong federation reflected the predominance in our labor movement of bargaining rather than political action, for which a powerful central body would have been more necessary to enable the movement to act in unison in election campaigns and lobbying efforts. In any event, the AFL was founded with the explicit understanding that the affiliated unions would retain their autonomy. Throughout its history, the federation had to rely, with mixed success, on persuasion and conciliation instead of exercising formal powers or sanctions. Even today the situation is not much changed. The AFL–CIO has acquired some power to investigate and suspend affiliates for corruption or Communist influence, but it has little or no authority over the bargaining and strike policies of its members, nor is it able to control their membership requirements or political activities.

There are other countries, notably Britain and Australia, where the central federation is also rather weak. But the situation is more often to the contrary. For example, the major Swedish federation negotiates directly with the central employers' organization to establish broad wage guidelines that are binding on its constituent unions. Member unions must also gain the consent of the federation before initiating a strike involving more than 3 percent of their membership and must agree to include various rules in their constitutions safeguarding the rights of individuals with respect to membership, discipline, transfers, and the like. Even in matters involving local grievances and discharges of workers, the federation has ultimate power to enter into binding settlements. In other European countries, the degree of power actually exercised by the central organizations is harder to assess, but certainly the Belgian and Dutch federations are highly centralized, and it is generally assumed that the dominant Communist federations in France and Italy have extensive control over the policies of their member unions.

The Near Unions

It has been assumed that everyone understands what a union is in this country. But any careful newspaper reader will agree that the definition of "union" has become decidedly vague in recent years. A decade ago, the National Education Association, an organization of a million schoolteachers and administrators, prided itself on its status as a thoroughly professional association. Today, the teachers affiliated with N.E.A. have embraced the idea of negotiation with school boards and have resorted to strikes and other collective sanctions to achieve their proposals. Professional associations of nurses have come to engage in mass resignations and other forms of economic pressure to achieve collective agreements. In professional athletics, football, basketball, and baseball associations have all sprung up seeking negotiations and uttering ominous threats of stopping play. Police officers' associations in a few localities have invented the "blue plague," an exotic illness known only to uniformed patrolmen in search of improved benefits. And in Southern California an erstwhile man of the cloth has even tried to organize Catholic priests. The near unions tend to have supervisory employees as members; their members are more independent, have higher incomes, and are more responsive to professional concerns than are members of conventional unions. It is unclear whether these organizations are in transition toward more conventional unions or constitute a more permanent form of employee organization.

Although the total size of the near unions is uncertain, their combined membership is certainly greater than two million persons. With the addition of the near unions, the composition of membership in all employee organizations is less heavily concentrated than in the AFL–CIO alone among certain income and occupational groups. It is also more diverse in its goals, its strategies and its political outlook.

The Union Leader

In contrast to the labor movements in other countries, unions in the United States boast a much higher number of full-time officials.* To some extent, this tendency may reflect a distinctive American attitude toward administration, for business enterprises, universities, and various other private organizations also seem to have particularly large staffs in this country. But the root of the matter, once again, lies in the decentralized pattern of union organization and labor relations in the United States. For the most part, collective bargaining has not consisted of negotiations with huge industrywide employer associations. The predominant tendency has been to conduct separate negotiations with individual plants and companies. As a result, there are a vast number of contracts to be negotiated. Because it is so decentralized, bargaining can also grapple with the particular working conditions of the individual plant to a degree not duplicated abroad. And once the agreement is signed, the local union is the natural agency for taking up the countless individual complaints and questions that arise concerning the application and administration of the contract. To perform all this work, a host of union officials is required.

Almost all labor leaders have come up from the ranks of the members working in the plants and crafts that the unions represent. Unlike the situation in several other countries, especially in the underdeveloped world, very few of these leaders have backgrounds as lawyers, politicians, editors, professors or intellectuals. Nor are their fathers predominantly found outside the ranks of labor. In a 1967 survey of union presidents, secretary-treasurers, and vice-presidents, 37 percent were found to have fathers who

---

* Ratio of officers to members

United States	1:300
Denmark	1:775
Australia	1:900
Sweden	1:1700
Great Britain	1:2000
Norway	1:2200

—Seymour M. Lipset, "Trade Unions and Social Structure: II," *Industrial Relations,* February 1962, p. 93.

were skilled workers; 17 percent were the sons of semiskilled and unskilled employees; 7 percent were the children of foremen. No more than 11 percent of the fathers owned a business and only 4 percent were executives.*

At first glance, these figures seem surprising. In a mobile society without marked class divisions, one might have expected that union leaders would be drawn to a larger extent from different areas of society. But other forces have tugged more strongly in the opposite direction. Intellectuals and professionals are most often drawn to a labor movement as a vehicle for their own political advancement or a force for promoting certain political and social ideals. The American labor movement has been rather unattractive for these purposes, for it has never been profoundly ideological, nor has it provided a particularly easy entry to a political career. Instead, the work of the unions has centered upon the bargaining process and, especially at the lowest levels of the union hierarchy, upon the day-to-day business of administering the working conditions in the shop and factory. These issues require an intimate knowledge of the workplace naturally acquired by union members who have worked in the trade. To the intellectual or the professional man, however, these matters are not only unfamiliar; they are also of precious little interest.

Emerging as he does from the rank and file, the union leader naturally tends to reflect many of the characteristics of his membership. For example, 83 percent of union presidents and secretary-treasurers are said to be Democrats, just as almost all unions have a majority of Democrats among their members. As for education, approximately half of all union leaders in the 1967 survey have no more than a high-school education; while 21 percent have completed college, 25 percent never graduated from high school. The proportion of college graduates among union leaders is appreciably higher than among union members, but it lags well behind the level achieved by businessmen, government officials, and other key groups within the society.

The average age of the national officer of a union is fifty-

---

* The remainder were distributed as follows: 11 percent had fathers who were farmers, 6 percent were clerks or salesmen, 6 percent were professional, and 1 percent were otherwise classified. These figures and those that follow are taken from Abraham Friedman "Characteristics of National and International Union Leaders," October 1967 (unpublished manuscript). We are indebted to Mr. Friedman for the preliminary results of his survey prepared for a Ph.D. dissertation at the University of Chicago.

three—about the same as for business executives at the vice-president and president level. According to the 1967 survey, the "typical" national officer is likely to have begun to work at roughly eighteen years of age. But he will probably not have become a union member until his early twenties and will not have joined his present union until three or four years later. Six or seven years after that he will have reached his first elective position in his union local. From local office, he will probably have taken an appointive staff position and then will have become a national officer at approximately age forty-five.

As one might expect, there are marked variations among officials and among unions. For example, union leaders tend to have higher levels of education if they belong to small unions or unions in the transportation, service, or government sectors. In most cases, these differences stem from variations in the type and background of the members in the various unions. Small elite crafts tend to be led by better-educated men. The Airline Pilots or Actors Equity will obviously produce a different kind of leader from that of the Mine Workers or the Laborers.

At one time, much was made of the differences between the leaders of CIO and AFL unions. According to the sociologist C. Wright Mills, "The AFL and CIO are not two differently shaped vessels filled with similar types of leaders. The split between them runs deep: It divides different types of men. They differ in their personal characteristics, in the union experience they have had, and in their social and political outlook."[15] When Mills was writing, the CIO was little more than a decade old. Its young unions were filled with young leaders. Their education was frequently superior to that of the AFL leaders. To Mills, therefore, the AFL seemed largely a gerontocracy—". . . at its top are older men who are relatively poorly educated and who have authority over much younger men who are relatively better educated."[16]

In the intervening years, these differences have all but disappeared. According to the 1967 survey, the average age of CIO leaders is fifty-three; for AFL leaders, fifty-six. The percentage of CIO leaders who have completed college is twelve; of AFL leaders, twenty-two. In sum, the divergent statistics that Mills developed were largely the accidents of history. They reflected the youth of the CIO and disappeared as soon as these unions increased in age. And as they disappeared, many of the differences in social and political outlook tended to diminish as well.

Appendix A

UNION MEMBERSHIP

Chart 1. Membership of national and international unions, 1930–1966*

Chart 2. Membership as a percent of total labor force and of employees in nonagricultural establishments, 1930–66†

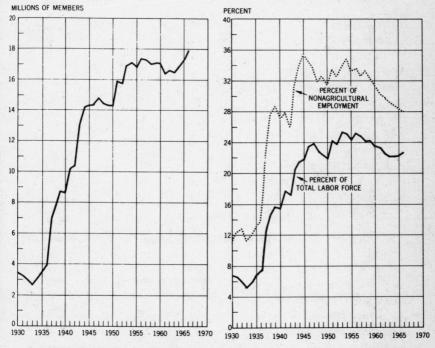

* Excludes Canadian membership, but includes members in other areas outside the United States. Members of AFL–CIO directly affiliated local unions are also included. For the years 1948–52, midpoints of membership estimates, which were expressed as ranges, were used.

† Excludes Canadian membership. The dotted line for the period since 1960 estimates the effect of including membership in "near unions."

SOURCE: United States Department of Labor, Bureau of Labor Statistics, *Directory of National and International Labor Unions in the United States 1967*, Bulletin No. 1596, p. 57.

Appendix B

UNION MEMBER ATTITUDES ON SOCIAL
AND POLITICAL QUESTIONS

What government programs would you cut first?
(Harris, May 8, 1968)

	Total queried	Union members	AFL–CIO	Teamsters
Space program	31%	37%	39%	24%
More highways	13	9	8	20
Welfare, relief	11	11	11	10
Anti-poverty program	10	8	7	4
Farm subsidies	7	6	5	10
Aid to cities	6	7	8	9
Financing Vietnam war	6	6	4	14
Anti- air, water pollution	4	4	4	1
Medicaid	3	1	1	—
Aid to education	1	1	—	3
Anti-crime, law enforcement	1	2	2	—
Not sure	9	8	11	5

What government programs would you most like to see kept?
(Harris, May 8, 1968)

	Total queried	Union members	AFL–CIO	Teamsters
Financing Vietnam war	23%	23%	18%	21%
Aid to education	19	20	20	31
Anti-crime, law enforcement	16	17	17	21
Medicaid	8	7	5	—
Anti-poverty program	8	8	8	5
Welfare, relief	6	5	7	3
Farm subsidies	4	3	2	—
Anti- air, water pollution	4	3	5	5
Space program	3	4	4	5
Aid to cities	3	3	3	5
More highways	1	1	2	—
Not sure	6	7	9	4

Do you favor subsidizing the poor through a negative income tax? (Harris, April 18, 1968)

	Total queried	Union members	AFL–CIO	Teamsters
Favor	27%	31%	21%	34%
Oppose	60	58	57	57
Not sure	13	12	12	9

Do you favor a $32 billion program to rebuild the cities? (Harris, April 15, 1968)

	Total queried	Union members	AFL–CIO	Teamsters
Favor	34%	37%	39%	23%
Oppose	52	51	51	62
Not sure	14	12	10	15

Do you favor such a program at the cost of paying $35 more in taxes? (Harris, April 15, 1968)

	Total queried	Union members	AFL–CIO	Teamsters
Favor	30%	30%	30%	15%
Oppose	59	62	62	77
Not sure	11	9	8	8

How much would you like to see the federal government owning and operating essential industries? (Opinion Research, August 1960)

	Nationwide public respondents	Union member households
A great deal	11%	12%
Fair amount	20	20
Very little	15	16
Nothing	36	36
No opinion	18	16

How satisfied are you with the results of the Marshall Plan to date? (Gallup, November 1, 1948)

	Non-unionists (1,915)	Union members (464)
Very well satisfied	13.5%	13.8%
Fairly well satisfied	49.3	48.7
Not at all satisfied	14.4	14.4
Not sure	22.8	23.1

*Should the United States give economic help to the poorer
countries even if those countries can't pay for it?* (Survey
Research, September–November 1956)

	Non-unionists (1,359)	Union members (403)
Strongly agree	21.8%	20.8%
Agree, but not very strongly	21.6	21.3
Not sure	15.2	13.9
Disagree, but not very strongly	9.5	9.9
Disagree strongly	15.9	17.1
No opinion	11.0	17.0

*President Johnson has proposed that Congress set aside
about $3.4 billion for aid in other parts of the world. . . .
Would you like to see this amount increased or decreased?*
(Gallup, February 17, 1965)

	Non-unionists (2,581)	Union members (485)
Increase aid	5.5%	8.5%
Keep at same level	32.9	36.5
Decrease aid	49.2	46.8
No opinion	12.4	8.2

*Would you like to see the Congress pass the (1964) Civil
Rights Act?* (Gallup, December 31, 1963)

	Non-unionists (3,214)	Union members (575)
Yes	59.4%	63.8%
No	32.4	27.5
Not sure	8.2	9.7

How do you feel about the Ku Klux Klan in America?
(Harris, May 31, 1968)

	Total queried	Union members	AFL–CIO
More good than harm	10%	9%	8%
More harm than good	68	69	70
Doesn't matter much	10	11	12
Not sure	13	11	10

Have Negroes tried to move too fast? (Harris, April 15, 1968)

	Total queried	Union members	AFL–CIO	Teamsters
Too fast	61%	69%	63%	66%
Too slow	9	6	6	4
About right	20	18	24	11
Not sure	10	6	7	19

All things considered, is the U.N. worthwhile? (Harris, April 16, 1968)

	Total queried	Union members	AFL–CIO	Teamsters
Worthwhile	83%	86%	89%	76%
Not worthwhile	12	11	8	16
Not sure	6	3	3	8

Which statement about Vietnam do you agree with most? (Harris, April 16, 1968)

	Total queried	Union members	AFL–CIO	Teamsters
I disagree with our present policy. We are not going far enough. We should go further, such as carrying the war more into North Vietnam.	21%	23%	27%	31%
I agree with what we are doing but we should increase our military effort.	38	41	37	44
I agree with what we are doing, but we should do more to bring about negotiations, such as stop bombing North Vietnam.	17	21	15	15
I disagree with our present policy. We should pull out our troops now.	15	10	13	11
Not sure.	9	6	8	—

Should Communist China be admitted to the U.N.? (Harris, April 16, 1968)

	Total queried	Union members	AFL– CIO	Teamsters
Yes	30%	27%	26%	22%
No	51	52	52	75
Not sure	19	20	22	3

Do you tend to feel left out of things going on around you? (Harris, May 16, 1968)

	Total queried	Union members	AFL– CIO	Teamsters
Yes	9%	9%	8%	8%
No	89	89	89	92
Not sure	3	2	2	—

Do you tend to feel that you don't have as good a chance to get ahead as most people? (Harris, May 16, 1968)

	Total queried	Union members	AFL– CIO	Teamsters
Yes	15%	15%	16%	14%
No	80	82	81	86
Not sure	5	2	3	—

Do you tend to feel that the rich get richer and the poor get poorer? (Harris, May 16, 1968)

	Total queried	Union members	AFL– CIO	Teamsters
Yes	44%	49%	44%	64%
No	48	45	51	32
Not sure	7	5	5	3

Do you tend to feel that what you think doesn't count very much? (Harris, May 16, 1968)

	Total queried	Union members	AFL– CIO	Teamsters
Yes	36%	38%	37%	36%
No	57	57	57	57
Not sure	7	5	6	7

> Do you tend to feel that people running the country don't
> really care what happens to people like yourself? (Harris,
> May 16, 1968)

	Total queried	Union members	AFL–CIO	Teamsters
Yes	26%	26%	22%	28%
No	67	68	71	64
Not sure	7	6	7	8

> Percentage voting for George Wallace by income (Harris,
> November 2, 1968)*

	Under $3,000	$3,000–4,999	$5,000–6,999	$7,000–9,999	$10,000–14,999	$15,000+
Total	14%	14%	16%	13%	11%	7%
Union members	4	9	17	15	11	20
Non-union members	15	14	15	11	11	5

* These figures suggest that substantial variations may appear among different subcategories within the total union membership. (The strong support for Wallace among union members with incomes over $15,000, however, must be treated with skepticism, since only a handful of union members were numbered among the 246 persons in this category polled by the Harris organization.)

3

Democracy, Union Government and the Interests of the Members

Corruption and Autocracy

During the past fifteen years, the subject of internal union affairs has been dominated by concern over corruption and autocratic behavior on the part of union leaders. Legislators have investigated these abuses, newspapers have reported a series of lurid scandals, and the American public has followed each step in the criminal proceedings against a Jimmy Hoffa or a Dave Beck. In view of the flamboyance of these subjects and the wide notoriety they have received, it seems best to confront them immediately before going on to consider the other aspects of union government.

Prior to 1920, Professor Robert F. Hoxie called attention to a type of labor organization that he designated "hold-up unionism" and characterized as "boss-ridden and corrupt," using methods of "open bargaining coupled with secret bribery and violence."[1] But these matters did not appear greatly to concern the public until the mid-fifties when the McClellan Committee began to investigate the internal affairs of unions. The disclosures were a revelation not only to the public but also to the president of the AFL–CIO, who declared that ". . . we thought we knew a few things about trade-union corruption, but we didn't know the half of it, one tenth of it, or the one hundredth part of it."[2] The Committee hearings unearthed several types of abuse. In some cases, local union leaders received kickbacks from employers in return for "sweetheart" contracts which provided wages and conditions below the prevailing scale. In other instances, union dues were used by officials to buy homes, take lush trips to exotic parts, or pad their expense accounts beyond any reasonable limit. On still other occasions, labor leaders won elections by throwing dissenting locals into trusteeship,* manufacturing votes from "paper" locals, or intimidating members by threats, physical beatings, or denying job referrals under union hiring halls.[3] Implicated in these practices were several well-known unions: the Teamsters, Bakery Workers, Operating Engineers, Carpenters, Meat Cutters, Barbers, and Restaurant Workers.†

Following the McClellan hearings, Congress passed the Landrum-Griffin Act in 1959 to outlaw many of these transgressions. Embezzlement or other improper use of union funds was made a criminal offense, and unions were prohibited from making loans to their officials in excess of two thousand dollars. The use of violence or threats to deny members their democratic rights was declared unlawful. Individuals convicted of serious crimes within the previous five years were barred from union office. And legal provisions were enacted to regulate the power of the international to maintain its locals in trusteeship.

In the same law, Congress attempted to strengthen democratic procedures and thus give power to the members to protect themselves against irresponsible leaders. Locals, intermediate bodies, and international unions were required to hold elections at stipulated intervals. Members were guaranteed a reasonable opportunity to nominate candidates and run for office, and their right freely to criticize candidates and union policies was secured. Incumbent officers were prohibited from using union funds to promote the election of any candidate and were enjoined not to disseminate propaganda for any candidate unless equivalent op-

---

* Placing a local union under trusteeship is a procedure typically provided for in the union constitution; it empowers the international to order the administration of the local placed under the control of a designated officer. The procedure is designed to enable the international to put a stop to misuse of the local's funds, violations of the collective-bargaining agreement on the part of members, violent factional conflict, or some other serious internal problem.

† Shocking as these disclosures were, it is only fair to point out that in several of these unions only a few locals were tainted out of the hundreds affiliated with the parent organization. And it is also true that these unions represented only a small, though important, minority of the 190-odd national unions in the country.

portunities were given to the opposition. To give the members
access to pertinent facts, union officials were required to file
information relating to the financial affairs of the union, its constitutional provisions, the names and salaries of its officers, and
financial dealings raising potential conflicts of interest. Finally, the
Secretary of Labor was empowered to investigate union elections
and to bring suit to overturn any election whose outcome might
have been affected by a violation of law or a breach of the union's
constitution and bylaws.

In the process of greatly strengthening the protections given
to the union member, the Landrum-Griffin Act has thrown light on
the incidence of corruption and undemocratic practices by providing statistics on the number of cases brought under its provisions.
Granted, violations may occur without resulting in a complaint, let
alone a conviction. Nevertheless, the official statistics offer some
suggestion of the magnitude of abuse and permit rough comparisons between unions and other groups in the society.

On grounds of corruption and dishonesty, sixty-one convictions were recorded in fiscal year 1968, of which fifty-three involved charges of embezzlement.[4] Since the law's enactment, the
Secretary of Labor has instituted only four civil actions to compel
compliance with the provisions relating to trusteeship imposed on
a local.[5] As for union elections, the Department of Labor issued
the following breakdown of cases resolved in the fiscal year ending
June 30, 1968.[6]

Election cases closed
No violation found   42
Insufficient evidence that violation affected outcome
    of election   24
Voluntary compliance   17
    a. Election rerun under
        Department supervision   11
    b. Election rerun without
        Department supervision   3
    c. Other corrective action   3
Civil actions filed to insure compliance   23
    Total Cases   106

In only eighteen elections was there reason to believe that
misconduct had occurred that may have affected the result. Some

of these cases could well have resulted from the ignorance of local officials rather than any deliberate desire to rig an election. More important, of the 51,656 labor organizations—locals, intermediate bodies, and international unions—filing reports with the Department of Labor in 1968, it is likely that at least 20,000 held elections that year. Thus, the incidence of proven violations is extremely small.

The record of criminal convictions yields no evidence that union officials are more prone to corrupt practices than other segments of society. During 1965, Department of Labor records suggest that convicted union embezzlers had their hands on an aggregate sum between $150,000 and $200,000.[7] At the same time, the National Crime Commission has estimated that roughly $200 million are embezzled each year in the country as a whole.[8] The fifty-three embezzlement convictions are also not large in comparison with conviction rates in the business sector. In the banking industry, for example, the Crime Commission reported that 100 bank presidents, 65 bank vice-presidents, 145 managers, 345 cashiers, and 490 other employees were all convicted for embezzlement in 1960 alone.[9]

Despite these comparisons, the fact remains that corruption and abuses of democratic procedures seemed to occur much more often in America than in the labor movements of Western Europe. Although no precise data are available, careful students of European unions have repeatedly stated that there is scarcely any evidence of corruption.[10] The behavior of labor leaders in these countries, moreover, has very rarely given rise to the public scandals or official investigations that one would expect if corruption were as prevalent there as it has been in the United States.

Critics have alleged that the abuses in our trade unions reflect the lack, in America, of the idealism and social purpose that seem to animate the labor movements in Europe. But America has probably never had a labor organization more imbued with social purpose than the International Workers of the World, and still a noted labor historian has reported:

Nothing was more striking in the recent [I.W.W.] convention than the stories of local financial losses. "All down the line," said one delegate, "we have had experience with secretaries who have absconded with funds." "No less than three have done the same thing [in our local]," was the testimony of

another. This has happened three times to one local in one
year according to a third statement. Indeed so loose is the
local financial control . . . that there appears to exist a body
of circulating professional agitators who make it their business
to go from locality to locality for the sole purpose of getting
themselves elected to the Treasurer's office and absconding
with the funds.[11]

In short, an explanation of the corruption that does exist requires
more than a passing reference to the lack of idealism in the
American labor movement.

In part, of course, the abuses in our unions merely reflect
patterns of behavior that pervade the society at large. Organized
crime appears to exist in America to a far greater extent than in
most European countries, and unions offer a tempting target for
the professional gangster in view of the opportunities presented to
collect dues and pressure employers. Most of the other familiar
abuses of union officials are also commonplace throughout society,
as evidenced by the prevalence of embezzlement and expense-
account manipulation, and the need for close regulation of corporate election procedures. In an open society it is not surprising that
certain union leaders should resort to morally reprehensible behavior, which they perceive so often in the world around them.

The likelihood of corruption has also been magnified in the
United States because of certain special features of the labor relations system. For example, companies have probably been more
tolerant of corruption because they have been subject to sharper
competition than has been typical in Europe. In industries marked
by a multiplicity of small businesses, keen competition, and a
casual labor market, employers have connived with union leaders
in corrupt practices that have promised to "stabilize" conditions. In
order to make a bigger profit—or simply to remain competitive—
individual employers also have offered payments to union officials
in return for wage agreements below the prevailing scale or covert
commitments not to enforce certain provisions of the collective-
bargaining contract.*

---

* "Not in the building trades, nor in the entertainment industry, nor in road
transportation, nor in any other industry seriously affected by amateur or
professional corruption, is there a public record of substantial employer opposition to the works of the corrupt. There was usually formal support for public
investigations and private crime commissions, but seldom loud protest or
effective action against the predators. In most cases there was only collaboration or silence."[12]

Internal union abuses have also been encouraged by the prevalence of strong local unions in our labor movement. In comparison with European labor organizations, local unions in this country enjoy considerable autonomy and have substantial power and financial strength. Under such circumstances, the opportunities for abuse have multiplied, simply because there are many more union positions worth fighting for and many more opportunities to profit from dishonest practices. The existence of semiautonomous, well-financed locals has also smoothed the path for individuals outside the labor movement who are tempted by the lure of appropriating dues and shaking down employers. History holds many examples of racketeers who have managed to gain a foothold in a union by "moving in" on locals in large metropolitan areas. These corrupting elements would have encountered much more difficulty in a country where it was necessary to capture an entire national organization before wielding significant power.

Finally, the presence of strong local unions has worked in another, more paradoxical way to increase the likelihood of autocracy and abuse. Decentralization of the labor movement has brought greater influence within reach of the rank and file than could ever be the case in a labor movement where significant decisions are regularly made by national officials far removed from the influence of any single group of members. Under these circumstances, local union elections are often vigorously contested to a point seldom matched in the more centralized labor organizations of Europe. While rivalry of this sort seems the very essence of democracy, it also increases the likelihood of abuse by creating great insecurity among local leaders, who, having achieved the power and prestige of full-time office in a strong local, are understandably reluctant to lose their position and return to the shop. As a result, strong temptations can arise to suppress criticism or engage in sharp election practices to remain in power.

Although the record in this country compares unfavorably with that of many other nations, legal safeguards now go far to curb dishonesty and encourage democratic behavior. Probably only a tiny fraction of all union officials in America would stoop to serious abuse. The overwhelming majority of labor leaders are honest men who take seriously their obligation to represent the interest of the members who have elected them to office.

The Role of Democratic Government
in the Union Movement

Democracy as applied to the union movement has meant different things to different critics of American labor. To some, democracy does not exist unless there is a two-party system wherein opposition to the incumbent administration is normal and institutionalized throughout the union. Others are concerned less with the particular political process employed than with rights of the individual member and the safeguards available to him in the event he faces discipline or expulsion by the organization. As used in this chapter, however, the term "democracy" refers to the processes that keep union leaders responsive to the members: principally the elections by which union leaders are chosen and union policies are ratified by the rank and file.

In a country founded upon a democratic system of government, it is perhaps natural that unions should be expected to conduct their affairs through democratic processes. But this premise is too often merely assumed and too rarely placed under serious scrutiny. Labor unions are not a part of the American governmental system; they are private organizations, and the American public does not insist that all large private institutions operate through vigorous democratic procedures. There has been no outcry, for example, over the lack of meaningful control by shareholders over the policies of corporations. Nor has the public been notably concerned over the lack of real democracy within the hierarchy of the church. In short, democratic procedures are not considered equally applicable to all organizations and institutions within the society. The real value of these procedures is determined largely by the purposes of the organization and the extent to which such processes can help it to achieve its goals. Thus, government by consent of the governed seems critical to the well-being of a municipality but clearly inappropriate to an army in the field.

Unions are expected to pursue several goals. Their primary aim is usually to promote the welfare of their members by bargaining with management over terms and conditions of employment. It is also widely conceded that unions should work more broadly for the interests of their members by participating in political and community affairs. In addition, like many other private associations, the union must not ignore the legitimate interests of individuals and minorities within its ranks. Nor should the union overlook the interests of the larger community, for labor organizations have important effects on many other groups in society. In sum, it is fair to say that the function that society has ascribed to unions is to promote the welfare of all their members as fairly and effectively as possible without interfering unduly with the interests of third parties.

In light of these purposes, there are at least three reasons for maintaining democratic procedures as the basis of union government. The principal reason is that these procedures permit the members to exert pressure on their leaders to pay attention to the needs and desires of the rank and file in formulating policies and programs. Perhaps most union officials would wish to promote the interests of their members even if their tenure in office were guaranteed. But even well-motivated leaders may do a poorer job of representing their members if they do not face a meaningful challenge at the polls. In England, for example, where top officials are often elected for life, many unions have not considered it appropriate to protect employees against arbitrary discipline even though their members have felt strongly enough to call repeated, unauthorized strikes to protest unjust dismissals.[13] In France, where the largest labor confederation has been strongly influenced by the Communist party, union policies on wages and strikes seem to have been shaped much more by party goals than the members would have directed had they been given a choice in the matter. Val R. Lorwin, who has observed the French labor movement, has written that "Party domination, which has given the C.G.T. unions a more solid bureaucracy and more capable administration than it has ever had, has taken most of the meaning out of the forms of membership control."[14]

A second reason for maintaining democratic procedures is that many employees value the sense of participation they derive from helping to select union officials and influence important policy decisions. These members would not wish to give up their political rights, even if their material needs were adequately protected by a well-meaning and paternal leader. Thus, democratic procedures are themselves an important rank-and-file interest which unions must respect in order to promote the wishes of their members.

Finally, the public has a stake in the democratic process within unions. The point is not that democracy will put an end to corruption or reduce the number of inconvenient strikes. It does not follow that the more responsive a union is to the wishes of its members, the more responsible it will be to the public. Nevertheless, unions have chosen to govern themselves by elections and related democratic procedures. As a result, there is a public interest in maintaining the integrity of these procedures, not only to protect the rights of individual candidates, but also to avoid the risk that dishonest practices will breed a cynicism toward governmental methods that are vital to our entire political system.

Although democratic procedures have a valuable place in union government, a real problem arises in determining how much—and what form of—democracy is appropriate to ensure that unions will respond to the desires of their members while giving due regard to the interests of the public. Two notes of caution are in order. To begin with, elections and other formal democratic procedures are not the only ways of keeping labor leaders responsive to their constituents. Moreover, to affirm the value of democratic government is not to insist that every policy and decision in a union should be voted upon by the members. In private organizations, just as in politics, the constant use of the ballot can prove too cumbersome and expensive, too inhibiting to creative leadership, too likely to pressure the officers into policies that slight the ultimate purposes of the institution or harm the interests of the public. Instead of asking whether the formal procedures of union government satisfy some preconceived democratic norm, one should inquire: *First,* in what ways can members influence the behavior of a union and how effective is their influence? *Second,* to what extent will efforts to enlarge this influence by strengthening democratic procedures cause labor leaders to promote the members' interests more faithfully without jeopardizing the other goäls that society ascribes to unions?

Methods of Influence by the Membership

ELECTIONS

One important way by which the rank and file can influence the leadership is through its power to vote for union officials.

Elections, of course, can only provide an opportunity to pass judgment on a candidate and the major policies with which he is identified; the voter cannot register his opinion on each of the many separate programs and policies pursued by a complex organization. Moreover, union elections often fail to give the members a meaningful choice, for many labor leaders run without opposition. This is particularly true of elections for the top posts in international unions. Rival candidates find it difficult to bid for these jobs, since they often lack sufficient money and organization to communicate their views effectively throughout the entire union. Yet contested elections do occur, and sometimes challengers succeed in defeating incumbents even at the highest level. Thus, Paul Jennings defeated James Carey in 1965 for the presidency of the International Union of Electrical Workers; I. W. Abel ousted David McDonald as president of the Steelworkers in the same year; and Jerry Wurf replaced long-time president Arnold S. Zander in the State, County and Municipal Employees Union in a close election in 1964. The risk of opposition doubtless serves in some degree to keep union presidents attentive to their members; in local unions, such pressure is even more pervasive.

REFERENDA

Almost all unions resort to voting, or referenda, to approve certain specified decisions. In most local unions of small and medium size, organizing campaigns, salaries of officers, new health or education programs, indeed almost every decision of any importance will be submitted to the membership meeting for approval. At the international level, new programs, salary increases, and other policy determinations are normally submitted to the convention, instead of being voted upon by the rank and file, but most internationals still require a vote of the members prior to calling a strike or finally approving a collective-bargaining agreement. Many unions also call for referenda before amending the constitution, and a few utilize this procedure in raising dues and per-capita payments.*

The referendum seems ideal as a device for impressing the will of the members on the organization. It forces the union leader

---

* Dues represent the periodic payments that members make to their union as a condition of membership. Per-capita payments are the portion of dues which the local unions are required to remit to their parent international.

to consider the wishes of the rank and file in framing policies and
to inform the members on the matters in issue and thus educate
them on the conduct of the union. In practice, however, the
technique is not without serious drawbacks for unions as for other
organizations. A meaningful vote requires that the members be
reasonably informed on the issues involved, and it is usually very
difficult to reach the entire electorate and engage their interest in
the matters at issue. Indeed, it is often impossible even to induce a
large portion of the members to cast a ballot. Local meetings
normally draw less than 10 to 15 percent of the members unless
some particularly vital issue is at stake. And referenda in international unions have often brought forth an average vote of less than
20 percent of the eligible members. Such meager turnouts would
not pose a great problem if the voters were reasonably typical of
the membership as a whole, but such is often not the case. Local
meetings may be heavily manned by workers with particular
loyalties to the incumbent officers. At other times, it is the dissi-
dents who are aroused to cast a ballot against the administration,
while satisfied members are not sufficiently interested to vote in
large numbers. In either case, the election results may not reflect
the sentiments of the entire membership. Nevertheless, the prospect of a referendum plainly forces union leaders to be more sensitive to members' wishes.

UNION CONVENTIONS

Every union constitution provides for a periodic convention of
delegates who are selected, in the main, by the various locals in
the organization. As in state and national legislatures, many problems have arisen in devising voting and representation methods
that will accommodate the interests of different areas and different-
size locals. In general, however, the conventions are reasonably
representative of the entire membership, and many unions have
gone so far as to establish funds to ensure the presence of delegates from more remote areas and from smaller locals with meager
treasuries.

At these conventions, many policy issues are worked over in
committee and then discussed and voted upon by the delegates as
a whole. Amendments to the constitution, dues increases, and
major new programs are almost invariably matters for convention
debate, along with resolutions relating to collective-bargaining

goals and matters to be pressed before state and national legislatures. And almost every convention will provide an opportunity to air particular grievances and concerns about the administration of the union.

As a device for reflecting membership sentiment, the convention is undoubtedly deficient in several respects. The national officers have a definite advantage through their power to appoint the members of the committees and to influence the order and timing of the issues on the agenda. Moreover, as in every representative body, the interests of the delegates do not precisely reflect the views of their constituents. Once again, the incumbents will normally hold the advantage. A small fraction of the delegates will usually consist of members from the international staff, who presumably have strong loyalties to the administration. Other local officials who serve as delegates may be partial to the incumbents because of past services received or hoped-for favors in the future. Conceding all of this, however, conventions still provide a useful forum for the expression of member sentiment and a device for forcing administration policies to conform with the wishes of the rank and file. One can cite countless examples in which important administration proposals have gone down to defeat, and open revolts on the convention floor are not unknown. The incumbent officials are normally most reluctant to run a risk of such defeats with their attendant harm to the administration's programs and prestige. Thus, national officers work hard to ensure that their proposals conform with the views of the delegates. A veteran delegate pointed out in explaining the lack of controversy in his union conventions:

> Well, you see, whenever a new matter comes up the President takes it to the Executive Board and talks it over with them, making whatever modifications he thinks necessary to win the approval of the Board. With these adjustments, the President then takes it to a number of key locals and finds out their reactions. Through this process, agreements are reached behind the scenes and there are no differences which need to be resolved at a convention.[15]

THE "STRIKE IN DETAIL"

Fifty years ago Professor Carleton H. Parker referred to the "strike in detail" to describe the quiet resistance of individual workers to unpopular policies of employers.[16] Such resistance may take the form of excessive turnover, poor morale, low productivity, or lack of discipline. In a word, the employee simply becomes "undependable" to the employer. It is no less important to observe that union members can also become "undependable" to their leaders by calling wildcat strikes, refusing to honor a picket line, or engaging in a wide range of activity or inactivity that will frustrate the policies of the organization. The threat of such behavior helps to impress the sentiments of the rank and file upon their leaders whenever union policies depend to any significant degree upon the cooperation of the members.

DECERTIFICATION, RAIDING AND WITHDRAWAL
FROM THE BARGAINING UNIT

The law provides various ways in which employees can repudiate an unwanted union. The National Labor Relations Act states that workers in an established bargaining unit can petition for an election at appropriate intervals to decide whether to oust their bargaining representative. Under the same act, particular groups of employees with special skills or bargaining needs are allowed, under some circumstances, to vote to split off from a larger unit and be represented by another union. In addition, an incumbent organization may be "raided" by a rival union, which can petition for an N.L.R.B. election to allow the workers to decide whether to change their bargaining representative. Although this danger has greatly diminished beginning with the signing of the AFL–CIO no-raiding pact in 1953, many organizations still face a threat from unions outside the Federation, notably the Teamsters and District 50 of the Mine Workers. In practice, workers do not often take advantage of these opportunities to repudiate their bargaining representative.* But the risk of being ousted poses dangers that can spur the union to give closer attention to complaints or disaffection from particular groups within the membership.

---

* In the fiscal year ending June 30, 1967, the National Labor Relations Board conducted 234 elections involving 12,705 eligible voters to determine whether a union previously certified or currently recognized by the employer no longer represented a majority of the employees in the appropriate unit. Unions were ousted in 165 of these elections with almost 5,000 eligible employees. In the same fiscal year the N.L.R.B. conducted a total of 8,183 elections of all types with 623,711 employees eligible to vote.

Results of Membership Influence on Areas of Union Activity

With the help of these channels of influence, the rank and file can exert varying degrees of pressure depending on the type of issue involved.

COLLECTIVE BARGAINING

Because of the prime importance of bargaining, members tend to have strong opinions about negotiations, and union leaders are under heavy constraint to pay close attention to these sentiments. The views of the members are first expressed when the union formulates its initial demands. At this stage, particularly in local negotiations, proposals are usually submitted from groups or individuals within the union without much effort to limit aspirations or assign priorities. The initial union demands are often akin to shopping lists; some management negotiators call them dream books.

The aspirations of the members must be adjusted by union negotiators to accommodate *a)* the conflicting desires of different groups of members, *b)* the longer-run interests of the members, as the leaders perceive them, *c)* the survival and growth of the union as an organization, *d)* the demands and interests of management, and *e)* the reaction of the community at large and its impact on the interests of the union and its members. This process of accommodation would become impossibly cumbersome if the rank and file had to express its judgment at each turn of the negotiations. But the various interest groups will usually have their spokesmen within the bargaining committee, where the initial demands are trimmed and tailored to reach an agreement with management. Moreover, union officials, even in national negotiations, will generally have a great deal of communication with active members, shop stewards and committeemen, and other leaders of subgroups within the union. These exchanges typically take place over many weeks or months.

Union leaders are further restricted in the collective-bargaining process by the necessity of "selling" the agreement to the membership. A formal vote of ratification is not always required for this purpose. Some unions authorize their negotiators to make a binding settlement; others require the approval of a representative body, such as the elected wage-policy committee in basic steel or the joint council in certain construction unions. The vast majority of collective-bargaining agreements, however, are negotiated subject to a vote of approval by the membership.

Ratification is not a perfunctory matter but rather affords a genuine occasion for the expression of members' views. Statistics compiled by the Federal Mediation and Conciliation Service reveal a recent rise in membership rejections (in cases involving the active participation of Federal mediators) from 8.7 percent of proposed settlements in 1964 to 14.2 percent in 1967.[17] These figures do not mean that union members reject one out of seven agreements negotiated by their leaders, or even one out of seven of the situations in which the F.M.C.S. has been notified of a dispute; the rejection rate in these situations would be very much lower. Instead, the figures reflect a rejection rate of one in seven for the seven thousand disputes in 1967 that were sufficiently important or troublesome to call for the active participation of federal mediators. Even so, there is no doubt that the rejection rate has risen and that the ratification process must be taken seriously as an expression of rank-and-file sentiment.*

The union member may also make his views felt through his willingness to engage in a strike, whether authorized by the union or not. In extreme cases, some members may refuse to join an authorized strike or they may drift back to work after a period. Conversely, individual members or groups may reject the settle-

---

* It may be noted in passing that these figures on rejections by union members help to refute a view, often repeated in public discussions of collective bargaining and reflected in several pieces of legislation, to the effect that union members tend to be more "reasonable" than their elected officers and would accept management proposals for settlements turned down by union officers and negotiators. The War Labor Disputes Act of 1943 provided that workers should vote after rejecting management proposals in disputes "whether they will permit any such interruption of war production"; Congress stated that one purpose of this procedure was "in order that employees may have an opportunity to express themselves, free from restraint or coercion, as to whether they will permit such interruptions in wartime." The current emergency disputes procedures of the Taft-Hartley Act also provide for a vote of employees "on the question of whether they wish to accept the final offer of settlement made by their employer as stated by him." The experience with these last-offer votes conducted by the government has been a complete failure. The theory on which they were based, it is widely conceded, was unsound. There are few, if any, disputes in the country in which workers would, against the advice of their leaders, accept a settlement which had been rejected in negotiations by the union negotiators.

ment of the union and engage in a wildcat work stoppage to register their displeasure. On occasion, members may even walk out to protest a decision to continue negotiations past a deadline rather than call a previously authorized strike. These possibilities cause union leaders to pay close attention to rank-and-file sentiment in order to avoid the risk of suffering a defeat for the organization or a serious split in its membership.

THE GRIEVANCE PROCEDURE

It is often said that management gains a valuable channel of communication with the union and the employees by agreeing to discuss complaints by individual workers through the successive steps of a grievance procedure. But the grievance process is no less vital as a method of interaction between union members and their leaders, who thereby gain a better perspective on the myriad problems that individual employees encounter in the workplace.

If grievance meetings do not resolve the complaint, the union must decide whether to take the case to arbitration. In some unions, these decisions are made by representatives of the international staff; in other unions, local officials are empowered to make the choice. Still other organizations provide for a vote of the local membership. However the decision is made, the union leader must consider the interests of other members before pressing forward to arbitrate, for arbitrations require the expenditure of at least several hundred dollars of union funds and may result in precedents that will determine future cases. The procedure for taking cases to arbitration will often affect the weight accorded these other interests. If the matter is decided by a vote of the members (the method best calculated to reflect the sentiments of the rank and file), there is always the danger that a majority will compromise the legitimate claims of unpopular workers, ignore the interests of minority groups, or discriminate against employees who are in the bargaining unit but do not belong to the union. Decisions by international officials may be free of these dangers, but they may also be less responsive to the local nuances and intangible needs bound up with each case. On the other hand, if the decision is left to the local officials, a danger arises that the union and the employer will be burdened by an excessive use of arbitration. Although it is never easy for an elected officer to say no to an aggrieved constituent, a decision to arbitrate will seldom

arouse opposition from the members, since the effect of a single
arbitration on the membership is generally indirect and difficult to
perceive.

These considerations illustrate a recurring problem in seeking
appropriate participation by the members in union decisions.
Those who prefer a town-meeting democracy may instinctively
favor subjecting all possible decisions to membership approval.
But as the problem of grievances bears out, this procedure may
not adequately protect the other interests to which unions should
respond, notably those of individual members and employers.

DUES AND PER-CAPITA PAYMENTS

Union members normally pay periodic dues to their local,
which in turn makes per-capita contributions to the international
(and perhaps to regional or other intermediate bodies as well).*
Decisions over the amount of these payments represent one of the
most sensitive areas of union government. Local dues are typically
fixed by vote of the members, and efforts to change the amount
arouse a lively interest at union meetings. Normally, per-capita
payments are specified in the union constitution, and increases
require a constitutional amendment. Such amendments usually
call for a vote of the delegates to the convention, although roughly
half of the unions can resort to a referendum by the members, and
several require authorization both by the convention and by
referendum. A few unions have elected to fix dues and per-capita
contributions as a percentage of wages, so that the amount of dues
will automatically increase as wages rise. In most unions, however,
when rising costs call for increased revenue, the officers have
to apply to the convention or, by referendum, to the membership
for approval of increases in dues or per-capita payments.

---

* In the Carpenters' union, for example, the international-union constitution
establishes a minimum level of local dues of $4 per month. Local unions may
establish higher dues. Most local unions are required to make per-capita payments of $2.65 per month for each member to the international union. Of this
sum, $1.45 is used for the general management of the union and $1.20 is
placed in a special fund for retirement and pension purposes.
    . . . the data collected in 1960 from more than 48,000 local unions filed to
    meet the financial requirements of the Landrum-Griffin Act show that over
    half of the local unions charged dues of less than $4 a month. . . . Barely
    one percent of local unions reported dues higher than $10 a month. . . .
    The typical monthly dues payment cost the union member, in real terms,
    about two hours' work.[18]

Union officials face tight constraints from the rank and file when they seek increases in dues and per-capita payments. Proposals for higher dues are often voted down by local unions, for members are naturally unwilling to pay larger amounts unless the need is convincingly demonstrated. As for per-capita payments, the delegate to international conventions is no more inclined to grant increases than a member of Congress to raise taxes, since the result is to reduce the funds remaining to his local union or to require a rise in its dues. The officers of several internationals, such as the Painters and the Machinists, have suffered defeat in recent years on proposals for larger per-capita contributions.

The process of increasing dues and per-capita payments also serves to give the delegates and members an opportunity to review the over-all performance of the union and to express dissatisfactions. An increase in dues often provides an attractive issue to coalesce opposition against incumbent officials, as David McDonald, then president of the Steelworkers, discovered with the formation of the Dues Protest Committee in 1957. This protest culminated in a bitter election challenge that almost unseated McDonald; it also helped to lay the groundwork for the subsequent defeat that McDonald suffered in 1965. Such episodes are not lost upon union leaders, who will take pains to establish a record that will justify the desired dues increase.

ORGANIZING

Members are far less interested in the organizing of new members than they are in bargaining for wage increases for themselves. Nor do they exercise much direct influence over the millions of dollars that international unions spend each year for this purpose, for unless the international contemplates a major new organizing drive or seeks a special assessment for organizing purposes, the subject arouses little attention at conventions. The rank and file can nevertheless have an indirect influence on the nature and scope of organizing activities. Since these activities do not directly affect the interests of members, officials can cut them back easily when funds are scarce without arousing political opposition. Hence, the size of the union's organizing program is particularly sensitive to decisions that affect the level of dues. In many local unions, the rank and file can bring more direct pressures to bear on organizing efforts. By virtue of their control over dues, the members can block efforts to secure the money to hire full-time organizers on the local staff. Attempts to encourage local officials to devote more time to organizing are often stymied by complaints from the members that their needs are no longer receiving adequate attention. And where employment is low or is known to fluctuate, members frequently resist attempts to bring in new employees, who threaten to compete with them for scarce jobs.*

SERVICES FOR THE MEMBERSHIP

Many unions provide a variety of services for their members, outside the ordinary range of negotiated benefits. A few labor organizations have provided low-cost housing for members and their families; others offer credit unions, recreation facilities, free legal services, family counseling, or old-age homes. Many provide trained community counselors who advise members on their eligibility and rights under social legislation or point out the proper community agency or government office to visit in case of personal difficulty. Some of these services prove so successful that eventually they are expanded and financed through collectively bargained employer contributions. This has been notably true in the case of health and welfare programs.

Services of this type rarely come about through pressure from the members, whether the programs are launched at the international level or in a particular local. Instead, such activities usually develop from some special interest or inspiration in the mind of an energetic union leader. Nevertheless, the rank and file will normally have the last word, for if the members do not choose to avail themselves of the services provided, the program will eventually atrophy.

POLITICAL ACTION

In the last three decades, unions have paid increasing attention to political-action programs. Millions of dollars and countless man-hours are expended each year by organized labor in promoting desired legislation and assisting favored candidates. At first

---

* Members may be particularly disposed to support organizing efforts, however, where unorganized competitors have a direct and immediate effect upon jobs or levels of compensation negotiated with a management.

glance, these activities do not seem to be much influenced by the rank and file. The endorsement of candidates is often the task of the national, state, and local federations, which are well insulated from membership pressure. And though individual locals often make their own endorsements, their members often have little to say in the matter. The legislative program is likewise not a question with which the members are closely involved. The program is almost never subject to ratification procedures, and rarely does it command more than peripheral concern at union conventions.

At the same time, there is a much more important sense in which the rank and file does exert considerable influence over the political activities of the union. Political endorsements are not worth much unless they are backed by the support of union members at the polls. In fact, competent politicians avoid endorsements by unpopular leaders for fear they will have an adverse effect on the members. Legislators also discount the importance of union lobbying when the members are known to be uninterested or badly split on the subject at issue. More important still, labor makes its greatest political impact by contributing large amounts of money and time to political campaigns. In an attempt to elect candidates, union members and their wives register voters, get them to the polls, address and stamp envelopes, man telephone banks, and perform the countless little tasks involved in a campaign—efforts inevitably affected by the amount of enthusiasm within the membership for the issues and candidates backed by their organizations. Much of the money unions give to candidates must also be raised by voluntary contributions from the members, and though it is sometimes debatable just how "voluntary" these donations are, there is little doubt that contributions will decline substantially if labor's programs and favored candidates are unpopular with the rank and file.

These considerations help to explain the abundant evidence suggesting that the political objectives of unions are well in line with the views of their constituents. If labor tends to support Democratic candidates, it is also true that most union members favor the Democratic party and by much larger proportions than among the electorate as a whole—by more than 20 percent, for instance, in 1952 and 1956.[19] In the case of legislative programs, there can be little doubt of the heavy support of post-office workers for the postal pay increases sought by their unions, or the sympathy of maritime workers for union efforts to maintain ship-ping subsidies. As for more general issues, opinion polls suggest that more than 70 percent of union members support the efforts of organized labor to increase social-security benefits, expand unem-ployment compensation and increase the minimum wage.[20] Unions are on shaky ground with their members on very few issues—notably the removal of state authority to pass right-to-work laws and fair-housing legislation—and only on the latter question does a majority oppose the Federation, and by a very narrow margin at that.*

Is There Enough Democracy?

In sum, there is much broader rank-and-file influence and many more channels for exerting that influence than one might suspect by merely examining the formal institutions of union government. At the same time, the power of the members is limited in several important respects.

To begin with, most members are apathetic toward the day-to-day affairs of union government. Employees with higher educa-tion, more stable employment, and greater skills tend to be more involved in their union than poorly educated, low-skilled workers or employees in occupations with high rates of turnover. In almost every union, however, only a small minority take a continuing active interest in the affairs of their organization. The great majority are aroused only now and then, when a strike vote is taken or some other issue appears that touches directly upon their vital interests.

Union democracy is limited also by the special position occu-pied by the leaders of large labor organizations. When decisions are being made in a small local, the members can easily discuss the issues among themselves and communicate their views to the leaders. In a local of several thousand members, communication becomes more difficult. The leaders are usually separated from the rank and file by layers of business agents and stewards, and the members may not have ready access to one another. These prob-

---

* A poll conducted for the AFL–CIO indicates that 54 percent of the members supported the Federation on the union shop, with 23 percent opposed and 23 percent undecided. On open housing, 43 percent were in favor, 46 percent opposed, and 11 percent undecided.[21]

lems become still more pronounced at the level of the international headquarters. Additional layers of subordinates are interposed between leaders and members, and the latter are scattered in hundreds of locals throughout the country. Under these circumstances, the international officers occupy a peculiarly strategic position. In contrast to the typical leader in government, the official of an international union controls the media of communication within his organization; there are rarely any independent newspapers or television commentators to review or criticize his actions. Nor is it likely that any permanent, organized opposition will be found within the union. If the members, or local leaders, are sufficiently dissatisfied, a palace revolt may occur, and some well-known union figure will step forward to challenge the administration. But until the situation reaches this point, there will normally be no one with the necessary information, resources or means of communication who has an interest in informing the electorate or suggesting alternative policies for the union to follow.

These limitations allow a more careful definition of the influence of the rank and file. Where wages, hours, or other employment interests are involved, the members will normally have expectations that the leaders can ignore only at the risk of igniting strong opposition. Ordinarily, these expectations are high—sometimes even impossibly so, as when the workers believe that management can pay unrealistic wage increases or that the union can provide more services without raising dues. As a rule, however, the members impose leadership standards that reflect only their traditional needs and aspirations. They seldom make novel or imaginative demands, because they lack the knowledge, the vision, even the interest, to appreciate all that their union is capable of achieving. In matters of politics, community service, or even organizing, the members impose still lower standards, protesting only when union officials direct too much time and money to these activities at the expense of bargaining and settling grievances. In short, the members do have an important influence upon the leadership, but they rarely are a force for achieving innovation in the union or for realizing optimum levels of effective performance or efficient administration.

In light of this assessment, is there a need to find some ways of strengthening union democracy? Many commentators seem to believe so. Such critics are quick to assume that union democracy is simply an end in itself and to suggest reforms without pausing to consider the effect of their proposals on other purposes and interests which unions are asked to serve. The pitfalls in this approach can be perceived most vividly by considering one of the more obvious methods to increase the influence of the rank and file: developing a genuine two-party system within the union.

The International Typographical Union offers the only example of a two-party system among the 190-odd labor unions in the United States.[22] Two organized factions—the Progressives and the Independents—have regularly run candidates and exchanged office over the past fifty years. Although the circumstances giving rise to this unique political system are so special to the Typographical Union as virtually to preclude its adoption by other unions,* the I.T.U. experience illustrates some of the dilemmas inherent in union democracy.

There is little doubt that the two-party structure has succeeded in encouraging an active debate within the union over a range of important policy issues, so that incumbents have been subjected to more searching criticism, and members have probably received more detailed information about the conduct of union affairs. On the other hand, by emphasizing the role of the majority, the two-party system has had a dubious impact on minority and public interests. For example, neither party in the union advocated work sharing, wage cuts or other steps to assist unemployed members during the 1930's, since each concluded that the political advantage to be won from jobless constituents would be more than offset by opposition from the much larger group of employed members. During the same period, a minority of members employed as mailers received so little recognition for their special interests that they eventually seceded and formed a separate organization. These experiences led Professor Seymour Lipset to observe: "Where interest groups are inflexible and built into the occupational structure of the union (as they are in the vast majority of unions) it would appear that [two-party] democratic processes not only lead to oppression of the minority subgroup, but they probably lead to *more* oppression than would rule by one man."[23]

---

* Among these circumstances are the relatively high education of the members, their homogeneity, the high degree of skill demanded by their craft, the absorbing interest that most members have in their occupation, and the role of the union foreman in hiring new employees and arranging substitutions for regular employees temporarily absent.

In terms of the public interest, the I.T.U. experience raises questions on several counts. At the bargaining table, the strong political pressures within the union create obvious problems whenever the wishes of the majority collide with the public interest in avoiding unnecessary strikes or inflationary wage settlements. A. H. Raskin has observed in commenting on the strife that has attended newspaper negotiations in New York City:

> The knowledge that a strong opposition is always ready to make political capital of any rank-and-file grievance is no stimulus to reasonableness at the bargaining table. The party in control must regard each new contract as its platform for the next election. If the members are dissatisfied, they can always vote in a new administration.[24]

The Typographical Union's record in other areas of activity has also come into apparent conflict with the public interest. Very few Negroes can be found within the union. The I.T.U. has also won broad notoriety for retaining the system of "bogus type" and other make-work practices. In fact, the typographers allegedly campaigned against permanent voter registration in some localities on the ground that the yearly printing of registration lists provided work for their members. And in the late forties, the union achieved an almost unequaled position within organized labor by reaching a formal decision to disobey the provisions of the Taft-Hartley Act by insisting that employers continue to honor the closed shop.

This is not to say that unions that are responsive to their members are necessarily more likely than autocratically run organizations to oppose the law, discriminate against minorities, or engage in restrictive work practices.* Nevertheless, every serious student of unions would agree that members have generally been more inclined than their leaders to favor such dubious policies as racial restrictions, make-work practices, and strikes for inflationary settlements.† As a result, efforts to strengthen the influence of the

---

* Critics often point out that featherbedding and racial restrictions have flourished, not only in the I.T.U., but in organizations that are allegedly less democratic. But these tendencies may simply reflect the fact that the rank and file exerts a potent influence in all of these unions as a result of the various methods of pressure available to the rank and file as described above.

† Whatever the union—the Machinists, the Mine Workers, the I.T.U. or the Auto Workers—one can think of numerous instances in which the leadership has tried to persuade the members to abandon harmful practices, such as racial restrictions and make-work devices. It is much harder to identify occasions on which the leaders have been pressed to take such action by pressures emanating from the mainstream of the membership.

rank and file can easily bolster the forces that lead the union to favor positions opposed to the interests of the society at large.

Critics who urge more union "democracy" must also examine the impact of their proposals on the effective operation of the union. It is true that stronger grass-roots democracy will induce union leaders to pay closer heed to the wishes of the members. But will the leaders be able, as a result, to promote these interests more successfully? This question deserves much closer attention than it has received heretofore, for democracy can hamper the union in several ways.*

Because of political pressures, high union officials often feel compelled to bend their personnel decisions in questionable ways to curry favor among groups of constituents. For example, the appointment of staff representatives in the field is frequently influenced by political factors. Defeated local officers may have to be rewarded for past political services. Strong local leaders may pressure international officers to remove a potential rival by appointing him to a staff position. Other selections will be made to satisfy particular regions and minority groups.

Top officials may also bow to the opposition of particular groups of members and abandon programs that would eventually bring a larger benefit to the union as a whole. In many unions, membership pressure from high-wage locals has frequently blocked the efforts of the union to strengthen the economic power of larger groups of employees by creating area-wide bargaining agreements. In the Laborers union, national officers refrained for many years from establishing multi-local bargaining committees and holding regional conferences for fear of creating power blocs that might oppose their administration.†

---

* Many writers have observed that unions are "half army and half town meeting" and that democracy can cause disunity and weaken the organization during critical tests of strength with employers. But examples of this kind misconceive the nature of the tension between democracy and effective performance. Democratic procedures are seldom an impediment in crisis situations. In fact, unions often emphasize democracy at such times through strike votes and membership rallies, for they know that genuine support is vital to achieve their ends. The real conflicts between democracy and efficiency express themselves at other times and in a host of other ways.

† It might be noted in passing that a two-party system could easily aggravate these problems. Appointments might be made more often on political grounds as the party in power sought to reward faithful supporters and retain their allegiance. Since staff representatives would tend to become identified with one faction or another, excessive turnover might result when a change in administration took place. And surely the task of maintaining harmony and

Local officials can work in other ways to inhibit union policies that seem to threaten their political power. Education programs for the rank and file are frequently resisted by local officers who fear that discussions about union problems may stir up the membership or stimulate younger workers to oppose them for office. Efforts to organize new plants may be blocked because they promise to add new members to the local and thereby threaten its political stability. In fact, pressure of this kind is often a major factor inhibiting unions from extending their organizing activity to new occupational groups.

Unions can also suffer because the rank and file make demands without appreciating their long-run effects upon the organization. Members often have pushed their leaders to obtain wage increases that in the long run (and perhaps in the short run as well) threaten the jobs of union men and invite encroachments by unorganized competitors. And union members have frequently insisted on strikes under circumstances where the losses in pay promised to exceed any benefits likely to be achieved. Knowledgeable observers have asserted that both the Ford strike of 1967 and the Communications Workers' strike against A.T. & T. in 1968 took place because the expectations of the members exceeded the results realistically obtainable at the bargaining table. Similar problems have emerged in unions that have relied extensively on membership votes to approve major policy decisions. In summarizing the experience of many unions with the use of referenda, Professor Ulman has observed:

> Union members were reluctant to vote increases in dues at the same time that they were willing to liberalize benefit provisions or to approve strike and benefit petitions; they frequently enacted ill-considered and inconsistent legislation; and they frequently failed to vote at all.[25]

Critics may argue that such difficulties are simply the fault of union leaders who insist on playing politics and do too little to persuade the membership of the reasons for their policies. But these arguments are much more telling in the lecture hall than in actual practice. Although students of the labor movement often advocate "democracy" and disparage political maneuvering, the

---

teamwork among subordinate units would become more strained under a system in which important locals were controlled by elected leaders belonging to a rival party.

two can hardly be separated in the real world. And whereas unions could certainly do more to inform and educate their members, one must concede that at the end of a hard day's work, the intricacies of a pension program or an organizing drive will never compete with television for the attention of the average member. Even the most diligent of labor organizations have repeatedly been frustrated in trying to reach members and help them understand the details of union programs.

Conclusion

The point of this chapter is surely not to depreciate the value of democratic procedures or to suggest that Congress erred in seeking to guarantee free and fair elections and the rights of members to participate in union government and criticize their leaders. In certain respects, however, concern over these matters has been carried to excess. The extent of corruption in the labor movement has been exaggerated in many quarters. Scholarly critics have tended to underestimate the power of the rank and file by concentrating on the formal procedures of union government and ignoring the subtler sources of influence. And there has also been a tendency to judge union government by preconceived democratic norms without asking whether these norms are well suited to all the goals and interests that labor organizations serve.

Students of the labor movement have also been preoccupied with the issues of corruption and democracy to the virtual exclusion of other aspects of union administration. This tendency is curious, for union members have doubtless suffered far more from inefficient and unimaginative administration than they have ever lost through corruption and undemocratic procedures. Today, the key problem in union government is how to encourage innovation, a longer view of the union's role and interests, and greater effectiveness in carrying out the policies and programs of the organization. Democratic procedures do not ensure that union officials will be pushed to optimum levels in these respects, and efforts to strengthen democratic processes will not fill this need, but in some respects may make the problem worse.

With the passage of the Landrum-Griffin Act, the issue of union democracy should move away from broad legislative reform to a host of particular questions that vary greatly from one labor organization to another. Should both the local business agent *and* the assistant business agent be elected, or should the latter be appointed to ensure continuity and experience? What types of decisions should be subject to ratification? Should elections be held every year or every two or three years? Should the elections occur close to contract negotiations or will this force union officials to take irresponsible positions at the bargaining table? Few of these matters are fit subjects for legislation, and most should be judged according to the special circumstances of the particular union involved. In every case, the question should be, not whether any given change will make the union more democratic, but whether it will serve the ends of the modern union—to respond to the interests of the membership, to promote them effectively, to deal fairly with individuals and minorities within its ranks, and to exhibit a due regard for legitimate interests of those beyond its walls.

4

The Protection of Minority Interests

AS SOCIETY grows more complex, interest groups become more numerous and their aims increasingly variegated and intricate. Consequently, the points of friction among groups steadily mount in number and variety. In addition, as basic human needs come to be satisfied more widely throughout the population, more people feel free to turn their attention to matters of equity and status. As a result, minorities everywhere develop a heightened sensitivity to the treatment they receive as it compares with that of similar groups around them.

Reconciling the claims of competing interest groups is among the most difficult tasks of leadership in any institution. There is no simple method by which to weigh the demands of different minorities, and this is just as true in unions as in other organizations. To be sure, clear cases do crop up. No one can justify giving white employees better wages and conditions than blacks if they are performing the same work in the same plant. But flagrant cases of this sort are now rare. In most instances, the different demands of the various special interest groups are not unreasonable: older members may want higher pensions; younger employees prefer health and welfare benefits or higher hourly wages; assembly workers are concerned about the speed of the line; stenographers complain about the food in the company cafeteria. Since there is no easy calculus for striking a balance among such widely differing demands, the task of reconciling group interests is less a science than an art of leadership, and its highest expression lies in discovering imaginative ways of accommodating different interests and then convincing the groups involved that no better compromise can be found.

In certain respects, the problem of minorities can be more acute in labor organizations than in other private institutions. Many unions have a more heterogeneous membership than country clubs, churches, or trade associations. Although these members may share a common occupation, they differ in age, skill levels, job classifications, and sex; and these differences often lead to sharp conflicts over bargaining policies. In addition, a union has greater power over individuals and minorities than most other private associations, since the contract terms it negotiates bind all employees in the bargaining unit. Hence, a young employee who feels that too much of his pay is being diverted to a pension plan cannot gain relief merely by leaving the union; he can escape only by quitting his job and finding employment in another company where different policies prevail. Finally, employees often have a particularly vital stake in the affairs of their union, since union policies can affect the income, the working conditions, the very jobs of the members—matters that often loom larger to a worker than the interests he has in his church, his fraternal organization, or the other private associations to which he may belong.

Individual Freedom and Majority Rule

Minorities may try to protect their interests in various ways. They often seek legal intervention or use political channels to see to it that their position is given due weight in reaching decisions that concern them. In some instances, however, minorities will attempt to protect themselves by refusing to participate in the programs and policies of groups or institutions that would affect their lives. In the case of labor organizations, for example, a minority may seek to escape the union's authority altogether by persuading the government not to include them in a bargaining unit represented by that organization. Failing in this, they may try to avoid joining or paying dues. Even if they become members, they may refuse to go out on strike or to observe a picket line. Or they may seek to bring an independent court action to vindicate their rights under a collective-bargaining agreement instead of abiding by the grievance procedures established by the union and the employer.

In each of these situations, the union will normally try to prevent the minority from asserting its independence. As a result, the law has repeatedly been called upon to resolve the conflict. In deciding such cases, judges must inevitably come to grips with the basic reasons for allowing a majority to impose its will upon the minority. The principal arguments are four in number.

Majority rule may be necessary to prevent the minority from frustrating the objectives of the majority. This situation occurs quite plainly where the union establishes programs that cannot function without the participation of all members of the group. For example, a seniority program for layoffs and promotions cannot exist in any meaningful form unless all the members of the work group are included. Not all cases are so clear-cut. A strike by a minority of workers may not actually frustrate the aims of the majority; nevertheless, such a strike may close the plant and thus cause the majority such inconvenience and loss of pay that the minority cannot be granted this privilege.

Majority rule may also be upheld to prevent the minority from accepting the results of group action without helping to assume the burdens involved. Even if the minority is too small to harm the majority by withholding cooperation, compulsion can be defended on the principle that those who enjoy a benefit should pay a fair share of the costs.*

Majority rule may also be required to safeguard the interests of persons outside the organization. Thus, minority groups may be barred from striking not only because such action may harm other union members but also because it can jeopardize the interests of the employers, customers, and suppliers involved.

Finally, majority rule can sometimes be justified for administrative reasons. For example, a few members may have strong

---

* A special problem arises where the minority is compelled to accept the benefits that are said to give rise to the obligation to comply with majority rule. Intuitively, the case for imposing the obligation is not so strong as where the individual chooses to accept the benefits. Thus, the union member who joins voluntarily seems more obligated to respect the majority than the employee who is required to join by a union-shop provision. Even so, certain cases may exist wherein the obligation remains relatively clear-cut. If the benefit and burden take the same form—e.g., money—and the money the member receives exceeds what he is asked to pay to the organization, it is hard for him to argue that he should be allowed to escape the duty to contribute. For example, even an involuntary union member would be on shaky ground in trying to avoid paying dues if it could be demonstrated that he had received wage increases attributable to the union that substantially exceeded his payments to the organization.

reasons for refusing to cooperate with the programs of the majority, but it may be so difficult to identify these persons that any attempt to accommodate them will inevitably open the door to many other persons who have much less cause for refusing to conform. This argument is often cited to justify the practice of compelling citizens to pay their taxes in full even when they claim the most profound moral disapproval of military or other major expenditures.

These four principles do not automatically justify majority rule. They are simply factors to be weighed against the interests of the minority in deciding whether and when the majority should prevail. Often, as the following examples suggest, the competing interests are so dissimilar and embody such different values that they can be compared only with the greatest difficulty.

THE APPROPRIATE BARGAINING UNIT

The National Labor Relations Act prescribes procedures for holding an election to determine whether a majority of employees wish to be represented by a particular union. Once voted in, a union gains the exclusive right to bargain for all the employees involved until it becomes defunct or is turned out in a subsequent election. But before an election can be held, the National Labor Relations Board must decide among what group of employees the vote should be taken.[1] Should the election be among only a particular group of skilled employees in a plant? Among all production and maintenance employees in the plant? Among the production and maintenance employees in all the company's plants? Questions such as these may vitally affect the status of small groups of workers, for the answers will determine whether such groups will be submerged within a larger body of workers or given the right to make their own decision regarding union representation.

Many determinations as to the appropriate unit reflect the general principles suggested earlier, in explaining the majority's right to override minority interests. For example, the N.L.R.B. will normally prevent a few employees from voting as a separate unit if they perform work similar to that of other employees in the same plant. To allow a separate unit in such cases would be unjust, since the union voted in by the smaller group might negotiate shift schedules, shut down the plant, or take other actions that would vitally affect the employees outside the unit. In other cases, the Board may prevent employees in different departments of a plant from voting in separate departmental units, since multiple units will lead to multiple negotiations, inter-union rivalries, and possibly added strikes, which can unduly burden the employer and the public. On the other hand, where different groups in a single plant have distinctive skills or working conditions—such as electricians and draftsmen—the Board often allows separate units on the theory that these groups have such special needs that their claim to separate representation outweighs the interests of the other parties involved.

Although many of the Board's rules rest on perfectly sound principles, there are other troublesome cases where minority interests are disregarded for reasons that cannot be easily justified even on administrative grounds. In the retail field, for example, one can imagine a series of bargaining units that comprise separate groups within a single store, such as warehousemen, clerical workers, and sales employees. But one can also conceive of a unit encompassing all the employees in a single store—or even all employees in a group of stores within a metropolitan area. Employers have long argued for larger units, both because it is easier to deal with fewer unions and because larger units are usually harder for a union to organize. Unions, on the other hand, have tended to press for small units in cases where they are unable to organize larger groups.*

---

* Another troublesome problem has arisen where members working in a certain plant may wish to reject their union and split away from a bargaining unit consisting of the several installations in a single corporation. In one case, the desire to leave the unit may simply reflect the personal ambition of a local leader or a resentment arising from the international's refusal to approve an irresponsible strike. On another occasion, however, the employees involved may have been badly neglected by their union. The interests of the minority seem very different in these two cases. Nevertheless, the Board does not attempt to draw distinctions of this kind; it generally blocks any effort to split away from the larger unit so long as there is an active tradition of bargaining for the several installations in a single set of negotiations. Such rulings do not give evidence of any great desire by the Board to weigh minority and majority interests. On closer analysis, however, there are deeper problems that help explain the attitude of the Board. To weigh the interests of the minority in these cases would propel the Board into passing judgment on the quality of service rendered by the union to smaller groups within its membership. Is the government truly equipped to regulate union behavior in this way? Should a Board already burdened with a large and growing caseload undertake this added function? Is it wise for an agency already buffeted by partisan pressures to assume the sensitive task of passing judgment on the job done by individual unions? Critics may come to opposite conclusions in answering these questions, but the problems involved at least suggest how even the most conscientious agency may be led to soft-pedal minority interests to avoid serious administrative difficulties.

The N.L.R.B. has vacillated over the years between these positions. A decade ago, the Board seemed to favor the employer's view by requiring larger election units. More recently, the Board has moved toward a flexible policy that is much more favorable to the unions. In the insurance industry, the N.L.R.B. has approved individual offices as separate bargaining units at the union's request, but it has likewise approved units comprising groups of offices in a city or state when the union has sought a broader unit. With retail stores, unions have also been able to gain elections for individual departments in a single store, or entire stores, or even groups of stores. Apparently, each type of unit may now be considered appropriate, and the union is free to choose among them depending on the extent to which it is able to organize the employees involved.

These varying interpretations have important effects on the interests of minority groups. Under the earlier policies, employees in a single department or insurance office could never branch out on their own but were always bound by the wishes of larger units of workers. With the recent change in policy, these smaller units of employees have greater freedom in that they may select a union even though a majority of employees in the entire store, or group of stores, prefers to remain unorganized. Nevertheless, it is interesting to note that the N.L.R.B. accommodates the smaller groups only when it appears that they desire a union affiliation not wanted by the larger group. If the opposite occurs—so that the larger unit desires a union and the smaller group does not—the minority will not be given its head. This result is not easily explained. If the smaller unit can exercise self-determination in order to have a union, there is no obvious reason why it should not also be allowed to reject unionization. This example makes a point that recurs in various other contexts and guises. One can easily see the advantages to unions in the recent rulings of the Board just as one can perceive the benefits to employers in the earlier precedents. But one remains less sure that the interests of the minority have been adequately recognized in any of the rules that have been laid down.

THE UNION SHOP[2]

No issue has aroused greater furor in the field of labor relations than the status of the union shop.* Prior to the advent of
modern labor legislation, strikes to make employers accept union-
security provisions were condemned by the courts in many jurisdictions. With the passage of the Wagner Act, the union shop was
expressly permitted by federal law, and labor organizations were
normally allowed to negotiate contracts providing for the dismissal
of any employee who either refused to join the union or was
denied membership by it. But twelve years later, in the course of
passing the Taft-Hartley Act, Congress seriously qualified the right
to negotiate union-shop provisions. Under the Act, unions cannot
bar an employee from membership and then compel the employer
to dismiss him; the individual is fully protected in his job except
when he refuses to pay the regular dues and initiation fees. In
addition, Congress enacted the right-to-work proviso,† which
allowed individual states to pass legislation prohibiting any form
of compulsory union membership. Union leaders objected vocifer-
ously to this provision and have fought continuously for its repeal.
But though they succeeded in amending the Railway Labor Act to
authorize union-shop clauses unconditionally in the railroad and
airline industries, the provisions of the Taft-Hartley Act have
remained in force throughout the rest of the economy. By the mid-
sixties, after many spectacular referendum campaigns, right-to-
work legislation was on the statute books in nineteen of the fifty
states.

---

* A union-security provision of a collective-bargaining agreement is a clause
which requires employees to become members of a union or assume some
financial obligation to the union. Among the more common forms of union-
security clause are the union shop, which requires membership as a condition
of continued employment after a specified number of days of employment
have elapsed. The law further provides that no employer shall discriminate
against any employee for nonmembership if membership was denied or
terminated for reasons other than the payment of periodic dues and initiation
fees uniformly required. An agency shop does not require membership but only
the payment of periodic dues and assessments. A maintenance-of-membership
provision requires present members to maintain their membership status but
does not require other employees to join. The closed shop, illegal since 1947,
requires membership in a labor organization before a worker can take a job
with the employer involved.

† Section 14 (b) provides: "Nothing in this Act shall be construed as authorizing the execution or application of agreements requiring membership in a
labor organization as a condition of employment in any State or Territory in
which such execution or application is prohibited by State or Territorial law."

Many dubious arguments have been repeated during the long debate over the union-shop issue. For example, right-to-work advocates have consistently urged that the union shop violates the individual's right of free association by compelling him to join a union against his will. Yet this argument seems weak, for the law merely allows the union to compel individual workers to pay dues; it does not permit labor organizations to force employees to attend meetings or associate with other members. On the union side, labor spokesmen have tried to justify the union shop by analogizing it to the government's power to require all citizens to pay taxes. This argument is also questionable, for unions and governments are very different institutions with different claims upon the individual. Clearly, if the shoe is on the other foot, labor leaders are only too quick to deny that Constitutional restrictions limiting the government should equally bind their own organizations.

The major argument for the union shop is that individual workers should not be able to accept the benefits secured by their union without helping to pay for the expenses involved. Apart from any analogies with the government, the fact remains that unions expend large sums in negotiating better wages and working conditions for all employees in the bargaining unit. They are also compelled by law to process grievances and extend contract terms without discrimination to members and nonmembers alike. Under these circumstances, it is arguably unfair for a minority to refuse to pay dues while taking advantage of the benefits purchased by their fellow workers.*

While this argument is forceful, one troublesome point remains. It is true that many unions secure greater benefits for their constituents. But it is not clear that *every* employee is better off when he is represented by a union. There are local unions that have done little or nothing for their members. And there are individual members, even in well-run labor organizations, who might

---

* There is yet another, though less compelling, argument for the union shop. Some employers believe that union-security provisions can improve the quality of labor relations in their companies by allowing a local leader to take more responsible positions without fear of losing dues-paying members who disagree with his decisions. Hence, after studying the effects of right-to-work laws in Texas, Frederic Meyers observed that many employers willingly supported the union shop in practice (even though some of them continued to approve of right-to-work as a matter of general principle).[3] To the extent that these observations are correct, right-to-work laws will exact a cost by forcing some employers to choose between accepting more turbulent labor relations or violating the law covertly to achieve their private ends.

legitimately prefer to work without union representation. Certain skilled employees may find their wages held below "free market" rates in order to secure greater benefits for larger numbers of less-skilled workers. Other individuals may object to particular union policies or leaders to an extent that outweighs any satisfaction they derive from better wages and working conditions. Unlike the taxpayer—who almost always benefits from the existence of a government, even though he might prefer another administration in power—a worker may insist that he would be better off if there were no union at all. And if he does, it seems unfair to make him pay for representation he would prefer to do without.

Despite its surface appeal, this argument has its difficulties. The critical flaw is that those who refuse to join the union are often not the ones who do not receive fair value for their dues. Many nonmembers are simply freeloaders who are happy to accept the benefits of organization without having to pay money to the union. Although there are others who stay out because they dislike the union leaders or disapprove of certain of its policies, many of these individuals may actually be getting ample benefits for their dues. In most cases, they cannot even know whether they are getting a fair return, for no one can state what wages and conditions would be like if there were no union in the industry. Certainly, the wages paid in unorganized plants provide no index, for nonunion employers often adjust their wages in response to changes in the union scale in order to hold their workers and forestall organization. Under these circumstances, the case for the open shop seems insubstantial. Although a few workers might be justified in not paying dues, they can be accommodated only by opening the door to many others who will escape without any real justification.

POLITICAL EXPENDITURES

A more limited attack has been made against the union shop by those who object to having any portion of their dues expended for political purposes. Federal law has long forbidden the union to use dues to contribute directly to political campaigns.[4] But even these provisions do not prevent labor organizations from drawing upon dues to defray the costs of lobbying and pay for political articles and radio programs for their members. In 1959, certain members who were compelled to join a union brought suit to protest the use of their dues for such purposes. The issue eventually came to the Supreme Court in the case of *I.A.M. v. Street,* and a majority of the Court declared that the minority could not be forced to contribute dues for these ends.[5]

The problem posed by the *Street* case is not an easy one to resolve. The key issue is whether some vital personal freedom is infringed by requiring employees to pay dues that are used in part for political programs. In this connection, lawyers will argue that it is particularly repugnant to be forced to contribute to political causes with which one does not agree. But this is a point that will appeal much more to a judge than to a worker in a factory. The individual employee can clearly be compelled to pay for strikes of which he disapproves, to underwrite a drive to organize Negro laborers for whom he feels no concern, or to support union leaders whom he dislikes. Under these circumstances, he is unlikely to comprehend why the law should protect him from having to contribute to campaigns for the passage of a minimum-wage law, a social-security increase or a candidate who promises to vote for these and other labor-backed proposals. It is also difficult to find any real infringement on the employee's political freedom. The member is not prevented from supporting the candidates or the issues of his choice. When unions have sought to penalize the member for giving such support the courts have properly enjoined them from doing so. The issue is simply whether the union can support its legislative program and publicize candidates with funds obtained from regular dues. The impact on the individual seems hardly greater than it is when he is forced to pay taxes for a war which he dislikes or to support the private utility lobbies by purchasing gas, electricity or telephone service.

An argument may yet be made that our system of government will be unstabilized if one interest group can compel its members to support its political activities. But this fear seems grossly exaggerated. The use of dues for such purposes is not materially different from the practice of industrywide associations, which finance their lobbying activities out of revenues collected from the consumer. Moreover, the amounts of money affected by the Supreme Court decision are actually minuscule, since it seems unlikely that workers will take advantage of their newly won legal right to claim a refund of the few cents expended from their monthly dues for political purposes. In the end, one wonders why a lawsuit was ever brought on the question, for the court costs may well have exceeded the dues reclaimed by dissenting members across the nation. The answer to this question is revealing. In fact, the case is said to have been launched by businessmen who hoped to seize on political expenditures as a lever to overturn statutory authorization for the union shop. The genesis of this litigation tells much about the entire union-shop debate. In a very real sense, the worker is often little more than a pawn in a battle for larger stakes between companies and unions. To the businessmen who finance right-to-work campaigns, the issue is only partly one of individual rights. Many of these men are much more concerned by the unions' ability to enlarge their treasuries with compulsory dues and thereby finance added strikes and organizing campaigns. Unions, in turn, are most anxious to fatten their treasuries through compulsory membership. In short, the controversy over the union shop involves much more than minority rights, and the intensity of the struggle will never be understood by merely looking to the principles expounded by each side.

MAJORITY RULE IN BARGAINING AND CONTRACT ADMINISTRATION

Labor legislation in America has generally recognized the union's right to negotiate terms and conditions that bind all employees in the bargaining unit whether or not they belong to the union. This principle can be defended on several grounds. Many contract terms, such as seniority provisions and shift schedules, cannot operate effectively unless they apply to all the workers involved. To be sure, unions could bargain for their members alone in negotiating wages and certain other terms of employment, but this practice would invite resentment and abuse by allowing the employer to discriminate among employees doing similar work, often for the purpose of discouraging membership in the union. In addition, if a labor organization could not negotiate for all employees in the unit, minority unions might spring up, creating dangers of multiple strikes and unstabilizing rivalries between the competing organizations.

These arguments are generally accepted today by unions and employers. But disagreement remains over the extent to which majority rule should apply in negotiating and administering contracts. Two issues predominate. Should unions be allowed to force unwilling minorities to join in strikes over new agreements? And once an agreement is signed, should employees be allowed to go to court and litigate their individual grievances under the contract if the union has chosen to settle their case instead of insisting that it be decided by an outside, neutral arbitrator?

Looking first at the individual's right to litigate his claims, the "majoritarian" view has stressed two dangers that may arise if the union is not given power to settle grievances.[6] To begin with, many employees may bring frivolous cases to court and thus put the union and the employer to unnecessary expense. Individuals who insist on pressing their grievances may also prejudice other employees by obtaining decisions that either create unwelcome precedents for the future or give undue advantage to the aggrieved at the expense of other workers. Hence, the union must control the grievance process in order to carry out its essential role of accommodating the interests of diverse groups to produce the greatest benefit for the unit as a whole. The majoritarian view recognizes that a union will, because of ineptitude, laziness, or even petty personal reasons, sometimes abuse its power and refuse to process grievances. But rather than permit the individual to have a court resolve his contract claim, majoritarians urge that he merely be allowed to sue the union for failing to handle his grievance in a fair and impartial manner.

Such a position has apparently been adopted by the Supreme Court,[7] as well as by the courts of most states.* But several academic critics have argued forcefully that the employee cannot be adequately protected by simply allowing him to sue his union for improper representation.[8] Too few employees have enough money or knowledge of the law to bring a suit of this kind. And it is usually difficult in an individual case to prove that the union failed to go to arbitration for unfair or inadequate reasons. Thus, libertarian critics insist that the individual cannot be protected unless he is allowed to sue directly on the contract. According to this view, the right to litigate can easily be tailored to respect the legitimate interests of others.† The union and employer can insist that the aggrieved bring his case before an arbitrator rather than have the matter resolved by a judge, less experienced in the

---

* There is some judicial authority to the effect that an individual employee can petition the National Labor Relations Board to issue unfair-labor-practice charges against a union that fails to prosecute a grievance. But even these cases would not go beyond simply requiring the union to handle grievances fairly and impartially.

† This process raises a number of technical issues that will not be discussed here—such as how to apportion costs and how to select an impartial arbitrator.[9]

peculiarities of collective-bargaining agreements. In addition, to counter the risk of frivolous complaints, the aggrieved can be compelled to assume all the costs of arbitration unless he prevails before the arbitrator, or at least is judged to have brought a substantial case. The risk of having to pay several hundred dollars or more in costs will, it is argued, serve to deter employees from resorting too lightly to arbitration.[10]

When the opposing arguments are clearly exposed, it is apparent that the issue is more one of fact than one of principle. Would the libertarian view provoke a substantial number of groundless cases? Would it result in ill-considered opinions having disruptive effects upon the interests of other employees in the unit? It is difficult to resolve these questions empirically, since the individual has so rarely been allowed to take his grievances to court. But what evidence there is suggests that the employee could be given such a right without much danger of adverse consequences, provided that the right is appropriately qualified by the safeguards referred to above. Experience in other areas of labor law indicates that few employees will press their claims when they run the risk of having to pay substantial litigation costs. And those who do bring action are likely to do so only where they have a strong interest at stake. Thus, the overwhelming number of individual court cases in the past have involved situations where the aggrieved has been discharged from employment. It is in these cases that inept or discriminatory treatment causes the greatest harm and injustice to the employee. And it is these cases that create the least risk of jeopardizing the interests of other employees, since the issues involved are generally matters peculiar to the case at hand, such as whether the aggrieved actually misbehaved, whether he was adequately warned, whether his conduct was justified under the circumstances, and so forth. To be sure, other cases may arise involving broader principles that can affect other groups of employees. But if the union and the management can insist that the matter be heard by an arbitrator, they will be free to explain the ramifications of the case to a man experienced in the subtleties of labor relations. As a last resort, they can even renegotiate the contract to nullify an undesirable ruling for the future. All things considered, therefore, access to the grievance process— at least in discipline and discharge cases—seems an appropriate area in which to give greater freedom to the individual without undue risk to the legitimate concerns of the majority.

The rights of individual workers during a strike present very different problems of accommodating majority and minority interests. The individual union member may, for several reasons, wish not to strike. He may feel strongly that the burdens of a strike do not justify the added gains being sought by the union. Even if he agrees with the union's position, his own financial position may make it difficult to bear even a temporary loss of wages. He may even fear, especially if he is a junior employee, that the company will hire a permanent replacement when he strikes and thus deprive him of his job.

The union will react very strongly against any member who refuses to join in a strike—so much so that it will often expel the strikebreaker or subject him to a fine or some other penalty. The point is not that the leaders want to compel a majority of workers to strike against their will. Unions normally poll their members before a strike; these votes typically result in overwhelming majorities, or the strike would have little chance of success, regardless of any fines imposed. The major arguments for exacting penalties are twofold: *1)* The union considers it highly disloyal for a minority to remain at work and avoid the losses and risks of the walkout; and *2)* The union fears that the minority may jeopardize the strike itself either by helping the company keep its plant in operation or by sapping morale and tempting others to break ranks.

Faced with these conflicting interests, what action can the union take against those who will not join in a strike? In the first place, the law is clear that the union can expel such individuals from membership. On this point, the law seems plainly correct. Bear in mind that the union cannot have the employees fired or discriminated against with respect to their wages or working conditions; it can only deprive them of their union membership. And since the strike is central to the purpose of the union, an employee who jeopardizes its success by refusing to participate can hardly complain if the organization does not wish to retain him as a member.

The problem is more difficult when the union seeks to fine the offending member and enforce the fine in court. If the union exercises this power, it can virtually compel participation in the strike, for even a member who would rather quit than strike may have to yield if he faces a prohibitive fine. Yet, what is wrong with giving this power to the union? Why should individuals be free to avoid the strike and thus endanger the objectives, and even the jobs, of the majority? After all, the minority must adhere to the terms of employment negotiated by the majority. Why should it not also be compelled to comply with a strike that is called to achieve these terms?*

The Supreme Court appears to have sided with the union on this issue, for it has affirmed the right to enforce fines of a reasonable amount, at least against those who have joined the organization voluntarily. But many critics strongly disagree. They argue that strikers may actually be replaced and lose their jobs and that the majority should not be allowed to force the individual worker to run a risk of such magnitude. This point has a certain appeal, particularly if the Court means to uphold the fining of members who were compelled, by a union-shop provision, to join, and thus never agreed to accept the risks entailed by a strike. But to concede this argument is not to say that the union should be unable to exact some payment from nonstrikers.

At least two arguments can be made in the union's behalf. To begin with, even if the nonstriker is allowed to protect himself from losing his job, he should not be permitted to avoid the loss of income that the majority suffered in its effort to extract better terms from the employer. Thus, the union should be allowed to collect a fine so long as the amount does not exceed the pay received by the nonstriker during the walkout (less any strike benefits he would have been eligible to receive from the union). Some observers would object to this reasoning, arguing that the minority should not be forced to accept even a temporary loss of wages during the strike. This argument goes very far to protect the individual at the expense of majority interests. But even putting this problem aside, the union can make the further point that individuals should not be able to eat their cake and have it, too, by escaping the burdens of the strike while sharing in the benefits that are eventually won. Under this approach, the union could legitimately force nonstrikers to pay any amount not exceeding the value of the added benefits achieved by the strike. Of course, there are practical problems in measuring these benefits. It may be unclear just what the employer would have offered had the dispute been settled on the eve of the strike. Nor can one know if a

---

* It is well to bear in mind that the minority will generally be very small; for practical and political reasons, the union will seldom be prepared to levy fines where a substantial proportion of the membership involved has refused to strike.

lost strike may eventually bear fruit by making the union's threats more credible in future negotiations. Despite these complications, most cases could be resolved easily enough by allowing the union to fine nonstrikers, provided that the amount collected does not exceed the income the members would have lost by striking or the added benefits they will receive over the terms of the new agreement as a result of the walkout.* By adopting this standard, the courts would do no more than respect the legitimate claims of the majority against the worker who refuses to walk out with his fellow members.

CONCLUSION

The rights of minorities to avoid majority rule are often analyzed in ways that do not take adequate account of the competing interests involved. But if the law has reached questionable results, it has not done so by consistently favoring either side. Whereas majority interests have been slighted in the area of right-to-work and political contributions, they have been exaggerated in the case of aggrieved individuals and in some of the appropriate unit determinations.

A wayward thread running through these cases is the tendency for minority rights to become a cat's-paw in the struggle between larger, organized interest groups. Employers may well perceive an interest in protecting the minority against the union shop, while unions will champion smaller bargaining units when it serves their organizing objectives. Yet the danger remains that neither employers nor unions may have interests that precisely coincide with those of the minority. When this situation occurs, minority interests are specially vulnerable, for it is usually employers and unions that bring the cases, marshal the arguments and generate the pressures that help to shape public policy. Thus, it is probably no accident that minority interests have received the least sympathetic treatment from the N.L.R.B. and the courts in cases where the minority stands largely alone—where individuals try to pursue their grievance against the wishes of the union and

---

*Most unions provide that fines levied by local unions may be reviewed by the international. In the process of review, it should be relatively simple in most cases for the union to make certain that the fine does not run a risk of being declared invalid under the principles set forth above.

the employer, or employees in a single store seek to avoid representation, or workers in a single plant petition to split off from a multi-plant bargaining unit.

Decentralization and Local Autonomy

Individuals and minorities do not always try to promote their special interests by avoiding the union entirely or escaping the fundamental obligations of membership. Instead, they may simply wish a measure of autonomy to pursue their special interests while continuing to work within the basic framework of union rules and obligations. This tendency has been most visible in the area of collective bargaining.

In theory at least, the union will maximize the welfare of its members by decentralizing its bargaining in order to give as much autonomy to particular groups as it can without jeopardizing the interests of the larger body of members. Most union officials would subscribe to this principle. Nevertheless, collective bargaining has become somewhat more centralized in many industries, and it is important to grasp precisely why this process has occurred. Five contributing factors can be cited.

BARGAINING POWER

In many instances, the union can increase its bargaining power by negotiating for a larger group of employees.* For example, workers in a single plant may have little power in bargaining with a management that has other plants it can operate profitably during a strike. If the union hopes to extract greater concessions, it will have to negotiate simultaneously for all the employer's plants on a companywide basis, or at least for those serving common markets. Similar reasons explain the recent efforts by several unions to join forces and engage in coordinated bargaining with giant diversified companies such as Union Carbide and General Electric.

---

* This is not always so. A small group of key craftsmen may exert enormous leverage if they bargain separately, since they can bring an entire plant to a standstill by walking out.

PRODUCT MARKET COMPETITION

Where different plants and companies vie with one another in the same market, the union may have to insist upon a common wage scale for all competing units. If a multi-plant firm is allowed to pay lower wages at one installation, it may expand its operations there at the expense of jobs in its other plants. If one company can pay lower wages than its rivals, it may undersell them and thereby force the other firms to insist that the union reduce their rates to competitive levels. Over the years, pressures of this kind have been a major force in centralizing wage negotiations. The process of centralization, moreover, has gone forward in many industries where advances in transport, storage and sales techniques have continuously enlarged the geographic area in which firms compete.

EQUITY

As union members become aware of conditions in other plants, they are likely to protest if they receive lower wages and benefits than members doing similar work elsewhere. As a political institution, the union is sensitive to pressures of this kind. Hence, the desire for "equity" often reinforces competition as a force for standardizing wages and benefits. In fact, the demand for equity may even lead to uniform wages and conditions among firms that are not actually competing with one another.

ADMINISTRATIVE CONSIDERATIONS

Centralized negotiations can offer a variety of administrative advantages. For example, in markets made up of many small firms, unions and associations of employers may find it cheaper and more convenient to conduct a single set of negotiations for the entire group of companies. Pension plans and other funded benefits also have led to more centralized bargaining because they can often be administered more economically when negotiated for larger groups of employees. In fragmented industries, these savings may result in multi-employer bargaining; in many large corporations, fringe benefits have been a major force in moving from plant to companywide bargaining. More recently, these tendencies have been reinforced by a desire for even larger multi-employer plans in order to permit workers to carry accumulated benefits with them when they transfer from one plant or company to another.

EMPLOYER INTERESTS

Even if a union wishes to maintain local autonomy, it may encounter heavy pressure from employers to move toward more centralized bargaining. Where a management's several plants are highly integrated, it may insist on companywide bargaining in order to minimize the risk of strikes in particular installations that can cripple the company's entire operation. In competitive industries, companies may demand multi-employer bargaining to avoid whipsaw tactics by which individual employers are threatened with being shut down while their competitors continue operating.

These various pressures have expanded the scope of negotiations in many industries to include increasing numbers of plants and employees. In view of such developments, several critics have raised the alarm of excessive centralization, claiming that too many issues are being decided at levels far removed from the workers involved. Yet there is very little hard evidence with which to evaluate these fears. Although one can point to obvious dangers in centralized bargaining, it is hard to demonstrate that these costs outweigh the benefits that can accrue to the members through greater uniformity, efficiency, and bargaining power.*

These problems are so complex and the circumstances so varied from one industry to another that the government would be ill-advised to fix the appropriate level of negotiations by statute. Moreover, the extent of centralization or decentralization in decision making varies among issues in the same collective bargaining relationship. If a proper degree of local autonomy is to be preserved, it will have to result in large part from the play of political forces within unions and management associations. These forces are not insubstantial. National officers must normally win approval from local leaders in order to shift collective bargaining to a higher level of authority. Like most officials, local leaders do not like to see their power diminished, and they will resist the international unless more centralized bargaining promises to yield better results. Various types of pressure can also be exerted from the ranks to

---

* Chapter 8 considers the consequences of an enlarged area of bargaining upon economic conflict and the public interest.

counteract excessive centralization. The grievance process provides an apt illustration. If the parties concentrate too much on resolving grievances at higher levels, foremen and local union leaders may begin to pass on disputes without making serious efforts to resolve them in the plant. Dissatisfaction with this process may then result in a larger number of grievances being filed. In time the grievance machinery will become so overloaded that officials on both sides will begin to think about decentralizing the process to encourage settlement at the plant level.

Much the same process has emerged in multi-plant negotiations over the question of local issues.[11] In order to maximize its bargaining power, one side or the other may insist that local problems—involving such matters as parking facilities, wash-up time, or distribution of overtime—be considered in the company-wide negotiations. In the auto industry, for example, many thousands of issues of this type have been presented in negotiations with the major companies. The immediate result has been to overburden the bargaining process to such a point as to preclude any thoughtful discussion of the issues involved. Once again, however, the ensuing difficulties create a growing pressure to find some way of resolving genuine local questions at the plant level.

These are but a few examples of the pressures that work against undue centralization. Employees may also resort to wildcat strikes or decertification petitions to convey their dissatisfaction with the treatment of problems at a remote level of negotiations. In other situations, a disgruntled rank and file will turn its local leaders out of office. Taken as a whole, therefore, this battery of constraints tugs insistently against excessive centralization.

The process of decentralization need not always stop at the level of the plant or the department. Even among individual salesmen, maintenance men, or pipe fitters, there will be important differences of opinion that are submerged by collective decisions that subject all members to a uniform decision. These differing interests cannot be fully accommodated without providing a generous measure of autonomy for each of the workers involved. The problem, of course, is to determine how much autonomy can be granted without interfering unduly with the operation of the enterprise.

Even now, a good deal of individual choice remains under the normal collective-bargaining contract. In the usual case, the employee is free to accept or refuse an opportunity for a promotion.

He can work overtime or refuse to do so. Under many contracts he can choose whether to take a vacation with pay or remain at work with extra compensation. Piecework systems allow many workers to decide, within limits, their own pace of work. It is possible, however, to conceive of a much larger scope for individual choice. In particular, one can imagine unions and companies bargaining over a standard increase in compensation, leaving to each employee an opportunity to distribute the added amount as he sees fit among such alternatives as a pension plan, a vacation fund, a health and welfare program, or a straight wage increase. With the help of the computer, a large company can now implement such proposals by leaping over the enormous complexities of costing different benefits and administering the thousands of varying decisions as to how paychecks will be distributed.

To be sure, serious problems remain to be solved before putting such a system into effect. For example, critics may argue that the healthy and the young should be required to help defray the cost of providing for the sick and the retired and that bachelors should share the cost of the medical benefits that go chiefly to the families of married employees. Employers may also insist that free choice be subject to requirements of minimum coverage for old age, disability, sickness and the like. Otherwise, managements, as well as union leaders, may suffer the consequences of disgruntled employees who have made improvident choices. With all these problems, however, the possibilities seem most intriguing. Providing more options to employees will increase their freedom and should enhance the welfare of the group, at least if certain minimum coverage is assumed. In fact, management itself may benefit by escaping in part from the prevailing system of bargaining in which unions can often satisfy their more important minority groups only by pushing hard to extract concessions for everyone.

The Fair Accommodation of Minority Interests

Up to now, consideration has been given to how much autonomy can be yielded to minorities without undue prejudice to the needs of the larger group. In many situations, however, it is clear that the claims of different groups conflict in such a way that it is impossible to satisfy one without sacrificing the interests of another. Ideally, union leaders seek a compromise that gives appropriate weight to the merits of each claim. But can the leaders meet this responsibility under political pressure from their members? Can a handful of women expect a union committee to press for their demand for more promotion opportunities into jobs now held by men? Will union negotiators support a large wage-rate increase for employees in a single classification who are suffering a wage inequity, particularly if this can be done only by dropping a demand for a slightly higher increase for all the employees in the plant? There is no end to these conflicts, for the accommodation of different groups is the very essence of collective bargaining.

THE INTERESTS OF OCCUPATIONAL MINORITIES

In negotiating a contract, the union typically begins by soliciting demands from all segments of its membership. These demands often reflect the special interests of various occupational groups, such as workers in a particular department or employees with some special skill. In cases of this kind, the union officers would seem to be under pressure to accede to the wishes of the largest number without regard to the merits of the competing claims. For example, the late Henry Simons concluded that rational union members would periodically insist on higher wages, at the expense of stunting the business and laying off junior employees, until the company finally collapsed just as the last affluent member retired.[12] In practice, however, the process works very differently. Most negotiations do not consist of clear-cut choices between majority and minority interests. Rather, the union works with many demands that are pressed with varying degrees of intensity by different groups. Under these circumstances, the typical union member is not simply identified with the majority or the minority; his interests lie with different groups on different issues. On wages, he may belong to a majority; on fringe benefits to the minority; on working conditions, he may simply belong to one of the many minorities that are backing special demands relevant to particular job classifications or departments. Under these conditions, the union negotiator has no easy calculus to decide which contract will win the largest following in the union. Nor do the members typically count on any particular set of results. More often, the rank and file simply have certain minimum expectations, and this

minimum normally leaves the negotiator with a measure of free
play in formulating his position.

In exercising this discretion, the negotiator will try hard to
satisfy the demands that are felt most keenly by particular groups.
He will also push ahead with the demands on which management
appears to be most accommodating. And he will probably emphasize claims that seem particularly meritorious, since he will normally consider them more important, easier to argue for, and more
likely to be accepted by the employer. Although this process is
hardly perfect, it tends, on the whole, to make union strategy
conform to the intensity of feeling among different groups of
members and to the relative merits of the claims they have
advanced.

It is true, of course, that situations do arise in which the
demands of a minority plainly clash with the interests of a larger
group of members. The desire of skilled workers to increase their
wage differential, for example, will often conflict with the wishes
of a larger body of less-skilled operatives for a uniform cents-per-
hour wage increase. Under these circumstances, there is an evident
danger that the skilled workers will simply be voted down regardless of the merits of their position. Yet even here, there are a
number of protective devices that help to safeguard the interests of
the minority.

Under certain circumstances, the employer himself will insist
on recognizing the special claims of the minority in order to keep
his work force and maintain morale. This is particularly likely in
the case of skilled craftsmen who may look for work elsewhere if
their wages fall below the prevailing scale in the area.

Minority groups may also protect their interests through the
normal democratic processes in the union. They may gain concessions for themselves by agreeing to support other policies of the
officers. They may participate more actively in union meetings and
vote as a bloc in order to expand their influence. If they are highly
skilled, their superior status and education may win them a disproportionate share of union posts and a high degree of influence
among their fellow workers.

As a last resort, occupational minorities may find ways of
making such trouble for union officers that the officers will be
forced to accommodate the special minority interests. Skilled
employees may be able to split off and join a rival union. Workers

in a single plant may threaten to decertify and abandon the union. Wildcat strikes may be used with telling effect by strategically placed minorities. All these forces can serve as threats to extract concessions from the leaders.

The effects of these safeguards are most clearly visible in the case of skilled minorities in industrial unions. In several unions, particularly those where the proportion of skilled workers has been substantial, normal political processes have served to ensure that continuing attention is given to the interests of the skilled groups. As a result, the wage differentials enjoyed by these groups have not narrowed appreciably vis-à-vis the semiskilled operatives. In other unions, where a narrowing has taken place, various forms of protest have eventually resulted in special procedures to ensure greater attention to skilled interests. In several organizations, skilled-trades departments were established to examine the special needs of craftsmen and make proposals to union bargaining committees. The U.A.W. and I.U.E. have gone further to provide representation for craftsmen on the bargaining committees in negotiation with major companies. In almost all instances, these changes appear to have caused an improvement in the relative position of skilled-wage levels.

Such processes do not work perfectly by any means. But it is important to recognize that deficiencies can occur in either direction. In some cases, a minority achieves a degree of power that seems quite out of proportion, as in the Auto Workers, where the skilled workers have possibly obtained the right to veto the entire contract if they object to its provisions. In other cases, particular groups do not have sufficient power to protect their interests. Minorities may have little influence where their numerical strength is small; this is particularly true of workers who do not have special skills or occupational interests that are sufficiently distinct for the law to provide extra leverage to the group by granting the right to split off or seek decertification. Other minorities will be overlooked because they lack the cohesion and the determination to bring maximum influence to bear. For example, there are many organizations that include scattered groups of employees in jobs unrelated to those of the great bulk of the members. In such cases, the satellite groups have often been ignored for years without arousing enough resentment among the workers involved to lead them to decertify or seek another union.

But these cases should not obscure the fact that there are many forms of access and leverage that allow most occupational minorities to press their interests quite forcefully upon their union leaders.

Unions and Racial Minorities

In the mosaic of different groups that make up a union, not all the divisions of interest are built along occupational lines. Older workers may have special bargaining interests that diverge from those of younger employees, women employees do not necessarily share the same priorities as men, and urban workers do not always have the same preferences as those employed in rural plants. These differences can be expanded in number and detail. Here, emphasis is given to the situation of the Negro worker, since this is a topic of particularly pressing concern to American society.

The subject elicits deep emotions. The following statements are illustrative:

> Union concepts of security and seniority were formulated in the period of struggle between company and union. Now the struggle is between the Negroes and the unions. . . . It is our position that a basic conflict exists between labor-union concepts and civil-rights concepts. Something has to give. [John Doar, former United States Assistant Attorney General and President of the Board of Education, New York City][13]

> DRUM is an organization of oppressed and exploited black workers. It realizes that black workers are victims of inhumane slavery at the expense of white racist plant managers. . . . The Union has consistently and systematically failed us time and time again. . . . The U.A.W. bureaucracy is just as guilty, its hands are just as bloody, as the white racist management of this corporation [Chrysler]. [DRUM, Dodge Revolutionary Union Movement][14]

> If the failure of organized labor to introduce the spirit of equality and democracy into the workplace has been a heavy burden for Negroes, it is also the tragedy of American labor as a social institution. [Herbert Hill][15]

> I believe that, when we look at the whole picture, labor is strongly on the side of social justice and equal rights. It performed a great service in pulling the rug out from under George Wallace's attempts to rack up a large blue-collar vote

for his message of hate. . . . All unions ought to be educating their members to the dangers of bigotry, and to the fact that racism damages white workers as well as blacks. But on the whole, organized labor is as good a friend of black efforts for equality as exists in our imperfect society. [Whitney Young, Urban League][16]

I promised you a talk today on a subject which some of you might find hard to swallow—and that is the recently adopted affirmative action program of the Building and Construction Trades Department. . . . It is more important than COPE donations, more important than getting our people registered and out to the polls on Election Day. . . . Above all, I ask that you not try to circumvent the whole issue with some kind of phony solution that is no solution at all. A general advertising for candidates that brings a thousand applicants for ten openings is no solution to our problem. Much better a single Negro prospect than a thousand white ones. . . . [Peter T. Schoemann, General President, Plumbers][17]

These statements are as passionate and as widely divergent as any to be found on any aspect of union activities. As a result, the subject requires a sterner commitment to objectivity and to the quest for facts than almost any other subject discussed in this volume.

HISTORICAL BACKGROUND[18]

From the outset of the AFL in the 1880's, its announced policy was to organize workers without regard to race or religion. In the language of the 1890 convention, the Federation ". . . looked with disfavor upon trade unions having provisions in their constitutions excluding from membership persons on account of race and color and they requested they be expunged."[19]

The Federation encountered difficulty in these early years in dealing with constituent national unions on the issue of race. The problems are illustrated by its relations to the International Association of Machinists. This important national union was founded in Atlanta by railroad machinists in 1888. It reflected what Professor Mark Perlman has called the "Southern influence"—non-egalitarian, emphasizing the superiority of a particular type of white, fully trained craftsmen.[20] An early circular offered membership to ". . . none but white, free born citizens . . . who must be practical machinists capable of commanding the average rate of wages given in some regulated machine shop and the trade at the time of their election."[21]

Gompers was anxious to have the Machinists affiliated with the AFL. He attended and addressed the 1893 convention of the union.

> Gompers recognized that the major block to affiliation was his own insistence on the deletion of the "white-only clause." He held true to his principles; while urging the delegates to vote affiliation, he told them that the "white-only" qualification was wrong and would have to be dropped before he would consent to taking the I.A.M. into the AFL. The delegates refused to remove the offending phrase at that time.[22]

In 1895, while Gompers was out of office for a year, the I.A.M. was admitted to the Federation. The "white" qualification was removed from the union's constitution; but to assuage its Southern locals—which, it was feared, might secede—the "white-only" clause was incorporated into the secret ritual.*

The 1900 AFL convention reviewed the racial problems of organizing, particularly in the South. It concluded that:

> . . . while we do not in any way abate the policy laid down by the American Federation of Labor, namely, that the trade union is open to all regardless of race, sex, nationality, creed or color, we recommend that the laws be so amended as to permit of charters being granted to separate local unions and central bodies composed of colored workers.[23]

The concept of racially separated locals—reminiscent of the separate-but-equal doctrine sanctioned by the courts until 1954—was applied by the Federation to directly affiliated locals and central labor unions, largely in the South, where an integrated policy was unacceptable to many whites. A number of national unions followed similar policies. Although Gompers found segregated locals distasteful, he concluded that unless they were permitted, there would simply not be unions in the South.

---

* The racial restriction in the ritual was to remain until 1947. In the 1945 convention, the Committee on the Ritual voted 10 to 3 to recommend dropping the clause. The matter was put to a roll call vote and was defeated 2,173 to 1,958. Late in 1947, faced with litigation and loss of representation rights, the Executive Council of the international union, on its own motion, amended the ritual and eradicated the race clause. This action was upheld at the following convention.

As the AFL grew in size, member unions that practiced discrimination asserted the principle of autonomy set forth in the Federation constitution and refused to change their racial policies. The Federation felt itself powerless to require the affiliated unions to mend their ways. Outside the AFL, the operating crafts on the railroads did not admit Negroes, and the Federation feared that member unions might disaffiliate if pressure were brought upon them because of their discriminatory policies.

Commencing in World War I, there was a considerable migration of blacks from the old South toward industrial centers in the North. The wartime shortage of labor and the sudden shutdown of immigration from Europe encouraged this internal migration. While 12 percent of Negroes lived outside the states of the Confederacy in 1910, the percentage increased to 26 percent by 1930 and to more than half by the mid-sixties. This migration was to bring Negroes from agriculture into urban centers, and into industrial employment and increasing contact with unions.

As time passed, Negroes gradually gained jobs in such industries as steel, meat packing, coal and ore mining, and automobiles. As these industries were organized by the CIO, Negroes were taken into the unions, which recognized the decisive importance of organizing all workers regardless of race if they were to engage in a successful strike for economic benefits.

As late as the 1930's, there were eleven international unions affiliated with the AFL with formal race bars, almost all of them associated with the railroad industry.* (There were thirteen other international unions with such formal restrictions outside the Federation also largely in transportation industries.)[24] In contrast, no national union affiliated with the CIO excluded Negroes by constitutional provisions, tacit consent of locals, or segregated local unions of minorities. A closer relationship developed between the leaders of the Negro community and the CIO unions than had generally prevailed with other labor leaders. Philip Murray and Walter Reuther served as members of the N.A.A.C.P. Board of Directors.

As CIO unions succeeded in organizing skilled and unskilled

---

* The policies of the railroad unions can be explained by the fact that many were formed in the South or border states. Early railroad unions were fraternal and social organizations; many started as insurance societies at a time when many insurance companies considered the transportation business too risky; railroad jobs were often considered "prestige jobs" in smaller cities and towns, and from 1920 on, the level of employment in the industry declined steadily.

workers alike, competition for members forced many AFL international unions, such as the Machinists and the Electricians, to modify their policies in order to take in unskilled and semiskilled groups which they had previously found difficult to organize or had shown little interest in enrolling. The same competitive forces compelled these AFL affiliates to show more interest in the organization of Negroes.

Civil-rights organizations and other critics also began to exert a gradually increasing pressure on unions to abandon discriminatory practices. The rise of the Sleeping Car Porters union and its affiliation with the AFL in 1936 was to prove a particularly significant event because of the role that A. Philip Randolph, its president, was to play in the relations between the Federation and Negroes. Professor Taft has well said:

> More than any single man he has been responsible for the formal ending of discrimination by a number of unions. . . . Randolph, by publicly revealing the prejudice of organizations which were themselves suppliants for rights, not only showed their contradictory and unconscionable conduct, but compelled the leaders of the federation as well as the heads of the unions to seek changes.[25]

In 1939, the AFL discontinued the practice of giving charters to racially segregated central labor organizations. Thereafter, economic forces lent added pressure to break down restrictive policies. Tight labor markets during World War II greatly accelerated the employment of Negroes in industry, and these workers automatically joined labor organizations pursuant to union-shop provisions. As labor continued to organize successfully in one industry after another, the number of Negro members steadily increased.*

After the war, the principle of nondiscrimination was more explicitly recognized within the union movement. The constitution of the merged federation in 1955 declared as one of its objects and principles, "To encourage all workers without regard to race, creed, color, national origin or ancestry to share equally in the full benefits of union organization."[26] A. Philip Randolph and Willard

---

* It is estimated there were 61,000 Negroes in AFL unions in 1928, when total membership of the Federation was 2.9 million. There were 1.5 million Negroes in unions in 1956, when membership reached 17.5 million in all unions. In 1928, Negro membership was 2.1 percent compared to 8.6 percent in 1956. The 1968 Negro trade-union membership has been estimated to be approaching 2 million members, or about 10 percent of the total.

Townsend were the first two Negroes elected to the executive council of the Federation. Arthur J. Goldberg, who played a major role in the merger negotiations, wrote shortly thereafter:

> The leaders of the AFL-CIO intend to seek achievement of this civil rights goal in as practical and speedy a manner as possible.
>
> I am so certain of this that I would be prepared, a few years hence, to measure the record of the AFL-CIO in this field alongside of the record of any organization in America.[27]

In 1961, the AFL-CIO convention adopted a comprehensive resolution urging equal treatment of minorities. Negro trade-unionists wanted a more forceful policy; but, while the Federation was willing to persuade and to preach to its affiliates and to work through an enlarged and more vigorous civil-rights department, it was unwilling to use the sanction of expulsion.

By the mid-sixties, then, the grosser forms of union discrimination had greatly diminished. The number of unions expressly barring Negroes from membership had dwindled from 27 unions in 1930 to 14 in 1943 to none after 1964. Segregated locals had also declined, and, of the few that lingered on, many were maintained because the officers and members of colored locals did not wish to lose their identity by merging with larger white counterparts. The impact of discrimination on Negro employment had also changed significantly. For several decades after the Civil War, unions in the construction, shipbuilding and railroad industries used their economic power to displace substantial numbers of Negroes who had previously held skilled jobs. After World War II, however, restrictive practices may have slowed the entry of Negroes into higher-paying jobs, but they were not used to push Negroes out of skilled occupations to any significant degree.

In recent years, discrimination on the part of unions has taken two principal forms, almost always with the cooperation or tacit consent of employers. In a number of skilled crafts, unions exercise a degree of control over employment through joint apprenticeship programs and by administering hiring halls. Many of these local unions have managed to impede entry into their trade by requiring difficult qualifying tests, failing to publicize openings in apprenticeship programs, and other informal devices that keep Negroes out of their organizations. These exclusionary tactics have aroused particular attention in the building trades. There are also crafts in other industries that have pursued similar policies. Thus, very few Negroes can be found in skilled jobs controlled by such organizations as the Air Line Pilots Association, certain railway brotherhoods, and the printing crafts.

Industrial unions rarely try to exclude Negroes from membership, nor do they have much influence over the hiring policies of employers. But many industrial locals, particularly in the South, have lent active support in collective-bargaining negotiations to seniority districts and rules that tend to relegate Negro workers to lower-paying and less desirable jobs. National officers in a few industrial unions—notably the Auto Workers and the Packinghouse Workers—have moved aggressively to stamp out these practices, even at the risk of losing some of their locals. But government investigations have continued to unearth cases of discriminatory practices and contract provisions among unionized plants in the steel, rubber, paper, and other manufacturing industries.

GOVERNMENT POLICIES[28]

Commencing in the early 1940's, the government developed increasingly stringent policies to protect racial minorities from discrimination in employment (and in labor organizations). In 1944, the Supreme Court's landmark decision in *Steele v. Louisville and N.R.R.*[29] announced that a union under the Railway Labor Act must represent nonunion or minority union members ". . . without hostile discrimination, fairly, impartially, and in good faith." According to the Court, if unions were to enjoy the rights of exclusive representation, under which they bargain for all employees in the unit whether union members or not, they had to assume an affirmative duty to act fairly toward all these employees. This doctrine has come to be known as the duty of fair representation; it compels every union in bargaining to refrain from discriminating against Negroes with respect to such matters as wages, discharges, layoffs, job assignments, promotions or grievance handling.*

---

* In the fifteen years following enactment of the Taft-Hartley law (1947), the N.L.R.B. did not consider that violation of the duty of fair representation constituted unfair labor practices under the N.L.R.A. Then, in a sharp reversal of policy the Board held in 1962 that unions with rights of representation are prohibited from ". . . taking action against any employee upon considerations or classifications which are irrelevant, invidious or unfair."[30] While the Board's

Although the Steele doctrine doubtless caused certain unions, such as the Machinists, to put an end to some discriminatory practices, it suffered from glaring weaknesses. Most Negro workers were unfamiliar with the law and unable to afford a lawyer; as a result, they brought only a handful of cases to compel fair representation. More serious still, employers were not subject to a correlative obligation; in fact, Southern employers sometimes urged white employees to vote against unions on the grounds that labor organizations would have to work to remove existing discriminatory privileges if they were selected as bargaining representative.

These defects were in part remedied by Title VII of the Civil Rights Act of 1964. This statute makes it an unlawful practice for an employer to discriminate against any individual with respect to employment or compensation because of race, color, religion, sex or national origin.[31] Similarly, the law makes it an unlawful employment practice for a union to exclude from membership, to segregate or classify its membership, to refuse to refer to employment, or cause an employer to discriminate against an individual by reason of race, color, religion, sex or national origin.

---

judicial arguments for its actions have had a mixed reception in the courts, it has sought to provide administrative redress for violations of the union's duty of fair representation, including cases arising from racial discrimination. Although resort to the N.L.R.B. in such cases has the advantage to the aggrieved individual employee that litigation costs are borne by the government, only a handful of cases have in fact been brought under this new Board doctrine.

The executive arm of government has also sought, from at least 1941, to use its power as a purchaser of goods and supplies and as an employer to eliminate racial discrimination in employment. In Executive Order 8802, establishing the Fair Employment Practices Committee (F.E.P.C.), President Roosevelt stated:

I do hereby reaffirm the policy of the United States that there shall be no discrimination in the employment of workers in defense industries or government because of race, creed, color or national origin, and I do hereby declare that it is the duty of employers and labor organizations . . . to provide for the full and equitable participation of all workers . . . without discrimination. . . .

Each succeeding President has fashioned similar orders, and more than half the states and a number of cities have enacted statutes with a similar purpose. Executive Order 11246 of September 24, 1965, provided that, as a condition of a contract with the federal government, the employer agrees that he will ". . . not discriminate against any employee or applicant for employment because of race, creed, color or national origin. The contractor will take affirmative action to ensure that applicants are employed, and that employees are treated during employment, without regard to their race." The Office of Federal Contract Compliance, in the Labor Department, is charged with responsibility for coordination of compliance, including the definition of programs of "affirmative action."

From the very outset, both the AFL and CIO were strong advocates of fair-employment-practices legislation before Congress.[32] When the legislation that was to become the Civil Rights Act of 1964 was introduced into Congress, the Kennedy administration had not included a Title VII, on the grounds that its inclusion might defeat the legislation as a whole. George Meany promptly urged the inclusion of equal-employment-opportunity provisions,* and the Federation carried on a vigorous campaign for the legislation. According to Clarence Mitchell, director of the N.A.A.C.P.'s Washington Bureau:

> Organized labor gave unfailing, consistent and massive support where it counted most. . . . It is frequently necessary to work nights, Sundays and holidays to achieve our objectives. The members of organized labor were always present at the right time and in the right places.[33]

The Federation supported the legislation, despite the fact that it would be used against some local unions, not merely on grounds of principle but also because it understood that many local leaders felt inhibited by rank-and-file views in pursuing adequate civil-rights policies. National and local leaders would be in a stronger position in dealing with members if they could point to the necessity of conforming with a federal law.

THE STATISTICAL PICTURE

In view of the bitter charges and countercharges on the subject, a discussion of discrimination calls for facts and statistics rather than general statements. Unfortunately, the statistics are not as helpful as one might wish. Nevertheless, the changing occupa-

---

* A telegram from George Meany to President Kennedy (June 5, 1963) stated: The action taken by President Kennedy yesterday, and the further steps he announced that he intends to take in the campaign to wipe out racial discrimination in employment, have long been urged by AFL-CIO conventions. We welcome the full use of the President's administrative power in this area, but we hope it will be followed up by equal-employment-opportunity legislation covering all enterprises engaged in commerce.
  The AFL-CIO has long pressed for such legislation, for racial discrimination is not merely unpalatable, it is intolerable.
  The trade-union movement has made progress in the fight against discrimination, but none of us can be nor will be satisfied until discrimination is eliminated in its entirety. We are happy therefore to have the greater assistance of the federal government, which we have sought for years, in eliminating this blight from American life.

tional distribution of nonwhite workers provides an initial perspective from which to consider the impact of collective bargaining and union organization. The following tabulation shows for selected recent years the percentage of nonwhite workers in an occupational group.[34] If discrimination were truly a major factor in blocking Negroes from jobs, one would expect to find lower proportions of blacks working in heavily unionized occupations, such as craftsmen, foremen, operatives and laborers.* But such is not the case.

	NONWHITE WORKERS AS A PERCENTAGE OF TOTAL EMPLOYMENT BY OCCUPATION			
	1954	1960	1964	1967
Total, all occupations	10.3%	10.6%	10.6%	10.8%
Professional, technical	3.9	4.4	5.8	6.0
Managers, officials	2.1	2.5	2.6	2.8
Clerical	3.7	5.2	5.4	7.3
Sales	2.3	2.6	3.1	3.0
Craftsmen, foremen	3.8	4.8	5.8	6.3
Operatives	10.7	11.8	11.8	13.6
Private household workers	51.4	45.4	43.6	47.2
Service workers	21.2	20.1	20.2	20.1
Farmers and farm managers	10.0	7.8	6.3	5.4
Farm laborers and foremen	23.6	25.0	23.8	20.0
Laborers, excluding farm and mine	27.6	26.5	26.9	25.4

Neither do the rates of expansion (or contraction) in nonwhite penetration of employment show any relation to the extent of union organization.

A similar impression emerges from data showing the change in employment in absolute numbers and the comparative change in nonwhite and white employment in the period 1960–67:

---

* As Chapter 2 noted, the highest concentration of union membership is in these occupational groups.

CHANGES IN EMPLOYMENT, 1960–1967

	Absolute numbers (in thousands)		Percentage change	
	Nonwhite	White	Nonwhite	White
Total	970	6,721	+14%	+11%
Professional and technical	263	2,141	+80	+30
Managers, officials	31	396	+17	+ 6
Clerical	391	2,158	+77	+23
Sales	25	99	+22	+ 2
Craftsmen, foremen	203	1,083	+49	+13
Operatives	465	1,434	+33	+14
Service workers	287	1,136	+23	+23
Private household workers	−169	− 278	−17	−23
Non-farm laborers	− 70	− 61	− 7	− 2
Farmers and farm workers	−453	−1,389	−52	−31

The occupational changes are clearly in the direction of more integration.[35] Nonwhites are expanding much faster than whites in the highly skilled occupational groups, and nonwhites are declining more rapidly than whites in the lowest-skilled groups. While private and public policies relating to equal employment opportunities may have played a role, the largest factor in these changes is undoubtedly high employment levels and tight labor markets.[36]

Another view of the relation of unionization and minority employment is provided by the following tabulation for 1966. The Negro percentage of skilled craftsmen and other blue-collar workers is shown for two groups of industries, one with little union organization and the other in which collective bargaining is much more extensive.[37]

	NEGROES AS A PERCENTAGE OF:	
Low unionization	*Skilled craftsmen*	*Other blue collar*
Manufactured textile mill products	2.6%	10.4%
Lumber and wood products	5.2	20.0
Leather and its products	2.3	5.1
Furniture and fixtures	6.1	16.0
Instruments and related products	1.9	7.8
Wholesale trade	5.0	18.1

Low unionization	NEGROES AS A PERCENTAGE OF:	
	Skilled craftsmen	Other blue collar
Retail trade	5.8	17.5
Finance	4.2	26.5
Insurance	4.3	25.3
High unionization		
Transportation	2.9%	16.0%
Transportation equipment	4.1	16.2
Contract construction	5.2	29.1
Food and kindred products	7.0	16.8
Apparel and other products	7.4	9.8
Communications	1.2	22.9
Mining	1.9	6.1
Stone, clay and related products	3.2	2.7
Primary metal industry	5.8	19.0
Fabricated metal products	3.5	11.4
Rubber and miscellaneous plastics	3.0	10.7
Machinery, except electrical	2.2	8.2
Electrical machinery	3.0	9.0
Utilities	1.5	11.2
Printing and publishing	1.2	12.5

While many factors influence the industrial distribution of minority groups,* it is clear that there is no simple inverse relationship between unionization and the extent of employment of Negroes in skilled and blue-collar occupations.

Further insight into the extent of Negro employment by occupation may be seen from the following data, also for 1966, from two industries, automobiles and aerospace,[38] which are highly organized. The executives of the major automobile companies and Walter Reuther have long expressed strong support for equal-employment-opportunity programs. The aerospace industry is particularly sensitive to public policy, since the government is its major customer. Nevertheless, the penetration of Negroes into higher-paid and higher-skilled categories is even lower in these

---

* Among these factors are the skill and occupational composition of the industry, the extent to which employment has expanded in recent years, and the location of the industry.

industries than in the skilled construction crafts, where discriminatory practices have been widely publicized.

	NEGRO EMPLOYMENT AS A PERCENTAGE OF TOTAL EMPLOYMENT	
	Big three automobile companies	*21 aerospace companies*
Officials and managers	1.2%	.4%
Professionals	.6	.8
Technicians	1.2	1.9
Sales, office and clerical	3.8	
Sales workers		.3
Office and clerical		2.8
Craftsmen	3.0	4.6
Operatives	20.2	11.9
Laborers	27.6	22.4
Service workers	27.2	22.2
Total	13.5	4.8

Further perspective on these data is provided by examining
the racial composition of the half million or more "wage board
employees" of the federal government. In general, these employees
are blue-collar workers in navy yards, arsenals and Air Force
installations, and manual employees of civilian government
agencies.[39] The occupational distribution can be inferred from the
tabulation of the proportion of Negroes by four categories of
annual wage level.

Annual wages	Percentage Negro
Up through $4,499	43.1%
$4,500 through $6,499	25.3
$6,500 through $7,999	9.4
$8,000 and over	2.9

While there is no easy way of translating these data into occupational categories, it is clear that in 1966 the proportion of Negroes
among the skilled craftsmen or supervisory personnel in these government installations was not markedly different from the percentage in comparable private industry, where most employees in these
categories would be earning above $8,000 a year.

These various statistical data showing the relatively small,
albeit growing, proportion of Negroes in professional, technical,

managerial, clerical, sales and craftsmen occupations, and their high concentration in semiskilled and unskilled jobs that ordinarily are lower-paid, suggest that factors other than collective bargaining and union policies have been primarily responsible. This is not to gainsay that some unions and collective-bargaining relations have been overtly discriminatory (although others have sought specifically to promote Negro employment). But if federal government agencies* and employers and unions with a reputation for long dedication to civil rights do not reflect significantly higher proportions of Negroes in skilled and clerical positions than comparable industries, more pervasive factors of social discrimination must be the primary factors at work. These added factors, of course, involve such problems as lack of adequate education, lack of transportation to jobs, lack of training programs, and—in many cases—the stunted ambitions, the narrow expectations, and the insecurities brought on by past decades of restricted opportunities and discrimination. The importance of these factors also indicates that prohibitions on overt discrimination, as in Title VII of the Civil Rights Act, are unlikely to do much to increase the penetration of blacks into managerial, technical, professional and skilled occupations without the addition of affirmative programs of manpower training, education and development.

In view of the heated debate over discrimination in the construction industry, a brief comment is in order.[40] Even if all overt forms of discrimination were eliminated (and that has still to be done), many of the industry's basic features, which are found in organized and unorganized firms alike, make penetration difficult for racial minority groups, and indeed for others without substantial training or experience in related work. The high wage scales, now often $6 or $8 an hour for journeymen in large cities, require that a worker produce to this standard as soon as he is employed; otherwise he faces discharge or early layoff, except in periods of the most stringent labor shortages. Since projects are of limited duration, the individual contractor has little incentive to invest in training for his workers who are likely to be working for a competitor in a few weeks. The contractor prefers to draw his

---

* In June 1965, the Department of Justice reported five Negroes out of 538 (.9 percent) wage board employees with over $8,000-a-year salary. By November 1967, employment in this category had increased to 953 with twelve Negroes (1.3 percent). The percentage in the $6,500-to-$7,999 bracket increased markedly from 1.9 percent to 16.8 percent.

labor from a local or regional pool according to his needs, and he is interested in only the most competent and skilled labor available. He is anxious to have workers whom he has employed satisfactorily previously.

Untrained workers are at a further disadvantage in that, except for a few crafts such as operating engineers or teamsters, there are no job classification ladders of promotion as in heavy industry by which a less skilled employee can learn the job gradually. There is also relatively little supervision to help the worker improve his skills. Additional problems result from the great instability in employment and the marked seasonality. These factors place a premium on broad training in a craft, for workers must have the versatility to perform several types of work in order to stay employed long enough to earn a more adequate annual income. A worker with a limited range of skills is likely to get much less work per year and eventually leave construction. Some of the necessary skills can be difficult to acquire. The mechanical crafts,* for example, call for blue-print reading and related skills which require a degree of formal education and mathematical preparation that disadvantaged groups are less likely to possess. The shifting sites of work, often over substantial distances for some specialty crafts, demand the use of private transportation and Negro workers are less likely to have cars. Such features of the construction industry would reduce the proportion of blacks in some of the crafts even if collective bargaining did not exist. Thus, when skilled crafts or contractors have simply advertised for applicants on a nondiscriminatory basis, typically only a handful of black workers have applied and many have proved unqualified. Union discrimination cannot adequately explain the problem. Negroes appear to have no greater participation rate in the nonunion sector of the industry, except among the few small black contractors in some central city areas.

FURTHER STEPS TO ENHANCE THE INTERESTS OF RACIAL MINORITIES

In the next decade, the main challenge for labor in the field of race relations will be to develop programs of affirmative action that will enable Negro workers to overcome the effects of decades of discrimination and deprivation. In the construction industry, for

---

* The mechanical crafts include the plumbers, steamfitters, electricians, millwrights, structural and ornamental iron workers, elevator constructors, boilermakers and sheet-metal workers.

example, the elimination of overt discrimination alone will not appreciably increase the representation of minority groups in these skilled crafts, and particularly among the mechanical crafts. Only programs of aggressive "affirmative action" by the parties to collective bargaining, in cooperation with the government and civil-rights groups, show promise of producing substantial results. Two types of programs are essential: apprenticeship "outreach" to attract applicants to regular apprenticeship programs and trainee programs to attract partially trained workers or those beyond the usual apprenticeship age to the mainstream of construction operations. The successful experience of the Workers Defense League, which pioneered apprenticeship recruitment with the New York City unions and contractors, has now been extended by the Urban League, local building trades councils, and other organizations. These outreach programs show that the recruitment of blacks and other minority groups requires an active program of seeking out youth and providing specialized orientation, training, coaching, and follow-up.[41] By October 1969, such programs had been established in fifty-five major industrial areas with federal government financial support.[42] In December 1968, Under Secretary of Labor James J. Reynolds reported that the number of minority representatives in registered apprenticeships in the construction industry had increased from 4,000 in 1966 to 10,500 in July 1968.[43] The 10,500 figure represented about 7 percent of all the apprentices in construction.* This proportion compared with 3.6 percent of the 115,000 apprentices registered in 1966 and 2.5 percent of the apprentices in 1960. The apprenticeship outreach programs alone indentured almost 4,000

---

* Since apprenticeship programs are typically four or five years in duration, the minority groups constituted a much higher percentage of the entering class in 1967 and 1968. Nonwhite workers constituted 26.9 percent of *construction laborers* in 1967.

Nonwhite workers as a percentage of *craftsmen and foremen* in construction are shown in the following tabulation:

	1957	1962	1967
Carpenters	3.9%	5.4%	6.2%
Construction, excluding carpenters	5.5	6.5	8.2

As of the end of 1968, the percentage of minority apprentices in programs registered with the federal government was reported among industries as follows:

Construction	7.2%
Metal manufacturing	4.3
Non-metal manufacturing	5.3

minority youth in the two years following the commencement of the federally funded program in 1967.

But an effective strategy to bring racial minorities into construction crafts requires more than an outreach program for apprenticeship. In most cities there are black workers with some limited experience in construction, or related work, who should be taken into employment in the industry at training rates (below the journeyman scale) and provided systematic instruction, both in related classroom training and on the job training, so that they can move up rapidly to journeyman status and wage scales. In July 1968, the Building Trades Unions adopted a policy statement and guidelines to promote such programs. Agreements incorporating this policy are in effect in a few cities, usually with the assistance of federal manpower funds, but such programs need to be vastly expanded. Some branches of the industry have developed intermediate job classifications to facilitate the entry of workers with less than standard qualifications. Thus, the electricians have developed a two-year residential electrician apprenticeship program. The expansion of such journeyman training and the apprenticeship outreach programs provide the best way of developing more blacks in the skilled workforce of the construction industry.

Affirmative efforts are also needed on the part of other sectors such as printing, insurance, and radio and television, where Negro employment is woefully small. In most instances, the position of racial minorities can probably be influenced more effectively through collective bargaining than through independent action by labor organizations.* Collective-bargaining agreements may be modified in some respects to facilitate the recruitment, employment and promotion of minority groups. While a few agreements contain provisions violative of federal laws and regulations, the pressing need in most instances is to go beyond the legal requirements and make voluntary revisions to improve the position of racial minorities. In some cases, the union may negotiate to insure promotion opportunities for minority-group members to higher

---

* It is well to recognize that in negotiations either side may find it convenient to blame the other for the position of racial minorities, and either side may make a proposal which is favorable to minorities but suits its own current special interests. Thus, some construction contractors who have had no previous interest in civil rights and have rejected proposals to spend funds on training to increase the pool of skilled labor, now in a tight labor market have suddenly become champions of Negroes to increase the labor supply. Unions in turn may point out that managements have had ample opportunity to hire blacks in the past and did not.

positions outside the bargaining unit. More often, ways must be found to create opportunities in the unit for workers with less than the normal qualifications. Here the problem is to favor the minority without arousing resentment among other employees. For example, the probationary period, normally of thirty to sixty days, may have to be extended to six months for disadvantaged groups to permit them greater opportunity to prove themselves, since a short probationary period leads many managements to refuse to continue an employee of uncertain performance for fear of difficulty in making a subsequent discharge. Under piecework or incentive systems of pay, a lower minimum guarantee may be appropriate for disadvantaged employees with less preparation and with a different learning pattern from that of most new employees. In dealing with disadvantaged employees, efforts to be tolerant in matters of discipline, tardiness and absenteeism can easily lead to charges of favoritism and an undermining of standards among all workers. To overcome these problems will require great patience and imagination.[44] The appropriate accommodations in the collective-bargaining agreement or its administration to favor the employment and advancement of racial minorities will necessarily vary widely among enterprises and industries.*

Another highly significant and sensitive area of relations between labor unions and the Negro community concerns the rate of advancement of Negroes to elective and appointive offices in local and national unions. Representation of occupational or ethnic minorities in union hierarchies has generally lagged behind the numerical strength of the groups involved. Negroes are no exception to the rule. In a growing number of international unions, such as the Steelworkers and the Auto Workers, there have been black caucuses at conventions designed to secure the election of black members to office or their appointment to staff positions. White members have often resisted these efforts with the result that top union leaders have sometimes been impelled to intervene. Thus, Mr. Reuther is reported to have persuaded two white candidates to drop out of the election contest for the directorship of the

---

* An illustration is afforded by the Boston residential construction and rehabilitation agreement, which provides a new category, "trainee," for the construction industry, and a new means of legitimate entry.[45] Another instance is the proposal to maintain employment for recently hired minority groups when a plant faces a decline in production, by laying off for a limited period some senior men, who are fully protected by unemployment compensation and private supplements.

75,000-member Region 1A in Detroit to make sure that a black candidate would win.[46] And I. W. Abel, president of the Steelworkers,
unsuccessfully backed the candidacy of a Negro staff representative for the directorship of District 8 headquartered in Baltimore.
In most cases, however, the influence of the union leader is sharply
curtailed by the necessity of selecting union officials by majority
vote of the members.

THE PROBLEM IN PERSPECTIVE

The record of organized labor in racial matters has always
varied greatly at different levels in the union hierarchy. At the
federation level, the AFL–CIO has consistently been opposed to
racial discrimination. Historically, it has been in the forefront of
organizations supporting government programs to implement
equal employment opportunities by executive action and by
F.E.P.C. legislation in the states and in Congress.

The situation is very different at the local level. Racial prejudice is much more prevalent among the rank and file than among
union leaders, and this has been true since the days of the
National Labor Union in the 1860's and the Knights of Labor in
the 1880's. This difference in attitude is starkly revealed in the
following unpublished survey of a large industrial union taken in
the mid-sixties.

*Do you feel desegregation of schools, housing, and job
opportunities for American Negroes has recently proceeded
too fast, not fast enough, or as fast as it should?*

(WHITE RESPONDENTS ONLY)

	Too fast	About right	Too slow	Don't know
International staff	0%	28.1%	69.2%	1.8%
Convention delegates	21.2	37.7	35.1	5.1
Local officers	36.5	28.7	25.2	8.7
Rank and file	31.6	31.2	20.9	16.3

Moreover, opinion surveys consistently have shown that racial bias
is more widespread on the average among blue-collar workers than
among segments of society with higher levels of income and
education.[47] It is hardly surprising, therefore, that many local
unions include a substantial group of members who have strong

prejudices on race issues. There are also unions in which members who are not markedly prejudiced will work to exclude Negroes along with any other outsiders, either because they fear that new members will raise a threat of unemployment or because they prefer to reserve the highly paid union jobs for relatives and friends. Under these circumstances, elective officials in these locals have had much to lose and little to gain by working to improve the position of racial minorities. And given the high rate of turnover in local union office, and the natural inclination to remain in power, it is not surprising that many local union leaders have not chosen to run the risks involved, although some have been courageous and imaginative in facilitating civil-rights programs.*

While leaders of the Federation have sought to use their influence and persuasion to change the policies of some national and local unions, they have been unwilling to support the drastic penalty of expulsion, for fear of widespread secession from uncooperative unions. As for the national and international unions, their leaders have chosen to reserve their limited powers of compulsion, such as trusteeship, for occasions involving political struggles for control of a local, corruption, and maintaining authority in disputes with employers. Most leaders have felt that they could not afford to be very far in front of their rank and file in the extent to which they advocated specific policies to eliminate discrimination at the workplace. They have preferred to improve the welfare of Negroes indirectly by the conventional union methods of organizing the unorganized, collective bargaining, and supporting social legislation rather than by pressing for racial policies that might split the union in internal conflict. In this respect labor unions have not behaved much differently from churches, schools and universities, medical institutions, and other bodies with lofty ideals.

The vigorous initiative and support which the AFL–CIO provided in the enactment of the Civil Rights Act of 1964 is better understood in this perspective. The law provided the labor leadership with a leverage that its voluntary internal government had been unable to produce. After the passage of the statute, national

---

* In these circumstances, it is fatuous for scholars to extol the virtues of union democracy in one chapter, only to castigate local leaders in another for perpetuating discrimination. A local union can hardly practice an enlightened autocracy on racial matters while operating in a vigorous democratic environment on other issues.

labor leaders were able to tell their local unions and members that they had the option of voluntarily merging the few remaining segregated locals and taking affirmative steps to recruit and train racial minorities or being required to do so by government agencies or the courts.[48] To buttress this effort, the Federation has conducted an extensive educational program and strengthened its civil-rights department to provide technical assistance to affiliated unions.*

It is probably correct to say that greater progress has been made in securing equal opportunity in employment than in any other field of American life. Yet, employment is so vital that Negro leaders are understandably impatient with the obstacles still to be overcome. Whether unions can surmount this challenge is a question of profound importance, but the answer remains obscure. With the aid of full employment and more adequate government training programs, the problem may eventually be overcome without great turmoil. On the other hand, rejection of Negro claims may lead to attempts to form black unions in the ghettos and complete alienation from the labor movement. In this respect, the unions are but a microcosm of the larger problems confronting all of American society.

Conclusion

The foregoing discussion suggests the complexity of union responsibility toward the many minority groups within its membership. Adequate lines of communication are clearly needed, to begin with, to ensure that union leaders are aware of the special needs of particular groups. Once aware of these needs, the leader-

---

* The experience of the Federation with civil-rights issues is to be compared to its concern over corruption in some unions, considered in Chapter 3, and the problems it has faced over the years in developing viable machinery for the resolution of internal jurisdictional disputes and conflicting representation claims. These issues have been transferred into the public arena, with governmental agencies and the courts empowered to make decisions. But the statutes have preserved a large role for voluntary action. See Chapter 6. The Federation has been able to use expulsion as an effective club in cases of corruption but not in cases of internal jurisdictional conflicts or instances of discrimination, since the roots of corruption are in union officials, who are more sensitive to the threat of being expelled. Discrimination, on the other hand, is rooted in the attitudes of the rank and file, who are much less moved by the threat of expulsion. Hence, the Federation has chosen not to use this remedy since it would remove all possibility of influence without any offsetting benefit.

ship must be prepared to curb the demands of powerful minorities when necessary for the greater good of the larger number. Yet they must also take pains not to overlook the legitimate interests of minority groups or discriminate against them on arbitrary grounds.

Several forces are at work to induce labor leaders to live up to these responsibilities. Of major importance is the natural disposition of most union officials to take account of the interests of particular groups within the organization. True, minorities cannot rely upon good will alone, and this is particularly true where their interests collide with those of larger groups. But political levers often are available to support the claims of the minority, especially where it is large enough to press its case in meetings and conventions, or strategically enough placed to mutiny effectively. And where these methods do not avail, many groups can fall back upon legal safeguards that provide them with the threat of eliminating the union certification, joining a rival organization, or demanding fair representation in a court of law.

These safeguards hardly do a perfect job of representing all minority interests. Some groups are too small and too poorly situated to make effective use of political pressure. Legal safeguards too may fail, since the law is administered by laymen who hesitate to intervene unless discrimination is blatant or minority interests are so obvious or meritorious as to call out for protection. Nevertheless, the combination of restraints—human, political and legal—does provide a measure of protection for a wide variety of separate interests within the union. There is doubtless more that unions could do to enlarge the area of autonomy of various groups within their organization and avoid undue discrimination against particular groups. But given the limitations inherent in all human institutions, the position of minorities may well be better rather than worse in the union movement than in most collective bodies.

The Administration of Unions

The Developing Field of Administration

The administration of unions is a subject about which very little is known. This information gap grows increasingly serious in an era when the techniques of management have become highly sophisticated and the importance of administration so widely understood. In recent years, such terms of modern management as "systems analysis," "program budgeting," "cost effectiveness," and "strategic planning" have left the domain of the specialist to become matters of common parlance in magazines and newspapers. Although these methods have been developed most intensively in business, they are being adapted increasingly for use in government agencies, educational institutions and other nonprofit organizations. It is worth asking, therefore, whether more sophisticated administrative techniques could be used to advantage in the operation of labor unions as well.

The following analysis of union administration is based on several principles:

1) The structure of an organization should be periodically evaluated to ensure that it fits the goals and strategies currently being pursued.

2) The informal methods of administration that often work well when an organization is small tend to become unsatisfactory as the organization grows in size and complexity. As this process develops, more formal techniques are needed to enable managers to obtain adequate information and make rational decisions.

3) When organizations grow large, it becomes increasingly important to develop an explicit planning process. Although the methods of planning may vary in sophistication from one type of organization to another, it will at least be necessary to make a conscious effort to define goals and consider how to progress most effectively toward them.

4) After plans are established, it is generally helpful to establish an operating budget which indicates how resources will be allocated among the various programs and units of the organization. The use of such a budget is most effective when it is prepared in a manner which allows officials at all levels to participate in deciding how their efforts can best be deployed in the succeeding period.

5) The operating budget serves the added function of informing subordinate officials what they are expected to accomplish in the ensuing period. But many other categories of information should also be developed and communicated throughout the organization. Facts about the external environment are necessary to plan future actions; data on the costs and results of existing programs are needed to evaluate and improve these activities; information about employees is indispensable for making intelligent personnel decisions.

6) An environment must be created that minimizes conflict between the goals of the organization and the individuals who choose to work in it. The system of promotions, salaries and nonmonetary rewards must be carefully related to performance in the light of organizational programs and objectives.

7) To provide effective leadership in the future, the organization must recruit systematically, acquire information relating to the qualifications of actual and potential officials and staff, and provide training, as needed, at all levels in the organization.

In a general way these principles of administration are little more than common sense, and labor leaders are instinctively aware of most of them. With few exceptions, however, union officials have not devoted much conscious effort to implement these precepts. If a labor leader is asked whether he has considered the use of planning or program budgets, he is likely to reply that his union is devoted to helping its members and has no need for the techniques developed by business concerns in their search for larger profits. But this is too easy an answer. If administrative methods have been more highly developed by business executives, it is largely because the stresses of the marketplace have put particular pressure upon them to operate efficiently. But the methods themselves can be adapted for use in a wide variety of organizations, for they are simply ways of using men and resources more efficiently to achieve any given set of organizational goals.

A more serious reservation is often entered by thoughtful labor leaders who claim that management techniques are not readily transplanted to an organization that is as frankly and explicitly political as a union. There is undoubtedly a problem here. Democracy may interfere with the efficiency of a society or an organization, at least in the short run. But it would be idle to insist that good management is irrelevant for union officials, who are chronically short of the resources they need to achieve their goals. And even though management methods may have to be adapted or delayed to take account of political considerations, it would be erroneous to assume that such methods are irrelevant to a union, just as it would be ridiculous to ignore them in the operation of the various agencies of a government established through political processes.

The Laborers' International Union

The subject of management is often broken down into a series of conventional topics: planning, organization, personnel administration, and the like. But administration can become very dry when it is treated in abstract terms. The subject comes to life only when one examines an actual organization to observe how it has sought to achieve a challenging series of goals.

The union described in the following pages—the Laborers' International Union of North America—is not typical of the entire labor movement. No union is. But the problems of organization and administration encountered by the Laborers are similar to those of many other unions. Moreover, the Laborers provide an interesting case study in several respects. With approximately half a million members, they are the eighth-largest union in the United States, easily big enough to be beset by a number of complex administrative questions. In addition, although the bulk of their members perform relatively unskilled jobs in the construction industry, the union has also recruited workers in manufacturing and government services, so that its jurisdiction covers a variety of occupations and industrial settings. More important still, the Laborers in recent years have made major changes in their objectives and methods of operation, and these offer an absorbing study of the problems of union administration.

In the early 1960's, the Laborers' International Union looked back upon a fifty-year history in which the organization had grown to include more than 400,000 members. Its organization was similar to that of many other unions. In a modern office building near the White House, the president and secretary-treasurer presided over the union, assisted by a handful of staff members, including a general counsel, a research director, and specialists in jurisdictional disputes and other matters important to construction unions. Throughout the United States and Canada, the international headquarters exercised its authority through sixteen regional managers, each with a small staff of roving representatives. At the grass roots, almost nine hundred local unions had been chartered, some of them loosely federated into state or area-wide councils to coordinate collective bargaining.

Despite its impressive size, the union faced serious problems. Total membership had been declining at a rate of roughly 20,000 per year since 1958. Many of the regional managers and vice-presidents were well advanced in age and had already been in office for many years. Much of the administrative authority had gravitated into the hands of the general counsel, who had achieved considerable influence decades before, after extricating the international from lawsuits involving malfeasance and defiance on the part of various local officials. Under his guidance, the international pursued a policy of strengthening and protecting the rights of individual members while minimizing any close involvement in the bargaining and economic activities of the local unions. As a result, much time was devoted to investigating individual complaints, but the international did not make serious efforts to organize new members; nor did it provide educational courses for its officers and staff or an established political-action program to pursue its legislative objectives. In short, the international office conceived of its role in very narrow terms. It performed certain functions that could not be carried out by its local affiliates: presented jurisdictional disputes to the private machinery established in the construction industry, argued cases before the N.L.R.B. and the courts, published a newspaper, and represented the union in the AFL–CIO and its Building and Construction Trades Department. It also used its influence to induce local unions to respect the right of individual members to vote in union elections, to participate in union meetings, and to enjoy a fair hearing before being disciplined for infractions of union rules. It intervened to straighten out occasional strikes and local abuses that threatened the welfare of other segments of the organization. It also joined with a few other international unions in the successful organization of cross-country pipeline construction and in the unionization of heavy and highway construction in some areas. But the international headquarters was rarely an innovating force within the union. It did not serve as a major source of new ideas or a stimulus for achieving more effective organizing, bargaining, or grievance processing throughout the union.

By 1964, the situation had begun to change with great suddenness. Several vice-presidents died, retired or resigned. The general counsel made the mistake of asserting his power too openly and was relieved of office. Other staff positions changed hands, bringing younger, fresher faces to the fore. Progressive ideas that had accumulated over past years began to be expressed at international headquarters. Many of them found their way into a fifteen-page memorandum entitled "A Proposed Organizational Program," which came to be referred to by the union's president as "the Magna Carta of our organization."

Underlying this document was concern about the disturbing trend in union membership, a trend that seemed to many of the more vigorous officials to symbolize a lack of dynamism within the organization. The memorandum stressed the need for addressing more systematic attention to this problem. The opening paragraph states: "In this age of automation, when machines are rapidly replacing men, and workmen are becoming more versatile in the application of their skills, our membership will decline unless we look to the future and plan to build and build to plan." Drawing upon the first membership survey ever conducted, the memorandum disclosed that even in the construction industry, where most of the members were concentrated, fewer than half the workers within its jurisdiction were organized. In addition, the memorandum pointed out that the union had a small but potentially significant membership among government employees and in plants which supplied the construction industry. To expand the union's strength in each of these fields, a number of steps were recommended. A full-time official should be put in charge of organizing government employees. Efforts should be made to work more closely with other unions by participating actively in the Industrial Union Department of the AFL–CIO and reactivating the four-way pact which provided for cooperative organizing with the Teamsters, the Operating Engineers and the Carpenters. More important still, an attempt should be made to develop a staff of men trained to plan an effective organizing campaign and motivate other employees to join the union. An inventory of talent should be created to provide names and background data of former local officials and other men who might be used to good effect in organizing efforts. Training programs should be established to equip local officers with the legal and tactical knowledge required to organize successfully. And locals should be urged to combine in district councils which could support the full-time organizing staff that small individual locals could not afford.

The 1964 memorandum was favorably received by the president and the executive board, and the international moved to put its recommendations into effect. The organizing department, already in existence under the supervision of a resident vice-president, was strengthened by providing a deputy and adding assistants specializing in heavy industry, highways, construction, and the industrial sector. Special efforts were needed, however, to make progress in the neglected field of public employment, where the problems of organizing and servicing government workers were unfamiliar to a union concentrated in the construction industry. A unique opportunity was presented by the recent change in leadership in the American Federation of State, County and Municipal Employees. Taking advantage of the turnover in staff at the AFSCME, the Laborers attracted a core of experienced men to help in organizing and in administering their public-employee activities. A former member of the AFSCME staff was placed in charge of the program at international headquarters, and a new publication was created to deal with the special interests of these members.

Having established a framework at the international level, the union turned its attention to mobilizing its officials in the field where the actual job of organizing had to be done. The international staff was aware that a vigorous program could not be launched by merely issuing orders and directives. Instead, the major problem was to marshal the cooperation and enthusiasm of a host of subordinate officials who were unused to serious organizing work and, in some cases, were even hostile to the thought of bringing new members and new occupational groups into the political units they controlled. The problem was sufficiently difficult to cause the international officers to refrain from setting specific goals or defining the types of units and employees to be organized. Instead, they began by exhorting local officials to go after any worker and installation that could be organized. Careful planning would have to wait until the necessary enthusiasm had been engendered up and down the entire union hierarchy.

To get its point across, the international emphasized organizing in its official journal, *The Laborer*. International officers instructed regional managers and representatives to stress the importance of organizing to the local unions and district councils. In addition, the international arranged for regional conferences throughout the country at which the top leadership and staff could discuss the problems of organizing with local officials. At these conferences, the international provided instruction and made it clear that help would be forthcoming in the form of subsidies, leaflets, legal assistance, and international representatives for local unions engaged in serious organizing. With greater experience, these techniques were improved and refined. For example, when it became clear that certain local leaders might lack sufficient drive and enthusiasm, the international arranged for meetings with the entire executive board of the local in the hope that the local board members would prod their local officers and prevent them from blaming their inactivity on a lack of cooperation from headquarters.

Although the response to these efforts was uneven, there is little doubt that the international succeeded in channeling much greater energy to the job of organizing in many localities. These very energies, however, soon brought home the need for more careful planning to direct the efforts in the field. New units were being added that could not be serviced, since they were too small to support a full-time officer. Enthusiastic local leaders began organizing ham factories, mattress plants and other units with economic conditions and employment problems that were quite foreign to the competence of a union staff whose experience lay in the construction industry. A hasty decision to organize farm workers caused the union to divert its energies to a fruitless effort to sign up employees who were constantly on the move, quickly intimidated, easily replaced, poorly educated, and often unable to read or speak English. Hundreds of thousands of dollars were expended for this purpose without visible results, until the union was able to extricate itself by handing the job over to another labor organization.

Once the spirit of organizing had begun to take hold, international officers felt freer to counteract these problems by fixing rough guidelines to direct the efforts of subordinate officials. Accordingly, the executive board agreed that organizing should be concentrated in three sectors in diminishing order of importance: construction laborers, employees in plants supplying the construction industry, and government workers. These priorities were not to be enforced by fiat. Rather, the international would simply refuse to give money to support organizing campaigns that did not meet the desired specifications. In order to allow more careful planning, international representatives were also called upon to prepare lists of unorganized government units and supplier plants in their respective areas. Finally, regional managers were asked by headquarters to submit plans outlining their targets for organizing during the following year.

The effort to expand union membership also brought home the importance of achieving economies of scale among locals so that they could support full-time officials who could organize. To afford a single full-time officer, it was estimated that a local union would have to include approximately two hundred members.* Four hundred members might be needed to add another official and a secretary. Yet the union's statistics revealed that over 400 of its 911 locals had fewer than two hundred members and that only a third of the locals had a membership in excess of four hundred.

To overcome this problem the international asked its regional managers to try to persuade officials of smaller locals to merge whenever possible. But many officials balked at losing power and prestige by being absorbed in this fashion. In such instances, the regional manager would sometimes go directly to the members to convince them of the better service they would receive by being

---

* Such a rule of thumb is derived from an estimated level of local union dues, salary of the local officer and related administrative expenses.

part of a larger organization. If this tactic would not work, the regional manager could ask that the local charter be revoked in order to force the members to affiliate with another local. Subject to review by the international, he could also issue an order to the officials involved to show cause why their locals should not merge.

Once again, however, the actual power of the top leadership was less than it would appear from reading the constitution and by-laws. Arranging voluntary mergers consumed much valuable time of higher officials and forcing two unions to combine took even more time and threatened to create opposition, litigation and disunity. For these or other reasons, progress was very limited. By 1965, the number of locals with fewer than two hundred members was barely below what it had been in 1962, while the number of locals with more than four hundred members increased by only twenty-seven.

The international, however, had another method of achieving economies of scale: the creation of district councils, or federations of local unions. In certain sections of the country, district councils had been established for decades, but new councils had been discouraged in recent years out of fear of creating important power blocs that might oppose the international officers. So important was it to coordinate the work of neighboring locals and create organizations which could support a full-time staff that the international now put its weight behind the district councils, and several of these organizations had been added in the South and the Midwest by 1966. In a few areas, where the organization of public employees was more advanced, such as Washington, D.C., special district councils were also formed for government workers.

The process of organizing also laid bare the need for capable officials—a problem that was particularly acute for a union so heavily composed of low-income, poorly educated workers. To a limited extent, the international could, and did, bring in outsiders, but for the bulk of its first-line leaders, the union had to rely upon its own internal resources. In order to get experienced people and avoid political repercussions, the international was forced to look almost entirely to the corps of local union officers, who were chosen in elections over which the international could exercise little or no influence. Thus, an effective training program was essential to make the best possible use of the talent available.

Although the need was acute, the international had to cope with considerable resistance from its local officials. Education programs represented a radical departure for the union. The very idea of education was disquieting to many subordinate leaders in a union where the level of schooling was extremely low. As a result, the international proceeded with extreme caution. A study committee was appointed to devise a "conservative bare-bones" education program. On the basis of the committee's report, the union agreed, with some misgivings, to establish an education department. Although the job of directing the department might have seemed to require an outside man with broad educational experience, the international felt that such a step would complicate the job of selling the program to the entire union. As a result, the union turned to one of its own international representatives, the son of a well-known Laborers' official, a former football player and a graduate of the University of Missouri and the Harvard Trade Union Program. Even at this point, it was considered unwise to launch a full-scale training program for staff and subordinate officials. Instead, the union began in a more unobtrusive manner by creating job-training programs in regions of the union receptive to upgrading the skills of their members. Training of this kind could be accepted as a step toward higher earnings for the members; it also appealed to union leaders who perceived it as something akin to the apprentice programs of the more highly skilled construction trades. As the idea took hold and spread to other regions, the international staff began to urge literacy training and basic education, on the grounds that many members could not profit from vocational training without such preliminary instruction. Initially relying on federal funds, the union soon began to bargain with employers to establish jointly administered training programs. By mid-1968, the Laborers had reached agreements of this kind with employers' associations in more than twenty states.* In 1969, it negotiated with the Associated General Contractors of America, Inc. a national training fund to be supported by contributions from the local and state funds. Only when such programs were established and accepted did the international feel ready to move toward the unfamiliar and politically sensitive area of staff and leadership training.

These events caused a transformation in the life of the Laborers.

---

* Typically these agreements provided for five cents an hour to be placed into a fund to be jointly administered by the union and the contractor association. In a sense, these funds are wages which union members agree to devote to training purposes.

The international headquarters has added new staff members with responsibilities for organizing, education, public relations, and legislative affairs. A professional comptroller was attracted from a business enterprise to institute improved records and develop a modern internal information system. Efforts have been made to build a more systematic base for the programs in education and organizing by polling local leaders on educational needs and surveying the occupational distribution of the membership. Much more important, the headquarters has significantly altered its role within the union. Once passive and narrowly limited in its functions, the international has become an innovator —initiating training programs, new publications, new organizing efforts and actively working to improve the structure of its local affiliates through stimulating mergers and regional bodies. Interestingly enough, these changes have not come about by pressure from the rank and file, nor is it likely that enough members could have conceived of such innovations to exert any influence on the union's leaders. At the same time, the international officers have seldom been prepared to dictate new programs to the union. The implementation of these policies has depended much more on finding ways to inform, motivate, and persuade lower levels in the hierarchy to move along the desired lines.

What has actually been accomplished by these initiatives? The union has established a better staff for organizing purposes, and many subordinate officials seem to be devoting more of their time and energies to attracting new members. More important, these changes seem to have yielded concrete results. The total membership of the union rose from 420,000 in 1963 to 485,000 in 1967, and mergers with the Mail Handlers and Stone Cutters helped bring the membership to 550,000 by mid-1968.

But serious problems remain. The education program is still in a preliminary, experimental stage, despite an acute need for staff training. The number of inefficiently sized locals remains almost as large as before. And many local leaders are still reluctant to engage in serious efforts to organize public employees for fear of unstabilizing the political situation within their union through the addition of new members from different occupational fields.

More germane are the administrative problems that continue to hamper the union's activities. Despite the recent rise in membership, no one can say how much of this growth is really attributable to union organizing, for much of it may result from larger employment in already organized firms. Indeed, one can argue that most of the Laborers' recent growth stems from prosperity in the construction industry, just as much of the decline prior to 1962 grew out of the industry's stagnation. The union simply lacks the data to find out how many new members have been netted by its organizers. Neither does it know how fast it is growing in particular occupational fields. The official in charge of public-employee organizing, for example, guesses that the growth rate in this sector is about 10 percent, but other officials make widely different estimates. There is also little hard knowledge of the costs of organizing. The international headquarters keeps track of the subsidies it disburses for organizing activities, but it cannot say how much time is being spent on organizing by its own field staff, nor is it aware of the time and money being devoted by local and district council officers.

These basic gaps in information obviously hamper the union severely in evaluating its programs and allocating its resources. It may be that the union would be well advised to mobilize fifty organizers instead of five in the public-employee sector or to concentrate more of its efforts in the thinly organized Southern regions. But the union lacks the information to make these judgments or to convince subordinates of their wisdom, for it does not know how much it is spending on organizing, nor does it know the relative effectiveness of its efforts in different areas and occupational fields. It is true that the union talks of planning and that regional managers are now being asked to formulate programs for the following year. Lacking adequate information and guidance, however, the managers are doing little more than expressing an intention to continue along present lines with a few broad proposals, like New Year's resolutions, thrown in for good measure.

The experience of the Laborers is not altogether typical. Many of the larger unions have long since established education programs, and some internationals have traditionally played a more active role in giving leadership and direction to their local affiliates. But the problems of planning and administration encountered by the Laborers are not fundamentally different from those of other unions. The quality of administration in most unions is still at a primitive level, lagging behind the standards achieved not only in large businesses, but in many of the better-run foundations, hospitals, and government departments.

Despite these deficiencies, scant work has been done to study the process and problems of running a union. In this respect, business and labor have had an entirely different experience. Comparatively little has been written on the subject of democracy within the corporation, while mountains of literature have accumulated on the techniques of administering business organizations. In the case of unions, the very opposite has occurred. The remainder of this chapter will be devoted to constructing a framework to open up the neglected field of union administration. This is admittedly a subject that may chiefly interest the union official and the student of organized labor. The general reader may, understandably, prefer to pass immediately to the Conclusion of this chapter.

The Structure of Labor Unions

Although there are many variations among unions, the structure of the Laborers is reasonably typical. The basic unit is the local, which may include only the employees in a single large plant or extend to numerous small employers in a defined geographic area. If the local has several hundred members, its treasury is usually large enough to support at least one full-time officer; the largest locals, with several thousand members, may actually have a dozen or more full-time staff members. But if the local has fewer than several hundred members, it cannot afford to pay salaries and the elected officers must somehow attend to bargaining, settling grievances, and organizing new members while continuing to hold down their regular jobs.

As in many other unions, a second layer of organization has been created in the Laborers by federating groups of locals into district or area councils. These councils are designed either to coordinate bargaining throughout a local or regional product market, or simply to achieve an organization of sufficient size to support a full-time staff. Above the councils stands the regional offices, each with a director. Some of the regional directors are also vice-presidents of the international, elected at conventions held every five years. Each regional office has under its supervision a group of field representatives. The field representatives are appointed by the international rather than elected by the members. The representatives normally travel extensively among the local unions in their area, helping them negotiate and adjust contract disputes with employers, organizing new plants, and trying to cope with factional disputes within individual locals. Since local officials are elected and turnover is frequent, traveling representatives provide a measure of continuity and experience as well as a check to ensure that the policies of the international are carried out.

At the apex of the union is the international headquarters, with the elected general officers, supported by a variety of staff departments—for education, research, organizing, legal counsel and the clerical and record-keeping units. These officers keep in close touch with international representatives and leaders of key locals as to the progress of negotiations, strikes and organizing campaigns; they travel widely to regional or state meetings of locals, and they are often in consultation with representatives of managements and government agencies over problems affecting their industry and membership. An increasing number of international union headquarters have been moved to Washington, D.C.*

There is nothing intrinsically wrong with this basic structure. Each of the layers of organization has an important function to perform. In practice, however, several problems of structure crop up repeatedly in a wide variety of unions.

EXCESSIVE DECENTRALIZATION

A common defect is a lack of sufficient integration among the different levels in the union hierarchy. In its grossest form, the problem is simply that the international lacks power to compel its locals to observe important union policies. Of course, local autonomy is not necessarily undesirable; it can allow adaptation to local conditions and give greater self-determination to the rank-and-file members. On the other hand, the international must surely be given power to prevent a local from violating the law, endangering union wage scales, or taking other action that might jeopardize other parts of the union. Yet many internationals lack this power, at least in their dealings with large, powerful locals.

The roots of this problem lie in the political structure of the union. Since local officers are elected by the members, the international cannot exercise the power available in other types of organizations where the chief executive can hire and fire subordi-

---

* In 1966, 56 international union headquarters were reported in Washington, D.C., 30 in New York, and 13 in Chicago, out of 119 international unions reporting headquarters offices.

nates at every level. The leader of a strong local, moreover, can also exert various forms of leverage not readily available in a corporation or a government department; for example, he may threaten to oppose the administration at the next convention or even to pull his local out of the union entirely. He may passively resist the advice, admonition, or general direction of the national office, recognizing that busy general officers are unlikely to have the time or the inclination to devote extended time to the affairs of a particular local except under extreme provocation. The dragging of local feet frustrates more national union policies than any formal opposition.

By imposing sharp limits upon the international, the political system can hamper the effectiveness of the entire organization. Yet the system itself has such obvious value that these drawbacks should perhaps be shrugged off as a price that must be paid to achieve a democratic union. Even so, many internationals could still do much to integrate their locals more effectively. The method of communication between locals and the international, for example, often leaves much to be desired. Locals do file regular statements with the international to record new members and dues payments, but seldom will they report systematically on their activities. In many unions, the international staff tends to concentrate almost exclusively on particular crises: strikes, jurisdictional disputes, rank-and-file unrest, and the like, so that there is little contact with a local unless it is experiencing obvious difficulties. Perhaps this is a wise allocation of time for a small staff. Nevertheless, the fact remains that many internationals lack adequate information about the activities of many locals and do not make systematic efforts to review the work of local officers or enlist their cooperation in formulating plans and priorities for the future. The inevitable result is inadequate performance in such areas as education, community service, new organizing, and even collective bargaining.

EXCESSIVE CENTRALIZATION

If there is too much local autonomy in many unions, there are also internationals that have suffered from excessive centralization. This is particularly a problem for some industrial unions that do the bulk of their bargaining on a national basis. In such organizations, local unions are often left with very little work to perform.

In basic steel, for example, the Steelworkers bargain on an industry-wide basis; organizing is largely carried out by international representatives, and grievances pass out of the hands of the local after the second step of the grievance procedure. Even dues are paid directly to the international and later remitted to the locals. There are several dangers in such a highly centralized system. Union policies may become too uniform and rigid to adapt to local conditions; for example, industrywide contracts may not take adequate account of the special problems of individual plants, and local officials may lack power to innovate by bargaining for health and recreation facilities or other special programs for their members. Under these circumstances, positions of leadership within the local may not seem challenging enough to appeal to the ablest members. The rank and file may grow more apathetic and more inclined to view the union simply as a service agency. Indeed, so much of the union's work may be carried on by the remote international office that the union will not seem to play a vital part in the lives of the members. As a result, the danger arises of a growing alienation that will erupt in rejected contracts or an overthrow of established leaders.

ECONOMIES OF SCALE

Still another problem of structure exists in many unions because so many locals are too small to function efficiently. In 1966, over half of the locals in the union movement contained fewer than one hundred members, and fewer than 15 percent of the locals had a membership in excess of five hundred.* In certain internationals, on the other hand, locals tend to be larger. In such unions as the Auto Workers and Operating Engineers, more than 40 percent of the locals were larger than 500 in 1966, while more than 50 percent of the locals were at least this size in the Retail Clerks and the Teamsters.

---

* The number of local unions with fewer than 100 members appears to have declined slowly in recent years. These figures were derived by Professor Leo Troy.

Size of local	1962	1966
0–50	14,926	14,801
50–100	7,165	6,847
100–500	13,315	13,129
500–1,000	2,882	2,971
1,000–5,000	2,571	2,876
5,000 and above	274	358

The small local creates many problems. Its resources are inadequate to support even a single full-time officer. By multiplying the number of separate units, small locals complicate the task of coordination and supervision from the international. The result may be ineffective performance even in such important functions as bargaining and grievance administration; other tasks, such as organizing, education, and training, will often not be undertaken at all.* If the international wishes to counteract these problems, it will have to devote so much time and effort to servicing small locals that these units will be carried at a deficit.

There is no general rule to define the minimum size for an efficiently run local. The answer will vary from one union to another, depending on the functions the local is to perform and the level of dues paid by the members. Presumably, each unit should be large enough to support at least one full-time officer. If the local is expected to assume responsibility for bargaining and organizing, two or more full-time officials may be needed. It would seem desirable for every union to establish a basic minimum appropriate to its dues structure and to the functions performed by its locals. Thus far, very few unions have taken this step.

Even after a minimum figure is established, the international will seldom be able to reach it in every case, and progress will be slow. Opposition from local unions will delay or frustrate many efforts to merge units to achieve effective size. In certain cases, locals will exist in small towns that are too remote to permit a worthwhile merger. Nevertheless, it is reasonably clear that much could be done in many unions to achieve a more effective scale of operations either by merger or, failing this, by establishing stronger district councils with an active full-time staff. There is increasing concern among national unions with the problems of small locals,

---

* In this regard, it is interesting to note that in the period 1962–66 small locals showed a much greater tendency to stagnate or decline than was true of larger locals. Union growth was much more highly concentrated in larger locals. As the extent of union growth increased late in the period, a larger proportion of all locals showed growth, but the differences between small and large locals persisted. The following figures are illustrative.

	1962–1963			1965–1966		
Size of local	Increase	No change	Decrease	Increase	No change	Decrease
0–50	1,308	7,204	4,058	1,578	10,952	2,195
50–100	1,356	1,958	2,870	1,969	3,167	1,709
100–500	3,871	1,808	6,593	5,784	3,048	4,296
500–1,000	1,190	141	1,539	1,663	223	1,085
1,000–5,000	1,487	71	1,234	1,808	99	969
5,000 and up	222	1	127	243	1	114

and experience in a few unions demonstrates what can be done by effective leadership from the international. In the Meat Cutters, for example, it was made mandatory for locals of fewer than 100 members to merge within a year. Other internationals, such as the Carpenters, have provided constitutional authority to the president, with the approval of the executive board, to require merger of local unions, and a policy has been enunciated requiring locals smaller than 250 members to merge. In most cases, the terms of local mergers have been worked out by mutual agreement.

The problem of achieving economies of scale applies to international unions as well as local units. The membership must be large enough to permit the bulk of the locals to achieve a size that will support the necessary number of full-time officials. The union must also be large enough to finance a field staff that can give adequate support and service to all its locals. In addition, its headquarters must be able to maintain a group of specialists with experts in legal matters, education, organizing, research, and so forth. Once again, the minimum requisite size will vary with such factors as the level of dues, the occupational structure of the membership, and its geographic concentration. But many internationals seem clearly too small to function efficiently. In 1966, for example, 64 of the 190 national or international unions reported a membership of 10,000 or fewer, while another 27 unions had fewer than 25,000 members.

Some unions that are too small to afford an effective organization at the international level can conceivably grow to sufficient size through an aggressive organizing program. But most are confronted with strong rival unions or are confined to a narrow occupation, with the result that the opportunities for needed growth are extremely limited. For these organizations, the issue is whether to merge with a larger union or remain at a size too small for efficient operation. This question need not be answered in only one way. Although considerations of efficiency may call for a merger, efficiency may not be paramount to the individual union member. He may prefer to have his separate union, fearing that his interests will be submerged if it joins a larger organization. Where a majority of the members feel this way, there is little reason not to continue the status quo. But experience suggests that many small unions persist, not because of genuine separatist sentiments, but simply because the leaders do not wish to lose their status and influence through merger.

GROWTH AND DIVERSIFICATION

When unions make an effort to grow, a common structural problem is whether the organization should confine itself to a single industry or craft, or seek instead to gather members from different occupations. The Bricklayers have been noticeably reluctant to "dilute the craft" by signing up members of lower skills. The Teamsters and the Communications Workers have gone to the opposite extreme by deliberately trying to organize workers in many industries. The Laborers have steered a middle course by seeking to confine their growth to a few selected occupations.

There are obvious advantages in diversification. For a union in a narrow occupational field, such a policy may be essential if the organization is ever to achieve an effective scale of operations. Even large unions may find it necessary to diversify in order to avoid maintaining many locals of inefficient size in sparsely populated areas. Still other labor organizations may try to represent workers in different levels of production in order to obtain greater leverage in bargaining and organizing. It is partly for this reason that the Meat Cutters have sought to organize processing plants as well as retail outlets. And similar reasons have caused the Laborers to move more aggressively to organize the firms that sell materials and supplies to the construction industry.

With all its advantages, diversification can create difficulties, particularly if it is pushed to extremes. The process of bargaining may grow more disorganized as the work force in plants, companies and industries becomes split haphazardly among a variety of unions. Union leaders may find that it is harder to administer a union with a heterogeneous membership. For example, low-wage members may not be able to afford the dues that are appropriate for more highly paid members, yet the latter may object if they are asked to pay more. Occupational differences may also cause increasing strains and political factionalism within the union. More important still, it may be difficult for the union to provide effective service for a wide variety of occupations. Employees in different industries and trades have widely differing needs and problems. The law, regulations, and employment problems of government employees differ profoundly from those of workers in the private sector (see Chapter 11). The needs and desires of white-collar workers are very different from those of manual workers. As a result, when a union leaves its major field of interest and enters a variety of new occupations, it may well lack the experience to represent its new members effectively. Under these circumstances, the union will have to expend large amounts of time and money to train its staff to understand the financial and market conditions of the new industry and the peculiarities of training, job skills, and working conditions of its new members. The more likely alternative is simply to allow the new members to make do with inadequate service.

In view of these problems, there are strong reasons for a moderate, planned diversification. A union adopting this course will look for a few occupations not unrelated to those of its existing areas of concentration. It may also seek mergers with unions that already are in these fields and can provide it with a nucleus of staff and leadership experienced in representing the new classes of employees. The reader will recall that these are precisely the steps that the Laborers followed in trying to limit their expansion to government employees and workers in firms supplying the construction industry.

ADAPTING STRUCTURE TO STRATEGY

Even if a union plans its growth in this fashion, there are important problems to overcome in building a structure that fits its new strategy. The time, effort and attention needed to organize new occupational groups will not be spent unless the structure of the union is altered to ensure that the affairs of the new groups receive attention from the highest policy-making bodies down through subordinate staff levels. Changes of this kind are hard to make. As a political institution, a union will naturally face insistent pressures to attract money and attention away from new occupational fields toward the traditional sectors in which the preponderance of members and leaders have their roots. These pressures—of habit and tradition as well as politics—can easily undermine new organizing efforts despite the good intentions of the top leaders. Tensions of this kind have been evident in the Laborers, where the staff responsible for organizing government employees has a high rate of turnover and still occupies a somewhat ambiguous position at international headquarters.

The difficulties are even more strikingly revealed in the efforts of the Auto Workers to organize white-collar workers. Walter

Reuther and other top U.A.W. leaders became intensely aware in the fifties of the changing composition of the work force and the resulting need to organize the white-collar sector. U.A.W. Vice-President Woodcock observed at the 1957 convention:

> It is an inescapable fact that if we cannot achieve the organization of professional and technical and engineering employees, and also office workers, this union will become an increasingly less effective force.

Despite such pronouncements, the U.A.W. failed completely to make progress. From 1950 to 1960, approximately 250,000 white-collar workers were employed by the automobile, aerospace, and farm-implement companies organized by the union. Nevertheless, white-collar membership in the U.A.W., which was estimated at 80,000 in 1953, not only failed to grow, but by 1961 had actually sunk to 55,000. Many factors were involved—some of them quite beyond the union's control. Nevertheless, there was an evident lack of urgency in the U.A.W.'s own efforts. Only a minute portion of union funds was directed to the white-collar sector. More pertinent still, several structural defects persisted that helped to blunt any serious attempt to expand white-collar membership.

To begin with, the union failed to take decisive action on the question of whether white-collar members should be grouped in separate locals or lumped together with production workers. According to one white-collar leader in a report to the U.A.W. Executive Board:

> It is an established fact that the most vital and active office and technical groups are those who have remained the masters of their own destiny. Experience has shown that when a group of workers of intelligence and varying degrees of skill are put in a position of being just a small segment of a large mass of workers in the production plants, they are often disgruntled, indifferent, or actively hostile to our unions. . . . It would seem that the worst deterrent to organizing, and the point most successfully made by management groups, is the placement of white-collar workers into production and maintenance units.

Notwithstanding this testimony, the U.A.W. continued with a hodgepodge of locals, some mixed and some exclusively white-collar.

The lack of a separate, specialized structure extended well beyond the local level. Although a Technical, Office and Professional Department was established at U.A.W. headquarters in 1953 for white-collar workers, it regularly received less than 2 percent of all staff department expenditures. In 1963, one writer noted that the funds, staff, and talent appropriated to the department were sharply limited. For one or all of these reasons it has been unable to do more than a minimum job of servicing the existing white-collar units. Aside from the department, the organization structure of the U.A.W. white-collar units did not permit adequate communication, coordination, and pursuit of the common interests of white-collar workers. Even in organizing new groups of white-collar workers, no separate structure was provided to ensure specialized competence. The organizers were drawn from the regular regional staffs; their background was in production, since appointments to the staff tended to reflect the political dominance of the much more numerous blue-collar members. As a result, organizers came to the job without an instinctive appreciation of the special needs of white-collar members or an awareness of the skepticism that many of these workers felt toward the union shop, the seniority system, and other traditions firmly imbedded in the blue-collar units.

At the root of these structural deficiencies was a lack of representation for the white-collar members in the higher councils of the union. Without such representation, the interests of these members could not be pushed at critical policy levels in the U.A.W. Only in 1962, when the white-collar units organized themselves in a political caucus, could they press their views with sufficient force to induce the union to devote greater attention to their problems.

Following protests by white-collar members, the U.A.W. finally decided to create an adequate structure for organizing such employees. The Technical, Office and Professional Department was allotted more funds and put under new leadership. Special organizers were recruited from the white-collar membership. New groups of members were given the choice of forming their own local, joining an existing white-collar local, or merging with a unit of production workers. (As one could have predicted, the members almost invariably chose to remain separate from the production units.) In order to improve communication between the international and the white-collar members, a special newsletter was initiated, and advisory councils were established to discuss the international's activities and make recommendations on behalf of white-collar members concerning bargaining demands, education programs and other matters affecting their interests.

These innovations did not immediately produce startling successes in organizing; the problems of attracting white-collar members are too deeply imbedded to be overcome by structural changes alone. Nevertheless, the U.A.W. did succeed in halting the downward trend in white-collar membership and replacing it with a slow but accelerating rate of growth. In 1962, for example, the union held only six white-collar elections involving 300 employees. By 1965, the number of victories climbed to 29, and 1,886 new members were added to the rolls. In 1967, the union was successful in 37 campaigns comprising 5,400 employees. Overall, then, the U.A.W. experience appeared to confirm the maxim that an organization must adapt its structure to its strategy in order to make adequate progress toward its objectives.

Planning

LONG-RANGE PLANNING

Long-range planning involves several steps. In order to know what to plan for, leaders must first make clear the purposes of the organization and their relative importance in view of the traditions of the organization, its resources, and the needs of those it serves. With these purposes in mind, the leaders must inform themselves about emerging problems and opportunities that may affect the ability of the organization to pursue its aims over a period of years. In light of this information, more precise objectives can be fixed over the period in question and strategies can be devised by which to reach these goals.

Defining the Purposes of the Union. Although the aims of unions may vary in detail, almost every labor leader would affirm that his organization seeks to increase the economic welfare and job security of the members, to increase the membership and thereby extend the benefits of unionism to new groups of employees, and to render constructive service to the community. In most instances, however, these objectives are left so vague as to obscure many important issues from view. For example, many unions are unclear as to just what "economic welfare" implies. Does it merely involve wages, fringe benefits, work schedules, and the like, or does it also include an effort to improve the design of the job in such a way as to increase the employee's satisfaction in his work? Does it involve only conditions of employment, or should the union make active efforts to furnish legal services, psychiatric counseling, cultural activities, recreational facilities, and the like? The union leader may reply that the answer to these questions must depend on what the members want, but as a practical matter, the members may never react one way or the other unless the leaders take the initiative in defining alternatives and putting them to an actual test.

Many unions are even more unclear on the meaning and importance of expanding their membership. Does union growth imply a planned expansion into new occupations? If so, what occupations and unorganized groups should receive priority? Is growth worthwhile only insofar as it pays for itself through economies of scale and increased dues and initiation fees? Is it important to add new members for social welfare reasons and how much are these objectives worth to the present union members? Do existing wage policies conflict with organizing goals by putting standard union rates so high that it becomes economically impossible to represent workers in related fields of employment? If so, how should these conflicts be resolved?

To give yet another example, most unions are not entirely clear why they should participate in community activities. Are these activities worthwhile merely to improve the union's image? To increase its political influence? To make a contribution to society? What types of community activity promise to accomplish the most for the particular objectives the union wishes to stress?

Unions run several risks in failing to be more precise in defining their purposes and establishing their relative importance. An evident danger is that they will overlook opportunities to perform valuable new functions. For example, if unions simply assume that they exist primarily to serve the traditional economic needs of their members, they are likely to continue bargaining over wages and working conditions and to adjust their aims only when they encounter pressure from the rank and file to do something about rising medical costs, racial tensions, or some other emerging problem. Thus, they may fail to anticipate new needs until dis-

satisfaction from the members breaks upon them, leaving too little
time to identify the needs and take corrective action. Or it may be
that the membership, accepting the union's narrow traditional
province, will never ask the leaders to pioneer new programs,
even though some of these might be well within the bargaining
process and, thus, well within the union's special competence. For
example, many students of industrial psychology believe that
employees often press for higher wages in response to unarticu-
lated discontent over the monotony of work and the lack of
responsibility and recognition for the tasks they perform. If a
union does not play an active role in probing these possibilities, it
may continue to concentrate on traditional bargaining goals at the
expense of other sources of satisfaction in work that might do more
to enhance the welfare of its members.

Unions can also run a serious risk of misallocating their
resources if they fail to think carefully enough about the relative
importance of their goals and programs. The problem of union
growth presents an apt illustration. In some cases, organizing new
plants may protect the union's wage scales, enhance its political
influence, and provide economies of scale to support an adequate
staff. In other situations, organizing campaigns may yield little
benefit to existing members beyond the satisfaction of extending the
advantages of bargaining to new groups of employees. These
varying results should be explicitly considered and weighed in
deciding whether it is worthwhile to finance new organizing
campaigns, for such outlays can only be made in place of other
expenditures, such as hiring additional staff to service local unions,
that may be much desired by the rank and file. Nevertheless, top
officials are not always clear about their purposes and priorities in
organizing; the underlying issues are left to be resolved *ad hoc* by
subordinates in the field, with the result that organizing efforts
throughout the union become haphazard and inconsistent.

Union participation in community affairs offers still another
example of the problems resulting from a failure to define organizational goals. In most communities, local leaders have tried to
participate in charitable, educational, and governmental activities.
In a few cases, these activities are undertaken to achieve some
specific objective, such as the protection of favorable building
codes or maintenance of prevailing wage policies. But local leaders
usually participate without a clear sense of what they expect to
accomplish for the community or their own organizations. When

this occurs, the union can easily dissipate the time and energies of its staff. Since local officials are normally hard-pressed simply to fulfill their essential union tasks, they generally have barely enough time even to attend the meetings of the community organizations. As a result, the union representatives can easily create ill will by failing to prepare for meetings or to carry out assignments. More often, they simply pass unnoticed. As one writer has observed, unions ". . . have not brought to the decision-making process [in community organizations] a new set of interests, a new program, a new ideology. They do not have a specific labor program but they have accepted the community welfare program at face value."[1] In short, so long as union leaders are content to leave their objectives undefined, one wonders whether these community activities do not merely squander the valuable time of local officials in return for very meager benefits to the organization and the community.

Although unions might perform more effectively by formulating their goals more precisely, a few readers may object on democratic grounds, arguing that the union's purposes should be defined by the members rather than the leadership. But nothing that has been said need detract from the authority of the members. A conscientious attempt to clarify the union's purposes will require continuing efforts to ascertain the needs and sentiments of the members. With the help of such information, of course, the leaders must take the initiative in defining the aims of the organization. Once formulated, however, these purposes will have to pass the test of rank-and-file approval or they will eventually atrophy for lack of cooperation and support.

Developing Specific Goals and Strategies.   Most unions understand their purposes sufficiently well to begin establishing specific long-run goals and developing strategies for achieving them. In a few instances, fairly elaborate work of this kind has been carried out. The Communications Workers, for example, commissioned an independent survey to study the long-term impact of automation on jobs in the communications field. In addition, the union has developed a series of targets for union growth over the ensuing decade, as well as programs of education and community action to help achieve these goals. In the United Automobile Workers, long-range plans have been devised to organize the poor and to develop education programs to meet emerging trends in member attitudes which the union has detected through surveys of the rank and file. But careful staff work of this kind is rare. To be sure, officials in almost every union will have thought about the steps to be taken over a period of years to accomplish certain objectives. Jimmy Hoffa had a clear sense of the long-range need to centralize bargaining in the trucking industry. One or two members of the Laborers' staff had formulated a series of stages by which to move over a period of years toward a full-fledged education program and a vigorous organizing effort. John L. Lewis had a rather clear vision of how he wished the Mine Workers' Welfare Fund to evolve.

Yet truly systematic planning does not often take place, for no one has been explicitly assigned the task of studying the environment methodically and making detailed investigations of long-range opportunities and problems. The needs and attitudes of the members are only just beginning to be surveyed by a few unions. The questions asked are seldom fully thought out, and there has not yet been an opportunity to repeat the surveys over a period of time to discover trends and shifts in attitude.

The larger problem, however, is not simply that there are no systematic procedures or assigned responsibilities. In many cases, the prevailing climate in union headquarters is not conducive to the development of new goals and new programs. To return to the Laborers, many subordinate leaders were aware, long before 1964, of the lack of vigorous organizing and the need for education and training programs. Yet they were dissuaded from pressing these ideas because of a pervasive feeling that new programs would meet with disinterest or even opposition at international headquarters. Conversely, the major factor in the revitalization of the Laborers has been the emergence of key officials who have changed this climate by communicating the sense that new ideas, if they are found to have merit, will be welcomed and pushed hard at headquarters.

The failure in many unions to create a favorable atmosphere for planning and innovation has deeper causes than a simple disinterest on the part of the leadership. The political nature of the union contributes in several ways to this deficiency. Innovation often implies a criticism of the status quo and thus may be upsetting to elected officers of an organization. In addition, planning can easily be distorted in the political climate of union headquarters. For example, a union president who is anxious to create a successful and dynamic image may be disinclined to set a modest target for union growth, however realistic such a goal may be. Thus, it is not surprising that the Communications Workers fixed a series of long-range membership goals that now seem unrealistic and quite out of line with the effort and resources that the union was actually prepared to commit to the task.*

The day-to-day pressures of running a union also seem to leave little time for planning. Unlike the top officials in many other large institutions, union leaders have not been successful in delegating enough responsibility to free themselves to think about the development of their organizations. To some extent, this problem may again result from the political nature of the organization. Like Congressmen, union leaders feel that they must spend major amounts of time in performing ceremonial functions and attending personally to the problems of their constituents and subordinates. Some top officials boast of signing every check and approving every expenditure—an understandable but highly inefficient method of insuring against a politically explosive incident of corruption within the international. These explanations, however, are not entirely convincing, for there are several large unions whose presidents have succeeded in delegating the bulk of their routine administrative tasks (though not for the purpose of gaining time to plan the development of their organizations). Hence, a deeper cause in many unions may simply be that the leaders lack the training and background for giving careful attention to long-range problems. Many of these officials have risen to the top through political skill and an ability to deal effectively with one immediate crisis after another. By the time they reach high union office, they may be unable to detach themselves from the day-to-day affairs of their organizations.

What is lost by all this? Surely, no one would allege that the union movement will perish if it fails to devote more effort to planning of this sort. Yet there are dangers for the unions in continuing their present practices. The major risk is that the organization will get a late start in developing adequate programs to meet emerging needs. Such tardiness can be costly. Unions may overlook valuable opportunities that will not recur in such a favorable posture. Abuses in union government cannot be dealt with so

---

* Although the target set for 1970 is 750,000 members, total membership at the end of 1967 was 344,557, an increase of only 9,000 over the preceding year. Moreover, appropriations for organizing were running far below the requests submitted by the appropriate officials.

flexibly if unions wait until Congress has had to treat them by legislation. Federal training programs may offer much less promise once they have hardened into established molds or changes in administration have occurred. Public employment and other burgeoning new areas for organization will not be captured so readily after other unions have begun to occupy the field. Racial problems may prove intractable once they have erupted into violence and open hostility. Technological developments may create new jobs that will fall to other unions if the organization has not prepared itself and trained its members to adapt to the changing skills required. Competitive developments may destroy jobs and undermine long established benefits unless the danger is recognized early and policies are formulated promptly to deal with it.

In failing to assign staff responsibility for long-range planning, unions have also lost a valuable opportunity to provide greater vitality and creativity within their organizations. As Amitai Etzioni has pointed out, planners and developers in large corporations ". . . tend to define for the organization successively higher levels of satisfaction by raising the standard of what is considered 'all right.' In this way organizations have been able to build in mechanisms to make themselves 'rationally dissatisfied' and continue in search of improvement."[2]

In the end, of course, no one can be certain of exactly what has been lost by not providing for systematic long-range planning. Nevertheless, since organized labor has been widely criticized for its lack of innovation, one may suspect that the gap has taken its toll. If a competent planner had done no more than capitalize on the computer at an early date and hasten its effective application to record keeping, he could have saved many unions enough to pay his salary for years to come.

SHORT-RUN PLANNING AND BUDGETING

Very seldom does a union headquarters collect the data required to allocate money and manpower systematically among its various short-term programs. Instead, allocations tend to be made *ad hoc* as individual requests and contingencies arise. Budgets are seldom employed, and unions that use them generally regard them simply as a method of ensuring that the organization live within its means. There is little recognition of the budget as a vehicle for permitting the staff to cooperate in planning an overall program for the union. There is almost no use of the budget-making process as a procedure to assign priorities to operations which yield greatest benefits to the union and to shift resources from one purpose to another. In these respects, the operation of the Laborers' union provides a typical illustration.

It has already been pointed out that the Laborers lack sufficient data about the costs and achievements of their organizing program to permit careful planning or resource allocation. Similar difficulties exist in other program areas. In the field of jurisdictional disputes, neither the Laborers nor the other construction crafts have any precise information on the manpower and money expended in protecting their jobs from being taken over by other unions.* Nor have these unions attempted to measure the benefits they derive from these expenditures.

To be sure, such matters are not entirely overlooked. In the Laborers, for example, a few regional managers have been troubled by the vast expenditure of time devoted by their staff to jurisdictional problems and have tried to reduce these costs by reaching agreements with other unions. Yet, the clear impression remains that by failing to make a systematic appraisal of the costs and benefits involved, neither the Laborers nor the other construction crafts have seriously grappled with the possibility that they may be spending far more on jurisdictional disputes than any net return they can secure for their members.†

---

* In response to private inquiries by the authors, a number of top union officials in the building and construction industry have made rough estimates that approximately half the time of their field representatives is spent in handling jurisdictional disputes.

† An interesting parallel is provided in the history of efforts by international unions to raid one another's members. The Joint Committee on Labor Unity, which helped to pave the way for the AFL–CIO merger, made a study of N.L.R.B. contested elections between two or more unions in 1951–52 and reported as follows:

In the labor board representation cases involving 366,470 employees, the petitioning union was successful in gaining certification as the collective-bargaining representative for approximately 62,000 employees, or only 17 percent of the total number of employees involved. Of these 62,000 employees, approximately 35,000 were won from a CIO union by a union affiliated with the AFL. Approximately 27,000 were won by a CIO union from a union affiliated with the AFL. The net change, therefore, of these raids involving 366,470 employees was 8,000 or only approximately 2 percent of the total number of employees involved. AFL–CIO, *Constitution of the AFL–CIO and Other Official Documents Relating to the Achievement of Labor Unity*, January 1956, p. 36.

These revelations helped pave the way for the no-raiding pact, which largely eliminated raiding by one affiliated union of employees represented by another affiliate.

Much the same analysis can be made of less important programs of the Laborers, such as publishing their magazine and newspaper. Here, the union is likely to have a better idea of its costs, since the regular financial statements assign a specific category for publication expenses. On the other hand, like most unions, the Laborers have not troubled to hire a consultant or conduct a survey to determine the impact of their publications on the membership. As a result, the union does not know how many members read its publications, which portions or subjects are read most carefully, or what impact has been produced upon the reader. At best, the editor simply obtains a random assortment of first- or secondhand comments passed along by other officials at meetings or other union gatherings. Lacking more systematic data, the union is obviously handicapped in deciding how much to spend on publications or whether to cut back certain portions of its journal, expand others, or initiate further changes to increase its effectiveness.

Acquiring the necessary data is only one step in preparing an adequate planning budget. To illustrate the process more concretely, it is useful to return to the Laborers and discuss the methods that might be applied to the field of organizing.

If effective planning and budgeting are to be carried on by the Laborers, it is vital to build an adequate body of data by obtaining more specific reports from representatives in the field. Even now, periodic reports are submitted to headquarters but they vary enormously in form and content. Some are transmitted orally and some in writing. Some are submitted daily and others monthly. Some offer suggestions for the future, while others do not. Most of the reports consist, by and large, of sketchy narratives of past activities—"I spent a couple of days helping Local 134 in Greenville and then headed down to Biloxi." In place of these accounts, representatives might be asked to submit periodic reports that would include the time spent on each organizing campaign, the estimated time spent by paid local officials, and an evaluation of the results of the campaigns, including the number of new members and their occupational classifications.* In addition, representatives should maintain a list of unorganized firms in their assigned areas and include, for each one, the number and

---

* The Communications Workers and several other unions require their field representatives to fill out printed report forms for this very purpose.

type of employees involved, a record of prior organizing efforts and an evaluation of the prospects for a successful attempt in the future.

With the help of this information, regional managers and headquarters staff could develop a keener sense of the strengths and weaknesses of their organizing program and staff. They could also identify more readily the areas and occupational groups in which the organizing dollar might be spent with greatest effect. In order to plan systematically, however, further analysis would be needed to develop an adequate set of organizing goals. The Laborers have already taken tentative steps in this direction by resolving that organizing resources should be devoted to construction laborers, construction suppliers, and government employees, in diminishing order of importance. These priorities, however, are much too crude, for they measure only the relative benefits to the union of organizing different categories of employees. To be specific, the priorities reflect the fact that it is often more important to organize construction laborers than to organize government employees since unorganized construction workers are more likely to jeopardize the wage scales of union members in competing firms. But it is quite conceivable that there are groups of public employees who are so ripe for organization that they can be signed up at a cost sufficiently low to make them a more attractive target than a group of construction workers who are skeptical of unions and hence very difficult and expensive to organize. In short, a set of priorities for organizing must be based on an appreciation of costs as well as benefits.

An approach of this kind might lead the staff to evaluate organizing opportunities within the following rough framework:

A. *Benefits*

  1. Direct economic benefits—dues and initiation fees payable by new members when the target plant is organized.
  2. Indirect economic benefits—for example, the protection to union wage scales derived from organizing competing employers.
  3. Social benefits—the satisfaction to the union of extending the benefits of representation and membership to new groups of employees.

B. Costs

1. Estimated organizing expenses (salaries of organizers, cost of leaflets, etc.) adjusted to reflect the risk of failure (which will cause a total loss of organizing expenditures).
2. Estimated cost of providing staff and other expenditures required to service new members.
3. Miscellany (risk of inviting retaliatory organizing efforts by another union, etcetera).

This general framework is not designed to yield any precise quantitative figure; several of the items call for rough estimates or value judgments that cannot be reduced to dollars and cents. At the same time, it should be possible to develop certain rules of thumb that will help in making organizing decisions. For example, units of a certain size may return enough in initiation fees and dues to exceed anticipated expenses without even considering the more intangible social and strategic benefits to be achieved. Hence, targets of this sort should always be attacked, unless the prospects of success are distinctly unfavorable. Conversely, other types of targets can be defined that would be considered undesirable, however attractive the prospects of success, because the size, location, or occupational structure of the unit will impose a drain on the union treasury so great as to outweigh any conceivable benefits to be achieved.

The most important function of the framework described above, however, would be to encourage union officials to make a more conscious, systematic assessment of organizing opportunities and to provide a more rational basis for allocating organizing resources. Lacking adequate data, the international tends at present to distribute resources among the regions on an *ad hoc* basis that reflects the relative size of the membership in each area or the personal influence of the regional manager. Hence, money and manpower can easily be expended on small unorganized pockets in heavily organized areas while leaving inadequate resources to cover much more attractive targets elsewhere.

Ideally, systematic planning should begin in the field. Within each region, international representatives and officials of large locals would be encouraged to analyze the targets in their area and to develop an organizing plan for the forthcoming year. With staff assistance, the regional manager could then incorporate these plans in a proposed budget that would reflect the amounts of money and manpower to be expended on organizing in his area and the targets to which these resources would be devoted. Thereafter, an overall plan and budget would be prepared at international headquarters in consultation with the regional managers. The final planning process would be directed toward several objectives: to determine the overall sum to be devoted to organizing within the international in light of the needs of other union programs; to review the regional plans and allocate resources among regions and occupational groups in light of past experience and current prospects; and to analyze the results in the different regions in order to spread successful techniques to other regions and identify problems that require corrective action.

Many union officials will doubtless recoil from the procedures outlined here. Some will protest that these procedures make a business out of organizing and undermine the social purposes of bringing the benefits of unionization to underpaid employees. Others will insist that planning budgets will straitjacket the union and prevent it from responding flexibly to changing opportunities to organize. Still others may argue that the prospects for organizing are too uncertain to permit reliable planning estimates.

None of these objections seems fatal, so long as the planning process is properly understood. As for making a business out of organizing, the procedures described do not imply that unions should overlook the social benefits of organization. On the contrary, the very object is to consider these advantages explicitly, along with other costs and benefits of organization, so that the union can make a full evaluation of the attractiveness of each potential target. Nor need the planning budget prevent the union from adjusting to new situations as they arise. The budget is intended to reflect no more than a tentative set of objectives and expenses. Resources can and should be shifted as old opportunities fade and new ones arise. Indeed, it is the present *ad hoc* system that is likely to be inflexible, for some of the regional managers will be forced to ignore attractive targets so long as scarce resources are allocated among regions on the basis of haphazard factors such as tradition, size of membership, and personal influence instead of a realistic assessment of where the organizing dollar can be put to most effective use.

The problem of making reliable estimates is admittedly more troublesome, for no one can deny that these are often speculative. Nevertheless, the problems of uncertainty will exist whatever the union does, for decisions must be reached whether they are made in the present *ad hoc* manner or with the help of advance planning. Increasingly, large organizations in other fields are finding that careful planning with adequate data produces better results even in areas such as the development of new weapons systems and research programs—fields that seem still more uncertain than an organizing program. Conceivably, there may be other areas of activity that are simply too speculative for careful planning. Strikes afford one obvious example, for it is often extremely difficult to know whether stoppages will occur and how long they will last. Jurisdictional disputes are also hard to estimate in advance; a union cannot easily predict the campaigns that may be launched against it by rival unions. But these uncertainties can be prepared for by strike funds and other contingency accounts. And in many other fields—such as lobbying, community activities, education, and the like—planning should prove even easier than in the area of organizing new members, since the costs involved are usually well known and largely within the control of the union. In the last analysis, the process of drawing up a planning budget can be valuable simply by forcing the leaders and staff of an organization to collect accurate data on the costs and results of its various programs and to join in analyzing the information to determine from experience how programs can be improved and resources rearranged to obtain better results in the future. There is little reason to believe that unions are any less in need of this procedure than other large organizations.

Problems of Personnel

Every union of substantial size is administered with the help of a large body of officials and staff. Some of these individuals occupy routine or clerical positions. A handful are professionals specializing in law, accounting, economics, or public relations. But the largest and most influential group are the union members who have risen to elective or appointive positions of authority at the local, regional, and national level.

As in other large unions,* the typical official in the Laborers will have begun his career by rising from the ranks to win an office in his local. If the local is small, he will hold this position while continuing in his regular job, since the local treasury will not be large enough to support a full-time official. In a larger local, however, he may leave his job and work only for the union. In either case, he may subsequently rise to become an officer or staff member of the district council in his area or he may move directly to a job as international representative attached to a regional office. An international representative may well continue in that position until retirement, but it is possible that he will be tapped to become a regional manager or to fill an opening on the headquarters staff. Further up in the hierarchy are the nine vice-presidents, who may be selected from among the thirteen regional directors or from the leaders of the larger locals. Once selected, these officials often take on their new office while retaining their regular jobs as regional manager or local officer (save for two or three vice-presidents who occupy full-time positions at international headquarters). Above the vice-presidents stand the president and secretary-treasurer. In theory, at least, any union member may be elected to these positions; in practice, such openings will almost certainly be filled by elevating one of the vice-presidents.

Each position in the union hierarchy has its own characteristic problems. For example, at the lowest rung of the ladder, the shop steward tends to suffer from too little authority from the top and too much abuse from beneath. His power to process grievances is constantly whittled away by his superiors, but he is often blamed by members when disappointing decisions are handed down. These pressures make it increasingly difficult to persuade good men to run for steward positions.[4] The effect upon the union is serious, for the steward is the immediate representative of the union to the

---

* According to one recent survey of more than 430 international union officers, the typical official joined his present union in his early twenties and gained his first office, usually in his local, at about the age of thirty. Though there are wide variations, the average international union president—of 56 surveyed—reached his present position at the age of approximately fifty years. The corresponding age for vice-presidents surveyed was 45. Among the vice-presidents, 64 percent rose from some lower position on the international staff while 36 percent were elevated directly from office in a local. Of 69 secretary-treasurers, 75 percent were chosen from the ranks of vice-presidents, while 83 percent of the union presidents were elected from the position of vice-president.[3]

members, and there is evidence that the performance of these officials has much to do with shaping the attitudes and loyalties of the rank and file toward the organization.[5]

The professional staff members, to take one other illustration, have an entire catalogue of occupational complaints.[6] Whether they are economists, accountants, actuaries, or educational directors, their salaries are low and their opportunities for promotion are meager. They frequently suffer from the peculiar insecurities and demands of working for a political administration. Outside the union, their professional status is low, while within the organization, they often work in an atmosphere that is distinctly anti-intellectual. These problems are easier to cope with in a union that offers the professional full scope for his talents or the possibility, at least, of contributing to the achievement of his social ideals. In many unions, however, even these opportunities are stunted, with the result that the professional often becomes actively disillusioned or a passive routineer.

These problems could be analyzed and elaborated in detail in a study of greater length. For present purposes, however, the more essential task is to focus attention on certain fundamental problems of personnel that cut across almost the entire official hierarchy of the union.

PROBLEMS OF SELECTION AND PROMOTION

Almost all unions are alike in choosing the bulk of their leaders from within the organization. To be sure, unions will look beyond their ranks to fill professional positions—lawyers, accountants, statisticians, and the like—and a few unions will recruit outsiders, usually from other unions, when it is not possible to find the necessary talent within their own organization. For example, the Laborers have recruited from other construction crafts in thinly organized regions where potential leaders are in short supply; they have also hired representatives from the Federation of State, County and Municipal Employees to help organize in the new and very different field of public employment. The Ladies' Garment Workers Union, with a heavy proportion of women members, has often looked outside its ranks to find male staff representatives. But these cases are relatively rare, not only for internal political reasons but also because unions tend to feel that only individuals who have worked in their industry and understand its problems and folkways can win the confidence of other union members and service their needs effectively.

Although there are good reasons for selecting officials from the ranks, this practice poses serious problems for most unions. Looking within the ranks implies selecting higher officials from the pool of elected local officers. But the international has very little influence over this pool, since any attempt to interfere with local elections would generally cause serious resentment. Unfortunately, able members often are unwilling to run, and promising leaders frequently are defeated for reelection before they have the time or experience to make a real contribution to the union. In addition, the quality of the candidates among the rank and file is probably lower than it was two or three decades ago. Although educational levels have been rising, employers have become more sophisticated in spotting promising workers for supervisory positions. Able young people, who once had to seek employment in mill and factory, now find abundant opportunities to go to college and prepare for positions in management and the professions. As a result, while the job of the union official has grown more demanding, the pool of talent to fill these jobs seems to have diminished.

In a few unions, these pressures may lead top officers to reconsider the possibility of filling more subordinate jobs with persons recruited outside the organization. In most unions, however, the critical need will be not to look to the outside but to develop methods for drawing more effectively on the talent already available within the organization and, specifically, for motivating able members to run for office and thereby enter the pool from which the union will choose its higher officials. The international can rarely risk persuading a member to run, let alone openly support his candidacy, for if the candidate should fail to win, top officials would find themselves in an extremely awkward position in dealing with the local. Nevertheless, the international may be able to work indirectly to encourage its members to seek office. Mergers of locals will make possible full-time, better-paid union posts that may be attractive to more members. Education programs and publicity in the union paper may arouse greater interest in union affairs. Particular individuals may be motivated by being asked to attend conferences and special programs. Some international representatives and regional directors already employ these methods to stimulate interest among promising members.

In the longer run, it is possible that certain unions will have to consider even bolder techniques to ensure adequate leadership at the local level. For example, larger locals might be required to hire a staff representative for certain functions, such as organizing, and the international might participate in selecting these officials. Conceivably, locals might elect boards of directors to provide a democratic process for establishing policy, but the chief adminis- trative officer would be appointed with the assistance of the international. Such a proposal might be impractical for some unions and politically impossible for others, and changes in federal law may well be required before the experiment could even be tried. Nevertheless, the fact remains that the election of top local officers is not necessarily the only way, or even the best way, of combining representative government with efficient administration.

At higher levels in the union hierarchy, leaders face additional problems in promoting local officials to positions on the inter- national staff. At times the difficulty is one of incentive. The repre- sentative's salary in certain unions is below the pay of higher- skilled members in their regular job. This is true not only for organizations with highly paid members such as the Air Line Pilots, but also for a union such as the Meat Cutters. A somewhat similar problem arises in the Laborers. In many of the large locals, the top official enjoys a salary comparable to that of an interna- tional representative; he is politically secure and relatively free of outside direction. For such a man, the constant traveling and close supervision involved in the representative's job can often make it unappealing. Thus, promotions to the staff may be rejected by the very individuals who have the greatest ability and experience for the job.

Even if a few promising individuals are uninterested, there will normally be many aspirants for openings on the staff. These positions provide considerable security and thus appeal to the local official who no longer wishes to return to the shop but fears that he will be ousted in some future election. Such attractions often generate pressure to have promotions made for reasons other than the candidates' qualifications for the job. In some unions, nepotism has apparently played a role, although its significance may be on the wane. More often, the pressures are political. The international may be strongly urged to offer the job to a loyal but ineffective local official who has recently been defeated for office. Or a powerful local leader may insist on placing his man on the international payroll. At the very least, the international may feel compelled to give the job to someone from a particular union local or ethnic group to avoid resentment and charges of discrimination. The strength of these pressures varies from one union to another. In general, the problem seems more acute where promotions are made by elected regional directors, particularly where the director is politically insecure. But it is a rare union that can honestly claim to make its appointments strictly on merit.

Even if there are no compelling political pressures, the international headquarters may lack sufficient information to make an adequate selection or even to be aware of all of the promising candidates for the position. In the larger unions, where this difficulty is most acute, top officials try to overcome the problem by relying heavily on the regional director, who is most likely to know the qualifications of all the candidates in the area. Nevertheless, even this system has its shortcomings. Top officials may lack sufficient information to check the recommendations of the director and thereby guard against errors of judgment or unnecessary political compromises. In addition, by relying on the regional director, the international must accept the appointment of a man from that region even though there may be individuals in other areas who could do a better job.

These problems can never be overcome completely. Nevertheless, many unions could make better choices if they could have recourse to the data developed through the planning and budgeting process described earlier. With more systematic information on how subordinates spend their time and the results that they achieve, the international could more readily identify a larger number of promising candidates for promotion. And with greater experience in setting goals and evaluating results for subordinate units, the union might develop better measures for helping appraise the performance of its officials. Even with such information, of course, the union will not always be able to resist political pressure to appoint certain candidates. At the same time, promotions are seldom *purely* political. In most cases, candidates will receive strong political support only if it is possible to make some plausible argument that they will do an effective job. As a result, the international's hand will be considerably strengthened if top officials have the data to make a convincing case that some other candidate has demonstrated superior ability for the position.

INCENTIVES AND REWARDS

Unions offer a wide variety of rewards and sanctions that affect the behavior of their officials. For elected local officers, the dominant motivation will often be to ensure reelection to office. As an incentive, the desire for reelection has the virtue of forcing local officers to pay close attention to the needs of their constituents. Nevertheless, it is apparent that this incentive will not always work to the best interests of the union. The local official may feel compelled to promote the interests of his local even when they conflict with the aims of the union as a whole. He may neglect membership growth and other longer-run interests of the local in order to respond to the immediate desires of his constituents. And in some cases, the local leader may for a period escape real pressure from his members by resorting to autocratic methods or by capitalizing on the indifference of the rank and file.

These dangers can be immaterial in the case of local leaders who happen to be devoted to the international union and the labor movement. Nevertheless, some local officials will not be strongly motivated in this way. As a result, every international union seeks to supplement election pressures by other rewards and sanctions that will induce local leaders to conform with organization goals. As positive inducements, the international holds out the prospect of promotion to a secure staff post and the promise of cooperation and financial support to assist the leader in time of strikes, collective bargaining, or factional disputes within the local.

In addition, the international normally carries a threat of sanctions in the form of trusteeship, fines, or compulsory merger. This network of incentives, however, leaves important gaps. Financial assistance may not be needed by the local official, and the prospect of promotion is often too speculative to exert much influence. Trusteeship and other negative sanctions cannot be employed very frequently without overtaxing the resources of the international and creating political repercussions within the union. Hence, these techniques tend to be more effective in curbing overt abuses than in spurring officials to optimum standards of performance. And the techniques are particularly ineffective in dealing with officials in large locals, who will often have the resources and political power to resist the efforts of the international to control their activities.

These difficulties are hard to correct and probably cannot be overcome without endangering the valuable practice of selecting grass-roots leaders by the vote of their constituents. Nevertheless, certain measures may sometimes produce modest progress. In some unions, it may be possible to gear the salaries of officials to the size of their local in order to provide a stronger incentive to organize new members. Experience in other organizations also suggests that performance often improves markedly when officials are given specific goals to achieve. As a result, a system of planning that assigns realistic objectives to local unions may stimulate greater effort by their leaders. In addition, by publicizing these goals as well as the results achieved by local unions, the international may help to shape the standards which the members employ in electing their officials and judging their performance. Finally, well-designed training programs may help to strengthen the psychic rewards of good leadership in addition to equipping local officials to carry out their functions more effectively.

The international has much greater control over the incentives affecting the members of its own staff. It selects these officials, fixes their salaries, prescribes their duties, holds before them the prospect of promotions and retirement benefits, and can dismiss them for poor performance. In many unions, however, these powers have not been used to maximum effect. The problems involved can be illustrated by the field representatives, or general organizers, who normally make up the largest part of the international staff.

In many unions the rewards given the representatives are too weakly related to achievement to provide an adequate incentive. Salary scales often are standardized with little room to vary compensation according to performance. And even where advancement is normally based on merit, the limited number of openings, often aggravated by the lack of a retirement policy, makes promotion too speculative to serve as an effective inducement. On the negative side, dismissal is available in case of poor performance; former President Dubinsky of the Ladies' Garment Workers tried to keep his staff on its toes by compelling each official to present him with an undated resignation. In most unions, however, it is not practical to fire a staff member except in the most serious cases of incompetence or abuse. Finally, the nature of staff jobs is often ill-suited to ensure continued high performance. The task of the field representative, in particular, is extremely arduous; it has recurrent crises and frustrations, and involves a large amount of travel and time away from home. The representative is generally appointed in his thirties and remains in the job for many years, often without much hope of substantial salary increases or promotion. Under these circumstances, it is not surprising that many unions face a problem of "burnt-out" representatives who cease to function effectively after a number of years in the job.*

In some respects, these problems are not amenable to the same solutions employed in corporations and other organizations. The traditions of the union in protecting workers against discharge may condition them against resorting to disciplinary sanctions. The venerable union tradition of "equal pay for equal work" may make it difficult for union leaders to vary compensation according to performance. In many unions, staff representatives may not even respond to the same types of rewards and ambitions that motivate business and professional people.

Despite these important differences, there are several alternatives that may be worth a trial. In some unions, particularly those in more affluent, white-collar occupations, it may be wise to widen the salary scale and gear pay increases more closely to performance. In other instances, the union would do well to intensify and publicize the opportunities for promotion based on achievement. Greater use of planning goals may likewise help to focus the energies of the representative and motivate him to greater effort.

Early retirement schemes may help to overcome the problem of the "burnt-out" representative. As unions grow and their staffs increase in size and specialization, it is also possible to provide more attractive opportunities for promotion and new jobs. For example, it is conceivable that a union like the Laborers will wish to create additional staff positions at the regional level to assist in collecting data, in budgeting, and in planning. It may also be necessary to establish appointive positions for officials to serve in

---

* It is noteworthy that in recent years the international representatives of a number of unions, such as the Machinists, Steelworkers and Garment Workers, and the Federation, have formed themselves into unions of their own to deal with the top officers of the international unions on such matters as salaries and job security. In some of these instances the international unions have opposed as strongly as other managers the organization of their employees. The N.L.R.B. has required some international unions to cease any interference with the organization of these employees. International union officers have been concerned that such organizations of their employees may seek to exert an influence in union policy making and in the internal political life of the union.[7]

auditing local unions or as chief administrative officer of regional councils. New positions of this kind not only will enhance promotion opportunities, but also may provide constructive ways of shifting field representatives out of jobs involving much traveling and irregular hours. Finally, a personnel policy might well make provision for some systematic rotation of promising representatives to the staff of the Federation, to government agencies, to assignments abroad, and to local communities for limited periods, in order to provide more interesting and broadening experiences.

EDUCATION AND TRAINING

Training programs are especially important for unions in view of the special constraints that limit labor organizations in selecting their leaders and staff. Having been recruited from the shop and the factory, union leaders tend to bring a lower level of education to their work than officials in other large, complex organizations. A survey of union presidents, secretaries, and vice-presidents reveals that only 17 percent have completed college. Fewer than half received any college training; more than a quarter have not completed high school. In contrast, studies of executives in large and medium corporations show that over 80 percent have completed college.[8]

Despite the apparent need, union training programs have not penetrated very deeply. In the study of union leaders referred to above, only 30 percent reported taking leadership training. The extent of training was most pronounced among union vice-presidents, with 34 percent reporting that they had attended some sort of program. In contrast, only 19.6 percent of the union presidents and 21.4 percent of the secretary-treasurers indicated that they had taken such training.

The nature and scope of training vary widely among the international unions.* The great majority of these organizations have virtually no training program beyond an occasional short conference to consider organizing, pension plans, or some other special topic. Although many of these unions are small, the list

---

* The following information has been derived largely from the files of Lawrence Rogin, former director of education of the AFL–CIO, who has undertaken a study of union education programs for the National Institute of Labor Education.

includes such established organizations as the Carpenters, the Musicians, the Iron Workers, and the Locomotive Engineers.

At the opposite extreme, a handful of unions have developed quite extensive training programs. For example, the Communications Workers and the Auto Workers have established a series of courses reaching almost every level of staff and leadership. In addition to special conferences and seminars on a variety of specific topics, both these unions provide regular programs for the field staff, for local leaders, and for shop stewards. The courses have been developed sufficiently to reach a high proportion of officials in each of these categories. Thus, every new staff appointee in the Communications Workers must take a six-month course combining supervised field experience with classroom instruction emphasizing the humanities. All members of the U.A.W. staff have taken its basic three-week program of training in labor law, organizing, grievance processing, and local union administration. And more than 75 percent of the eligible officers participate in the basic orientation courses which both of these unions provide for new local officials.

Between these extremes lie a variety of programs offered by other large internationals. In general, three modes of training are most commonly used: the one-week course for staff members or local leaders; the one- to three-day conference on some particular problem, such as pensions or political action; and the training manual, which is designed to provide officials at different levels with a simple, clearly indexed summary of information relating to their duties and responsibilities. With few exceptions, the courses and conferences do not reach nearly all of the leaders or staff representatives at any given level in the union hierarchy. Attendance is rarely compulsory, and often only a minority of the eligible officials will attend.

Outside the labor movement, universities and other independent groups sponsor a number of classes for union leaders. The range of programs is very wide. For example, the Harvard Trade Union Program, wholly controlled by the university except for an advisory committee, gives a thirteen-week course that each year attracts approximately thirty representatives from a variety of unions. The program includes courses in economics, union administration, labor law, trade-unionism abroad, collective bargaining, and health and welfare plans; most of the participants are local union officers and international representatives. The University of Wisconsin School for Workers offers a two-week course each summer for two hundred or more local leaders. The National Institute of Labor Education has provided four-week seminars for top staff members from the South and shorter seminars for top union officials on current labor and domestic problems.

Labor-education centers at some of the larger universities also conduct courses for local unions in their vicinity. In 1965–66, for example, the Cornell labor-education program enrolled more than two thousand members and officials from locals of twenty-four different international unions in New York City. For the most part, the courses consisted of six to eight evening or weekend sessions on such basic subjects as collective bargaining, labor history, and grievance administration. The Cornell program is unique in its size and scope, but similar courses are offered at the University of California, Michigan State, Illinois, Rutgers, and other institutions.

In recent years, the larger unions have been making greater efforts to develop training programs for leaders and staff. Nevertheless, the record to date can be criticized on a number of grounds. Many leaders and staff personnel still receive no training at all, and an even larger number have attended only short conferences on one or more special topics. With very few exceptions, the programs offered are extremely short—a week or less— and the material covered is highly elementary. Indeed, after examining the typical curriculum—with a morning or two for labor law, a few afternoons for collective bargaining, three or four hours for pension plans—one cannot but wonder about the competence of the union officials who have *not* been exposed to even these rudiments. A further criticism of many programs has to do with the teaching methods employed. Despite numerous exceptions, the typical program is still built around the expository lecture, with little opportunity for problem-solving, role-playing, and other advanced learning methods.

Another drawback is that there are so few courses that draw together officials from several unions.* Without more of these programs, unions lose a valuable opportunity to broaden the horizons of their staff by exposing them to the experience and insights of leaders who have confronted similar problems in other organizations. Finally, there are a number of union programs that

---

* The Brookings Institution program, lasting a week, for top union officials drawn from various international unions is an exception.

are too much tinged with the dogma and doctrine of the sponsoring organizations. To recall one lurid example, the education director of the United Textile Workers (AFL) once observed that his programs were designed to imbue the members with ". . . the necessary spirit of loyalty to their union . . . and to inoculate them against the false slogans and ideological attacks of our major enemy, the Textile Workers of America (CIO)."[9] This sort of propagandizing may be extreme, but it is reasonably clear that a heavy dose of indoctrination creeps into many union programs. And it is likewise clear that there are few programs that allow a really frank and open discussion about union policies.

A number of rationalizations are commonly advanced to explain the deficiencies of training programs. Perhaps the basic claim is simply that experience is the best teacher for the intensely practical job of leading a union. This is a common argument among older officials who have risen to prominence without the benefit of formal training. And it is an argument that is always hard to refute; the value of education is seldom capable of objective demonstration. At the same time, several counterbalancing facts of union life argue in favor of systematic training. For example, in most unions there is a frequent turnover in local officers and stewards; many serve no more than two years. With so little time to learn by experience, there are obvious values in a program that will at least convey a basic knowledge to the official when he takes office. In addition, the job of most union officials includes a growing list of subjects that are sufficiently technical to require some formal training. It may be possible to rely on experience to gain a knowledge of labor law, pension programs, time study, and job evaluation, but it is surely more economical to receive a basic understanding of these subjects through classroom instruction.

Another familiar argument is that union officials cannot spare the time to engage in training programs. There are doubtless many unions in which leaders and staff are heavily burdened. But if training will enable these officials to do their job more effectively, it is extremely shortsighted not to provide the necessary courses for them. Moreover, the entire argument is increasingly discredited by the experience of unions which have found it possible to offer comprehensive education programs.

It is also claimed that longer training programs are impractical, even for promising leaders who are destined for higher jobs in their union. The usual argument is that officials will be impatient with these programs or will suffer politically if they are absent from their posts for more than a week or two at a time. These points are heard so often that one suspects that the underlying problems must be real. Yet the Communications Workers have long maintained their six-month training program for new staff members without apparent ill effects. Even in the case of established officials, the experience of Harvard's thirteen-week program again suggests that the difficulties are overstated. This program has attracted staff representatives and local officials from a number of international unions. Despite the lengthy interruption in their normal duties, all but two of ninety-five graduates responding to a Harvard questionnaire indicated that the program helped them to perform more effectively in their jobs, and over 60 percent of the graduates asserted that the training had helped them to advance more rapidly in their unions.

The real difficulties in gaining support for such programs lie much deeper. The root cause is not a simple distrust of the value of education. On the contrary, surveys reveal that the overwhelming majority of union leaders approve of education programs, at least in principle.[10] The political complexion of the union, however, works in several ways to undermine effective training. As in most political organizations, immediate problems and crises are constantly arising to attract attention away from programs of a more intangible, long-range importance. The time and effort of top union leaders are inexorably drawn from education programs into such tasks as bargaining, coordinating strikes, settling local disputes, persuading subordinates in the field to take this or that course of action, and curbing incipient revolts among segments of the membership. In addition to these pressures, active opposition may arise at lower levels in the union hierarchy. Staff members often resist training because they are unsure of their own capacities and afraid that their careers may be jeopardized by poor performance in an education program. Many union leaders do not wish to have their subordinates undergo extensive training for fear that the latter will become more competent, more self-assured, and more willing to run against their superiors in union elections. According to one union delegate to an education conference: "A lot of our top officers in our locals have to be educated. They don't seem to want anybody to become educated for fear that somebody is going to get their jobs."[11]

Other leaders have different reasons for distrusting education programs, especially those that are independently run. Some feel that participants may be led to become less militant; others fear that education will lead young activists to criticize the union movement and question its policies. Older officials still remember Brookwood and other labor colleges of the twenties and thirties, which graduated many vocal critics of the labor establishment.

Whatever the explanation, union training programs have attracted much criticism over the years. According to the education director of one union: "The cultural lag in the labor movement with respect to leadership programs is frightening. No other institution in American society is so careless of the technical and intellectual preparation of its staff and of the training and retraining of its leadership."[12] It is hard to know what to make of such statements; the importance of education is so inherently speculative and intangible. But in an era in which the union movement fails to grow as rapidly as the labor force, in which large portions of the rank and file are still unregistered and unwilling to vote, and in which leaders are often unable to obtain ratification of bargaining contracts, one cannot help but wonder whether the lack of adequate training is not taking its toll. At the very least, the risks seem far too large for any well-run organization to tolerate.

Conclusion

Judged by contemporary standards of administration, the typical international union leaves much to be desired. Little effort is devoted to systematic research and long-range planning. Careful procedures for budgeting and resource allocation are virtually unknown. The methods for selecting, training, and motivating officials are often haphazard and not well designed to elevate the ablest, best-trained men to union office. The process of communication up and down the union hierarchy does not produce the information required for formulating and implementing effective policy. And the structure of the union is often ill-adapted to the programs of the organization.

With these problems, what are the possibilities for introducing better methods of administration into the international union? Clearly, any estimate must take account of the political system in which unions operate. This system is one which is highly valuable and even guaranteed by law. The political process, however, interferes with administration on several fronts: It diverts the energies of leaders, weakens their controls over subordinates, particularly at the local level, interrupts continuity in office, and may impede the leadership in such important tasks as raising dues to finance the organization. In addition, the political process leaves its mark upon the selection and development of leaders. It greatly limits the opportunity for attracting leadership from outside the organization and allows the administration virtually no opportunity to influence the composition of the pool of local officials from which higher leaders must be drawn. More important still, the election process offers slight assurance that leaders will be chosen for their administrative talents. Unlike the corporation, where these capacities are an explicit criterion for advancement, a labor leader may be elected for reasons that have little to do with his ability to formulate imaginative goals and implement them effectively.

These handicaps are compounded by several other pressures from the environment. For example, the development of union leaders is doubtless affected by the low estate that unions occupy in the public mind. In one survey comparing the prestige of ninety occupations, officials of international unions stood fortieth, ranking behind farm owners, public schoolteachers, railroad engineers, Army captains, airline pilots, and a variety of other callings.[13] Officials of local unions ranked sixty-second in the same survey; higher ratings were given to plumbers, policemen, auto-repairmen, bookkeepers, undertakers, and traveling salesmen.[14] Under these circumstances, it is hardly surprising that few college graduates seek careers in union administration. Nor is it shocking to find the following statement in a staff report to the General Electric Company: "Given a choice between a foreman's and a shop steward's position, the typical union member will—nine times out of ten—elect to climb the management ladder." And yet, if this statement is even half correct, it carries very serious implications for the quality of union leadership.

Apart from its effect upon the development of leaders, the environment in which a union operates lacks many of the incentives that push the leaders of other organizations toward higher levels of efficiency. Unions do not compete with one another to provide better service at lower cost. Unlike the typical business executive, the union leader is not goaded by market pressure, nor

need he fear that his administrative shortcomings will be exposed
in any balance sheet or marketing figures. As a result, unions will
be slower to develop better methods of administration and organization, and successful innovations will be transmitted less rapidly
throughout the labor movement than in the world of large corporations.

In light of these limitations, can international unions be
expected to make significant improvements in their administrative
practices? It is hard to escape the conclusion that there are many
unions that do not possess a leadership with sufficient imagination
and talent to institute effective programs of planning, budgeting,
cost control, and personnel development. And there are others
with internal political problems that are sufficiently troublesome to
preclude, for the time being, any sustained attack upon basic
administrative problems. At the same time, a number of organizations possess leaders and staff who seem clearly able to make substantial progress along these lines. And it is also plain that if the
environment of a union is not conducive to such progress, it is not
necessarily fatal to it. An energetic labor leader is constrained to
think carefully about the use of his resources, because it is often
difficult to obtain the dues increases that are needed to finance all
of the programs he desires. The intricacies of health and pension
programs have exposed increasing numbers of union officers to consultants using more advanced administrative techniques. The
advent of computers has also led many leaders to pay closer attention to more elaborate ways of gathering and storing information.
As a result of these and other pressures, the methods of administration in many unions today—whatever their deficiencies—are still a
substantial improvement over the techniques in use several decades
ago.

In sum, it is probably not unrealistic to expect significant
advances in administration over the next generation. The needed
improvements will have to be made through experimentation by
unions that are more generously endowed with creative, talented
leaders. And the process of emulation by other labor organizations
may not be as rapid as it would be if unions were forced by the
demands of the marketplace to be efficient. But significant progress can still be made, and its realization will bring to the members
benefits that may well be more important than those achieved
through further refinements in the democratic process.

The AFL–CIO:

Vital Force or Rope of Sand? [*]

STANDING ABOVE the vast mosaic of local and international unions is the American Federation of Labor-Congress of Industrial Organizations—the AFL–CIO. To this body belong more than 120 international unions. Not affiliated with the Federation are the United Auto Workers and the Brotherhood of Teamsters, the two largest international unions. With more than 13 million members, however, the AFL–CIO claims allegiance from over 70 percent of the American labor movement. At its apex in Washington is George Meany, who has served as its president since the merger of the AFL and CIO in 1955.[†] In the field, subordinate federations have been created to represent the AFL–CIO in every state and major community.

The Functions of the Federation

A central confederation of unions serves five important functions in the United States.

---

[*] When the AFL and CIO merged in 1955, John L. Lewis, in self-exile from both groups, criticized the new organization as a "rope of sand." Samuel Gompers had earlier used the same phrase in a favorable manner to describe the Federation.

[†] Meany, who had been secretary-treasurer of the AFL from 1940, became president following the death of William Green on November 21, 1952. William Green became president of the AFL in 1924 on the death of Samuel Gompers, who had been president from 1886 except for the year 1894–95.

1) To resolve disputes between two or more member unions. The international unions have traditionally fought with one another, especially in the area of jurisdiction over jobs. While conflicts of this type can be settled by governmental machinery, unions quite naturally prefer to resolve their own problems without outside intervention. A federation provides a logical instrument to perform this task by issuing decisions, administering agreements between the competing unions, or helping to bring about a merger.

2) To represent the labor movement on matters of common concern. This function is best illustrated in the process of lobbying and political action. International unions share many interests in the work of executive and legislative bodies, and these interests will be promoted more effectively if the efforts of the separate internationals are coordinated by a central body such as the federation. A central federation is also essential to represent the interests of American workers in international organizations of labor movements, such as the International Confederation of Free Trade Unions, and in the International Labor Organization, which brings together labor confederations, management associations, and governments from more than a hundred countries.

3) To improve the image of the labor movement. Here, too, unions share a common interest that can often be promoted more effectively and economically through the efforts of a central body.

4) To restrain particular unions that are jeopardizing the interests of other elements in the labor movement. By flagrant acts of corruption or highly disruptive, inconvenient strikes, individual labor organizations can impair the reputation of the entire movement or call forth the threat of punitive or restrictive legislation. A federation is a natural mechanism for bringing pressure to bear on an offending union to protect the movement as a whole.

5) To strengthen weak links within the labor movement. Certain unions may be too small to function efficiently—for example, labor organizations in newly emerging fields. Even large unions may lack the will or imagination to organize new members, train their staff adequately, or perform other tasks effectively. By offering advice, encouraging mergers between unions, providing research and education facilities, and supplying money and trained personnel, the Federation can strengthen member unions in these areas and thereby add to the growth and effectiveness of the movement as a whole.

From its founding in the 1880's, the Federation engaged in these functions. A legislative committee represented labor's interests before Congress, while representatives were appointed by the Federation to meet with international labor bodies. The AFL annual convention and the Executive Council tried to resolve jurisdictional squabbles between member unions. New federal locals and international unions were organized with the help of the Federation. In countless speeches and public appearances, Samuel Gompers sought to explain the aims and practices of organized labor to the public at large.

Despite these activities, the Federation was scarcely an imposing body by present standards. Its staff was tiny; its budget meager. Above all, its powers were extremely limited. The member unions retained complete autonomy over their internal affairs and bargaining activities. The AFL convention, or by delegation, the Executive Council—composed of international union officers*— did have formal authority to settle jurisdictional disputes between affiliated organizations. But strong member unions might simply refuse to comply, knowing that the Federation would do no more than threaten them with expulsion.

During the past half century, the labor movement has undergone profound changes. The CIO emerged as a rival to the AFL in 1935, and union membership grew from 3.7 million to 14.8 million members by 1945. Ten years later, following two decades of strife, the CIO and AFL eventually agreed to merge, with a new constitution and organizational structure.

Despite these changes, the formal powers of the AFL–CIO remain extremely weak. The member unions enjoy formal autonomy over collective bargaining. With respect to their internal affairs, the AFL–CIO constitution does allow the Executive Council† to investigate affiliates for corruption or Communist or other totalitarian influence, to order corrective measures, and by a two-thirds vote to suspend recalcitrant members. These powers have actually been used on several occasions against corruption-ridden affiliates, but the ultimate sanction of suspension still suffers from its ancient weakness; the Teamsters have shown that it is possible

---

* The 1934 convention increased the number of members of the Executive Council from eight to fifteen plus the president, secretary, and treasurer.
† The Executive Council in the period 1955–69 consisted of twenty-seven vice-presidents and the president and secretary-treasurer elected at biennial conventions. In 1969, the number of vice-presidents was increased to thirty-three.

for a strong union to survive and even flourish after being expelled from the Federation. As in earlier decades, the Federation's authority is greatest in the area of interunion rivalry. Much more effective machinery has been created through a constitutional provision specifying outside umpires to resolve disputes over raiding and jurisdiction, subject to review by the Executive Council and the final authority of the convention. Yet even here, the ultimate sanction is still expulsion, and the merged Federation has yet to employ this remedy in disputes between rival unions.

Formal powers, however, do not provide an adequate measure of the Federation's importance. The impact of a Federation on the labor movement can best be determined by its success in influencing the conduct of its member unions, and by this index the AFL–CIO is a much more significant body than the AFL of several decades ago.

One mark of this change is reflected in the size of the Federation's staff. In the early years, Gompers worked with only one assistant. Today, more than a hundred staff members serve in Washington in a number of departments* and committees charged with such problems as legislation, political education, civil rights, social security, community services, international affairs, research, education, and, most recently, urban problems. These departments have no authority to dictate to the member unions, but they do make use of a variety of techniques to exert a growing influence on the internationals.

The Committee on Political Education (COPE), for example, seeks to persuade international unions and state and local federations to make greater efforts in mobilizing money and manpower for political campaigns. In doing so, the committee has resorted to a whole battery of techniques. A large political fund, contributed by the member unions, provides an important source of leverage. Matching grants are provided from this fund to stimulate registration drives and get-out-the-vote campaigns. Additional grants are made to enable twenty-two of the smaller state federations to appoint full-time political directors. COPE's own field staff of

---

* These staff departments are to be distinguished from others which bring together international unions in an industry or a sector. Among the latter departments are the Building and Construction Department, the Industrial Union Department, Maritime Trades Department, Metal Trades Department, Railway Employes' Department, Union Label and Service Trades Department, Government and Service Trades Department, Government Employes Council and the Scientific, Professional and Cultural Employees Council.

twenty men is also deployed to strengthen particular campaigns. Pilot programs are conducted to establish the value of new methods such as computerized mailings to union members in particular localities. With the help of periodic meetings of political directors, international unions are persuaded to donate money, membership lists, and manpower, which can then be deployed under the guidance of COPE. And reinforcing all the committee's efforts is a constant series of meetings, conferences, and literature to persuade union leaders at all levels to increase their efforts to work together toward common political goals.

The Organizing Department uses somewhat similar techniques in trying to induce member internationals to improve the quality of their organizing efforts. Grants of money may be given to encourage experimental programs in which various unions cooperate in identifying unorganized firms, allocating them among the participating unions, and pooling information and even manpower to get these target companies organized. A field staff of trained organizers has been assembled for loan to particular unions or use in carrying out Federation-sponsored campaigns of special importance. In either case, a principal aim of the staff is to provide a demonstration of effective campaign tactics—how to decide whether to try to organize a particular plant, how to plan the campaign, pick the in-plant organizing committee, prepare the campaign leaflets, counter the employer's tactics, and avoid unfair-labor-practice charges. The same purpose underlies the preparation of campaign literature which the Organizing Department distributes on request to member unions. Services of this kind help to awaken an interest among the member unions for training programs put on by the department. Through these programs, all of the union's organizers in a given area receive intensive instruction for periods up to a week in the methods and tactics recommended by the Washington office.

The Civil Rights Department, to take a third example, works in somewhat different ways from those of the Organizing Department and COPE. It has sought to establish itself as a center for complaints from union members claiming discrimination on racial grounds. It also has tried to make arrangements with interested government agencies to ensure that it is informed of civil-rights charges in order to obtain voluntary compliance and possible settlement. Once a complaint is received, the department goes to work with the international union involved to persuade the offending local to resolve the underlying problem. The department also has worked through conferences and individual conversations to persuade union leaders to modify restrictive policies. In these meetings, Federation officials have not merely relied upon humanitarian arguments, but also have emphasized the dangers to the union of failing to take active measures to increase the proportion of Negro members. With the craft unions, in particular, they have stressed the growing political strength of Negroes in urban areas and the danger that politicians will respond to the demand for jobs by beating down craft standards and forcing locals to admit poorly qualified applicants. Through efforts of this kind, the Washington office has persuaded craft unions in more than fifty cities to cooperate in programs to seek out and give preapprentice training to members of minority groups.[1]

Dissatisfaction with the Federation

During the past decade, the AFL–CIO has attracted a number of critics both in and out of the labor movement. Some observers within the movement have been particularly disappointed by the failure of organized labor to grow more rapidly.[2] When the AFL and CIO were united, many labor spokesmen felt, in characteristic fashion, that by stilling much of the rivalry between unions, the merger would greatly simplify the task of organizing.* Some union officials actually talked of doubling the membership in a few years.[4] As events worked out, the Federation managed to develop several coordinated drives and worked in various ways to improve the level of training and tactics. But union membership did not double. Indeed, as noted in Chapter 2, the labor movement did not grow even as fast as the total nonagricultural work force from 1955–68.

In the wake of this experience, several critics have urged the Federation to take the lead in mounting a massive membership campaign. The United Auto Workers has even suggested that the

---

* "Historically and constitutionally, the primary responsibility for the organization of a particular area of employment has rested with the international union or unions having that jurisdiction, with the AFL–CIO playing a cooperative, supporting and promotional role. Where conflicts between affiliates legitimately involved in an organizing campaign cannot be resolved by voluntary agreement, the Federation has adhered to the principle that it cannot use the resources provided by an affiliate to work against that affiliate, and accordingly withdraws from participation in that particular campaign."[3]

Federation raise a special fund of more than $14 million per year for organizing over a period of at least six years.[5]

One difficulty with this proposal is its premise that money will open the door to massive organizing successes. There is some historical support for this position, for the money that the United Mine Workers contributed to organizing committees in the thirties provided the staff and paid for the litigation that helped produce the unprecedented breakthroughs in the mass-production industries. Yet one can legitimately question whether this simple prescription fits the circumstances of the seventies. The history of the labor movement suggests that there are certain periods when circumstances are ripe for large organizing gains. In these critical periods, money may be needed to bring the opportunities to fruition, but if the circumstances themselves are not ripe, large expenditures may produce very meager results.

The current period presents a mixed picture from the standpoint of union organizing. Government service represents a newly emerging area in which larger expenditures for staff and publicity might accelerate union growth. But few knowledgeable observers would agree that money alone is the answer to the major organizing challenges posed by white-collar workers, female employees, or persons employed by the larger nonunion companies in the manufacturing sector. In the case of manufacturing firms, for example, if unions spend more money in representation elections, employers will doubtless do likewise. In this process of escalation, there is little assurance that labor will prevail, or that it can conquer the central problem of winning over employees who are already being paid the union scale, without the threat of strikes and union dues. In the white-collar field, money seems to have little to do with the fact that only teachers in the large cities are willing to join the AFL–CIO–affiliated American Federation of Teachers, while in the towns and suburbs teachers seem to shun an avowed union like the A.F.T. in favor of the National Education Association. Dollars alone will hardly do much to overcome the evident coolness of engineers and technicians toward the idea of belonging to a union. And as for organizing poor people in the ghettos into community unions, U.A.W. efforts to date seemed to have failed almost entirely (see Chapter 15), thus suggesting that much remains to be learned about the techniques of building viable organizations in this new, uncharted field.

In short, there are stubborn tactical and psychological problems that must be overcome before real progress can be made in many unorganized areas where employment is expanding most rapidly. Thus far, critics have not had much advice to offer on how these problems can be met, save for an occasional plea for more coordinated organizing drives. But experience to date does not demonstrate that coordination will net substantial gains or that it has much to do with the problems of organizing in the rapidly growing white-collar occupations. Whether in Los Angeles, in Boston, or in Greensboro, the results of coordinated drives have not been particularly impressive, and many of the participating unions seem to be disenchanted with the program. In short, unless union organizers are armed with greater knowledge and sophistication, or aided by a climate more favorable to organizing, there is little assurance that added funds will bring dramatic membership gains.

Beyond these difficulties lie other troublesome issues. The millions of dollars recommended for massive organizing drives must be contributed by union members. How much money do they want to contribute for these purposes? How much should they have to contribute in a democratically run union? Most members are probably not particularly interested in helping the American Federation of Teachers wean members away from the National Education Association or even in extending the benefits of unionization to such groups as the farm workers and the urban poor.* And though union officials may argue that membership growth will enhance the political strength and prestige of the labor movement, the evidence for these propositions is none too solid; at least there is reason to think that the millions of dollars involved could be better spent for registration drives and political-education programs to achieve the same ends. It is possible, of course, that growing membership will bring important, albeit subtle, advantages to organized labor by enhancing its influence, its vitality, and above all, its own self-confidence and *esprit*. But these points are not self-evident to many union leaders, who are slow to lend support to costly organizing drives, especially when it is so unclear that heavy expenditures will succeed in bringing large membership gains.

A different group of critics has maintained that the Federation

---

* Organizing, of course, can sometimes benefit members directly by protecting them from lower wages and substandard conditions in competing firms. But unions already spend large sums on organizing drives for these purposes, and it is doubtful that these efforts need to be supplemented by a massive Federation effort.

should assume greater control over negotiations and strikes that may adversely affect the public interest. A crippling strike may help to lay the groundwork for regulatory legislation distasteful to organized labor. Therefore, it is argued, the AFL–CIO has a natural interest in curbing strikes that may prejudice the entire movement. At the same time, being freer from grass-roots pressure and more closely attuned to the needs and demands of the larger public, the Federation is expected to take a more statesmanlike view of important strikes and thus do a better job of reflecting the public interest in avoiding unnecessary and harmful stoppages.

There are several difficulties with this suggestion, but the principal one is simply that it is unrealistic. Since the conduct of a strike is vital to the political position of a labor leader, union presidents will never cede such power to the Federation unless they or their oganizations clearly stand to gain by doing so. Thus, member unions might take this step if there were an imminent threat of restrictive legislation, for then a major strike by any affiliate would become a matter of serious concern to all unions in the Federation. Moreover, if some central organization were to emerge on the employer side, with power to initiate lockouts and compel member firms to participate therein, comparable authority might be given to the Federation, as has been done in Scandinavia. For the present, however, these possibilities are remote. The notion of a powerful employers' confederation is quite alien to the American experience, and there are no indications of any departure from this tradition. As for legislation, Congress is always so unpredictable in labor matters that the threat of regulation may never seem imminent enough to move union leaders to relinquish their independence.

Although the Federation is unlikely to receive formal power over strikes, it already exercises an informal influence in certain cases. As early as 1901, Gompers tried to mediate a major steel strike, and he again lent assistance in the anthracite dispute a year later. In recent years, George Meany has worked with government and union representatives in an effort to resolve many strikes, including railroad, electrical manufacturing and copper disputes.

While the Federation has only rarely played a decisive part in settling strikes, its influence in the future could grow as a result of two institutional developments: the use of coordinated bargaining, and the increasing government involvement in the settlement of strikes. Where unions join in negotiations, they may naturally turn to the Federation when disputes arise between them, particularly during strikes arousing wide public concern. More frequent official intervention during strikes also gives added leverage to the AFL–CIO, because of its special influence with government bodies and key administrative officials. If the AFL–CIO is asked to intervene in the councils of government, the Federation is naturally in a position to make reciprocal suggestions to the unions involved. In fact, the mere possibility that a striking union will have to call for help from the Federation gives the latter a degree of influence. In a period of restiveness and legislative ferment in the area of public-employee strikes, the Federation might use this influence to persuade the various unions involved to develop a common position that would be sufficiently responsible and realistic to have some prospect for success. In the private sector, the Federation might encourage unions in strike-prone sectors to participate in efforts to reappraise their bargaining procedures and search for methods to minimize the risk of work stoppages. Even these possibilities, however, fall far short of granting power to the Federation to veto strikes or impress settlement terms upon the unions involved.

The Contemporary Role of the Federation

From one viewpoint, the Federation is a very limited body. It clearly has little power to order individual unions to do what they do not wish to do, and circumstances make it unlikely that the situation will change in the near future. Authority of this kind may exist in a labor movement where the sense of common purpose or ideological control is so great that unions will accept the direction of a federation rather than embarrass their sister unions and jeopardize the prestige of the movement as a whole. But solidarity of this kind has been noticeably weak in the United States, with its heterogeneous labor force, its vast geographic area, and its lack of class consciousness. A federation may also gain authority if some mutual danger or objective is sufficiently compelling to cause individual unions to accept a common course of action in order to avoid the risk of being harmed or blocked from reaching a valued goal. But these conditions, too, have been lacking in the United States, where the main preoccupation of unions and their members has been with collective bargaining, a process which each union has normally conducted on a highly decentralized basis with its own group of individual firms and employer associations.

These observations will not please the independent critics who are chiefly concerned by what they consider to be the transgressions of the unions and hopeful that the Federation can somehow wield the power to put a stop to such behavior. Nevertheless, the AFL–CIO is much better situated to leave its mark through a quieter type of influence.

The real opportunity for the Federation lies in helping the leaders of its affiliated unions to understand their long-run interests and informing them how they can proceed most effectively to achieve these goals.

The position of the Federation is special in that it is twice removed from the rank and file and is situated in the nation's capital, where it has regular access to legislators and other public officials. From this vantage point, Federation officials are further removed than the individual unions from rank-and-file pressures and better situated to take a longer view of union policies and to observe the implications of broad political and economic forces for the labor movement as a whole. In addition, the Federation is in a superior position to serve as a source of new ideas and new knowledge for its member unions. Without substantial responsibilities in the field, and supported financially by over 120 unions, it can afford a much larger education department and a more specialized research and legislative staff than even its largest affiliates can support. And with an atmosphere that is not quite so subject to grass-roots political pressures, the Federation should find it somewhat easier to avoid making staff appointments on political grounds or allowing the entire staff to become embroiled in day-to-day problems.

As previously pointed out, the Federation has been trading on its special advantages by gradually expanding the range and scope of its influence. The effects of its efforts, however, are hard to estimate. Like so many institutions, the AFL–CIO cannot convincingly demonstrate what it has accomplished, for no one can be certain of what laws might have been passed and what membership gains might have been recorded if the Federation had not been in existence. Yet the AFL–CIO already seems to have had an influence upon its affiliates in several areas of their activity.

Through the impetus of the Federation's Industrial Union

Department, many unions have been persuaded to join in coordinated bargaining with large conglomerate companies, such as General Electric Company. In this way, these unions are at least making an effort to respond to the diversified growth of modern corporations and overcome the weakness of having each labor organization bargain with the capability of shutting down only a small fraction of the company's total operations. In the field of organizing, aside from encouraging local unions to participate in several coordinated campaigns, the Federation has contributed staff and about $2 million to the growth of the approximately four-thousand-member Farm Workers Union in California. In relations among member unions, the Federation has succeeded, through the no-raiding and internal-disputes agreements, in reducing to minimal proportions the efforts of member unions to launch campaigns to lure away one another's members. But it is in the political sphere that the AFL–CIO has had its greatest impact. Voluntary contributions from member unions have risen from $2 million to $5 million. In the 1968 campaign, approximately five hundred staff representatives were placed by member unions under the direction of the AFL–CIO to work for periods ranging from six days to six months in a variety of political races. After years of having unions balk at sharing membership lists (for fear of inviting raids or exposing shortages in per-capita contributions), all but a few international unions made their lists available on a state-by-state basis in 1968 to allow the Federation to experiment with computerized mailings in four large areas. And on Capitol Hill, the Federation has also made progress by welding the Washington lobbyists of its member unions into a more highly coordinated body that is much less prone than in earlier years to take inconsistent and conflicting positions on legislation of common interest.

It is understandable that the AFL–CIO should have its greatest influence in the political sphere. Since unions have common interests in getting certain bills passed and certain candidates elected, they naturally look to the Federation for coordination and guidance. It follows that the influence of the AFL–CIO has inevitably grown as the federal government's activities have continued to expand and member unions have come to appreciate more clearly how profound is the impact of federal policies on employment, profits, and other aspects of the business climate that help determine the success of collective bargaining.

These trends are likely to continue and spread. As urban

renewal, relations with public employees, fair-employment policies and other government programs grow more important to unions at the metropolitan level, local federations should become increasingly influential. In addition, the importance of politics forces the union movement at all levels to become more conscious of the impact of its behavior on public opinion, and the Federation is the natural body to express this common concern. Thus, it is no accident that the Federation took the unprecedented step of expelling member unions for corruption in the fifties and that it should press unions in the sixties to accept such racially oriented programs as preapprentice training for Negroes and the elimination of segregated locals. What, then, is the role of the Federation? To revert to the title of this chapter, the AFL–CIO may well come to be regarded *both* as a rope of sand *and* as a vital force within the labor movement. Established unions that dislike Federation policies can resist its wishes and even break away from the fold entirely. Yet the AFL–CIO also has the capacity to wield considerable influence. If it is to utilize this capacity fully, however, there are several steps which it could profitably consider taking.

New Steps for the Federation

Perhaps the most serious weakness in the AFL–CIO is the lack of influence of the Washington office over the subordinate federations. These state and local bodies bear the brunt of lobbying, political organization, participating in community-service work, and developing closer ties with universities and other civic organizations. All these tasks are important, and they will become more so in the future. As currently constituted, however, the subordinate federations are often unable to perform this work effectively. They are financed by contributions from unions in the area that wish to affiliate. But only 53 percent of the locals of member internationals have chosen to affiliate with a state federation, and the extent of affiliation with local bodies is probably even lower. In addition, many federations constantly face the threat of losing member locals, and since finances depend upon these members, the subordinate bodies are influenced much more by the locals in their area than by the national office in Washington.

In theory, decentralization of this kind may be desirable, since it fosters local initiative and allows flexibility to adapt to local conditions. But these advantages can be realized only where the local unions are genuinely interested in creating an active and effective federation. In all too many cases, this desire is not present; local leaders are either preoccupied with the affairs of their own union or divided by internal rivalries and animosities. As a result, many local federations are underfinanced, poorly staffed, and unable to formulate and execute vigorous programs to stimulate organizing, political action, or community service.

To counteract these problems, some observers have urged that local unions be compelled to affiliate with their state and local federations. This proposal would yield higher revenues to the federations and would strengthen their hand vis-à-vis the locals in their area, since the federation would no longer face the constant threat of disaffiliation. On the other hand, compulsory affiliation would not do much to ensure better appointments or more imaginative programs. Nor is it clear just how the obligation could be enforced. International unions might well be unable or unwilling to take action against recalcitrant locals, and it seems unrealistic to expect the AFL–CIO to threaten the suspension of internationals that refused to bring their locals into compliance.

In view of these problems, a more promising alternative might be to abolish per-capita contributions to state and local bodies, increase contributions to the AFL–CIO in Washington, and have the national office supply the funds to the subordinate federations. By this device, the AFL–CIO would gain a greater leverage to encourage better staff appointments and more effective planning by the Federation in its relations with state and local bodies. At the same time, the leaders of the state and local bodies would still be elected by the unions in their jurisdiction. And since no local federation could hope to make much progress without the co-operation of the locals in its area, the Washington office would have to pay attention to the wishes of local leaders in influencing the activity of its subordinate bodies. In this fashion, central financing might well succeed in bringing national and local influence into a more constructive balance.

Efforts to improve the structure of the Federation are important, but still more important are the goals to which it directs its energies. One major task is suggested by the lack of knowledge within the labor movement about any number of questions critical to union activities. In contrast to other institutions, unions have shown little capacity for research except in its most rudimentary and practical forms. Although analogies cannot be pressed too far, many institutions share the common goal of attempting to understand and satisfy the needs of constituents. Increasingly, the more progressive of these institutions find it useful to rely heavily on systematic methods of developing information about the attitudes of those whom they serve and their success in satisfying these needs. Yet most unions continue to rely on habit and intuition, in spite of a persistent lack of growth, widespread refusals by the memberships to ratify bargaining settlements, and other signs that they are failing to secure the workers' loyalties. If the Federation wishes to exert a more vital, constructive influence, it might do well to help fill this gap.

For example, little sophisticated research has been done on such questions as why certain organizing drives succeed while others fail, whether coordinated organizing yields superior results, why employees join or refuse to join unions, why unionism has flourished in certain white-collar fields, such as airlines and theater, while failing to take root among engineers, salesmen and many other groups.* There is also much to be learned about the attitudes of members toward political activity, the changes taking place in these attitudes, and the effect of unionization and political programs on the registration and voting of members. Except for one recent opinion survey, the Federation has not explored these questions systematically. Collective bargaining presents many other relevant issues. Are wages becoming less important to members than other goals? How can the desires of the workers be more reliably ascertained? What types of studies can be undertaken in specific industries to develop useful information on future trends in manpower needs and skill requirements, technological change, and industry growth? Still other questions arise concerning the attitudes of members toward their union. What are the critical factors that affect these attitudes? Bargaining gains? Opportunities for more meaningful participation in union affairs? The performance of stewards and other first-line leaders? More extensive union programs in such fields as health care, recreation, education, and the like?

Another opportunity for the Federation has to do with long-

---

* The Industrial Union Department has begun to collect the results of campaigns and store the data in a computer. But this much-publicized effort will yield very meager results unless a serious attempt is made to identify the most pressing problems and to develop research methods to explore them.

range planning on matters of common interest. Reference has already been made to the work of the Federation's Civil Rights Department in anticipating political changes in the government of large cities and relating these changes to the racial policies of craft union locals. Even more important are the current efforts of the Federation to examine the problems of the younger members and to establish pilot programs to experiment with education programs and other ways to make unions more appealing to this new generation. There are many other long-run problems worth exploring—problems such as the effects of growing affluence on the attitudes of union members, the impact on political and community action resulting from the dispersion of members to the suburbs, the possibilities for large-scale urban programs and their effect on union opportunities and goals, the recent growth of more militant professional organizations among teachers, nurses, and the like, and their possible relationships with the labor movement. The day-to-day pressures in international unions make it difficult to pay adequate attention to such projects. With the aid of an expanded research program, the Federation might fill this gap and provide data to help union leaders take a longer view of the programs and policies of their organizations.

The Federation could also help member unions to improve their methods of administration and organization. Since many internationals are short on administrative talent, they are likely to continue paying little attention to better management. It is possible, of course, to hire outside consultants to offer advice, but many union officials will not know which firms are most competent, and few management consultants will have experience with unions or a "feel" for their special needs and constraints. Thus, on the few occasions when a union has called upon a consulting firm, the reports have almost invariably been of inferior quality and often entirely misdirected in their recommendations.

In view of these problems, the Federation could render a great service by developing a consulting office for problems of organization and administration. Such an agency could develop trained people to advise on matters ranging from planning and budgeting, personnel practices, organizational design, accounting, and cost-control techniques to new uses for computers and communications technology. As an arm of the Federation, such an office might command greater confidence than a consulting agency accustomed to servicing corporate clients. And after working with a number of organizations, the office could become increasingly useful as a clearinghouse to enable unions to profit from the experience of their fellow organizations in attacking common problems.

A related activity of the Federation that deserves further emphasis is the encouragement of mergers among international union affiliates. More than a third of these unions have fewer than 25,000 members, and another third report between 25,000 and 100,000 members. As noted in Chapter 5, many of these unions are so small that they cannot serve their members well and provide economically the staff assistance needed for effective bargaining, administration and community activity. In recent years the higher costs of union administration and declining employment in some industries have stimulated interest in mergers. The amalgamation in 1968 of four operating railroad brotherhoods and the merger of the Amalgamated Meat Cutters and Butcher Workmen and the United Packinghouse Workers were significant developments. But merging unions is a delicate business, often frustrated by the clash of strong personalities and the complexities of integrating staffs with varying pay structures and treasuries in differing stages of health. The Federation might do more to overcome these problems by appointing distinguished leaders to serve as mediators and by marshaling the experience gained in other amalgamations to formulate proposals and compromise solutions when the unions involved have reached an impasse.

Education provides another promising area for further work by the Federation. The foundation for such an effort may have been laid in the form of the AFL–CIO Labor Studies Center approved in February 1969. The critical test is whether the Federation will work to create more than just another forum for offering brief training courses—better taught, perhaps, but patterned along the usual union lines. If the Center is to have any enduring significance, its training must either perform a function not currently achieved within the affiliated unions or provide a substantial advance in quality for the member unions to emulate.

Several possibilities come to mind. A major component of this Center should presumably be a program of at least several weeks' duration for younger leaders who seem likely to rise to key positions in their internationals. In addition to this central course, shorter programs could be offered to groups not commonly reached by the educational offerings of a single union. For example, courses might be provided for directors of organization or research personnel to expose them to new techniques or new research findings developed within the Federation and elsewhere. With so many internationals now located in Washington, it should also be feasible to offer other programs to union presidents, vice-presidents, and secretary-treasurers on topics ranging from techniques of union administration to economic and political developments of significance to their organizations.

Although the main function of the Center should be to impart new skills and information to union officials, other important results could be achieved. The Center could presumably serve as a focal point for the development of better materials and methods of instruction. Its staff could provide a source of talent for eventual service as education directors of international unions. The Center might also serve as an obvious link between the labor movement and the universities by enlisting the advice and participation of outside experts. In addition, its programs could afford a much-needed forum to bring together officials from many different unions and offer them an easy opportunity to exchange ideas and experience. Above all, the Center should serve as yet another channel through which the Federation could suggest ideas, opportunities, and higher standards of performance to the representatives of member unions.*

In order to fill these needs, the Federation will have to make a major effort to add individuals of high competence to its staff and to develop closer ties with universities and perhaps foundations as well. But such efforts will not represent a radical departure from the evolution that is already taking place in the Federation. This movement is sound and deserves to be continued. The greatest contributions of a federation do not necessarily lie in preventing affiliates from doing what they want to do, nor is it realistic to expect member unions to tolerate this type of interference. In the long run, ideas will be much more important than authority in furthering the progress of the labor movement.

---

* There are additional opportunities for the Federation in helping to confront the variety of urban problems that beset the country. These matters are taken up in Chapter 15.

Collective Bargaining in the United States:

An Overview[1]

THE DEMOCRATIC character of labor organizations and the nature of their internal operations have aroused particular interest in the United States. If unions were largely devoted to political action or social reform, rather than collective bargaining, their internal affairs might have attracted no more attention than those of the American Medical Association or the National Association of Manufacturers. But unions have traditionally been preoccupied with collective bargaining, and this preoccupation has given labor organizations a significance that has stimulated interest in almost every phase of union activity and has created a series of problems for employers and for the economy as a whole.

Although the practice of collective bargaining has been known for more than one hundred fifty years, the term itself seems to have been first used in 1891 by Mrs. Sidney Webb, the Fabian writer and, in collaboration with her husband, historian of the British labor movement.[2] As the Webbs stated, "In unorganized trades the individual workman, applying for a job, accepts or refuses the terms offered by the employer without communication with his fellow workmen. . . . But if a group of workmen concert together, and send representatives to conduct bargaining on behalf of the whole body, the position is at once changed."[3] Individual bargaining is thus transformed into collective bargaining.

The Special Character of
Collective Bargaining in the United States

Collective bargaining is carried on within a framework of law, custom and institutional structure that varies considerably from one country to another. The framework of bargaining in the United States has certain characteristics that sharply distinguish it from that of most other industrial democracies.

DECENTRALIZATION

Perhaps the most significant characteristic of the American collective-bargaining system is that it is highly decentralized. There are approximately 150,000 separate union-management agreements now in force in the United States. A majority of union members work under contracts negotiated by their union with a single employer or for a single plant. Only 40 percent of employees covered by collective agreements involve multi-employer negotiations, and the great bulk of these negotiations are confined to single metropolitan areas.

In Europe and Australia, on the other hand, the great majority of union members are covered by general agreements negotiated for large groups of employees on a multi-employer basis. Collective bargaining in Sweden, for example, is normally carried out within the framework of a national agreement negotiated by the central confederation of labor unions and its counterpart on the management side. Subsidiary agreements then are hammered out in negotiations conducted on an industrywide basis. Additional negotiation takes place at the plant level. Since each of these levels of negotiation may cover some of the same subjects, such as wages, the bargaining arrangements may be said to consist of three tiers, in contrast to the single tier that is more typical in the United States. In Great Britain, there are normally two separate tiers, an industrywide negotiation followed by bargaining at the plant level.[4] In France the dominant pattern of bargaining is initially regional. In the typical case, a general agreement covering a large section of the country is negotiated by an association representing a group of loosely related industries. Thus, a key French negotiation takes place within the greater Paris region involving the metalworks sector—a group which includes a variety of industries ranging from steel plants and automobile factories to jewelry shops and repair establishments. In addition to regional negotiation, bargaining may also take place at the plant level, usually with individual workers but sometimes through regular plantwide negotiations with the unions.

The prevalence of plant and company negotiations in the United States is a natural outgrowth of the patterns of organization among employers and unions, the great size of this country, and the highly competitive character of its economy. National negotiations, along Scandinavian lines, are hardly feasible, since the AFL–CIO has much less authority over its affiliates than the central confederations in most other industrial democracies (with the possible exception of Great Britain), and managements also are less centralized in their decisions on labor-relations issues. The manager in America has been strongly inclined to act independently in working out his labor and personnel policies. To be sure, multi-employer bargaining associations are not unknown; they are quite common on the local level and exist on a nationwide basis in a few industries, as in railroads. Nevertheless, it is difficult to envisage American employers following the example of their Swedish counterparts by forming a single national confederation with power to veto any important bargaining concession by a member firm or to compel any member to join in a lockout. Nor is it likely that American employers will follow the lead of those abroad in forming powerful bargaining associations in virtually all major industries.

EXCLUSIVE JURISDICTION

In the United States, unlike most countries in Western Europe, one union serves as the sole representative for all the employees in a plant or other appropriate bargaining unit.* This practice conforms to the American political custom of electing single representatives by majority vote. It also can be traced back to the tradition of conflict among the autonomous international

---

* Government employment, however, provides some exceptions to exclusive representation. Executive Order 10988 provided for more than one form of recognition by a government agency, so that two or more unions may legitimately be recognized in federal employment. In New York City government, different unions may represent the same worker for different purposes, one for grievances and another for wages and benefits.

unions. To restrain such conflict, the American Federation of Labor—as far back as the 1880's—developed the concept of exclusive jurisdiction. Under this principle, only one union was authorized to represent employees in a particular occupation, a group of jobs, or, occasionally, an industry. Employers generally accepted exclusivity since it stabilized labor relations by diminishing disputes among competing unions. It was natural, therefore, for the principle to be embodied in public policy when the government began to develop detailed regulation over collective bargaining. Thus, during World War I and under the Railway Labor Act of 1926, a system of elections was adopted to enable groups of employees to select a single representative by majority vote. The same procedures were subsequently carried forward on a broader scale in the National Labor Relations Act of 1935 and its subsequent amendments.

A different system of representation prevails in most other industrial democracies.[5] In a few countries, as in West Germany, the federation is made up of unions neatly divided along industrial lines so that there is less need for an explicit doctrine of exclusive jurisdiction in order to curb union rivalries. There also are a number of nations where the labor movement is split along political or religious lines that reflect fundamental ideological cleavages in the society. Under such circumstances, there are obvious objections to any system that would give one union exclusive rights over its rivals. In France, for example, neither employers nor the political parties in power would accept a system that would allow the Communist-controlled unions to win exclusive bargaining rights wherever they could enlist a majority of employees against the opposing Socialist and Catholic organizations. Instead, each of the rival unions is simply given the right to represent its members, and collective bargaining normally takes place through uneasy coalitions among the three major labor federations.

INDIVIDUAL BARGAINING

Under almost any system, collective bargaining leaves room for a degree of individual negotiation over certain terms and conditions of employment. Even in the United States, the law explicitly provides that an employee can discuss individual grievances with representatives of management.[6] And in a few fields— for example, the performing arts—agreements typically leave employees free to bargain individually for salaries above the minimum. For the most part, however, collective agreements in the United States specify the actual wages and terms of employment which in fact govern the workers in the bargaining unit, and individual employees do not negotiate different terms on their own behalf.

In most other industrial democracies, the scope for individual or small-group bargaining is much greater. Collective agreements generally do no more than provide minimum wages and conditions. In the tight labor markets that have prevailed in so many of these countries, actual wages have drifted well above the contract rates in the great majority of plants. As a result, though negotiated pay increases put upward pressure on wage levels, the actual rates of pay are largely fixed by individual bargaining, often initiated by employers seeking to keep their work force from going elsewhere.[7]

Collective agreements in the United States also tend to specify many more conditions of employment than is the case in other countries. In Western Europe, for example, a union contract normally obliges the employer to observe little more than a minimum-wage scale and a few basic provisions relating to working conditions and perhaps a few fringe benefits. In this country, on the other hand, agreements are extremely detailed and far-reaching in their content. Collective bargaining typically regulates standards for discipline, promotion criteria, transfers and layoffs, priorities for determining who will be laid off and recalled, shift schedules, procedures for resolving grievances and a wide variety of other matters.

The decentralized structure of the American industrial-relations system does much to explain the greater reach of the collective agreement and the more restricted role for individual and small-group bargaining and unilateral action by the employer. In Europe, where negotiations normally embrace entire industries or groups of related industries in particular regions and where so many diverse employers participate in the negotiations, it is extremely difficult to write a detailed set of contract rules applicable to each participating firm. As a result, the parties have been content to negotiate contracts containing only a limited number of minimum terms and conditions.

In this country, on the other hand, the pattern of plant and companywide bargaining enables unions to negotiate contracts specifying a detailed system of wages and working conditions to be observed at each workplace. Even in industries where multi-employer bargaining has prevailed, unions have been sufficiently organized at the plant level to negotiate supplementary provisions to take account of special conditions in particular plants. But in most European countries, where plant locals scarcely exist, this process has been much slower to develop. Lacking strong organizations at the workplace, unions have left many terms of employment to be resolved through individual bargaining or by consultation with workers' councils,[8] which often are established by law and are not formally a part of the union hierarchy.

THE ROLE OF LAW IN FIXING CONDITIONS OF EMPLOYMENT

Just as individual bargaining plays a part, along with collective negotiations, in setting terms and conditions of employment, so also does the law have a role in the process. In every industrialized country, legislation has been passed to perform such functions as fixing minimum wages or maximum hours, or providing safety requirements, or requiring payroll deductions for social security and other welfare programs. In at least one respect, however, the law performs a broader function abroad than it does in the United States. In other industrial democracies, outside the Scandinavian bloc, legislation has been passed that can be used to extend the terms of collective agreements to nonunion enterprises in the same industry. In a few countries, the extension of the collective agreement is ordered by a labor tribunal or a regular court. More often, either the union or the employers' association can petition a designated public official who has discretion to extend the terms of the agreement throughout the industry in question. In the United States, however, no comparable procedure exists.*

---

* One consequence of the arrangements in the United States is that the economically weak—agricultural labor and those employed in small retail establishments, for example—have relatively little protection. They are excluded from much social legislation and do not enjoy the benefits of collective bargaining. The Davis-Bacon Act does, however, specify that the Secretary of Labor shall predetermine the wage rates and benefits to be paid to workers employed on construction projects under federal government contract; and the Walsh-Healy Act empowers the Secretary to prescribe the prevailing minimum wages in connection with the government's purchases. In Great Britain the Wages Councils, and in Australia the arbitration courts, provide more egalitarian conditions of employment for the unorganized without bargaining power; they extend to such workers benefits comparable to those developed by parties to collective bargaining.

The absence of any authority in law to extend a collective-bargaining contract to others who have not accepted the agreement is rooted in the structure of the American industrial-relations system. It is comparatively easy to extend a contract containing a few minimum terms and conditions, particularly when the contract has been negotiated by an association representing a large and representative group of firms. In the United States, however, where rival unions may coexist in a single industry, where contract terms set actual rather than minimum requirements, and where provisions are highly complex and often vary from one firm to another, it would be very difficult to find a single set of terms that would be suitable for all firms in the industry.

In another respect, the structure of bargaining in this country has caused the law to play a more ambitious role in collective negotiations than it does abroad. Although we rely less heavily on legislation to fix the substantive terms of employment, there is much more regulation in the United States over the tactics and procedures of bargaining.

This difference largely reflects the special tensions and pressures that arise in a highly decentralized system of bargaining. Under plantwide or companywide negotiations, the individual employer must confront the union in his enterprise, instead of leaving negotiations to his employer association to be conducted on a regional or industrywide basis. The bargaining process reaches into the details of his business, seeking to regulate every aspect of working conditions in his plant. The contract terms do not merely set minimum standards but also fix the actual conditions to be observed. Above all, the institution of bargaining threatens to subject him to contract obligations that may put him at a disadvantage with his nonunion competitor or even other organized enterprises. Under these circumstances, the bargaining process is accompanied by greater tension, and the employer often resists the union more strenuously than is common abroad. In turn, the law responds to these strains and seeks to contain antagonisms within reasonable bounds. Thus, law in the United States defines the subjects that must be bargained about. It requires the parties to "bargain in good faith" and clothes this obligation with detailed rules proscribing stalling tactics, withholding of relevant information, and other forms of behavior that are considered unfair. The net result is a complex of regulations that greatly exceeds anything to be found in other industrialized countries.[9]

The Role of the Parties in
Determining the Structure of Bargaining

These special characteristics help to define the framework of the American system of collective bargaining. Within these contours, several types of negotiation go on. The most familiar aspect of bargaining involves the discussions between the parties over the terms and conditions of employment for the workers involved. But a vital part of the bargaining process has to do with determining the structure and the procedures through which these discussions will take place.

One question of structure has to do with the level at which different issues should be resolved. This problem is particularly significant in any negotiation that affects more than one place of work. In a situation of this kind, the parties must decide which issues should be agreed upon at the negotiating table and incorporated into a master agreement and which should be left for labor and management representatives to settle at the company, plant, or departmental level.[10] Agreements made at these subsidiary levels are called local supplements. Sometimes the interdependence between the two settlements creates problems. Is one settlement contingent upon the other, and is a failure to conclude one a basis for a strike or lockout in all units? Which settlement will be made first?

These questions are often difficult to resolve. In a multi-plant company, for instance, such matters as the amount of time allowed for wash-up before the end of a shift or the allocation of parking facilities might be best handled at the plant level. But it is also clear that policies or precedents on these matters at one plant may influence decisions elsewhere. Considerations of bargaining power and market competition may also influence the level at which particular issues are treated. As technological and market changes take place, it may be necessary to alter these arrangements and provide for more centralization on some issues, as with the introduction of containers in the East Coast longshore industry, and greater decentralization in other instances, such as the determination of the number of trainmen in a crew on the railroads. Since conditions vary widely from one plant or industry to another, there is little uniformity among collective-bargaining relationships in the pattern of centralization and decentralization in negotiations.

A second problem in arranging negotiation procedures concerns the range of jobs, territory, and employees to be governed by the ensuing agreement. Several illustrations may be helpful. The basic steel companies took major strikes in 1946 in part to achieve separate negotiations for their fabricating facilities from their basic steel operations. As a result, separate agreements with different expiration dates and different wage scales now are negotiated at different times, reflecting the different competitive conditions that affect these two types of operations. In view of differing market conditions for the different products involved, the major rubber companies have on occasion insisted on differential wage increases for tire plants and those plants making rubber shoes and other rubber products. Conversely, twenty-six cooperating international unions sustained an eight-month strike in the copper negotiations of 1967–68 in an effort to obtain collective-bargaining agreements with the same expiration dates and identical wage increases for all employees of a company.

A third set of structural problems has to do with the relations among different craft unions bargaining with a common employer. In recent years, the newspaper printing industry, the West Coast shipbuilding industry, and the construction industry have suffered many strikes growing out of disagreements over the wage pattern or sequence of settlements among a group of interrelated crafts agreements. For example, the 114-day New York newspaper strike of 1962–63 was fought by Bertram Powers, president of Local 6 of the International Typographical Union, largely to change a system of bargaining which had existed since the early 1950's. Under the prior agreement, wage settlements had been made with the Newspaper Guild and then extended to other newspaper unions. As a result of the strike, contract expiration dates were negotiated which removed the five-week lead the Guild had previously held and thus eliminated its ability to impose an industrywide pattern on the other unions before they ever got to the bargaining table. Thus, the strike enabled Powers to put an end to a follow-the-leader pattern that had deprived his union of any real power to negotiate its own wage agreements.[11]

Serious questions may arise also in deciding which subjects should be encompassed within the scope of collective bargaining.

The subjects that are dealt with vary widely, reflecting in each contract the problems of the relevant workplace and industry. Some maritime agreements specify the quality of meals and even the number of bars of soap, towels, and sheets that management is to furnish to the crew. Such provisions are natural subjects for negotiation, since they are vital to men at sea, but they would make no sense in a normal manufacturing agreement. In some contracts in the ladies' garment industry, companies agree to be efficient and to allow a union industrial engineer to make studies of company performance. These provisions would be regarded as ludicrous in the automobile industry. Detailed procedures respecting control over hiring are central to collective bargaining in industries with casual employment, where employees shift continually from one employer to another, as in construction and stevedoring; but in factory and office employment, new hiring typically is left to the discretion of management. In this fashion, the topics raised in collective bargaining tend to reflect the problems of the particular workplace and industry.

The law also plays a part in deciding the subjects for negotiation, since the National Labor Relations Act (Section 9a) requires the parties to bargain in good faith over "rates of pay, wages, hours of employment, or other conditions of employment." Pursuant to this Act, the National Labor Relations Board and the courts have decided which subjects are mandatory topics for collective bargaining and which are optional. In some instances, particular subjects or bargaining proposals have been held to be improper or illegal and hence nonnegotiable, such as a union's insistence on a closed shop or an employer's demand that the union bargain through a particular form of negotiating committee or take a secret ballot prior to calling a strike. On the whole, however, the Board and the courts have steadily broadened the scope of mandatory bargaining to include Christmas bonuses, pensions, information on plant shutdowns, subcontracting, provisions for checkoff of union dues, and many other topics.

The provisions of the National Labor Relations Act would appear to make legal rulings decisive as to the scope of bargaining. And on a few issues, such as pension plans, litigation undoubtedly played a significant role. In the main, however, although the law may help to define the outer limits of bargaining, the actual scope of negotiations is largely decided by the parties themselves.

The Process of Bargaining:
Negotiation, Administration, and Consultation

In common parlance, "collective bargaining" is used to refer to three separate forms of labor-management activity: negotiations for a new contract, administration of an existing agreement, and informal consultation on matters of common interest to the parties.

NEGOTIATION

The process of negotiating a new agreement varies widely from one firm to another. In a number of industries, for example, the smaller firms will usually follow the pattern set by a larger competitor; bargaining for them will mean little more than seeking to make a few minor adjustments in the pattern-setting agreement to take account of special conditions. In larger firms—and particularly in the pattern-setting companies—bargaining will be a much more elaborate and difficult process.

When bargaining involves more than simply accepting a standard agreement, there will normally be much preparation on both sides. The union will develop a series of demands through local meetings, consultation among officials, and sometimes the use of surveys and questionnaires. Management will likewise develop its position through meetings among its officers and staff. Both parties will normally arm themselves with research data; for example, they may study the nature of prior grievances, draw upon studies of market and employment trends, and analyze the financial and competitive position of the firm itself.

Once these preparations are complete, the process of bargaining often proceeds through a series of stages. At the outset, the union customarily presents a long and extravagant list of demands. In many instances, the company will respond by submitting its own proposals, which are typically far apart from those of the union. Although this exchange may seem as irrelevant and ritualistic as the mating dance of the great crested grebe, it can serve a variety of purposes. By putting forward many exaggerated demands, the parties create trading material for later stages of negotiations. They disguise their real position and thus give themselves room for maneuver as bargaining progresses. They explore a wide range of problems that may have been bothering each side, and they have the opportunity to explain concerns to each other. They manage to satisfy their constituents or principals by seeming to back numerous proposals, only to scale down many of the demands or abandon them altogether later on in the negotiations when it is more expedient to do so. A proposal may be advanced and explored, only to be put aside for more serious negotiation in subsequent years.

After the initial presentations, there normally is a period of exploration in which each side tries to clarify the proposals of the other and marshal arguments against them. At this stage of negotiation, little change can be expected in the positions of the parties. As bargaining progresses, each side will begin to formulate a combination of proposals, or "package," which it considers an appropriate basis for settlement. The package offered by each side gives the other party a clearer sense of the priorities attached to various items and the possible concessions to be gained. In this process, more than one package may be put forward by either side.

Eventually, before or after a stoppage, an agreement will be reached. The meeting of the minds will normally be arrived at first during informal talks between key negotiators, and the proposed settlement will then be discussed before the full negotiating committees on either side. Thereafter, the tentative agreement must be reduced to contract language, usually with the advice of lawyers and after much further discussion over details of wording.

After the agreement is reduced to writing, ordinarily it must be ratified or approved by the principals involved. On the union side, ratification may be required by the membership of the union, by a specified group of elected delegates, or by an elected wage policy committee, as in the case of the basic-steel agreement. Management negotiators in a single company will need the approval of the president or the board of directors. In association bargaining, the approval of the elected directors or the full membership of the association is typically required.

The ratification of settlements by union members serves a variety of purposes. By obtaining an explicit vote of approval for the settlement, subsequent enforcement of the agreement by management, by union officers, or by an arbitrator is made easier. Ratification also requires union negotiators to explain and "sell" the agreement to the membership. In doing so, ratification provides a check to insure that the negotiators keep in touch with the rank and file and reflect their interests in the bargaining process.

The quality of union leadership and its influence on the membership are subtly reflected in collective bargaining and ratification. In many bargaining relationships, ratification on the union side is a formality. The negotiators, by common consent, are in touch with the membership or wage policy committee with power to ratify; the negotiators are highly respected, and their views and recommendations carry great weight. In other instances, the union leaders occupy a more tenuous position; they lack the influence and prestige to guarantee acceptance even of a satisfactory contract.

As previously observed, there has been a marked increase in the proportion of settlements that have been rejected in the ratification process. According to federal mediators, the most common reasons for rejection are dissatisfaction with the size of wage and fringe benefits, lack of understanding by the leaders of the real desires of the members, internal political rivalries, and inadequate ratification procedures that give undue weight to the views of dissident members. At times, however, a rejection can be a deliberate tactic in the bargaining process. Union representatives may take a management offer to the members to demonstrate the unity and the sentiments of the rank and file. They may appear to accept a proposal and later oppose ratification in order to extract further concessions from management. Such stratagems normally are harmful to bargaining relationships. Management is unlikely to make its best offer at the bargaining table once it has been burnt by the use of a rejection as a tactical maneuver; it will save its best offer for a later date, thus causing the agreement-making process to become more difficult.

ADMINISTRATION OF THE CONTRACT

Although many of the most important issues concerning the terms of employment will be settled explicitly in the collective agreement, controversies will continue to arise over its meaning and application. Such disputes are inevitable. Most collective agreements are highly complex documents covering a multitude of problems. Typically, they are negotiated within a limited period of time, often in an atmosphere of rush and crisis. As a result, certain problems are bound to be overlooked. Others arise from changing circumstances that could not possibly have been foreseen when the contract was signed. Still others reflect ambiguities which were deliberately created by the parties with the thought that not every controversy could be settled in negotiations if the agreement was ever to be signed within the time available.

Almost all collective agreements contain procedures to be used in resolving "grievances," or disputes over the application of the contract. In some cases, the procedures are very simple. In the construction industry, for example, where many contractors have a work force that changes constantly from one job to another, it is often not feasible to operate an elaborate grievance machinery. Hence, disputes often are settled at the workplace through informal discussions between the union representative and the employer. Similarly, grievances in small establishments often are resolved by having the aggrieved employee get in touch with the union representative, who then may take up the matter directly with the employer. Where larger numbers of employees are involved, however, the grievance machinery tends to become more elaborate.

Most contracts for larger plants provide several stages at which a grievance can be considered. Typically, the aggrieved employee will first present his complaint to the foreman or supervisor, with or without the assistance of a union representative. The great majority of grievances are settled at this stage; were it otherwise, higher management and union officials could easily become overwhelmed with the task of reviewing complaints. But where an accommodation cannot be reached at this early stage, the contract will provide one or more levels of appeal at which disputes can be considered by progressively higher echelons within the union and management hierarchy. If no settlement can be reached through this process, the agreement will typically provide for presentation to an outside arbitrator, who will issue a final and binding decision following a hearing of the parties.

Today, arbitration procedures can be found in an estimated 94 percent of all collective-bargaining agreements. Nevertheless, not all disputes are made subject to this procedure, even in contracts with fully developed grievance machinery. For example, contracts signed by the major automobile companies expressly provide that the arbitrator shall not decide disputes involving production standards used in the measured day-work system; in some of these firms, matters involving health and safety and rates of new jobs are likewise excluded from arbitration.[12] Despite such exceptions, it is fair to say that arbitration represents the dominant method for resolving grievances that the parties cannot settle by themselves. Through this procedure, a peaceful and impartial resolution of disputes is obtained without the delay and formality that might result from taking such matters to court or making the dispute a test of economic power.

In light of the experience in countless plants, it is clear beyond dispute that an effective, well-administered grievance procedure can play an indispensable role in improving labor relations and providing a measure of industrial due process to the workers involved. The advantages to be gained have been summed up in the following terms by a distinguished panel of labor relations experts:

> A major achievement of collective bargaining, perhaps its most important contribution to the American workplace, is the creation of a system of industrial jurisprudence, a system under which employer and employee rights are set forth in contractual form and disputes over the meaning of the contract are settled through a rational grievance process. . . . The gains from this system are especially noteworthy because of their effect on the recognition and dignity of the individual worker. This system helps prevent arbitrary action on questions of discipline, layoff, promotion, and transfer, and sets up orderly procedures for the handling of grievances. Wildcat strikes and other disorderly means of protest have been curtailed and effective work discipline generally established. In many situations, cooperative relationships marked by mutual respect between labor and management stand as an example of what can be done.[13]

JOINT CONSULTATION

In many labor-management relationships, the parties have fashioned machinery to consult with one another during the term of the collective agreement. Such arrangements may involve high-level officials from both sides or specialists concerned with particular technical problems. They may or may not include impartial representatives.

Many purposes can be served by discussions of this kind. A study committee may be useful in exploring some special question, such as a pension program or a new job evaluation plan, which is too complex to be handled satisfactorily in the limited time available for regular contract negotiations. In other cases, a committee may be needed to construct and administer special machinery for dealing with a large, continuing problem such as the displacement of personnel through automation or the closing of a plant. Regular consultation may be employed to develop information and exchange ideas with a view to narrowing the range of issues to be taken up in subsequent contract negotiations. In a strike-torn firm or industry, a committee may also be formed to search for ways of resolving underlying problems or redesigning bargaining procedures in order to eliminate the sources of controversy.[14]

These three processes—negotiation, administration, and joint consultation—are not always readily disentangled in practice. Discussions between representatives of the parties may be of a mixed character. They may talk over a particular grievance and in so doing agree to exchange letters which embody the solution of a more general problem. The administrative and the legislative functions are here closely intertwined. A joint study committee may, on occasion, find a resolution for some pending grievances, agree on some new provision in the contract, or simply provide an exchange of information and opinion. Nonetheless, it is helpful to distinguish these three types of interaction between labor and management organizations even though general usage may employ the term "collective bargaining" to describe them all.

The Social and Economic Functions of Collective Bargaining

If society is to evaluate the institution of collective bargaining and compare it with alternative procedures, its social and economic functions must be clearly perceived. Five functions seem particularly important.

ESTABLISHING THE RULES OF THE WORKPLACE

Collective bargaining is a mechanism for enabling workers and their representatives to participate in establishing and administering the rules of the workplace.* Bargaining has resulted in the development of arbitration and other safeguards to protect the employee against inequitable treatment and unfair disciplinary action. More important still, the sense of participation through bargaining serves to mitigate the fear of exploitation on the part of the workers. Whether or not wages would be lower in the absence of bargaining, many employees would doubtless feel that their interests would be compromised without the presence of a union or the power to elect a bargaining representative. In view of these sentiments, collective bargaining may well serve as a substitute for sweeping government controls over wages as a device for insuring adequate, visible safeguards to protect the interests of employees.

CHOOSING THE FORM OF COMPENSATION

Collective bargaining provides a procedure through which employees as a group may affect the distribution of compensation and the choices between money and hours of work. One of the most significant consequences of collective bargaining over the past two decades has been the growth of fringe benefits, such as pensions, paid holidays, health and welfare, and vacations with pay. If unions had not existed, it is unlikely that individual workers would have spent added income in exactly the same way; indeed, it is doubtful whether, in the absence of collective bargaining, health and pension plans at present prices would have grown widespread. Moreover, though speculations of this kind are treacherous, the history of social-insurance legislation in the United States suggests that, under a system where the government was responsible for setting wages and terms of employment, fringe benefits would not have grown to the extent they have.[15]

These fringe benefits have had a significant impact upon the whole economy. There can be little question that collective bargaining played a major role in focusing priorities and attention

---

* Some writers have contended that collective bargaining is a process of joint decision making or joint management. It is true that many rules are agreed to by the parties and written into the collective agreement. But many other functions are left exclusively to management. Moreover, labor agreements typically specify areas within which management takes the initiative, with unions being left to file grievances if they feel that management has violated the contract. Although management may consider it wise to consult with the union before taking certain types of action, it is normally not obligated to seek advance consent from the union. It is misleading to equate collective bargaining with joint management by unions and employers.

upon medical care in the past decade. With the growth of health and welfare plans, information about medical care has been widely disseminated and developed; a body of experts in business and labor have arisen, and the pressures for public programs in the medical field have been accelerated. In much the same way, the extent of expansion in vacation-oriented industries—motels, resorts, transportation, boating, and leisure goods—must be partly attributed to the emphasis in collective bargaining on greater vacation benefits for employees.

STANDARDIZATION OF COMPENSATION

Collective bargaining tends to establish a standard rate and standard benefits for enterprises in the same product market, be it local or national. Labor contracts in the ladies' garment industry seek to establish uniform piece rates (and labor costs) for all companies that produce the same item within the same general price brackets; all the firms in the basic steel industry confront virtually the same hourly wage schedule for all production and maintenance occupations; and all construction firms bidding on contracts in a locality confront known and uniform wage schedules.

Such uniformity is naturally sought by unions. As political institutions, they desire "equal pay for equal work" in order to avoid the sense of grievance that results when one group of members discovers that another group is performing the same job in another plant at a higher wage. Thus, unless there are strong economic reasons for maintaining wage differentials, unions will normally push hard for standardization.

From the standpoint of employers, it should be observed that uniform wage rates do not necessarily imply uniform labor costs. Firms paying the same hourly rates may have varying wage costs as a result of differences in equipment and managerial efficiency. But competition tends to remove these differences and promote more uniform labor costs among close rivals. In highly competitive industries, employers often have a keen regard for such standardization; it protects the enterprises from uncertain wage rate competition, at least among firms subject to the collective agreement.

From the standpoint of the economy as a whole, the effects of standardization are mixed. In some instances, wage uniformity may be broadened artificially beyond a product market area, as when the wage rates in a tire company are extended to apply to its rubber-shoe work. The effect is to produce a less efficient use of economic resources. The resulting premium over the wages paid in other rubber-shoe plants eventually will compel the tire companies to give up doing business in the rubber-shoe field. In a more important sense, however, the effect of uniformity has been positive in that it has favored the expansion of more profitable, more efficient firms. In a country like France, on the other hand, bargaining establishes only minimum rates, so that backward companies can often survive by paying lower wages than their competitors if they can somehow manage to retain the necessary work force.

DETERMINING PRIORITIES ON EACH SIDE

A major function of collective bargaining is to induce the parties to determine priorities and resolve differences within their respective organizations. In the clash and controversy between the two sides, it is easy to assume a homogeneous union struggling with a homogeneous management or association of employers. This view is erroneous and mischievous. In an important sense, collective bargaining consists of no less than three separate bargains—the agreement by different groups within the union to abandon certain claims and assign priorities to others; an analogous process of assessing priorities and trade-offs within a single company or association; and the eventual agreement that is made across the bargaining table.

A labor organization is composed of members with a conglomeration of conflicting and common interests. The skilled and the unskilled, the long-service and the junior employees, the pieceworkers and the day-rated workers, and those in expanding and contracting jobs often do not have the same preferences. A gain to one of these groups often will involve a loss to another. Thus, in George W. Taylor's words, "To an increasing extent, the union function involves a mediation between the conflicting interests of its own membership."[16]

Similarly, corporate officials may have differing views about the negotiations, even in a single company. The production department and the sales staff may assess differently the consequences of a strike. The financial officers may see an issue differently from the industrial-relations specialists. These divergences are compounded where an association of companies bargains with a union, for there are often vast differences among the member firms in their financial capacity, vulnerability to a strike, concern over specific issues, and philosophy toward the union.

One of the major reasons that initial demands of both parties often diverge so far from final settlements is that neither side may have yet established its own priorities or preferences, or assessed the priorities of the other side. In many cases, these relative priorities are established and articulated only during the actual bargaining process. (This view of the bargaining process helps to explain the sense of comradeship that labor and management negotiators often develop through the common task of dealing with their respective committees and constituents.)

This process of accommodation within labor and management is central to collective bargaining. It should not be disparaged as merely a matter of internal politics on either side. In working out these internal adjustments in a viable way, collective bargaining serves a social purpose of enormous significance. The effective resolution of these problems is essential to the strength of leadership and to the continued vitality of both the company and the union.

REDESIGNING THE MACHINERY OF BARGAINING

A most significant function of collective bargaining in this country is the continuing design and redesign of the institution itself. While it is true that the national labor policy—as reflected in legislation, administrative rulings, and court decisions—has a bearing on some features of collective bargaining, the nature of the institution is chiefly shaped by the parties themselves. As previously noted, the collective-bargaining process largely determines the respective roles of individual bargaining and union-management negotiations. It defines the subjects to be settled by collective bargaining. It determines the structure of bargaining relationships. It establishes the grievance procedures and prescribes the uses of arbitration and economic power in the administration of an agreement. It decides the degree of centralization and decentralization of decision making. It influences the ratification procedures of the parties. The results are seldom fixed. The bargaining parties must reshape their bargaining arrangements from time to time in response to experience and emerging new problems. Thus, the design of collective bargaining and its adaptation to new challenges and opportunities have much to do with its capacity to fulfill its social functions effectively and without undue cost to the public.

Five Major Issues

In certain respects, collective bargaining is being subjected to a closer scrutiny than in the past, because of the special circumstances in which the country now finds itself. On the one hand, it is plain that society is becoming more critical of its institutions and more demanding in the performance it expects of them. Collective bargaining must now be judged in the light of the American position in the world, which has created new demands for economic progress and monetary stability. The consequences of labor negotiations must be viewed in the light of more insistent demands for full employment. And though labor and management have grown more professional in their dealings with each other and more successful in avoiding strikes, Secretary of Labor Willard Wirtz could still observe that ". . . neither the traditional collective-bargaining procedures nor the present labor-dispute laws are working to the public's satisfaction, at least as far as major labor controversies are concerned."[17]

At the same time, the climate in which collective bargaining must operate has also become more trying. In recent years, bargaining has been spreading rapidly into the field of public employment, where the parties are often inexperienced in labor relations and the problems involved are in many respects more difficult than in the private sector. Full employment has also placed new strains upon the bargaining process. With jobs so plentiful employees are less amenable to discipline and control. Their demands have grown larger, particularly in an economy where the cost of living has been creeping upward. Labor shortages have likewise created difficulties by forcing managers to hire less-experienced and less-qualified employees.

From these pressures have emerged five groups of questions that have been debated increasingly in recent years. Each of these problem areas will form the subject of a subsequent chapter.

1) Economic strife and dispute settlement. What can be done to protect the public interest when the parties to collective bargaining engage in economic warfare? Is the exertion of economic and political pressure an appropriate way to resolve bargaining disputes? Would not compulsory arbitration be a superior procedure, substituting facts and reason for power? What can the parties themselves and the government do to improve the performance of collective bargaining?

2) *Efficiency and productivity.* What is the impact of collective bargaining upon managerial efficiency? How extensive and serious are restrictive work practices, and what can be done about them? Does the rule-making character of collective bargaining necessarily stifle management in its quest for reductions in labor costs? When is a rule of collective bargaining an appropriate protection of the health, safety, or convenience of a worker, and when is it an undue limitation of efficiency? How can uneconomic work practices be eliminated in the future?

3) *Inflation.* What are the consequences of collective bargaining for inflation? The experience of many Western countries since World War II, including our own, raises the question whether free collective bargaining, continuing high employment, and price stability are compatible. What can be done to make collective bargaining less conducive to inflation or to reduce its inflationary bias at high levels of employment?

4) *Public employees.* In recent years, the process of negotiations has been spreading rapidly to many sectors of public employment. Are the procedures of private bargaining appropriate to public employment? Is the strike a suitable means to induce agreement in the public sector? What is the proper relation between negotiations in the public sector and legislative bodies and civil service? What machinery is appropriate to resolve disputes in public employment?

5) *New opportunities for bargaining.* What are likely to be the new subjects of collective bargaining in the private sector in the years ahead? What are the new needs and opportunities to which collective bargaining procedures can fruitfully be applied?

8

Alternatives to Economic Conflict in the Private Sector

WE VALUE collective bargaining because it yields agreements that reflect the needs and desires of labor as well as management. We deplore strikes and lockouts because of the inconvenience they cause, especially to innocent bystanders. Yet the strike and the lockout are means of stimulating bargaining and inducing the parties to reach agreement. Economic conflict, or its threat, may cause a management to improve its offer or lead a union to reduce its demands; the prospect of a test of strength forces each side to reassess its position by carefully weighing its goals and priorities against the costs of conflict. A strike deadline minimizes stalling and indecision and forces the parties to face up to issues even though the solutions may not be ideal. In short, strikes and lockouts are tools in the agreement-making process. At the same time, it is important that every effort be made to minimize the outbreak of economic conflict.

Although the incidence of strikes in the United States is greater than in other Western democracies, much progress has been made over the past thirty years toward reducing the level of economic conflict. There has been a marked long-term decline in violence* in labor-management relations[1] and a reduction in the incidence of work stoppages. The average level of industrial strife

---

* In the period January 1, 1902, to September 30, 1904, it is estimated that 198 persons were killed and 1,966 injured in strikes and lockouts. The most important single cause of violence in labor disputes has been controversy over union recognition. The sharp decline in violence is to be attributed particularly to the Wagner Act (1935) and to procedures for representation elections.

in the eight years 1960–67, measured by the percentage of estimated working time, was .18 percent or 4.3 minutes per 40-hour
work week. This figure is less than 60 percent of the strike activity
during the preceding ten years and only one eighth of the peak
postwar year of strike activity in 1946. Furthermore, during the
Vietnam war only four occasions have arisen when it has been
necessary to use the emergency-dispute procedures of the Taft-
Hartley law to restore vital production. In comparison with the
Korean war period, the record of collective bargaining and constructive mediation has been outstanding.

The public strongly supports collective bargaining as a matter
of principle, and 61 percent of a nationwide sample has recently
expressed opposition to making all strikes illegal. Yet, despite the
declines in work stoppages, there is still considerable unease over
the continued outbreak of economic conflict. To be sure, the public
is far less concerned today than it was in the late 1940's when polls
revealed that strikes were regarded as the number-one national
issue. But substantial majorities still favor the use of compulsory
arbitration to put an end to strikes that last more than a few days
or weeks.* These polls may not yield entirely consistent opinions
and they may not reflect a sensitive appreciation of the problems
inherent in government intervention in labor-management negotiations, but they accurately mirror public irritation and hostility to
strikes and lockouts, particularly in the wake of a New York City
transit strike or an airline shutdown. These feelings are also reflected in the legislation introduced in each session of Congress to
establish a labor court or to provide for compulsory arbitration.[2]

Public opinion does not seem to have been assuaged by a
number of well-publicized instances of imaginative and constructive bargaining—the Kaiser Long-Range Sharing Plan, the Armour
Automation Committee, the Pacific Maritime Association Agreement and the Human Relations Committee in the basic steel

---

* A 1966 Gallup poll asked: "If a strike continued for seven days, with no agreement reached, would you favor or oppose the idea of a government-appointed
committee deciding the issue and compelling both sides to accept the terms?"
Of all persons asked, 54 percent were in favor, 36 percent were opposed, and
10 percent had no opinion. A 1967 Gallup poll put the question: "It has been
suggested that no strike be permitted to go on for more than 21 days. If after
21 days, the union and the employer cannot reach an agreement, the courts
would appoint a committee that would decide the issue and both be compelled to accept the terms." The responses indicated 68 percent favored the
idea, 22 percent were opposed, and 10 percent had no opinion.

industry, to name only a few.[3] Neither does the public seem to have been impressed by the views of some experts that there is little basis for concern over industrial "warfare." The arbitrator Theodore W. Kheel writes:

> I view the prospect of a strike or lockout as indispensable to collective bargaining, and collective bargaining as the best process any society has ever developed for voluntarily setting the relations of workers and their employers. Indeed, the "prospect" of a cessation of work is the most effective strike deterrent ever devised even though it doesn't work 100 percent of the time. . . .[4]

The public-opinion polls, however, seem more in keeping with the views of A. H. Raskin, assistant editor of the editorial page of *The New York Times:*

> It is nonsense to suggest that the right to make war deserves sacrosanct status in the labor field when the zenith of aspiration in every other field, including the global relations of sovereign powers, is to banish that right. When all people have to suffer because of the wilfulness or ineptitude of economic power blocs, the establishment of improved governmental machinery for breaking deadlocks is an affirmation—not a denial —of democracy.[5]

The Basis for Public Concern

Although experts may dismiss the man in the street as ignorant and misinformed about labor-management relations, his views cannot be discounted so easily. On the contrary, each of the arguments underlying the widespread public concern needs to be carefully stated before any judgment is expressed on the gravity and cure of the "strike problem."

HARM TO THE INNOCENT BYSTANDER

Economic conflict not only affects the disputing parties but characteristically has an adverse impact on third parties unable to influence the outcome of the negotiations.[6] An airlines stoppage may cause considerable financial loss to businesses and unemployment for workers at airports who are engaged in catering, vending, or enterprises dependent on plane deliveries. Merchants and their employees are adversely affected by strikes which shut down plants employing a significant part of the local population. Newspaper disputes can cause significant harm to retail establishments and businesses dependent on advertising. The New York City ten-day transit shutdown of January 1966 and the eight-month copper stoppage of 1967–68 both inflicted hardship on multitudes far beyond those directly involved in the disputes.* The industrial warriors do not shoot at each other alone; innocent bystanders are hurt as well.†

INTERNAL RIVALRIES

It is difficult for the public to appreciate or sympathize with economic conflict where division within the membership of unions or employer associations is a significant factor deterring settlement. Nor is the public likely to be tolerant of strikes when rivalry among unions or disagreement over their differing wage and benefit levels is a major cause of the dispute. Plumbers' Local 2 in New York City was on strike for six months in 1966–67 to the eventual detriment of much of the construction activity in the city. An advertisement of the Building Trades Employers' Association stated:

> Background to all this . . . is the fact that there is an intra-union tug-of-war. Recent press reports indicate a reluctance to approve and recommend any contract offer whatever—no matter how generous its terms—prior to the Union's election of new officers on December 10th, or even prior to the induction of the new President in January 1967.

---

* In theory, the problem of the innocent bystander could be taken care of by requiring the parties to share the costs of compensating such losses. In practice this approach leads to formidable difficulties. Apart from the burden of having to process the claims of a large number of third parties, there are extremely complex problems of deciding how much money, for example, a business has lost during a strike, how much of this amount is recovered after the strike's end, how much business may be permanently lost due to the temporary disruption of the strike, etc.

† Sometimes, too, innocent bystanders may reap unexpected gains as larger profits and greater employment and overtime go to competitive enterprises not shut down by the dispute. Radio and television advertising may gain during a newspaper strike, and one beer company may gain when a competitor is strikebound.

The Plumbers' strike is not an isolated example. It was widely known that rivalries and tensions within the Machinists and among the six shop craft unions* were a major contributing factor to the national railroad crisis in 1967.[7] Internecine warfare between pilots and flight engineers gave rise to strikes and government intervention in the early sixties. New York newspaper strikes have been aggravated by internal pulling and hauling over which craft union would set the pattern for wage increases. When several managements bargain together, conflicting interests among companies with different competitive markets and different spokesmen are quite often a significant deterrent to settlements. The 1959 basic steel shutdown, for instance, was complicated and prolonged by the different problems which the twelve individual companies confronted on local working conditions. Circumstances such as these arising from labor or management contribute to the disenchantment of the general public with collective bargaining and enhance the case for more governmental intervention.

DISREGARD OF AUTHORITY

Although instances have been relatively rare in the private sector, open defiance of governmental procedures and authority is a factor prejudicing the public against strikes and lockouts. At the end of World War II, public opinion was provoked by the refusal of John L. Lewis to heed the War Labor Board and the President and by his contempt of court in 1946, for which he and the Mine Workers paid a heavy fine. The Taft-Hartley Act was in part a response to these episodes. In recent years, strikes by public employees have produced a strong public reaction. Michael J. Quill, the head of the Transport Workers Union, tore up injunction papers on television and declared, "The judge can drop dead in his black robes."[8] Against this setting, the New York City transit strike of January 1966 could not fail to alienate public opinion no matter how high Quill's prestige rose within his own ranks or how much this popularity may have freed his hand in settling the negotiations. According to a poll conducted by the Opinion Research Corpora-

---

* The six unions are: International Brotherhood of Boilermakers, Iron Shipbuilders, Blacksmiths, Forgers and Helpers; International Brotherhood of Electrical Workers; International Brotherhood of Firemen and Oilers; International Association of Machinists and Aerospace Workers; Brotherhood of Railway Carmen of America; Sheet Metal Workers' International Association.

tion, 52 percent of the New Yorkers questioned said the transit strike made them less favorable to unions, 32 percent reported feeling about the same, and only 4 percent said the strike made them feel more favorable to unions.[9]

THE HIGH INCIDENCE OF STRIKES IN AMERICA

The incidence of industrial strife in the United States is materially higher than in most other advanced industrial countries. The number of days lost in work stoppages per employed person in the United States during the decade 1955–64 was three and a half times that in the United Kingdom, which in turn was more than twenty times higher than in Sweden. The following table reveals the extent of American "leadership."

Days Lost per 1,000 Persons Employed, in Mining, Manufacturing, Construction and Transport, 1955–64[10]

Australia	378
Belgium	498
Canada	597
France	336
Germany, (F.R.)	52
Italy	875
Japan	391
Netherlands	53
Sweden	14
United Kingdom	294
United States	1,044

There are many reasons for the higher incidence of industrial conflict in the United States. Decentralized negotiations create many more bargaining relationships in which breakdowns can occur. For the most part, these negotiations are too scattered and local in nature to be subject to strong government influence, and the officials involved are not always as skilled as those who would participate under more centralized negotiations. In addition, the larger number of important provisions in bargaining contracts— and the tradition of negotiating actual, rather than minimum, wages—make it harder to reach a peaceful agreement. The higher level of wage income in the United States, compared to Europe, permits American workers to sustain longer stoppages. Regardless of these reasons, however, the record of other major industrial countries forcibly raises the question, which concerns the American public, whether the incidence of industrial strife arising over the negotiation of collective-bargaining agreements cannot be appreciably reduced.*

DEMANDING MORE OF LABOR-MANAGEMENT INSTITUTIONS

The public appears to be asking for a higher level of performance from collective bargaining than was expected in an earlier day. One may well ask whether the public has come to expect too much of private bargaining. Collective-bargaining negotiations are expected to produce agreements that provide, to use the standards of editorial writers, noninflationary wage and benefit increases, that contain no inefficiencies, that provide new opportunities for minority groups, that are democratically negotiated and ratified, and that are reached without resulting in a strike or lockout.† These are very tall orders, particularly since certain of the demands are somewhat inconsistent; for example, economic conflict may inconvenience the public, but it also provides a measure of discipline in the private sector to restrain the aspirations of both labor and management. Nevertheless, larger demands have been placed on all our institutions, and there is no reason why collective bargaining should be an exception. Moreover, the public can well expect a lessening of conflict as more and more bargaining relationships grow older and more professional.

---

* It should not be too quickly concluded that the higher level of industrial strife in the United States is all deleterious. Peace may be purchased at too high a price; the relative decentralization in bargaining in this country may encourage plant-level managerial initiative and some strikes over work practices brought on by a strong managerial initiative may yield higher efficiency and productivity.

† These expectations are often fed by traditional and populist concerns over the power of private producer groups. In the words of Lionel Robbins:

"The Classical Economists sympathized with the state and with the individual citizens but not with intermediate bodies claiming coercive power. Their sympathies with the worker, which were real, were contingent upon his service to the consumer."[11]

In every corner of society one can discover traces of worry over the plight of the individual in the presence of huge impersonal organizations. In the field of labor relations, A. H. Raskin captures this mood when he says, "The real need is not more protection for the economic disputants but improved mechanisms to safeguard the public against abuses of the power bigness gives them to batter the economy."[12]

Compulsory Arbitration and Labor Courts

On first impression, at least, strikes could be easily done away with by simply prohibiting them and substituting impartial arbitration in their place. Thus, it is not surprising that the public dissatisfactions just described have fostered proposals for generalized compulsory arbitration and labor courts. In most proposals the compulsory procedures would be confined to a limited number of designated industries or to particular disputes that adversely affect the public interest of the nation to a substantial degree. To resolve these disputes, proposals have often been advanced to create special arbitral tribunals or establish a separate system of labor courts and a separate labor judiciary with the sole and exclusive function of deciding labor disputes which the parties themselves cannot settle. According to Judge Samuel I. Rosenman, one experienced proponent of such reforms, "With equality now reached by labor unions in nearly every industry, and insured for the future by our many labor laws, their right to strike should be curtailed when it is in conflict with the public interest, and . . . some form of final compulsory decision must be provided."[13] Although they differ in the precise machinery to be used, such proposals seek to specify in advance that the failure of negotiations will result in a final and binding determination and that any strike or lockout against the decision of the arbitration tribunal will be illegal. An overall compulsory-arbitration mechanism is to be distinguished from *ad hoc* legislation, such as the statutes requiring final determination of the railroad work-rules disputes in 1963 and the railroad shopcraft dispute in 1967.[14]

The Association of American Railroads and many airline and maritime managements have joined the critics who call for procedures for final and binding decisions in critical industries.* On the whole, however, labor and management are clearly against such measures. Even such strange bedfellows as the AFL–CIO and the

---

* It may be noted that in the railroad and airline industries rates and fares are regulated by governmental agencies and these managements believe they are already required as a practical matter to accept, although unions are not, the recommendations of emergency boards under the Railway Labor Act. Moreover, the fear of management that compulsory wage determination may lead to government price controls is of no concern in a regulated industry.

N.A.M. find themselves united in their opposition to compulsory arbitration and the establishment of a labor court.[15]

Although the arguments voiced by union and management spokesmen are often too doctrinaire to be convincing, there are compelling reasons for rejecting compulsory arbitration in the private sector. The arguments, however, are thoroughly pragmatic. They do not rest on ideological considerations, nor is it likely that ideology will prevail over practicalities in determining the ultimate form by which labor-management conflicts will be resolved in this country.

THE DANGER OF DESTROYING BARGAINING

Compulsory arbitration, even within a few industries, tends to undermine an important ingredient in productive labor-management relations, namely the willingness of the parties to bargain conscientiously over their differences. If both sides realize that their differences may ultimately go to arbitration, they may well be less willing to compromise—either because they prefer to pass the responsibility on to some third party or because they fear that in the event of arbitration any concessions they make will cause the arbitrator to reach a compromise settlement less favorable to their interests. These tendencies seem to have been confirmed by experience both here and abroad, for arbitration statutes have often led to an erosion of the bargaining process in favor of more frequent resort to the government tribunal.

The increased use of arbitration would greatly magnify the various problems of enforcement, rigidity, and bureaucracy that are described in the paragraphs to follow. To avoid this danger, many critics have proposed that arbitration be only one of several procedures—among which the government could choose to fit the circumstances of each dispute. This alternative might well reduce the likelihood of arbitration to such a point that the parties would not diminish their bargaining efforts in anticipation of a governmentally imposed solution. At the same time, proponents of this scheme rarely stop to point out that Congress can already impose arbitration or any other remedy it chooses if the usual emergency procedures fail to yield a solution. That is precisely what Congress has done on two occasions in recent years to avert nationwide strikes in the railroad industry. Viewed in this light, although the "choice of procedures" approach to emergency disputes may include new notions as to which official body should choose among the alternative remedies, the essence of the proposal does not provide any real advance over the practices already in use.

PROBLEMS OF ADMINISTERING THE AWARD

Compulsory arbitration also affects the willingness of union and management leaders to take responsibility for explaining, defending, and implementing the terms arrived at by the parties. The arbitration tribunal would be blamed for all unpopular decisions, and no consistent defense or advocacy of these decisions could be expected from union or management officials who disagreed with the terms imposed by the government. In time, resentment would arise among workers and employers through lack of understanding and sympathy for major decisions governing the workplace. This vacuum could not be filled from an outside source; the arbitration tribunal would have no standing to explain and advocate its decisions within a labor or management organization. Many issues, such as incentive-pay systems, seniority and adjustments to technological change are so complex that any unpopular decision of a tribunal could be expected to give rise to a burdensome stream of requests for clarifications, interpretations and other litigation. This is precisely what occurred after the railroad work-rules arbitration mandated by law. The resulting unrest may seriously affect productivity. There are thus serious limits in the industrial-relations arena to the effectiveness of legally imposed terms of employment.

DISPUTE SETTLEMENT VERSUS NATIONAL ECONOMIC POLICY

Sooner or later a labor court or continuing arbitration tribunal would have to install general wage policies and other economic yardsticks, or its decisions would appear haphazard and unfair. These general policies would not be limited to basic wage rates. Proposals for cost-of-living escalators would likely require a consistent policy. The tribunal would be confronted with the necessity to set precedents on skill differentials, severance pay and a variety of new demands for fringe benefits. Moreover, a tribunal with power to limit wage increases and preclude the strike or lockout would arouse strong political pressures for regulating price increases as a matter of common equity.

No tribunal could frame general wage and price standards

without adapting them to the economic policy of the government. If the tribunal enunciated its own independent wage policy, the national administration might well object. An administration would scarcely delegate so essential an ingredient of national economic policy to an independent tribunal; wage policy must be coordinated with monetary and fiscal policies to achieve the desired economic goals. Yet if the tribunal were restricted by the wage policy of the administration, a policy which would be unlikely to be accepted fully by labor and management, the parties before the tribunal would argue that their case had been prejudged and that the procedures were basically unfair. One or more parties might even refuse to appear. In the end, wage movements in a high-employment economy will inevitably be of major concern to a national adminstration and they are likely to become even more so in the future. Under these circumstances, it is awkward to give power over key negotiations to a judicial-type arbitration tribunal designed to prevent strikes and lockouts. The wrong man at the wrong place in the government would be making vital economic decisions.

ARBITRATION TENDS TO BE INFLEXIBLE

Compulsory arbitration on a continuing long-term basis could easily become rigid and bureaucratic, to the great detriment of labor-management relations in an economy of rapidly changing technology and competition. Major work stoppages seldom involve simple disputes over wages. The issues will often raise complex questions involving new fringe benefits, elimination of complex work practices, or new methods for responding to technological change. Many of the most serious impasses in recent years have not even involved wages and working conditions but have concerned new and uncharted procedures and structures for negotiations. Coalition bargaining provides an apt illustration. Arbitrators and judges are not likely to be imaginative or pioneering in treating such issues in industries and relationships they cannot know intimately. Their natural inclination will be to avoid experimenting with the lives and property of others and to continue instead to temporize with problems which require fresh approaches. These tendencies seem especially likely in the context of American traditions of government. The history of regulatory bodies in the United States does not inspire confidence in the quality of personnel who are attracted to these agencies after initial crusading periods. Nor is the process of arbitration well suited to the problems at hand. Professor Archibald Cox has said in arguing against compulsory arbitration, ". . . litigation is essentially a non-creative process in labor relations. It tends to freeze existing practices and past relations. . . . The resulting drag upon the mobility and fluidity of industry would be damaging to the economy."[16]

PROBLEMS OF GAINING COMPLIANCE

Compulsory arbitration creates serious risks that workers will refuse to comply with unpopular awards and will rebel, either by stopping work or by various covert tactics, such as slowdowns, sabotage, or working to rule, which can cripple the efficient operation of modern industry. In Australia, where compulsory arbitration is widely used, strikes are more serious than in most other industrial democracies where free collective bargaining prevails. While no exact parallels can be drawn between two countries, the Australian experience clearly demonstrates that compulsory arbitration does not automatically do away with strikes, or even reduce them to minimal proportions.

AN INOPPORTUNE SOLUTION

In view of the preceding arguments, compulsory arbitration seems decidedly inopportune at the present time. Government experience in encouraging the peaceful settlement of labor disputes is still developing. The complexities involved are great enough to call for continuing experimentation to develop better, more effective techniques and procedures short of a general system of compulsory arbitration. Innovation has in fact been going on in recent years both at the initiative of private parties and by government bodies in cases where intervention could not be avoided. There remains ample scope for further experimentation. In fact, a major purpose of this chapter will be to outline a variety of measures which the parties and the government might undertake short of compulsory arbitration to improve the performance of collective bargaining. It is not sound to cut short this process by imposing the sweeping solution of compulsory arbitration. Nor is it wise to impose fresh and uncomfortable controls in a period when respect for law is already so precarious in so many different areas of life. Decisive action might conceivably be called for if the problem of strikes in the private sector were growing steadily more serious. In fact, however, the burden of work stoppages has been steadily receding over the past three decades.

The Improvement of the Performance of Collective Bargaining

If a general system of compulsory arbitration or labor courts is unsatisfactory, what is to be done? The public concerns over economic conflict, cited at the outset of this chapter, cannot be brushed aside; they require a review and appraisal of alternative measures to reduce the amount of economic strife. A number of alternatives are available. They may be divided into three broad groups: *1)* measures to be taken by the parties themselves; *2)* measures to be taken by the parties with the cooperation, assistance and even the prodding of government; and *3)* further legislative action to improve the performance of collective bargaining.

WHAT CAN BE DONE BY PRIVATE PARTIES THEMSELVES

In the United States, collective bargaining is highly developed in prescribing detailed agreements to fix the terms of employment and elaborate mechanisms to resolve differences over the meaning and application of these terms. In contrast to many Western countries, however, the American industrial-relations system has been relatively underdeveloped and unimaginative in fashioning *procedures* to settle disputes over the terms of new or reopened agreements. The Taft-Hartley Act simply requires sixty days' notice to the other party of the proposed modification or termination prior to the expiration date of the agreement and thirty days' notice to the Federal Mediation and Conciliation Service. Rarely do the parties themselves agree on steps to improve upon the Taft-Hartley procedures. It is therefore worth inquiring whether private parties and government in this country can develop new ways to facilitate the resolution of conflict over the terms of agreements.

The cumulative experience of collective bargaining has de-

veloped a wide variety of measures to promote settlements
without resort to stoppages. Some of these devices are as old as
collective bargaining; others are new names for older developments, while some have come into prominence only recently. A
common element of these techniques is that the parties do not wait
until the eve of negotiations, when demands and tensions are
accelerating, to shape the course of bargaining; they work at
arrangements for peaceful negotiation during the term of the
agreement. Among the more common procedures are the following:

Prenegotiation conferences to influence the proposals that are
subsequently made by each side and to shape negotiation
steps.[17] The technique has been used historically particularly
in the garment, clothing and hosiery industries.

Advanced joint selection of specialists—actuaries, accountants,
engineers or economists—to secure agreed-upon cost estimates
of possible proposals or to gather specified wage and earnings
data in a form agreed to be relevant to negotiations.

Early negotiations carried out well in advance of the deadline.
The Armour and Company negotiations with the Packinghouse
Workers and Butcher Workmen completed in the spring of
1967, before the September 1 deadline, affords an apt illustration.

Private mediation, including possible fact finding and recommendations, by neutrals or a tripartite group selected by the
parties. The Kaiser Steel–Steelworkers Long-Range Sharing
Plan is illustrative.

National private joint machinery within an industry or sector
to assist in mediation of terms of agreements between parties
in a locality, or the commitment to settle nationally, disputes
over such agreements not settled locally. The Industrial Relations Council in the electrical branch of the construction industry, established in 1919, is a notable case.

A continuing joint study committee, or human-relations committee, which provides a forum for periodic discussion of
specific problems. These committees show wide variation in
function and scope of issues considered. The basic steel industry has provided examples.[18]

A formula-type arrangement under which the parties agree to resolve one or more issues by the adoption of a specified norm or formula, such as a measure of prevailing wages. Thus, occupational wage rates for the United Shoe Machinery Corporation employees are determined periodically by a B.L.S. machinery wage survey in the Boston area, and elevator constructors' wages are set in relation to the wages paid other construction crafts in the same locality.

An advance commitment to voluntary arbitration. The collective-bargaining agreements of Schrafft's Restaurants and Bickford Company, two chain restaurants in New York, have included such a provision; the transit industry in many localities historically included such provisions; in the airline industry, Pan American Airways is signatory to such agreements with several crafts. The agreement between the Airline Pilots and United Air Lines concerning cockpit-crew size for the Boeing 737 equipment provides for extensive fact finding under two crew-size patterns, with review of the experience and arbitration if the dispute is not resolved in joint negotiations.

Voluntary arbitration over the terms of unresolved disputed provisions of an agreement may be utilized without an advanced commitment, as a deadline approaches.[19]

Experienced mediators and neutrals have also sought to persuade parties to use these procedures. The preventive mediation program of the Federal Mediation and Conciliation Service and the American Arbitration Association, particularly through its Labor Management Institute, encourages private parties to adopt some of these steps, or fashion their own variants, to achieve settlements without work stoppages. The F.M.C.S. made 375 preventive mediation assignments in fiscal year 1963, and the number had increased to 1,175 in fiscal 1967, and 1,322 in fiscal 1968.[20] Federal mediators, in cooperation with the parties, seek to encourage prenegotiation conferences, training programs for management supervisors and union stewards and continuing joint study committees. The F.M.C.S. reports, "Substantial segments of labor and management have fully embraced the concept of preventive mediation as an extension of the free collective-bargaining procedures."[21]

Taken as a group, these voluntary procedures are no doubt

growing in American collective bargaining. President I. W. Abel of
the Steelworkers said in his 1967 Labor Day statement:

> Industry and labor themselves have a vital obligation to
> voluntarily strengthen and bring perfection to our free collec-
> tive bargaining system. Even before negotiations on new
> agreements begin, the parties might be able to agree on steps
> to be taken in event of a stalemate in collective bargaining. An
> approach of this type, developed freely by the parties them-
> selves, would go a long way toward perfecting our collective-
> bargaining system and preclude the need for government in-
> tervention.[22]

Work stoppages do not arise ordinarily as a result of a lack of
knowledge of techniques for settlement, but rather from the
absence of a mutual disposition to use the available procedures
more extensively. There are, however, some sources of conflict that
have been growing in significance in recent years and for which
parties to collective bargaining have been developing still other
procedures to facilitate settlement.

In a significant number of negotiations, the ratification of the
settlement agreed upon by the committees of the parties has been
rejected by the union membership or, less frequently, by the top
management or an association of employers leading to a strike or
lockout.[23] William E. Simkin, former director of the Federal Mediation and Conciliation Service, reported that union members have
rejected settlements in 10 to 15 percent* of the cases in which the
F.M.C.S. was actively involved.[24] The ratification procedures are
established by the customs, practices and constitutional requirements of the parties, and labor and management can often contribute to industrial peace by jointly reviewing these procedures. In
some cases, more authority should be given to negotiators to make
final settlements. In others, it would be well to review the question
of which members of a union, or which members of a management
association, should be allowed to vote on particular settlements;

---

* The following tabulation shows the percentage of F.M.C.S. cases actively
involving a mediator in which a settlement achieved by the negotiators was
rejected in the ratification process:

Fiscal	1964	8.7%
	1965	10.0
	1966	11.7
	1967	14.2
	1968	11.9

union members have sometimes been allowed to vote on contracts in which they have no direct interest and hence no duty to strike if the agreement is rejected. In many cases, ratification can more certainly be achieved if enough time is given before the vote to allow the leaders to explain the settlement carefully and advocate its approval effectively. Voting procedures, too, may need examination, since they influence the number and characteristics of the members who actually vote. The results of a ratification vote may be influenced by whether it takes place in open meeting, by secret ballot at a meeting, or by mail; a procedure that produces a light vote may prejudice the legions of satisfied, apathetic members in favor of the aroused and indignant minority. A vote against ratification of a settlement by union members also requires careful assessment, since a higher offer is not always the most appropriate response by management. Some rearrangement in the package settlement, or a new vote, may be all that is needed to settle the dispute. These procedural issues relating to ratification are vital to good-faith bargaining since the rejection of negotiated settlements tends to reduce the willingness of negotiators to put forward their best offer in future negotiations.

Careful and perceptive understanding of the problems of both bargaining-unit employees and supervisory personnel in advance of negotiation also can contribute substantially to the achievement of peaceful settlements. It is not enough for union officials to presume they know the problems of workers or for top management to assume that it has full knowledge of what is going on at the workplace. A long list of demands or proposals to amend the contract is also inadequate. It is important to know something of the intensity of views on various issues and the types of members or supervisors concerned with each. A workplace is not a monolith, and knowledge of the diversity of interests and views, and the way in which they change during the course of negotiations, is essential to agreement making. The use of surveys, questionnaires and small department meetings is growing and providing more precise knowledge for negotiators. In the course of negotiation as well, more care can be directed to the conscious choice of alternatives and formulation of priorities. Agreements might provide for more options, to permit individuals or groups to choose among alternative benefits (see Chapter 12). A savings plan, for instance, may be used for illness or specified emergencies or carried over to retirement. Greater sensitivity in ascertaining the problems and preferences of workers and supervisors and greater imagination in formulating package settlements will result in fewer rejections of agreements in ratification votes and lessen the prospects of a strike.

In many industries with local or regional negotiations, the quality of settlements can be improved by closer supervision on the part of international unions and national associations of employers. Many international union constitutions provide that a strike by a local union requires the prior authorization of the international union; in other instances, approval is required if strike benefits are to be paid from international union funds. International unions and national employer associations typically may be able to arrange a postponement of a deadline in local negotiations by offering to assist in efforts to achieve a settlement. The national representatives from both sides can bring detachment, broad experience and influence to deadlocked local negotiations. Strikes arising from misinformation or miscalculation can be significantly reduced.

Economic strife in collective bargaining is often related to the high and distorted expectations with which one side or both may enter the negotiation. The bargaining sessions may not fulfill one of their traditional functions, to deflate the aspirations of each side toward the area of realistic settlement. In recent years of high employment and substantial profits, there have been a number of instances in which experienced chief negotiators might well have reached agreement without a stoppage had they not decided that a limited strike was essential to cool the unrealistic aspirations of their constituents. The aspirations arising prior to negotiation may substantially influence the chances of peaceful settlement, and the internal politics of one side or the other may exaggerate these expectations. To avoid this danger, a number of parties have mutually taken special care to limit publicity, moderate their comments, and otherwise avoid raising the aspirations of their constituents prior to negotiations. Such conduct may make a substantial contribution to subsequent peaceful negotiations.

These suggestions scarcely exhaust the possibilities for constructive activities by the parties, alone or in cooperation with the F.M.C.S., to reduce the incidence of strikes and lockouts in collective bargaining. The essential suggestion is that creativity and imagination of the parties be directed to the perfection of the procedures and structure of bargaining.

WHAT CAN BE DONE BY PRIVATE PARTIES
WITH THE INITIATIVE OF GOVERNMENT

In the past, too little imagination has been expended on the opportunities for government to influence the conduct of collective bargaining. Discussions of the role of government have oscillated from proposals for drastic regulation to critiques of conventional mediation in particular disputes. Yet there is a vast underdeveloped world between these two forms of governmental involvement in private collective bargaining. An active industrial-relations policy would use the government to suggest, to stimulate, to research and to advocate a variety of measures to reduce conflict.

From the 150,000 agreements in the United States, it should be possible to develop a short list of those that produce the greatest concern, both by the frequency of stoppages resulting from a breakdown of negotiations and by the economic impact of the eventual settlements. The maritime, East Coast longshore, construction, newspaper, railroad, airline, and copper industries undoubtedly would be included on the list. Detailed studies of bargaining problems and bargaining structure should be arranged by government officials in each of these industries, preferably with the cooperation of the parties. As a general rule, the studies should be made apart from pending negotiations and disputes. Some investigations might be made in the executive branch of government;* others could be made by private bodies under government contract.[25] Some might be undertaken under legislative auspices if Congress could develop a greater capacity for making dispassionate inquiries into labor-management problems than it has managed to display in recent decades.†

---

* The Economic Report of the President, February 1, 1968, provided for a Cabinet Committee on Price Stability. The message stated that the Committee will study and recommend, both for private and for public action, ". . . measures which can improve efficiency, remove bottlenecks, and improve technology in industries which are the source of persistent inflation." While the scope of the activities of the Cabinet Committee was considerably broader than collective bargaining, the types of problem sectors identified earlier were clearly within its purview. While the concern of the Cabinet Committee was not primarily with collective bargaining, it could not avoid attention to labor-management negotiations in sectors with unsatisfactory price, productivity, and cost patterns. Such a cabinet committee might well constitute one appropriate body to undertake some of the studies and hold some of the hearings recommended above.

† In the last generation, legislative committees in the labor-management field, with a few exceptions, have been preoccupied with lurid investigation, partisan

Such studies would provide a careful review of recent experience, analyze the reasons for major difficulties, inform a wider audience of the problems, and formulate proposals for private and public discussion. The parties might, under the circumstances, be asked to react specifically to the analysis and the recommendations of a report. Through such procedures, an attempt could be made to create within the parties a sense of public accountability for their conduct and a resolve to improve their performance. These studies should also be designed to help labor and management leaders within a sector educate their constituents and members on the nature of the problems of the sector and the hard alternatives which confront the parties.*

In some of these problem sectors, and preferably after a detailed preliminary study, the executive branch should formally appoint a group of outsiders to work with the parties to assist them to develop procedures, or in some instances, actually propose legislation to improve the performance of collective bargaining.†
The nature of the sector and its problems should determine the type of outsider to be chosen. At times, the group might include leaders of the AFL–CIO and representatives of managements from other sectors; at other times it might include Congressional and executive department representatives; and on still other occasions it might be composed of private neutrals. The group should be

---

regulation, or a particular crisis. Too few legislators are well informed on the processes and problems of collective bargaining and their variations in different sectors. The present state of affairs stands in marked contrast to earlier years if one surveys the work of the U.S. Commission on Industrial Relations, 1912–15, composed of Congressional representatives, labor, management and public representatives, and the U.S. Industrial Commission, 1898–1901, which included ten Congressional members out of a total of nineteen. These commissions and their staffs held hearings and wrote constructive reports of outstanding quality. Even today, constructive Congressional intervention is not without precedent. In recent years, committees of Congress, often with cooperation across the aisle, have developed genuine expertise and provided significant initiative in the development of public policy in the related fields of health and medical research, and in manpower. The labor-relations field could be significantly affected by a similar approach. In some industries, a series of informed Congressional hearings could provide a valuable stimulus to labor and management. In turn, Congressional representatives would become very much better informed on vital industrial-relations issues.

* The proposed sector studies are to be distinguished from more comprehensive reports on industrial relations for the country as a whole. It is significant that both Great Britain and Canada completed such reports in 1968 and 1969.[26]

† On September 22, 1969, President Nixon established by Executive Order the Construction Industry Collective Bargaining Commission, a tripartite body, to undertake a number of studies, to improve the performance of collective bargaining and dispute settlement, and to meet other problems of the industry.

selected not only for its ability to work constructively with the parties, but also for its capacity to impress upon labor and management leaders, and their followers, the urgency of the public's concern.

Another approach to reducing excessive strikes and lockouts is to establish, at least for a limited period, an agency to resolve a range of collective-bargaining disputes in cases in which federal funds are substantially involved. The President's Missile Sites Labor Commission, which operated in the period 1961–67, and the Atomic Energy Labor Relations Panel are illustrative.[27] Both these bodies were created under Presidential authority and have exercised varying degrees of pressure (in addition to mediation) in the resolution of disputes over the terms of collective-bargaining agreements. The tripartite Missile Sites Commission and the all-public Atomic Energy Panel provided specialized mediation and made recommendations which typically resolved disputes over the terms of agreements between the parties. These bodies also provided a basis for discussion between labor and management and the operating personnel of government procurement agencies. The Missile Sites Commission was concerned with more than labor-management disputes; it was also given authority to make findings regarding uneconomic work practices and unreasonable provisions of collective-bargaining agreements. The authority of the government to approve costs for purposes of reimbursement at these missile, space and atomic-energy installations enhanced the influence of these public bodies in collective bargaining. National leaders of labor and management recognized the need for more orderly dispute settlement at those vital installations, and saw in such agencies a means to strengthen their hand in dealing with isolated and often independent local groups. The threat of other forms of government intervention, particularly legislation, likewise helped to secure the cooperation of labor and management.

These precedents suggest that national leaders might agree for a period to substitute a public board for the strike or lockout in disputes over the terms of agreements in which governmental funds are heavily involved, as they are in the construction and maritime industries. In some instances, the board might actually fix the terms of the new contract. In others, it would be useful simply to provide for the postponement of a local stoppage until a tripartite body had the opportunity to review the dispute and recommend a settlement around which negotiations should proceed.

WHAT CAN BE DONE THROUGH ADDITIONAL LEGISLATION

Additional general legislation for the settlement of serious disputes does not seem appropriate, at least until measures of the type proposed above have been given a fair opportunity. But this does not imply that certain procedural and *ad hoc* legislation may not be appropriate on occasion for particular industries or disputes.

The seriousness of the defects of collective bargaining in certain problem sectors, noted at the outset of this section, might be brought home more forcibly to the parties if Congress, rather than the executive branch, were to require the studies proposed above. Such action might help to bring the bargaining parties together and give national leaders of labor and management a greater degree of influence over their respective organizations and members. Congress might further require labor and management in specified sectors to submit their proposals for bargaining reform by a certain date.

In the event that stoppages continue to be a major problem in a particular sector, Congress could even provide, for a specified period, that no strike or lockout over the terms of an agreement would be legal until local parties had submitted the dispute to a national body established by labor and management in the sector and until this body had the opportunity to resolve the controversy. The body would be empowered to recommend settlement terms if it should deem that this step would contribute to the resolution of the dispute. These procedures would not prohibit the resort to economic conflict, but they would postpone strikes or lockouts until the procedures had been exhausted. The body might be tripartite and include government or neutral members.

There is probably no great urgency for going beyond these limited proposals to revise the procedures contained in the emergency dispute provisions of the Taft-Hartley Act.* To be sure,

---

* The Taft-Hartley law provides that whenever, in the opinion of the President, a labor dispute affecting an entire industry, or a substantial part, imperils the national health or safety, he may appoint a board of inquiry to find the facts but make no recommendations. The President may then direct the Attorney General to seek an injunction restoring work operations, or precluding a stoppage, for a period of eighty days. If the dispute remains unresolved between the sixtieth and seventy-fifth day of the injunction, the N.L.R.B. shall take a secret ballot of the employees on the question whether they wish to accept the final offer of the employer. If the dispute still remains unresolved at

these provisions contain many well-publicized defects. If taken literally, the definition of an "emergency" dispute is extremely narrow. Critics have also objected to the prohibition barring the statutory board of inquiry from making substantive recommendations for the settlement of the dispute.[28] The statutory provisions seem particularly futile in requiring that the employees vote on the employer's last offer; this provision was enacted on the mistaken assumption that union leaders caused unnecessary strikes that would be prevented if the members could only express their views on the matter. In spite of these flaws, the procedures have worked out better than might have been expected. The ingenuity of public officials in designing mediation and special fact-finding procedures has often compensated for the formal deficiencies of the law.[29] The possibility of legislative action if the procedures do not solve the dispute has been a factor helping to induce settlement. The courts have so defined "emergency dispute" that the law can be applied to some disputes in single plants. In all, the procedures in the Act have been invoked twenty-nine times in the past twenty years. Only in the longshore and maritime industries have strikes developed after the eighty-day period.

The record of the Railway Labor Act, which was developed for railroads in 1926, and applied to airlines in 1936, is less satisfactory.[30] The emergency procedures* were invoked in a total of 171 cases up to 1967; in the twenty-year period 1947–67, they were used on 127 occasions and strikes occurred in thirty-four cases after the procedures had been exhausted. In the period 1958–68, in the airline industry, the unions rejected recommendations of emergency boards in 60 percent of the disputes, and strikes occurred in all the principal cases. The procedures of the

---

the end of the eighty-day period, the injunction is dissolved and the President shall submit to the Congress a full report together with such recommendations as he may see fit to make for consideration and appropriate action. The law provides for no restraint on the strike or lockout after the eighty-day period.

* The Railway Labor Act provides that if a major dispute between a carrier and its employees, in the judgment of the National Mediation Board, threatens substantially to interrupt interstate commerce to a degree such as to deprive any section of the country of essential transportation service, after seeking to resolve the dispute by mediation and the proffer of voluntary arbitration, the Board shall notify the President, who may create an *ad hoc* emergency board to investigate and report respecting the particular dispute. By convention, the report almost invariably contains recommendations for the resolution of the dispute. The parties may not engage in strike or lockout, or change rules affecting rates of pay, rules, or working conditions for thirty days, during which the emergency board conducts its investigation and makes its report, and for thirty additional days. The law contains no restraint on the strike or lockout after that period.

Railway Labor Act have led to a situation in which the parties do little, if any, genuine bargaining until after the report and recommendations of an emergency board. In the early stages of collective bargaining, when it should be most vigorous, collective bargaining has often become perfunctory. The procedures have been invoked so frequently on individual carriers that the notion of an emergency has been diluted. The managements have felt compelled by virtue of their extensive regulation by government to accept the recommendations of emergency boards, and they have argued, with some justice, that recommendations have become a floor from which unions, backed by the threat of strike, demand higher settlements. The leading academic authority on the Railway Labor Act, Professor Benjamin Aaron, who is also a respected mediator and arbitrator, has proposed that the emergency procedures of the Railway Labor Act be repealed and railroads and airlines be included within the scope of Taft-Hartley.[31] The railroad and airlines industries were earlier noted to be two of the economic sectors with the greatest problems in structure and procedures for the negotiation of agreements. Even if one does not now accept the solution proposed by Professor Aaron, these industries are high on the list for the type of governmental study and joint discussions proposed earlier in this chapter.

Types of Disputes and Procedures to Match

In recent decades, many strikes have been averted through the development of specialized procedures for settling particular types of disputes. Bitter conflicts over determining the right of a union to represent employees, often accompanied by rivalry between competing unions, were responsible for some of the most serious strikes and lockouts in our history. Such disputes are now routinely handled through N.L.R.B. election procedures. Strikes that shut down operations during the term of a collective-bargaining agreement, including wildcat stoppages, have largely yielded in private industry to the discipline of the grievance procedure and arbitration over the interpretation and application of the agreement. Jurisdictional strife is generally subject to private arbitration machinery developed by the parties to avoid a binding determination by the N.L.R.B. With the growth of these various procedures, differences over the terms of new agreements remain the major category of disputes in the private sector without effective alternatives to the strike.*

Just as particular types of work stoppages have required special machinery, so great care must be taken to tailor the treatment of strikes over the terms of agreements to the particular circumstances of the dispute involved. There are vast differences among contract disputes and no single procedure is likely to be most effective in resolving all of these controversies.

In disputes over the terms of an agreement, there are three elements that may shape the procedures, beyond ordinary mediation, to be used for settling differences.† The first involves the *substantive terms* in dispute—wages, pensions, technological displacement, crew size, incentive systems, job evaluation, promotion criteria, and the like. Some subjects are more complex than others; some issues treat all employees equally, while the essence of others is that they involve differential treatment among groups of employees. Some questions are easily compromised; others arise from differences of principle or involve matters that vitally affect the institutional security and well-being of one or both of the parties.

The second critical feature of a dispute has to do with the *relations between the particular labor and management organizations.* The character of the negotiation may differ enormously between the first contract and, say, the fifteenth to be negotiated by the parties. One or both parties may be afflicted with intense internal leadership rivalry; expectations among constituents may be very high with respect to the results of negotiations, thereby complicating agreement-making and ratification; the preceding contract period may have been most difficult to administer, with the consequence of a large backlog of unresolved grievances that shape attitudes in the negotiations.

A third feature, present in some disputes, is the determination of one side to change the *structure of bargaining.* Such disputes

---

* Work stoppages over the renegotiation of collective-bargaining agreements in recent years have accounted for approximately 40 percent of the numbers of stoppages and 80 percent of the man-days idle. The inclusion of disputes over initial agreements results in making the figures 58 percent of the number of stoppages and 87 percent of the man-days idle.

† While no scheme is ideal for all purposes, practitioners will readily recognize the types of disputes which follow. These do not, of course, constitute an exhaustive list. In fact, disputes seldom occur in the pure forms here cited, since actual cases typically involve mixtures.

involve a change in the design of collective bargaining negotiations themselves—the scope of employees to be covered by the agreement, the timing of expiration dates of various agreements, the selection of a leader among a group of unions—as much as disagreement over wages, hours, and working conditions. Two subtypes are especially significant: (a) Disputes involving relationships of two or more unions, typically craft unions, bargaining with the same management or an association of employers, and (b) controversies over the range of plants or companies or employees to be included, formally or informally, within the scope of the negotiations. In cases of rivalry among unions, managements are often seeking to expand the scope of bargaining with a group of craft unions. In coalition bargaining[32] it is typically the union which seeks to expand the effective coverage of the agreement and enlarge the scope of possible future strikes.

Where the impasse relates to the substantive terms of employment, much turns on the complexity of the issue in dispute. At one extreme, there are disputes involving a relatively simple question, such as a general wage increase, between parties with a stable and uncomplicated relationship in a generous economic environment. At the other extreme, there are disputes involving a large number of complex issues, such as crew size and technological displacement, between parties plagued with intense internal rivalries, and with a history of serious conflict. The suitability of procedures, beyond ordinary mediation, and the chances of settlement without resort to strike are clearly quite different as one moves between these extremes.

A straightforward dispute over wages and simple benefits, without serious complications in the relationship of the parties, is more amenable and suitable to arbitration than are disputes involving more complex issues. Issues such as incentive systems and crew size involve greater penetration into the operating relationship of the parties and require more technical knowledge of the plant, with the consequence that arbitration is less suitable. Experience suggests that arbitration of these more complex and intimate issues, save in very few cases, will prove acceptable only after a long strike or as a settlement to a single issue otherwise unresolved in a negotiation involving many issues.[33]

Although more complicated issues are less suitable for arbitration, they are often helped by outside study. Thus, disputes over severe technological change may call for an extensive and dispassionate investigation of the magnitude of the changes, the manpower utilization patterns and prospects, age distributions, costs of various measures, such as relocation allowances and early retirement plans, to afford protection from displacement. Such inquiries played a useful role in the settlement of East Coast and West Coast longshore negotiations in the 1960's. In similar fashion, disputes involving pensions and other fringes with complicated problems of cost computation are likely to prove more tractable if jointly chosen experts or subcommittees can prepare cost estimates of various levels of benefits to be made available to negotiators. Such cost estimates facilitated the early negotiations of the Armour agreement in the spring of 1967.

In disputes with intense internal problems arising from rivalries or grievance backlogs, an experienced and respected neutral with powers of fact-finding and recommendation may prove the most effective procedure. The formalities of open hearings are likely to be less significant than the quiet mediation of positions within each side, the establishment of priorities, and the improvement of relations to permit the negotiation of an agreement.

If the relationship of the parties is significantly influenced by the government, particularly as a purchaser, dispute-settling procedures may be facilitated by government participation. The President's Missile Sites Labor Commission, 1961–67, is illustrative. The procedures used to resolve labor-management disputes at missile and space sites had to be tied directly into the defense procurement agencies, since many of the stoppages had their roots in procurement policies and the decisions of procurement officers over the letting of contracts. Since some of the disputes were held to involve conflicts between the manufacturing and construction sectors, representatives from both were included in the tripartite machinery. In this fashion, the Commission was deliberately tailored to fit the character of the underlying disputes; other machinery, such as the emergency disputes procedures of the Taft-Hartley law, would have been neither suitable nor effective.

In some collective-bargaining relationships, there may be persistent difficulty in securing ratification of settlements negotiated at the bargaining table. Union members or employer-association members may reject the proposed agreement. Two steps may be helpful in these circumstances. The first involves conducting negotiations so as to keep employees (members) and supervisors better informed and to involve them more fully in the gathering of data, the formulation of proposals, and the approval or rejection of alternatives. The second step involves a review, in cooperation with the appropriate international union involved, of the procedures and rules governing ratification votes.

In industries with local bargaining, the procedures for dispute settlement might well involve more formal assistance and participation from national union officers and national association staff. The Industrial Relations Council in the electrical branch of the construction industry provides an illustration of well-developed procedures to settle local disputes over local agreements, which cannot otherwise be resolved by joint national-level determination. The government could encourage other industries to develop similar procedures.

Disputes arising from attempts to change the structure of bargaining no doubt involve the most difficult negotiations, with the most serious and longest work stoppages. A list of the disputes and stoppages that have attracted the greatest public attention in the private sector in the past six years would include the following cases where the structure of bargaining was a major issue.*

New York City newspapers	1962–63	116 days
East Coast longshore industry	1964–65	60 days
Cleveland construction industry	1965	39 days
Maritime industry, East and Gulf Coasts	1965	78 days
Pacific Shipbuilding Association, electricians	1966	5 months
New York plumbers	1966–67	6 months
Railroad shop crafts	1967	1 day
San Diego shipbuilding	1967–68	4 months
Copper industry	1967–68	8 months
East Coast longshore industry	1968–69	2 months

Disputes over bargaining structure often lead to prolonged work stoppages and substantial money settlements without ultimately resolving the underlying structural issue. Since adjustments in bargaining structure are not readily negotiated, higher money

---

* Although these disputes often involved wages, benefits, and even adjustments to technological change, the most stubborn issue concerned a desire of a union or a management to change wage differentials or wage leadership, or to alter the past bargaining arrangements.

settlements are simply a rough compromise to postpone the ultimate day of reckoning. As a result, disputes over bargaining structure can persist over many years, with an accommodation in bargaining arrangements being made bit by bit through negotiations that are often characterized by prolonged stoppages. The following record for the San Diego shipbuilding industry, 1953–67, involving several companies and six or eight unions, illustrates the tenacity of the problem of rivalry among certain craft unions, such as the Machinists, Carpenters, Painters, Electricians, and Ironworkers, and the internal instability in the leadership of some of them. Five long strikes took place in the course of seven negotiations against a background of deep conflicts over wage differentials among crafts and wage relationships with shipbuilding in other ports.

Initiation of agreement	Expiration of agreement	Length of strike*
12/1/52	11/30/53	37 days
12/1/53	6/30/55	No strike
7/1/55	6/30/56	60 days
7/1/56	6/30/58	No strike
8/1/58	6/30/61	49 days
8/17/61	6/30/64	50 days
8/19/64	6/30/67	121 days

* The length of the strikes shown in the above tabulation applies to negotiations that followed the expiration of the agreement.

There is no easy solution to problems of this sort. In some instances, where several rival unions are involved, progress can be made by encouraging a merger of the respective international unions. In the railroad, printing and construction industries there has recently been some movement in this direction, often as a result of the high costs of operations among small internationals that are declining in membership. In other cases, it has been possible to agree upon a joint negotiating committee comprising all the crafts, rather than continue separate craft negotiations. A specific voting formula among the crafts has been negotiated with management in some cases, providing, for example, that two thirds of the crafts may bind the group as a whole. In still other instances, the negotiating unions may establish in advance their ratification procedures as was done by the Pacific Coast Metal Trades District Council following the 1966 prolonged strike by electricians.°

If disputes involving union rivalry have been troublesome, efforts to force management to change the structure of bargaining have proven no less intractable. The problem of coalition bargaining is the best-known recent example. There have been significant tests of strength on this issue in General Electric, Union Carbide, the copper industry, and Campbell Soup, to name some of the more prominent cases. In an era of rapidly growing conglomerates it is understandable that the unions should be seriously concerned over the ability of companies to sustain a strike by continuing production in other plants not involved in the dispute and by maintaining profits through diversified operations in other divisions of the enterprise. The unions are also concerned that managements may establish patterns of wages and benefits in plants with the weakest organization. The unions have not found consolidated bargaining easy against determined managements, and a number of prolonged strikes have resulted. In Union Carbide, for example, eleven plants went on strike in 1966–67. The longest strike lasted 246 days; the shortest was 44 days. In five plants the strike exceeded 200 days. The strike apparently achieved very little toward coordinated bargaining. Negotiations in these circumstances have also been hindered by interunion conflicts. Local unions and internationals which have not cooperated previously have found it difficult to withdraw their own demands to secure a concession for a relatively unknown partner elsewhere.

The experience to date with coalition bargaining points up a sobering but realistic fact. Despite the emphasis of this chapter on relating procedures to the type of dispute, not every dispute can be resolved by the happy choice of one of these techniques. In some situations, economic conflict seems to produce a catharsis that no alternative can achieve. Moreover, there appear to be no procedures distinctly suitable for resolving disputes in which one side seeks to change the previous structure of bargaining. Neverthe-

---

° The constitution of the District Council provides that when an agreement has been negotiated it shall carry a recommendation from a majority of the Board of the District Council for submission to the membership of all the affiliated locals. Before a vote can be taken the proposed agreement shall be submitted to the presidents of the international unions of the affiliated locals. If the presidents disapprove, the agreement is rejected; otherwise it is submitted to the members of all the locals. A majority vote of the membership as a whole binds all the unions.[34]

less, the record of collective bargaining has been generally improving in the private sector. It can undoubtedly be improved still further by devoting more attention to developing appropriate private or public settlement procedures carefully tailored to the specific dispute in issue.

The Impact of Collective Bargaining on Productivity

FOR MORE than a century and a half, economists have debated the effects of "combinations of workmen," or collective bargaining, on the efficiency of business enterprises. The literature is replete with conflicting appraisals of the impact of work stoppages, work rules, regulation of machinery, apprenticeship, and training on employee efficiency and managerial decisions. To quote an early source:

> This liability and strong proclivity of associations of working-men to intermeddle and dictate concerning the methods and courses of industry must be accepted as a valid, practical argument from human nature against trade-unions. [Francis A. Walker, 1886][1]

Yet, another well-known economist writing in the same period reached a very different conclusion:

> Unions have been at once a chief product and a chief cause of this constant elevation of the standard of life: where that standard is high, unions have sprung up naturally; where unions have been strong, the standard of life has generally risen. [Alfred Marshall, 1893][2]

These opposing conclusions are still widely echoed in contemporary discussions of unions and collective bargaining:

Unions are also undermining the system by undercutting managerial authority by changing the rules of control which are necessary to survival. [Charles E. Lindblom, 1949][3]

Two important effects are ascribed by foreign observers to the distinctive characteristics of American industrial relations—greater pressure on management to increase the productivity of labor and greater interest by the employees of each enterprise in the prosperity of the concern. [Sumner H. Slichter, 1955][4]

Conflicting views about the actual impact of unions are paralleled by divergent value judgments about the unions' role. On the one hand, collective bargaining is depicted as stifling enterprising management, constricting its operations with onerous work rules, and engaging in immoral behavior often characterized as "featherbedding." On the other hand, collective bargaining is also defended as a way of ensuring a reasonable compromise between the interests of management in efficiency and those of workers in security and job protection.

The Protean Influence of Collective Bargaining

In order to grasp the impact of bargaining on efficiency, it is important to distinguish the many different ways by which unions can affect the operation of a company.

OBSTRUCTING NEW TECHNOLOGY

Labor unions have sometimes sought to prohibit the introduction of new machines and new processes. The window-glass workers, with a strong craft tradition, tried to prevent the use of glassmaking machines when they were introduced in about 1908. The union did not organize the new machine plants and did not accept the machine operators into membership. In time, however, the new processes displaced the old, since they were much more efficient, and the window-glass union had to be formally disbanded in 1928. In the cigar-manufacturing industry, the local unions and members opposed the introduction of new methods that involved specialization and new machines. The national leaders worked from 1912 to 1927 to revise the constitution and overturn these policies, while the percentage of union organization in the industry declined from approximately 45 percent to 20 percent.

Because obstruction so often proves suicidal to the union, labor leaders have normally chosen to accept new methods and share in the gains which these innovations make possible. As Professor Sumner H. Slichter wrote in 1941:

> No stronger statements on the unwisdom and futility of opposing labor-saving devices can be found anywhere than those made by the leaders of organized labor themselves. Through bitter experience they have learned that the policy of obstruction is likely to involve the union in hopeless fights from which it emerges defeated and weakened.[5]

Thus, Samuel Gompers, the president of the AFL from its founding in 1886 until his death in 1924, admonished that it is " . . . absolutely futile for workmen to protest against or go on strike against the introduction of a new machine, a new device or a new tool."[6] Such general statements, of course, have not precluded members of isolated locals, in a decentralized system of collective bargaining, from opposing changes which they regard as a threat. Indeed, union members, particularly older members with a short remaining working life and with little interest in moving or learning new skills, may even find rational grounds for sacrificing their union in order to prolong their jobs until retirement.

PAYING FOR MORE LABOR THAN MANAGEMENT CONSIDERS NECESSARY

Collective bargaining may affect productivity through rules that require an enterprise to employ and pay for more hours of labor than the management would freely choose to utilize. These rules may take many forms. For example, a contract may specify that management must give a certain number of hours' pay or a whole day's wage to every employee called to work, even though management does not find that much work for him to perform. Other contracts require the company to pay an entire week's pay to anyone asked to report on the first work day of the week. Most guarantees apply to a day, or a week, rather than to a full year, and such yearly guarantees as do exist typically apply to a fraction of the employer's total work force. There are some agreements, however, which guarantee pay to every employee for a stated minimum length of time each year, with exception only in cases of retirement, death, and quits.[7]

In the construction industry, management may be required to

pay for more labor than it would choose to employ as a consequence of collective-bargaining rules which specify that workers told to report to work shall be paid for a stipulated number of hours, even though work is impossible by virtue of weather conditions. Moreover, safety rules insisted upon by a union may prescribe procedures with more hours of work than management in its judgment considers necessary. In the establishment of norms for incentive pay, management, under collective bargaining, may regard the effort and pace of work set for a normal day's pay or the actual amount of work performed as below its industrial-engineering standards; as a consequence more labor per unit of output is paid for than management considers essential.

There are still other rules which affect the amount of labor that management may be required to hire and are designed to preserve employment opportunities for particular employees against others in the same enterprise or outside the firm. Formal or informal rules may fix the amount of work to be performed in a day, and these rules may fall below management's estimate of what is reasonable or appropriate. The agreement may seek to require the performance of unnecessary work, or the use of obsolete methods of production, or procedures which utilize the immediate employees rather than others that management might prefer.

The consequences of such rules will depend, in the first instance, upon whether a management can, by improved planning or further mechanization, use the otherwise superfluous labor productively. If not, the effect in a highly competitive industry will be in part to raise prices to consumers and in part to reduce the returns of owners. In a monopolistic industry, economic analysis indicates that added costs imposed by a guarantee are analogous to a lump-sum tax and may be expected to increase output, decrease prices, and reduce the returns to owners.* [8]

CREW SIZE AND RELATED RESTRICTIONS

Provisions in some collective-bargaining agreements prescribe the proportions in which labor services are combined with capital

---

* If the collective-bargaining agreement provides a wage and employment guarantee within a certain range of output, then labor costs become fixed costs, and incremental labor costs within the range of output are zero. In these circumstances, the enterprise may be expected to expand output which reduces the returns to owners.

equipment. Rules of this kind specify the number of men on a particular type of printing press, the size of the crew in the cockpit of an airplane, the number of workers in a raising gang of structural-iron workers, the size of a longshore gang to unload a ship, or a crew to tend a furnace in a steel mill. The rules may be stated in terms of machines per man as in the case of the tending of looms in a weaving mill or the number of heaters per operating engineer. These restrictions may specify the total amount of labor hired—as discussed above—but they also have the essential characteristic of regulating the proportion of labor to capital, a condition not present in the cases previously discussed. This difference can be important. If collective bargaining merely specifies a limited employment guarantee or requires that unnecessary work be done, management is usually free to substitute machines and methods for relatively more expensive labor. But where collective bargaining fixes the crew sizes or proportions, such substitution is normally more difficult, unless management can make such substantial changes in the design of the capital equipment that the restrictions become obsolete.

The economic consequences of these rules stipulating crew size depend on how far they depart from the proportions in which management would use labor and capital in the absence of the rule. If the rule conforms to management choice, as such rules often do when they are first adopted, there will be little impact on efficiency. But when the rule forces management to hire more men than it would otherwise choose, the wage bill will normally be increased and resources will be used less productively than management would prefer.

WAGE DIFFERENTIALS AND INNOVATION

A large number of rules in collective bargaining, such as various types of wage differentials and premiums, influence the rate at which technological changes are introduced and the production methods which management chooses to employ. A wage premium for an operator of a more complex piece of construction equipment or a pilot of a larger and faster jet airplane may have entirely benign justifications: to compensate for higher skills and greater responsibility or to secure for employees part of the productivity gains associated with the new equipment. Yet premium rates for new equipment are sometimes high enough to suggest that a major objective is to slow or to control the rate of introduction of the new technology—particularly when higher skills or greater responsibilities are not involved.[9] Premium rates at double time for roller or spray painting in some localities, for instance, have had this character. In other cases, where motives of this kind were not present, high wages have had the opposite effect by encouraging management to reduce its costs through the development and use of labor-saving equipment. For example, the increase in wages in California agriculture and in retail trade have no doubt been one factor stimulating the development and introduction of such innovations as harvesting machinery and retail self-service.

TRAINING AND MOTIVATION

The quality of the labor force is decisive in relation to productivity in modern industry. Quality encompasses training, versatility and adaptability, the morale and attitudes toward supervision and management, and the skill, responsibility, and pace of performance. Modern management is not interested in merely having warm bodies on the job in a plant or office; it seeks the full involvement and loyalty of its employees in the destiny of the enterprise. All managers know that output can be increased appreciably if employees can somehow be more deeply motivated and committed to the fortunes of the enterprise. Managers everywhere have experimented with a variety of plans to entice greater effort and dedication—incentives, profit sharing, stock ownership, suggestion plans, workers' councils, and participation in management. Such schemes are designed not only to improve output and productivity but also to reduce turnover, accidents, and absenteeism, and to improve the quality of work. In this sense, the personnel function in the modern enterprise is substantially an investment to improve the quality of the work force.

In an enterprise with union representation, the quality of the labor force is inevitably influenced by collective-bargaining policies and labor-management relationships. In industrial plants the design and administration of seniority will affect the qualifications of employees for promotion to higher jobs; it may also affect their morale and the range of jobs that they are equipped to perform within the plant. In craft-oriented industries, the jointly administered apprenticeship and journeyman-retraining programs are basic factors shaping the quality of the labor force. In casual industries, where workers shift frequently from one employer to another, the quality of the work force is directly influenced by rules and procedures governing the recruitment and assignment of employees. Morale is often affected by the handling of grievances and the diffusion of tensions that are associated with the collective-bargaining relationship. The orderly introduction of technical and organizational changes on a day-to-day basis may be facilitated by the bargaining agreement and by the union's efforts to explain the new technology and the reasons for its adoption.

There is no rigorous way to measure the independent effect of collective bargaining on the quality of the work force in American industry. The effects are clearly not the same for all managements and unions. But there is reason to believe that the net effect of collective bargaining is to increase productivity through a higher quality of the labor force. In casual industries the skill levels of organized workers are generally conceded to be above those of the unorganized workers. Managers in unorganized plants have come increasingly to adopt many of the forms of collective bargaining— seniority, job classifications and wage scales, grievance procedures, and even arbitration by neutral "outsiders" of discharge cases. These developments are not merely designed to keep the union away; they reflect a belief in the usefulness of these procedures in motivating employees. In organized and unorganized companies, the operation of collective bargaining has compelled managements to pay much greater attention to the problems of the work force. A great deal of this induced management behavior improves the quality of the work force.

LABOR-MANAGEMENT COOPERATION

In a few collective-bargaining relationships, the management and the union have worked together to reduce costs and increase productivity. A number of these cases of labor-management cooperation have emerged out of a crisis for survival. The threat of a plant shutdown or a loss of jobs has led the parties to join in trying to improve the competitive position of the enterprise. In other instances, an unusual personality has been responsible for the development of a program to improve efficiency, or lower costs, or improve quality of output. On other occasions, some dramatic event such as a war or a strike has led to the creation of labor-management committees to improve industrial performance.[10]

These efforts have taken various forms. In the needle trades, for example, unions have played a key role in developing and enforcing industrial engineering procedures. In many collective-bargaining relationships, safety programs have been a focus of common interest, ordinarily with beneficial consequences with regard to frequency and severity of accidents as well as insurance rates. Unions have agreed with managements in a number of places to assist in correcting specific instances of inefficiency that have gotten badly out of hand—a piece-rate system with perverse effects on efficiency, a breakdown in discipline, or an increase in scrap or waste, and a decline in quality. In the main, the consequences of collective bargaining on productivity are indirect; there are comparatively few deliberate joint programs to increase efficiency or lower costs. Except for special circumstances, such as just outlined, management ordinarily carries the responsibility for taking steps to raise productivity.

QUALITY OF MANAGEMENT

One of the major economic effects of collective bargaining has been its impact on the internal policy making and organization of management. According to a major study sponsored by the Brookings Institution: "The challenge that unions presented to management has, if viewed broadly, created superior and better balanced management, even though some exceptions must be recognized."[11] Managements are compelled under collective bargaining to weigh explicitly industrial-relations considerations against other interests of the enterprise. Thus, the stabilization of employment and improved labor relations have often become objectives of management. In larger firms, collective bargaining has helped also to encourage longer-run planning with respect to product line, plant locations, employee-benefit policies and strategies in negotiations. These policies are designed to achieve greater control over costs and productivity.

One of the significant indications of the consequences of collective bargaining is that well-managed enterprises, after a period of initial internal readjustment, appear to have had little difficulty in maintaining high standards of efficiency and management performance under collective bargaining. The experience of

General Motors or General Electric is illustrative. In bargaining collectively over the past generation, the managements of these corporations have given every indication of being able to preserve high standards of management and increasing productivity. Conversely, when one studies the cases in which work rules under collective bargaining have been most onerous, one repeatedly discovers managements of inferior quality. There are exceptions, of course, but the correlation is high enough to underscore the critical importance of high-caliber management to productivity.

"Featherbedding" in Perspective

The public's view of the impact of unions on efficiency is dominated by the imagery of "featherbedding." This view is a distorted one, however, for the preceding discussion makes clear that through collective bargaining, unions affect productivity in a wide variety of ways, sometimes in a restrictive manner but often in a fashion that increases efficiency. It is this diversity in experience that makes it possible for Professor Lindblom to have voiced such dour opinions of labor's effect on efficiency, while Professor Slichter concluded that unions, on balance, had caused productivity to improve.

The exaggerated emphasis on featherbedding is only one of several misconceptions that arise with respect to this term. Many people speak of unions as though they had a unique propensity to block labor-saving devices and oppose efficient work practices. Yet Professor Benjamin Aaron reminds us how widespread the fear of change and displacement has been throughout history:

> In 1579 the hapless inventor of a weaving machine was ordered strangled by the Council of Danzig, on the ground that his device would reduce many workers to beggary. John Fitch, inventor of the steamboat, recorded in his memoirs that when in 1787 he appealed for financial support, he was treated 'more like a slave than a freeman' and was 'obliged to suffer . . . indignities from my landlord and be henpecked by the women.' When John Kay invented the flying shuttle in 1733 he was forced to leave England; workers invaded Hargreaves' home in 1768 and destroyed his spinning jennies; and Crompton, who invented the spinning mule in 1799, was forced into hiding as a reward for his work.[12]

Frederick Winslow Taylor, the father of scientific management, emphasized at the turn of the century the extensive and systematic tendency of groups of unorganized workers to withhold effort:

> The greater part of the *systematic soldiering*, however, is done by the men with the deliberate object of keeping their employers ignorant of how fast work can be done.

> So universal is soldiering for this purpose, that hardly a competent workman can be found in a large establishment, whether he works by the day or on piece work, contract work or under any of the ordinary systems of compensating labor, who does not devote a considerable part of his time to studying just how slowly he can work and still convince his employer that he is going at a good pace.[13]

In the past generation, Stanley Mathewson and Donald Roy have shown that individual workers, without union help, will regularly restrict output and resist change.[14] Indeed, the influence of the informal work group on output and performance has been a subject of intensive study by social scientists over the past several decades.[15] And in the reactions of many businessmen toward lowering tariffs, the hostility of many doctors toward group practice, and the opposition of lawyers toward insurance schemes for compensating automobile injuries without litigation, one sees how pervasive is the tendency to resist new ways that would abolish old privileges.

Many individuals also condemn instinctively every rule that forces the employer to hire more labor than he would choose if left to his own devices. Yet this view is hard to sustain. Rules that regulate crew size may actually reflect the wishes of the men for greater safety or easier work loads. Contract provisions restricting split shifts for bus operators embody a desire on the part of employees to work for one continuous period rather than split the day into early morning and late afternoon segments to conform with peak traffic loads. Regulations of this kind reflect understandable differences between management's concern with costs and efficiency and the worker's interest in his convenience, employment opportunities, pace of work and effort, job security, and health or safety. In setting work rules, collective bargaining strikes a balance

between these contending interests in much the same way as it
does in fixing the length of the work week or the amount of vacation to be granted. Each individual rule or practice needs to be
examined in detail if a judgment on its equity and reasonableness
is to be expressed.

There is also some tendency to overstate the effects of restrictive work practices. Consider a rule which requires management to
hire several employees it regards as unnecessary. The competitive
position of an individual enterprise may be adversely affected and
employment opportunities reduced if the rule is substantially out
of line with the practice among competitive firms. If the rule is
applied to the whole industry, the likely result will be an excess of
labor and a higher wage bill that will fall in varying proportions on
the companies and their customers. Yet the amount of the added
wage cost is easily overstated. A restrictive practice is often
accompanied by a lower hourly wage rate than the union might
otherwise secure. If the practice were removed, the employer
would probably have to pay a higher wage to the remaining
employees, both because the industry would have a greater capacity to pay and because, typically, collective bargaining would
provide some *quid pro quo* for abandoning the disputed rule.

It is also erroneous to assume automatically that all of the
extra workers constitute waste in a social sense. Such a conclusion
is warranted only if the excess workers could be readily absorbed
in other jobs requiring comparable skills. But this assumption may
not hold, either because the specialized skills of the employees are
not in demand by other employers, or because the workers live in
an isolated location, or because their age or the prevalence of
widespread unemployment makes it hard to find new jobs. At best,
these workers may have to accept employment at wages materially
below their existing wages, employment that will not require the
specialized skills they have developed over many years. The flight
engineers in the airlines[16] and the locomotive firemen in the
railroads fought tenaciously to perpetuate negotiated rules guaranteeing their jobs in part because they would not readily find new
positions without a grave reduction in skills, prestige and income.

With all of these qualifications, the fact remains that a number of work rules do provide for more labor than management
requires with some resulting burden on the public and the economy. And even though such rules may have the virtue of protecting the employee from the hardships of change, they generally

tend to do so in a manner that is much less acceptable from a social point of view than such measures as retraining, severance pay, relocation and early retirement.

The Historical Course of Work Rules

A survey of uneconomic work practices suggests a standard life cycle for such rules. "Make-work rules do not usually begin as attempts by unions to force employers to hire an excessive number of workers."[17] In the normal case the employer imposes a rule or agrees with the union on a rule which seems to make perfect sense under the conditions then prevailing. In the course of time, however, minor changes in working conditions or technology gradually diminish the appropriateness of the rule. The job may be simplified or made safer or more automatic, or the men working on the job may discover short cuts, so management comes to disregard the rule. In the early stages, however, management may not feel that it is worth a serious conflict to press for a change in the rule. As time passes, the gap between current conditions and those envisaged at the outset of the rule grow steadily wider. The more out-of-date the rule becomes, the larger the number of men who would be displaced if the rule were abandoned. Hence, there is growing opposition on the part of the members and the union to making a change. At the same time, as the inefficiency grows more apparent, management regards the perpetuation of the rule as a mounting threat to its competitive position. In short, the prospects rise for a major confrontation between the parties.

An apt illustration of this cycle is the case of the fireman on the diesel engine—the most renowned dispute over work rules in the United States during the past generation.[18] The fireman was essential to the operation of the steam engine; in particular, he was responsible for shoveling coal and keeping up the steam pressure. But these functions are not performed on the diesel engine. Diesels were first used in yard service in the 1920's without firemen. In 1937, the National Diesel Agreement was made between the Brotherhood of Locomotive Firemen and Enginemen (B.L.F.E.) and the carriers. This national rule provided that firemen would be assigned to all diesel locomotives but not to electric trains or small locomotives (less than 90,000 pounds on the driving wheels). At the time of the agreement, however, less than half of one percent of all locomotives were diesel. The negotiators for the carriers were uncertain as to future developments, but their committee of five representatives believed that electrification was more likely than the diesel to replace steam engines. After World War II, however, the great advantages of the diesel engine led to the rapid replacement of steam; by the early 1960's, the change-over was virtually complete. In 1937, there were 218 diesel engines and 43,624 steam engines; in 1959, there were 28,163 diesels but only 754 steam locomotives. In the wake of this transformation, management found itself with a highly uneconomic work rule.

In 1959, the carriers proposed rule changes to eliminate the fireman from the cab in freight and yard service.* This was not the first proposal to change the 1937 National Diesel Agreement. The firemen and certain maintenance crafts had sought in the early 1950's to add a man to each diesel unit comprising the locomotive. The carriers had sought to eliminate the fireman in notices of proposed changes in rules filed in 1956. Neither of these efforts had produced a major change in the rule.

During the 1959 negotiations, the B.L.F.E. and other unions contended that firemen " . . . perform functions essential to the safe and efficient operations of railroads."† Safety was the major contention. Union negotiators also stressed the lockout function in service, the relief which the firemen afforded the engineer and the role of the firemen as a source for future engineers. The carriers, in rebuttal, argued that the firemen contributed little, if anything, to safety and that the firemen's duties vanished with the elimination of steam power. The carriers sought the right to determine for themselves whether firemen should be assigned to engine crews.

It is not necessary here to review the sequence of events that followed the 1959 proposals to change the 1937 diesel rule nor to recount the public campaign of the carriers against featherbedding. The eventual resolution of the dispute took place after a

---

* In passenger service, the carriers did not seek to eliminate the firemen. The explanation lies in the fact that the freight and yard locomotives carry in the cab an engineer and head brakeman while the passenger engines have no head brakeman.

† Over the several decades after 1937, the quality of signal systems on the railroads had been improved, methods of detecting hot boxes had been perfected, and the mechanical performance of diesel engines and the procedures for maintenance had been made substantially more reliable. At the same time, the speed and length of trains had increased substantially. It was conceded by the carriers that there were some runs on which they would continue to use firemen in the absence of the national rule.

long list of public interventions, including recommendations by a tripartite Presidential commission, recommendations of Emergency Board No. 154, intensive mediation by the Secretary of Labor, Congressional legislation preventing a nationwide strike and requiring arbitration,[19] and the decision of a three-man arbitration board. The decision was followed by extended litigation and interpretations. In brief, the decision changed the old rule to eliminate the need for a fireman except on 10 percent of the runs and to provide, as earlier boards had recommended, for varying degrees of protection to incumbent employees according to length of service. As a result of the decision, almost 20,000 firemen out of 45,000 in road and yard service elected other railroad positions or accepted severance pay and left the industry. The cycle which started in 1937 with the National Diesel Agreement had finally run its course, although the union still seeks to reinstitute the old rule.

Not all uneconomic work practices lead to the same dramatic confrontation as occurred in the case of the firemen. In this regard, it is instructive to observe that boilermakers, who had been used in the repair of steam engines, were also displaced by the diesel, but this drastic change, involving even a larger number of men, was made without serious conflict. Unlike the firemen, boilermakers had a skill that was transferable, at higher wages, to other industries, such as construction and boiler shops. Since the boilermakers union is engaged in many industries, the elimination of railroad jobs posed no threat to the survival of the union as it did in the case of the firemen, with a membership confined to the railroad industry. Moreover, the boilermakers did not confront a serious rival in the railroad industry as did the firemen in the form of the engineers union, with its overlapping jurisdiction and membership. Economic conditions also made it difficult for the firemen to compromise on the work rules. The railroad industry was experiencing sharply declining employment in an economy which suffered from recurring unemployment in the 1950's and early 1960's. In the absence of a national public policy that either maintained favorable employment conditions or took vigorous steps to facilitate orderly adjustment to changes of this kind, the reaction of the union and its leaders was hardly surprising.

The West Coast Longshoremen's agreement of October 1960 illustrates another way by which fundamental changes can be made in work rules without a strike.[20] A number of troublesome practices had been initiated in the period 1935–40 and strengthened over the years. For example, there were rules requiring double handling of cargo and methods of loading that resulted in "witnesses" in the crew who merely watched the unloading in the hold aboard ship. These practices inflated costs and endangered the economic future of the industry and employment opportunities. After an intensive study and extended negotiations, the parties agreed to create a fund to provide a substantial degree of additional security and retirement benefits to employees; in exchange, the employers won a substantial degree of freedom for productivity improvements. As a result, output per man-hour was an estimated 40 percent higher in 1964 than in 1960, and most of the increase stemmed from the relaxation of restrictive rules.[21]

If uneconomic work rules continue for extended periods, managements may have ways of getting rid of the practices without confronting the union in a prolonged strike. In some instances, significant technological changes may permit the replacement of the equipment or process giving rise to the dispute. Much automated equipment has had this effect on issues involving crew size in mass-production industries. In a multi-plant company, management may also expand facilities at a new location or transfer production to a new plant, rather than battle the union over modernizing an old location. Thus, the Pittsburgh Plate Glass Company placed a new float process in a Cumberland, Maryland, plant instead of building it at Creighton, Pennsylvania, when its employees there failed to make suitable changes in rules or accept a day-rate method of pay instead of old incentives which masked idle time under conditions of continuing technological change. In some industries, competition among methods and materials is so extensive and entry so easy that high-cost procedures are quickly eroded. Although many factors were operative, the relative displacement of brick and masonry in construction work in the past decade and the growth of poured-concrete and curtain-wall construction were influenced by these factors. It is noteworthy that this relative decline has induced significant response among masonry contractors and their unions, thus causing the latter to pay considerable attention to new ways to achieve efficiency and to a pioneering program of winter work. These responses to uneconomic work practices do not usually emerge overnight; they are long-term. But typically, so is the development of a serious work-rule problem.

The Long-Term Decline of Uneconomic
Work Practices

The course of the firemen-diesel controversy invites the question of whether restrictive or uneconomic work rules are dying out in this country or whether new practices are being created faster than they are being eliminated. The information does not exist for a definitive response, but the available evidence suggests that there has been a perceptible decline in such practices and rules. The trend has not always been in this direction. In World War II, the emphasis on production on a cost-plus basis resulted in a substantial increase in inefficient work practices in American industry. After the War, labor relations became more sophisticated and professional, while increasing competition both at home and abroad forced management to pay careful attention to costs. Thus, the Brookings study of the late 1950's reported a drop in the extent and severity of such practices compared to 1947 or 1948.[22] It also concluded, "It is a fact of greatest importance in the industrial-relations history of the United States . . . that in most plants direct action by unions and appeasement by management are dying out."[23]

In the past decade these tendencies have continued. Although some important problems remain, substantial changes in work practices have been made in railroads, airlines, and longshoring on the West Coast and, to some extent, on the East and Gulf coasts. The rapid pace of technological change and mechanization has facilitated the elimination of other inefficient practices, since new capital equipment often provides the occasion to review and to alter previous rules. In construction, the ease of entry of new enterprises and the very keen competition among materials and processes have been decisive factors, although serious problems remain in some localities over the manning of heaters, the use of some tools and the assignment of work operations among some crafts and job classifications. The new industries such as oil, chemicals and electronics are often highly automated and do not present traditional manning issues. Modern industrial managers have become more alert to the necessity of meeting these issues at an early stage before they have been allowed to expand. These trends are offset to some extent by experience in sectors outside manufacturing. Practices such as limitations on the mix of occupations and restrictions on the work that may be performed outside the store may be growing in the service or trade[24] sectors, although competition provides some genuine checks. In government service, inefficient practices may prove even more severe, since public management has little experience with unions, and market pressures for greater efficiency are far less intense than in the private sector. On balance, however, the net result to date appears to be a gradual decline in the extent of uneconomic work practices. Future trends are not easy to assess. If prolonged high employment is maintained, the abundance of jobs may reduce the workers' concern over unemployment and may thereby reduce the pressure for make-work devices. On the other hand, labor scarcities and high production may also reduce the capacity of managers to risk controversy by resisting restrictive practices and eliminating inefficiencies at an early stage.

Toward the Further Elimination of Uneconomic Practices

COLLECTIVE BARGAINING

Although restrictive practices have been on the wane, it is worth considering how they may be further diminished. Since work rules are sanctioned by collective bargaining, the quest can be viewed initially as a problem in negotiations. Above all, management must be wary of work rules that may grow restrictive when circumstances change. And when such rules are already in the contract, company officials must be alert to bargain them away before they grow so severe as to involve a heavy displacement of employees. In so doing, every management should follow what is already becoming the accepted practice by taking the initiative in proposing changes in rules and practices which would provide greater efficiency or managerial flexibility. As Wayne T. Brooks, an experienced management negotiator in the steel industry, has said:

> Changes, corrections, new forms, new procedures, the timing of their introduction, the exchange of "something of value" for the surrender of an old privilege, or for taking on a new obliga-

tion or the gain of a new privilege for relief from an old obligation, are the very essence of collective bargaining.[25]

Negotiating away an entrenched practice is not easy. The workers immediately affected can be expected to object strongly. They may enjoy a high degree of leisure on the job, a light work load, a high wage premium, or a great deal of security, at least relative to other workers in the plant or industry. They have a "good thing," to which they have been acclimated over the years. Under such conditions, employees are not likely to volunteer a change desired by management. Nevertheless, a detailed and dispassionate study arranged through collective bargaining may provide a factual basis for negotiations, especially if it demonstrates the long-run effect of restrictive practices on the health of the industry in question.

The failure of negotiations may lead to a prolonged work stoppage in which the management's determination to change an entrenched and significantly adverse practice is pitted against the willingness of employees affected to make a trade. The long strike has been an important means of changing work rules in a number of industries, such as flat glass and the airlines. The prolonged stoppage helps to change the views of the employees affected, or to show that the cost of retaining the practice is not worth the continuation of conflict compared to negotiable alternatives, including various protections. In some industries, managements may believe that they cannot afford prolonged stoppages particularly in times of high employment; the possibilities of ameliorating work practices are appreciably reduced in these circumstances.

LEGISLATION

In view of the widespread antipathy toward featherbedding, it is not surprising that public officials have tried at times to wipe out uneconomic practices through the use of legal sanctions.[26] In November 1939, Assistant Attorney General Thurman Arnold announced a policy for prosecuting unions for restraints of trade under the antitrust statutes. He sought to preclude "unreasonable restraints designed to prevent the use of cheaper material, improved equipment, or more efficient methods" and "to compel the hiring of useless and unnecessary labor." The effect of this program would have been to ask the courts to pass judgment on the merits

of collective-bargaining agreements and practices; the courts would
have had to determine the efficient size of a press crew, the reasonableness of a sling load in longshoring, or the proper number of
men in an ironworkers' crew erecting various materials. In *United
States v. Hutcheson*,[27] however, the Supreme Court in effect made
the type of conduct complained of by the Justice Department
immune from prosecution under the Sherman Act. A number of
pending cases in the courts against work practices were then abandoned by the government.

A fresh legal assault was launched with the passage of the
Taft-Hartley Act of 1947. Section 8 (b) (6) of the Act declared it
to be an unfair labor practice for a labor organization " . . . to
cause or attempt to cause an employer to pay or deliver or agree to
pay or deliver any money or other thing of value, in the nature of an
exaction, for services which are not performed or not to be
performed." Senator Taft commented on the development of this
provision by the conference committee:

> The Senate conferees, while not approving the featherbedding
> practices, felt that it was impractical to give a board or a court
> the power to say that so many men are all right, and so many
> men are too many. It would require a practical application of
> the law by the courts in hundreds of different industries, and
> a determination of facts which it seemed to me would be al-
> most impossible. . . . However, we did accept one provision
> which makes it an unlawful labor practice for a union to accept
> money for people who do not work.[28]

The language of the statute is ambiguous; on its face it would not
appear to prohibit the setting of bogus copy in newspapers, the
stationing of firemen on the diesel engine, or the glazier resetting
glass on a construction site, or any of the work rules popularly discussed. It is hard to imagine any restrictive practice that could not
be cast in such a form as to comply with the statute. Thus, it is not
surprising that, when the Supreme Court was eventually asked to
interpret the provision, it " . . . reduced Section 8 (b) (6) to a
nullity, if the provision was ever in fact anything more."[29] At present, there is no recourse to the N.L.R.B. or the courts for a management which regards particular work practices as uneconomical or
for unions and employees who believe that work standards are excessive or unsafe. It is public policy to leave such questions to
collective bargaining, except when such an issue—like the firemen-
diesel impasse—leads to an emergency dispute.

FURTHER STEPS BY GOVERNMENT BODIES

Government officials might well stimulate or initiate detailed factual reports in sectors with serious work-practice problems. There is often widespread public misunderstanding of these questions, and it is often difficult in the middle of contract negotiations to assemble and evaluate the complex factors of technological change, manning, training, safety, variability in work operations, pace of work, practice, and other considerations which typically enter into the merits of such an issue. It is true that on occasion parties have conducted their own surveys or have asked the government to do so, as in the case of the East Coast Longshoremen's manning study and the Presidential Railroad Labor Commission established following agreement of the parties. But there are other sectors with no less significant problems—for example, maritime and certain branches of construction*—where detailed and dispassionate studies, even without recommendations, would make a contribution to the capacity of the parties to deal with these issues.

In the next chapter a suggestion is made for a continuing body such as the Cabinet Committee on Price Stability, announced in President Johnson's Economic Report of February 1968, or the National Board for Prices and Incomes, in England, to inquire and make recommendations in sectors of the economy with structural price and cost problems. Such a body might well be authorized to conduct detailed studies, preferably in cooperation with the parties, in industries which appear to have developed work practices which to a significant degree adversely influence productivity, costs and prices.

Of equal importance is the steady maintenance of high-employment conditions that are conducive to technological change. Refusal to change an uneconomic practice typically involves the fear of being thrown out of work. Full employment

---

* The National Commission on Urban Problems, under the chairmanship of Senator Paul H. Douglas, reported in 1968 as follows with respect to restrictive practices in construction:

To cut costs and to prevent capricious interruptions of production, the commission also strongly recommends that the project agreements for public and publicly subsidized housing be negotiated between the unions, the contractors, and the government, both national and local. These agreements should seek to guarantee a greater volume of employment and in return remove some of the obstacles to increased production and reduced costs. . . . The commission does not urge punitive legislative action or government compulsion to gain the abandonment of restrictive building practices.[30]

alone, however, may not suffice, especially in cases involving
employees such as firemen or flight engineers, who are unlikely to
find jobs at comparable pay in another industry. For such men, the
loss of a job threatens to produce a severe drop in income. To
counteract this problem, government and management must try
to provide such opportunities as training programs, early retirement, outright purchase of job rights, relocation allowances and
better job information to induce change and to reduce the impact
of displacement. At present, government programs of this kind lag
behind developments in some of the other advanced industrial
countries. So long as this situation persists, the nation will have to
pay an added price in labor strife and restrictive practices.

Collective Bargaining and Inflation

FEW SUBJECTS create more acrimony in popular discussions than the assignment of responsibility for inflation. Each interest group puts the blame on someone else. A financial columnist declares, "Everyone with an ounce of brains must know that the main inflationary force is the ability of labor unions to enforce wage increases in excess of gains in productivity." The chairman of the board of United States Steel Corporation says there is no longer any mystery about the true causes of inflation: "When government spends more than it gets and when labor gets more than it gives, that empty feeling in your pocket is inflation."[1] The Executive Council of the AFL–CIO understandably points the finger elsewhere: "Inflation in America is clearly and directly profit inflation. Profits have skyrocketed—moving up, far out of line with wages and salaries. . . . Wage and salary earners have not received a fair and adequate share of the benefits of the economy's forward advance."[2] Professor Milton Friedman, University of Chicago monetary economist, places the blame at still another door:

> The plain fact is that inflation is made in Washington, in that stately and impressive Grecian temple on Constitution Avenue that houses the Board of Governors of the Federal Reserve System. Prices have been rising at faster and faster rates because William McChesney Martin and the other distinguished men who govern the system have decreed that they shall.[3]

These conflicting views arise in an economy of continuing price and wage increases in the twentieth century. Price stability

has not been the normal state of the economy.* The first law of
money wages appears to be that they go up. Since 1900, consumer
prices increased almost threefold; total compensation per hour in
manufacturing (wages plus fringe benefits) increased almost
twenty times.† These rates of increase are 2 percent a year,
cumulatively, for consumer prices and 4.5 percent a year, cumulatively, for compensation per hour. The more rapid increase in
compensation reflects an improvement in labor productivity that
has permitted a fivefold rise in real compensation per hour over
the period at a cumulative rate of approximately 2.5 percent per
year.

The history of wages and prices since 1900 includes periods of
prosperity and recession; it reflects periods when unions were
weak as well as the recent decades of much more substantial
organization. But past trends cannot provide a wholly reliable
guide to the future. New forces are at work, and their overall
effect cannot be foretold with any confidence. On the one hand,
greater upward pressure on wages may be expected from tighter
labor markets, the pursuit of high and stable employment, expensive public programs to mitigate racial and urban problems, and
expanding labor organizations in new sectors, such as public
employment. On the other hand, contrary pressures may emanate
from higher rates of labor productivity resulting from greater expenditures on research, development and training, from increased
restraints on prices that arise from the competition of imports

---

* The index of consumer prices may not make entirely adequate allowance
for improvements in quality, and to this extent exaggerate the extent of consumer price increase. For some purposes, wholesale prices or G.N.P. deflators
are more appropriate measures of price changes.
† The movement in consumer prices and total compensation per hour of work
in manufacturing for selected dates since 1900 follows:[4]

Date	Consumer prices (1957–59 figure equals 100)	Total compensation per hour of work in manufacturing
1900	29.0	$ .15
1914	35.0	.22
1920	69.8	.553
1933	45.1	.441
1940	48.8	.67
1948	83.8	1.41
1953	93.2	1.94
1957	98.0	2.27
1961	104.2	2.59
1964	108.1	2.80
1967	116.3	3.11

and new products, and from improvements in the application of monetary and fiscal restraints.

Public discussions typically presume that it is self-evident that inflation is evil and to be avoided at all costs. But the reasons are too seldom articulated. The case against inflation emphasizes the inequity of transferring income through higher prices from pensioners, E-bond holders and others without power to raise their incomes, to recipients of profits, dividends, and those in a position to extract an increase in their compensation. This is why inflation has often been called "the cruelest tax." Inflation may also be so rapid that it dislocates business operations by creating uncertainties over the future course of wages, prices, and production and by fomenting bitter struggles over wages and prices in an attempt to transfer the burdens of inflation to others. Inflation can capriciously increase the money value of some assets such as land and equities, and decrease the real value of others such as savings accounts and life-insurance policies. Finally, if domestic prices and wages rise faster than those in other countries, the costs of exports will tend to increase, together with the demand for imports, adversely affecting the balance of payments and the international position of a currency.

On the other hand, a degree of inflation may be tolerable in order to avoid still less acceptable alternatives. For example, inflation may facilitate economic readjustment among industries and regions, a readjustment that could otherwise be made only through reductions in wages and prices that would be bitterly resisted. Mild inflation may also promote business expansion and help to maintain high employment. As the country discovered in the late fifties and early sixties, an effort to maintain complete price stability may only be realized at a heavy cost in unemployment, which in turn bears cruelly upon minority groups, low-skilled workers, part-time workers, women, and older employees. Moreover, the society has learned in some measure to live with a moderate inflation by providing periodic increases in social-security benefits, by raising interest rates on savings accounts in periods of inflation, and by other measures to offset in part the inequities of inflation. With the help of progressive income taxes, higher money incomes from higher wages and prices result in larger governmental revenues, which in recent years have led to a larger allocation of resources to the public sector.

All in all, the consequences of inflation depend very much upon its rate. A price level rising at 3.5 to 4 percent or more per year may be cause for serious concern. Yet a rate of 1.5 to 2 percent may well be tolerable, for experience in the United States and Western Europe over the past decade does not support the homily sometimes expressed that creeping inflation will inevitably turn into galloping inflation.[5] The view that even moderate inflation should be avoided because it inequitably transfers income must be tempered by a recognition that complete stability seems to be associated with unemployment rates that produce other inequities even more difficult to accommodate.

How Collective Bargaining Affects Inflation

Any effort to isolate the independent impact of collective-bargaining institutions on inflationary pressures is difficult since the economy is so interdependent; a great many other institutions and forces play upon wages and prices, and the latter, in turn, have their own effects on the performance of the economy. It is not possible, as in experimental sciences, to eliminate collective bargaining from an economy and then observe the course of wages and prices. It is necessary to thread one's way through diverse sets of indirect evidence in order to reach any judgment at all on the subject.

There is a natural tendency for labor leaders and managements alike to exaggerate the independent influence of collective bargaining on wage setting. Labor leaders are understandably proud of their negotiating skills; they naturally seek to enhance their position and strengthen their union by claiming great victories in behalf of the rank and file. Managements, in turn, often believe, after enduring the strike threats of a militant union, that lower levels of compensation would have resulted in the absence of bargaining. But appearances may deceive. In the fable of Cantillon, the cock flapped its wings and crowed each morning as the sun emerged over the horizon, and eventually persuaded himself that he alone was responsible for the sunrise. There is a good deal in the ritual, chest-thumping and crowing in collective-bargaining negotiations that is reminiscent of Cantillon's fable.

The comparative increases in hourly earnings among different industries in the years 1960–67 should make one pause before dispensing easy generalizations about the consequences of collective bargaining on wages. The largely unorganized industries of agriculture, services and retail trade showed much larger increases than the more highly organized manufacturing sector. The increases in agriculture and retail trade were 37 and 32 percent respectively, as compared to 25 percent in manufacturing. Although wage gains in unionized sectors may have had some indirect influence, the increases among the unorganized seem to have resulted much more from the tightening of labor markets independent of collective bargaining.

A first step toward a considered judgment on the effects of collective bargaining on inflation consists in identifying the major ways by which unions can influence the rate of wage and price increases.

MARKET POWER

The economic power of labor organizations is cited by certain economists as a major factor contributing to "excessive" wage increases and inflation. According to this argument, prices are often "pushed up" by rising costs caused by wage increases forced upon the economy by powerful unions issuing strike threats and aided by government policies.[6] In industries with rapid rates of increase in productivity, or labor costs that are a small percentage of sales, or monopolistic markets for their products, including markets sheltered by tariffs from foreign competition, strong unions can push up wages faster than average increases in productivity, particularly in times of high employment. Such increases lead to wage raises and price changes in still other sectors. Cost-push inflation is the result. From this point of view, full employment and stable prices cannot be had at the same time without a change in the present methods of collective bargaining.

This analysis has been disputed by economists no less conservative than those who have advanced it.[7] These critics insist that the American economy is largely competitive in its product markets, so when prices of a product are pushed up, competitive factors work to stimulate the entry of new, unorganized firms, reduce sales, create unemployment, reduce profits, and put restraining pressures on wages. While these competitive forces may not operate instantaneously, over a number of years they have a powerful effect. The history of bituminous coal in the 1950's and basic steel in the 1960's can be cited as examples of the eventual restraining effects of competition—from nonunion firms, from competitive products and industries, and from overseas.

To the charge that union power has contributed significantly to inflation, spokesmen for labor organizations respond by insisting that inflation is the result of business efforts to make excessive profits. Initially, prices rise, or fail to fall, in the face of declining costs. Only then do unions seek to cut into the larger corporate profits in order to benefit their members. In support of this argument, union spokesmen stress that after a prolonged period of stability in wholesale prices of manufactured goods and unit labor costs from 1958 to 1964, it was manufactured wholesale prices that rose first in mid-1964. Unit labor costs did not increase until eighteen months later, in 1966. This significant lag in unit labor costs is cited as strong evidence that it was business price policy rather than union wage power that destroyed the stability achieved at the cost of high unemployment in the early part of the period 1958–64 and started the acceleration in prices after 1964.

Since the issue of the impact of collective bargaining on inflation can be argued several different ways in the abstract, the critical need is for facts and measurement. Ideally, one would like to compare existing wage levels and differentials with those that would prevail in the absence of labor unions. A number of ingenious attempts have been made to resolve this question. After summarizing all the relevant statistical evidence, including twelve separate industry studies, Professor H. G. Lewis concluded that the average wage of union labor exceeded the average nonunion wage by 25 percent or more in the mid-thirties under depression conditions, by less than 5 percent in the period of rapid inflation, 1945–49, and by 10 to 15 percent in the late 1950's.[8]

Professor Lewis' findings may surprise many readers, since they suggest that union influence on wages was substantial during depression conditions and very slight in the period of greatest inflation. The reasons for this will come to light momentarily. In the end, however, neither Lewis' findings nor those of similar studies are likely to be very meaningful, for it is unrealistic to try to make comparisons with a world free of unions. Had there been no labor organizations, there might have been government wage fixing or some alternative device to protect employees, and no one can determine what effects these policies would have had on wages. It is also impossible to take a nonunion enterprise or economy and introduce the complex institutions of collective bargaining, leaving everything else the same, and then measure the independent effects of unionization. Widespread changes typically take place in management and supervision, internal communications, the quality and morale of the work force, systems of promotion and wage payment, and the responses of management through product lines, location and production methods. Collective bargaining also affects the surrounding product and labor markets. When all the factors that affect wages are so interdependent, the separate influence of unionization is not readily identified.[9] As a result, although one can find particular market situations and methods in which unions can push up wages and prices —notably in industries that face little or no competition from non-union firms and where entry is expensive or difficult—a reliable measurement of the overall effect of collective bargaining on inflation still eludes the economist's grasp.

BLOCKING WAGE DECREASES

Unions have had an effect on the secular rise of prices by contributing to the virtual disappearance of wage decreases. In the nineteenth century, long-term declines took place in money wages and prices in addition to short-run cuts in both during depression years. Thus, increases in money wages and prices in some periods were offset to some degree by decreases at other times. In the past generation, however, money wages and the price level have moved only upward. The last hints of wage cuts on any scale were associated with the recession of 1938. The virtual elimination of decreases in wage and price levels must be counted as a factor contributing to inflation over the long term.

Collective bargaining, of course, is only one of many influences which have placed a floor under wages and prices. Government policies to provide high levels of effective demand and employment have also played a role by eliminating periods of recession that give rise, particularly in highly competitive industries, to cut-throat competition in prices and wages. The intellectual climate has also changed, for modern economic analysis, rooted in the *General Theory* of John Maynard Keynes, rejects general wage reductions as an efficacious means to cure recessions and restore prosperity. The monetary authorities, reflecting public policies, have become more permissive, adjusting to wage and price levels. Sir John R. Hicks has noted:

> But the world we now live in is one in which the monetary system has become relatively elastic, so that it can accommodate itself to changes in wages, rather than the other way about. Instead of actual wages having to adjust themselves to an equilibrium level, monetary policy adjusts the equilibrium level of money wages so as to make it conform to the actual level. It is hardly an exaggeration to say that instead of being on a Gold Standard, we are on a Labor Standard.[10]

Collective bargaining has also played some role in this transformation in the pattern of wage and price movements. One lesson of the Great Depression in England and the United States was that attempts to reduce wages through collective bargaining tended to result in prolonged industrial strife and conflict. In an economy with widespread and decentralized collective bargaining, where unions possess a measure of political influence, economic policies which seek adjustments through extensive reductions in wages and prices are likely to prove highly disruptive; other measures involving expanding demand have been substituted, and these tend to be somewhat more inflationary over the long run.

INITIAL IMPACT OF UNIONIZATION

The introduction of collective bargaining into an industry or sector is likely to be associated with an initial rise in compensation. A successful organizing campaign calls for substantial wage increases for the newly organized. A union typically confronts management with a new operational situation that may require considerable adjustment, and these circumstances are likely to produce large wage and benefit increases in negotiations. Workers at many newly organized establishments, private or public, are relatively low paid; this very state of affairs may have helped to induce organization. Some managements faced with possible organization of employees grant increases hoping to forestall a union; when the tactic fails and further increases are negotiated by the union, the relative wages of the enterprise have been twice increased. The recent experience of voluntary hospitals and sectors of public employment illustrates these tendencies. After an initial phase, however, the relative wages of an organized sector or industry are likely to be influenced largely by factors other than the union, such as the profitability of the enterprise, the expansion in employment, skill composition, the tightness of the particular markets from which labor is recruited, and wage movements in other related industries and occupations that serve as yardsticks due to economic and industrial-relations considerations.

Other factors being equal, then, periods in which unions spread rapidly into previously unorganized enterprises and sectors will be periods in which the effects of collective bargaining on compensation may be substantial. The argument is not that collective bargaining has no effect whatsoever upon relative wages after an initial period; the wage-setting forces enumerated above operate through and are shaped by collective-bargaining institutions. Nevertheless, as Senator Paul H. Douglas concluded, after studying the role of trade unions in securing wage advances in the period from the 1890's to the 1920's, "The evidence seems to indicate that when labor organization becomes effective, it yields very appreciable results in its early stages, but that thereafter the rate of gain enjoyed by its members tends to slow down to a speed which does not appreciably exceed that of nonunion industries."[11]

THE EFFECT OF LONG-TERM AGREEMENTS

In collective-bargaining negotiation in the United States, wages are typically set for a specified period: one year, two years, three years, or more. Anticipation of the future course of living costs, profits, wage movements and other factors play an explicit role in the negotiation when a collective-bargaining agreement fixes wages for a definite period of time. In a nonunion situation—without the direct influence of union settlements—wages are not likely to be influenced so directly by such expectations, since pay rates can be adjusted at any time to meet changing conditions.

Long-term agreements can exert either an inflationary or a stabilizing influence on wages.[12] In a year of rapidly rising prices and wages, the size of collective-bargaining settlements, and the course of wages for the next several years, may turn out to be larger than short-term wage increases under nonunion conditions. Thus, the three-year basic steel and railroad negotiations in 1956, at a time of high profits and favorable outlook, led to larger wage increases in 1957 and 1958 under recession conditions than would have taken place with one-year agreements or under nonunion conditions. (It is partly for this reason that the estimates of H. G. Lewis show an increased effect of unions on wages in the late 1950's.) On the other hand, it is clear that longer-term agreements may appreciably restrain wage responses, as compared with non-union conditions, when inflationary pressures develop unexpectedly during the term of collective-bargaining agreements as they did at the outset of the Korean conflict in mid-1950.*

While it may not be possible to demonstrate the net effect of long-term contracts on inflationary processes, it is clear that such agreements affect the transmission of inflationary pressures and the sensitivity of the economy at high employment. Under some circumstances, depending on the timing of negotiations, these pressures may be magnified, as compared with nonunion conditions; under other circumstances collective bargaining may restrain or at least postpone the consequences of rising prices, high profits and tight labor markets on wage levels. On balance, the long-term agreement may be a stabilizing force, since it implies a long-term perspective in which short-term advantages to either side are not fully exploited. The longer-term agreement also facilitates longer-term planning and permits both parties freedom from annual negotiations to work more intensively on common problems affecting the relationship and productivity.

BARGAINING STRUCTURES

Collective bargaining may also contribute to inflationary pressures where union institutional rivalry is associated with enterprises that have a considerable degree of product-market power and where employers are not well organized to resist union pressures. In newspaper, construction, and maritime industries, employers bargain with several craft unions. Under these circumstances, wage

---

* It should be recognized, of course, that most long-term agreements provide for some adjustments in the wage schedule during the life of the agreement. The automobile company agreements with the U.A.W. provide for a cost-of-living adjustment. Inflationary periods bring forth demands by other unions to insert such provisions. In recent years, a number of agreements have included, at the initiative of management, a ceiling on the extent of wage increases under cost-of-living adjustments. The automobile agreements included such a provision for the first time following the 1967 negotiations. Most collective-bargaining agreements of several years' duration include specified step increases rather than a cost-of-living escalator. The automobile agreements provide for both the cost-of-living adjustment and an annual specified wage increase during the term of the agreement.

increases negotiated by one union may become a target to be exceeded by a second or third union, which in turn may require adjustment in the first settlement, and so on, in a cycle of more expensive negotiations.[13] When negotiations of this kind take place in an environment of tight labor markets, ample profits, and a climate of labor-management relations in which workers feel they have a past score to settle, then very large settlements may emerge, often after a long strike which, in itself, may raise the settlement price. These pathological bargaining structures are themselves a major independent factor contributing to wage inflation. Large wage increases gained in such circumstances are also contagious, affecting other negotiations in the same localities or in contiguous industries.

There is another way, often associated with bargaining structures, in which the institutions of collective bargaining may contribute independently to inflationary pressures. Occupational differentials between skilled and unskilled occupations, or among skilled classifications, may be unduly narrowed, in percentage terms, through many years of collective bargaining. The across-the-board cents-per-hour increases that were given over a period of thirty years in nonoperating railroad classifications afford a good illustration. Eventually, the compression in differentials leads to a revolt by some skilled workers and some unions. The problem cannot normally be resolved by reducing or holding down the wages of the unskilled. Very often, exceptional wage increases must be offered to the disgruntled groups in order to achieve a settlement. In this way, the bargaining policies of the past themselves contribute to very large settlements in the present.

INFLUENCE THROUGH GOVERNMENT POLICIES

Labor organizations have made major efforts to influence a wide variety of government programs and policies. The labor movement has been in the forefront of those advocating public policies to reduce unemployment and to maintain stable high employment. In recent years, it has urged even lower levels of unemployment than the four percent "interim goal" of the government, and it has pressed the government to achieve this objective more rapidly. The AFL–CIO has also advocated a multibillion-dollar-a-year program of public expenditures as its answer to the urban crisis.[14] Like other interested groups, the labor movement has sought to influence governmental decisions related to fiscal and monetary policy and to expenditures on social and welfare programs. The effects of these influences and pressures on government expenditures and inflation are not readily isolated. But in the main, union policies seem to have been heavily weighted in the direction of deficit spending and full employment, which in turn have created inflationary tendencies in the economy.

In a number of industries public policies advocated by both parties to collective bargaining may have some direct effects on wages and prices. Illustrations are provided by the subsidy policies and restrictions on use of foreign ships in maritime and shipbuilding industries; the advocacy of tariffs and import quotas, as most recently urged by both parties in the basic steel industry; and the prevailing-wage legislation for government purchases of goods and construction. Political power is used in such cases to insulate markets from competition. The appropriateness of such measures from the perspective of the public interest needs to be judged in each instance.

To identify the major mechanisms through which the institutions of collective bargaining affect the rate of wage and price increase leaves unresolved the actual role of collective bargaining in inflation. In approaching this subject, it is important to be clear about just what question is being asked, for several different inquiries are often jumbled together with a consequent loss of clarity.

To some, the relevant question is whether wages and prices would be materially higher in a world without unions. Most economists would express the judgment that collective bargaining has added only modestly to inflation in America since the end of World War II; a much larger role would be ascribed to monetary and fiscal policy and to the war-related expenditures of the government. But it is difficult to prove these conclusions. As previously mentioned, no one can know what the economy would be like without unions, let alone estimate the wage levels that would prevail. The situation is further complicated by the fact that there are many types of inflation, and the role of collective bargaining is not the same in each. In 1945–48, rising prices were chiefly the result of wartime shortages of goods and money balances. The 1950–51 price rises were substantially influenced by the rapid changes of expectations, particularly as they affected primary markets, associated with the Chinese invasion in the Korean War. Some of the price and wage increases in 1956–59, in the face of substantial unemployment, may be linked to cost-push arising from three-year collective bargaining agreements made in 1956 and 1957 on the mistaken assumption that business activity and profits would remain at a high level. As for the inflationary period after 1965, economists have stressed the importance of sharp increases in expenditures for capital goods and defense products resulting from the Vietnam war and the somewhat fortuitous rise in food prices that occurred in mid-1965. The chairman of the Council of Economic Advisers has said, "Nobody would deny that our price problems in 1965–66 and 1967–68 constituted demand inflation."[15] Another member of the Council emphasized that, "The speed of expansion—rather than the level of economic activity— was primarily responsible for the burst of inflation after mid-1965."[16] Amid this shifting array of factors, the independent role of collective bargaining is very hard to isolate.

Other critics seem more interested in asking whether union leaders can be blamed for rising prices. This inquiry is also blunted by the inability to measure the independent contribution of collective bargaining to inflation. In addition, one cannot gauge the responsibility of labor leaders without making value judgments of the most intractable kind. Should elected labor leaders be expected to stand up more resolutely against the demands of their constituents for higher wages, especially in a nation where unions are required by law to follow democratic procedures? How long would they last as elected leaders? When employers raise their prices following a negotiated wage increase, is the price rise attributable to the demands of the union, the unwillingness of management to accept any cut in its profit margin, or the rising cost of living caused by the monetary and fiscal policies of the government? These issues are more often matters of opinion than fact, and it is most unlikely that they will be answered to the satisfaction of everyone involved.

A more useful question to ask is whether there are feasible steps that private parties or the government can take with respect to collective bargaining, to make an appreciable contribution to checking inflation. Three possibilities come to mind.

First, to the extent that unions in some markets succeed in making added wage gains because their employers are insulated from outside competition, the government can conceivably exert a restraining influence by stimulating imports or taking other steps to bring corrective pressures to bear upon the markets involved.

Second, to the extent that wage levels in certain markets are pushed up by structural weaknesses, such as interunion rivalries or divisions within employer groups, measures can perhaps be devised to correct the weaknesses involved.

Third, it is possible that many employers and unions would find it to their mutual long-term advantage to exercise restraint over wages and prices. Granted, neither businessmen nor labor leaders will withstand the pressure to raise wages and prices if pay rates, costs, and prices are going up throughout the economy around them. But if some way could be found to impose a general restraint upon wages and prices, most of the parties involved might be better off. If so, it is worth asking whether some form of government intervention might provide the general inhibition that is needed to check the inflationary process.

It may well be that none of these steps could play a major role, by themselves, in moderating inflation. As previously mentioned, the consensus of informed observers is that collective bargaining is only a modest factor among many others that contribute to rising prices. Nevertheless, it is probable that an effective policy of stability will have to include many separate efforts on many different fronts if inflation is to be curbed without the cost of heavy unemployment. As a result, in exploring the many facets of a program for price stability, it is altogether appropriate to investigate the possible public and private measures that may restrain the inflationary propensities implicit in collective bargaining.

Incomes Policies

The American community, in common with other advanced industrial countries, seeks a variety of goals other than price stability, including economic growth, high employment, free collective bargaining, democratic unions, labor peace, the avoidance of government wage and price controls, overseas military objectives and economic aid, preservation of the price of gold and a satisfactory balance of payments. It would be pleasant indeed if the nation could achieve all these goals at the same time. But experience shows that some objectives must be sacrificed, at least in part, in order to come closer to achieving others. Thus, inflationary pressures might well be reduced if the government were prepared to accept some combination of more unemployment, more labor-management strife, unions which were less responsive to the rank-and-file members, less rapid economic growth, fewer foreign commitments, and less attachment to the present international monetary system. There is no single "correct" combination of these objectives; the ranking of goals is a matter ultimately to be decided through the political processes and values of the society.*

Not every advance toward one of these goals involves a sacrifice of other objectives. It is possible that certain adjustments and institutional changes may allow a closer accommodation of these diverse objectives. Thus, a major task of public policy is to determine what measures can be taken by private parties, government, or the two together, to reduce the inflationary costs of high employment without adversely affecting labor-management peace, democratic control of unions, economic growth and international economic relations. Such a question invites a searching examination to determine what can be done with the structure and process of bargaining, with labor markets, with education and training, and with policies affecting productivity, in order to mitigate inflation without inducing serious, unwanted side effects. Perhaps the effects of such efforts will be small. Nevertheless, even small diminutions in the rate of inflation can have large effects over a period of years; a price rise of 1.5 percent a year instead of 2.5 percent results in a cumulative increase of only 81 percent instead of 169 percent over a working life of forty years.

In the postwar period, many countries have fashioned some

---

* The public discussion of these issues would benefit from increased knowledge of the approximate costs of various trade-offs or priorities. For example, how much of a rise in unemployment would it take starting at a 4 percent unemployment rate to reduce wage and price increases by one percentage point a year? (It is estimated that an unemployment rate of 5 percent and an operating rate of 80 percent of industrial capacity are necessary to achieve industrial price stability which would be associated with 1 percent or 1.5 percent rate of increase in consumer prices as a consequence of the upward trend in service prices.) Or, how much additional labor-management strife (beyond the level of 40.5 million man-days lost in work stoppages in 1967) would be necessary to cut one percent off the rate of wage and salary increases? Or, how large a reduction in tariff barriers and how great an increase in domestic competition would it take to exercise a more significant restraint on prices and wages? Or, in more general terms, what changes in internal union government and what government intervention in the collective-bargaining process would be needed to achieve an appreciable reduction in the size of settlements under conditions of high employment?

form of "incomes policy" to achieve the ends just described. The major purpose of incomes policy has been to try to solve a universal riddle of modern economics: how to avoid inflation at full employment. Incomes policies have attempted to introduce into wage, nonwage income and price decisions criteria which would produce greater price stability without sacrificing employment objectives.[17] The experience of the United States and other advanced European nations may offer at least a preliminary view of the strengths and limitatons of government programs to accommodate these diverse economic goals.

THE EXPERIENCE IN THE UNITED STATES

Ever since the Employment Act of 1946, and the establishment of the Council of Economic Advisers as an agency of the federal government, there has been a lively and continuing debate over the policies appropriate to achieve a proper balance between price stability and maximum employment.[18] While great advances have been made during these two decades in the analysis of economic growth, the perfection of statistical measures, and even the application of fiscal and monetary policies, there has been little consensus on the appropriate and effective measures to achieve price stability or the deference to be accorded this goal. Inflation continues to be the unwanted stepchild of prosperity.[19]

From the early years of its existence, the Council urged that the average gains in productivity for the nation as a whole should provide the norm for increases in the average money-wage level. This view was commonly advanced by economists in discussions of the immediate postwar inflation.* From time to time in the 1950's the Council reiterated the principle and President Eisen-

---

* The following statements are illustrative:
    "The net result is a picture in which money wage and salary rates rise with average productivity and in which some prices rise and others fall, with the general level of prices about constant."—John T. Dunlop, 1947.[20]
    "There is wide support for the view that the general level of wage rates should as a matter of public policy rise in accordance with gains in productivity with a relatively constant price level."—John T. Dunlop, 1948.[21]
    "The soundest general formula, once wages, prices and profits are in a workable relationship, is for money wages to increase with productivity trends in the whole economy."—*Economic Report of the President,* 1950.[22]
    "But improvements in compensation rates must, on the average, remain within the limits of general productivity gains if reasonable stability of prices is to be achieved and maintained. Furthermore, price reductions warranted by especially rapid productivity gains must be a normal and frequent feature of the economy."—*Economic Report of the President,* 1960.[23]

hower, like President Truman before him, appealed publicly to business and labor for responsible price and wage decisions on this basis. When the Council in the Kennedy administration announced the "guideposts" in January 1962, it followed the same theme; but it also initiated new policies to restrain the rise of wages and prices while stimulating an economic expansion to reduce the high unemployment level of 6.7 percent in 1961.

The guideposts were formulated in the following propositions, one for wages and the other for prices:

> The general guide for noninflationary wage behavior is that the rate of increase in wage rates (including fringe benefits) in each industry be equal to the trend rate of overall productivity increase. General acceptance of this guide would maintain stability of labor cost per unit or output for the economy as a whole—though not, of course, for individual industries.

> The general guide for noninflationary price behavior calls for price reduction if the industry's rate of productivity increase exceeds the overall rate—for this would mean declining unit labor costs; it calls for an appropriate increase in price if the opposite relationship prevails; and it calls for stable prices if the two rates of productivity increase are equal.[24]

The Council also specified certain exceptions to these general principles. Higher wage increases would be appropriate where wage rates were inadequate to attract sufficient labor or where wages were exceptionally low. Subsequently, the Council recognized that an exception should also be made where changes in work rules created large gains in productivity and the human costs of adjustment required special compensation.[25] Smaller wage increases than the general productivity guidepost were also considered appropriate in a declining industry that could not provide jobs for its entire work force, with full employment in the economy generally, and in industries where wages were already exceptionally high because of union power.*

The guideposts were designed to prevent sectors with strong market power (union or management) from transforming expansionary measures into wage and price increases while the economy as a whole operated with considerable slack. They were advanced

---

* The Council also specified certain exceptions to the general price standard, primarily related to the need for capital to flow into or out of a sector or where costs other than labor costs had changed or where excessive market power alone had produced profits higher than elsewhere for comparable risks.

at a time of increasing concern over foreign competition and the balance of payments, particularly after the enactment of the Trade Expansion Act. They were formulated also to lessen the fears of conservative elements—in Congress, in the administration, and in the business community—who were not enamored of the New Economics or its tax-cut prescriptions to raise the economy to full employment. These forces had to be assuaged, for unwarranted fears of inflation could otherwise have created a major stumbling block for expansionist policies.[26]

In several respects, the guidepost era represented a new departure in public policy. For the first time, the guidepost for wages was translated into a specific number, 3.2 percent a year.* The Council also made extensive efforts to use the guideposts to increase public understanding of inflationary processes. As Walter Heller saw it, "In essence they pit the power of public opinion and Presidential persuasion against the market power of strong unions and strong businesses."[28] But the most significant reason that the guideposts represented a new style of public policy was the willingness of President Kennedy, and later President Johnson, to draw upon the considerable influence and powers of the Presidency to affect, and even to rescind, private wage and price decisions.

The high drama of the 1962 steel price confrontation saw a mobilization of executive power to compel the basic steel industry to rescind price increases it had announced. Arising at the early stages of the guideposts, this show of power succeeded for a time in making large and prominent business enterprises more sensitive about general price decisions. A measure of the Council's involvement in pricing is furnished in its report of January 1967, indicating that during the preceding year it had been involved in " . . . perhaps fifty product lines for which price increases were either imminent or had been announced by one or more firms." The Council was no less concerned with collective-bargaining negotiations. While no major public confrontations took place, there were repeated efforts to influence the size of wage settlements through both labor and management negotiators, and in some cases through government personnel involved in dispute settlement.

---

* The theory of the guideposts required a measure of the trend increase in productivity. The adoption of a five-year moving average as the "official" method of measurement was to create considerable difficulty in 1966 when the moving average method would have yielded 3.6 percent and the Council retained 3.2 percent as its measure of trend productivity.[27]

The guideposts flourished only briefly. The rank-and-file rejection of a wage agreement announced over national TV by President Johnson on July 28, 1966, in the five airlines-machinist cases brought to a close this period of intensive use of Presidential influence to apply the guideposts to particular wage and price decisions. The policies were not abandoned entirely, for the Administration remained faithful to the underlying analysis and objectives and continued to try to moderate private decisions. But, with living costs rising by 3 to 4 percent a year, with unemployment rates dipping below 4 percent and profits remaining high, it was no longer equitable or practicable to enunciate a wage guidepost of 3.2 percent a year. Union members could not be asked to take a cut in real wages when the gross national product continued to increase and other groups in the economy were enjoying continued prosperity.

The breakdown of the guideposts in 1966–67 is basically attributable to the inflationary pressures engendered by a sharp expansion in producer-goods expenditures and military outlays for the Vietnam war in an economy close to full employment. But there were other difficulties too. As full employment approached, tight labor markets and high demand stimulated prices and wages even in the most competitive markets. In fact, wages increased far more rapidly in unorganized sectors, such as agriculture, service trades, retail and wholesale trade, than they did in manufacturing. The Council was not equipped to deal with these sectors. The number of price and wage decisions that would have required Council review and possible intervention grew too large. The Council's adventures in the wage-and-price field also reduced its acceptability and sapped its energy in the area of general economic policy. Presidential influence, being a scarce resource, could not be used effectively in many cases. There were no sanctions against parties who openly flaunted the guideposts. The *ad hoc* executive intervention in wage and price decisions also raised questions of due process, since the Council intervened without the usual administrative safeguards. To many observers, the judgment that a wage or price increase contravened the public interest was a serious conclusion that warranted an impartial investigation, with full opportunity for the presentation of contesting views.

The use of mediation and fact finding in key labor disputes was also complicated by the guideposts, for serious disputes arose between the Council, with its interest in stability, and other agencies charged with the responsibility of maintaining labor-management peace. Tensions of this sort were inevitable, but they were further aggravated by the fact that the guideposts had not been developed with the cooperation and approval of labor and management representatives. Hence, unions and businessmen were quick to oppose the government's policies. Without such support, the guideposts could not be counted on as an effective policy tool in 1965 and 1966, when they were most needed. Strikes were even deliberately called against the guideposts in order to show militancy and win support of the rank and file, a tactic which illustrates the importance of obtaining advance commitment to stabilization policies from those to whom the policies are to be applied.

There were further difficulties of analysis and application. At high employment and near-capacity operations, actual productivity may advance at a rate well below the long-term average, with the result that guideposts based on normal productivity rates may become inflationary. The exceptions to the general guideposts are hard to specify in particular cases and each party sees his situation as an exception. It is also difficult, if not impossible, to secure price decreases in tight markets where productivity has increased more than the average. Decreases have even been resisted successfully in the airline industry, where there have been very rapid increases in productivity and where the government through the C.A.B. has the actual authority to set fares.

Experts differ as to whether the guideposts succeeded in dampening price and wage increases even temporarily. But it is clear that the new policies could not provide any lasting protection against the forces of inflation. As a result, it is worth looking briefly at the experience of other countries to determine whether they have been able to do any better.

TYPES OF INCOMES POLICY IN WESTERN EUROPE

The experience of the Netherlands reveals that a crisis of major proportions can provide support for a stringent incomes policy. The Dutch led the way in attempting to guide price and wage developments within the framework of an overall plan for the economy.[29] The enormous economic dislocations suffered in wartime, the need to hold down real incomes to facilitate reconstruction, the fact that nearly half of Dutch productivity is intended for exports, and the mutual confidence between unions and managements engendered in the wartime underground joined together to permit strict controls over wages and prices in the first decade after World War II.[30] In the Foundation of Labor, managements and unions together reviewed particular wage decisions as well as general wage policy. In the Social and Economic Council they met with public representatives selected by the government to discuss broad economic policies, including wage policy. A Board of Government Mediators was empowered to act as a wage-control body, and the Ministry of Economic Affairs was responsible for the conduct of price policy. The amount of wage and price increases for each year was related to detailed forecasts supplied by the Central Planning Bureau.

The Dutch system ran into serious difficulties, particularly after 1963, in an economy with very high demand and very tight labor markets.[31] Wages and prices rose substantially; compensation to employees increased by 15 percent in 1964 alone. Behind these developments lay a growing disenchantment among the unions. Labor leaders complained that wages were below those of neighboring countries, and wages were said to be restrained more than other incomes. In tight labor markets some employers paid "black wages" in excess of the official rates. The economic integration of the Dutch economy into the Common Market further limited the extent to which an independent incomes policy was feasible. In retrospect, the Dutch experience shows how incomes policies can disintegrate as the country draws away from the crisis conditions that led to the initial acceptance of controls. And once the controls are relaxed, wages and prices may rise very rapidly to offset the previous restraints.

The British experience suggests that if an economic crisis permits resort, for a time, to incomes policies, the critical question is whether these periods of restraint can be used to make some of the structural reforms on which enduring prosperity will depend. The British involvement in incomes policies has been closely related to efforts to overcome serious balance-of-payments difficulties. The continuing interest in incomes policies in recent years by both Conservative and Labour governments reflects a belief that some form of incomes policy is essential to break out of the cycle of boom and recession that has so often marked the postwar years.

On at least four occasions the attempt has been made to halt the rise in money incomes.[32] The recovery program of Sir Stafford Cripps and the Labour government involved a form of wage freeze, or wage pause, in the years 1948–49. In 1956, agreement was sought, but not achieved, to maintain price and wage levels. In 1961–62 a Conservative government sought, without success, to convert a temporary wage pause into a durable incomes policy. The Labour government that came to power in 1964 secured agreement from labor and management on "A First Step Towards an Income Policy." This Joint Statement of December 22, 1964, included an agreement from both groups that they would accept, as a major objective of national policy, " . . . to raise productivity and efficiency so that real national output can increase, and to keep increases in wages, salaries and other forms of income in line with this increase." The National Board of Prices and Incomes was created to investigate the facts and make recommendations on wages and prices in particular cases referred by the government. Its careful reports have had an impact on pay structures, distribution costs and work practices affecting productivity. In July 1966, the government reacted to an even more severe crisis by announcing a standstill on money incomes and prices until the end of the year to be followed by a further six-month period of severe restraint. In 1967–68, wage increases were to be allowed only under specified conditions, primarily if they could be justified as contributing to increased productivity.

The objective of the recent British policy has been to induce the parties to agree upon cost-savings through "productivity bargaining" as a condition for wage increases.[33] As a result, while the incomes policy appears to have had only relatively little effect on slowing down the rate of wage and price increase, Allan Flanders, of Nuffield College, Oxford, has persuasively argued that its most significant contribution " . . . may be expressed in the simple statement that restraint has been used to induce reform."[34] There is urgent need for both managements and unions to pay more attention to the workplace in order to eliminate inefficient work practices and related plant-level work stoppages. The British experiment may prove a significant instrument of overdue structural change in the nation's industrial relations system.[35]

Sweden boasts no official or formal incomes policy. According to the Finance Ministry, "The Swedish government has little confidence in the usefulness of a direct incomes policy as an instrument of price stabilization, irrespective of whether this policy be executed by exhortation or by a special machinery set up for the purpose."[36] To some extent, however, the attitude of the Swedish government is made possible by the existence of strong labor and management organizations that are prepared to fashion their own stabilization policies.

Labor and management in Sweden are organized into central federations with a long record of peaceful agreement-making on many questions. In consultation with the government, they negotiate a central agreement providing for general wage increases which constitute a framework for further negotiations at the industry level. In recent years, the increases provided for in the central agreement have accounted for less than half of the rise in hourly earnings, since additional increases (popularly referred to as "wage drift") result from negotiations in individual plants and with individual departments and workers. The government has been reluctant to intervene directly in wage and price decisions, because the record of labor-management peace is outstanding, and it is feared that an official incomes policy would tend to weaken private negotiations and the freedom of collective bargaining. Labor and management would not feel the same responsibility for their actions if the government intervened in the bargaining process.

Instead of advancing an official incomes policy, the Swedish government has tried to find a better accommodation between price stability and full employment by creating an active labor-market policy to reduce the manpower bottlenecks that arise in periods of full employment. This view is particularly associated with Gosta Rehn, although it was partly anticipated by both Bertil Ohlin and the Myrdal Commission of 1944. Rehn wished to push restrictive fiscal policy hard enough to exert some depressive pressures in the economy, but he proposed an active labor-market policy to prevent these pressures from causing substantial unemployment.[37] General economic policy in Sweden, including the stimulation of growth and technological change, is designed consciously to create problems of manpower adjustment and then to assign to national manpower policy the task of solving such problems by selective means.[38] Among the manpower measures introduced are extensive retraining programs that enroll one percent of the labor force (the equivalent of 750,000 workers in the United States if retraining were practiced on the same scale), measures to locate industry in areas of labor surplus, special financial payments to induce workers to move from one area to another, and a system of investment reserve funds which encourages business to make added outlays in periods of slack demand.[39]

If one compares the actual course of prices and hourly earnings in these three countries with those in the United States over the course of the post-war years, the rate of increase in America is significantly lower.* This record does not necessarily suggest, however, that public policy has been more successful in this country. Against the backdrop of Western Europe, the price of greater stability in the United States has been a higher rate of unemployment, a lower rate of economic growth (except for Great Britain), and a higher level of industrial strife, though the latter phenomenon has many other causes.

A review of the experience of those countries that have been seeking to restrain inflation at high employment levels by direct intervention in wage and price decisions suggests the following: Strong policies of direct controls over wages and prices have been associated with crises. There is a political temptation at such times to use incomes policies to restrain inflation instead of imposing stern enough fiscal and monetary measures. Yet, no Western country has had sustained success with incomes policies; their contribution has been much more modest. The imposition of direct limitations may be effective in slowing down the rates of increase for a short period, but the easing or removal of controls often appears to yield larger subsequent increases. Sustained high employment creates strong pressures; when held back, they ultimately lead to a wage-and-price explosion. Labor and management become restive, and regulations become unenforceable. On the other hand, incomes policies have provided a much-needed dampening of inflationary pressure for short periods following an economic crisis. Some forms of incomes policies and machinery to implement these policies may also facilitate structural adjustments in the economy. Price and wage increases may be made contingent upon manpower and reform measures designed to reduce the degree of inflation at continuing high employment. If manpower policies become more fully developed, they may even serve in lieu of incomes policies, as in

---

* In the period 1958–67, the Consumer Price Index increased 40 percent in the Netherlands, 39 percent in Sweden, 29 percent in the United Kingdom, compared to 15 percent in the United States. The comparative unemployment rates, adjusted to United States definitions for 1965, were 1.2 percent in Sweden, 2.2 percent in the United Kingdom, compared to 4.6 percent in the United States.

Sweden, to provide a means of making price stability and full employment more compatible.[40]

Stability, Full Employment and Collective Bargaining

The United States is at an important crossroads in the development of policies to make continuing high employment and price stability more compatible. The experiment in guideposts and *ad hoc* intervention has been abandoned at least temporarily. In these circumstances there is a need to reappraise the methods and institutional forms of intervention in private wage negotiation and price formation.

One conceivable alternative is to move in the direction of a formal system of wage and price controls. The Dutch experience would be illustrative. A policy of this sort would not necessarily flounder for lack of initial support. The labor movement has repeatedly stated: "If the President judges the situation to warrant the adoption of extraordinary stabilization methods—designed to bring all costs, prices and profits, as well as wages and salaries, under even-handed restraint—he can be assured of the support and cooperation of the AFL–CIO."[*] But there are strong objections to direct controls as a permanent feature of the economy. The dynamic and productive qualities of our enterprises and the voluntarism of our collective bargaining yield large enough material and psychological benefits to make the burden of continuing controls an unattractive prospect. The requisite bureaucracy is cumbersome, inefficient, and repugnant. The risk of misallocating resources is considerable. As the nation discovered in World War II, many individuals will react to such controls by cheating or inventing ways to get around the regulations. For these and other reasons, the experience abroad, as well as in this country in wartime, suggests that direct controls have a short effective life even in times of dire national emergency.

Another approach would be to foreswear any effort to rely on incomes policy and to concentrate on perfecting fiscal and monetary policy to provide an economic environment more conducive to

---

[*] Statement of the AFL–CIO Executive Committee on "The National Economy," August 23, 1966.

growth and stability. This alternative is in the spirit of the Swedish experience. But the situation in the United States is different in several crucial respects. Labor and management in this country are not highly enough organized at federation levels to work toward a responsible wage policy; thus far there has been little significant direct discussion among labor and management leaders on matters of this sort. The President's Committee on Labor-Management Policy, which included prominent union, management, and public representatives, did not suceed in making substantial progress along these lines. In contrast to their Swedish counterparts, the decentralized labor federation and management associations have little or no power to affect the wage decisions of their affiliates. With respect to monetary and fiscal policy, Washington has not yet displayed sufficient skill, nor have economists been sufficiently able to predict the future of an economy marked by so many centers of decision making, to avoid periods of inflation followed by unemployment, both of which appear in greater amounts than would seem to be necessary. In view of these differences, the most promising lesson to learn from Sweden is the development of an active, imaginative manpower policy. As yet, however, despite promising beginnings, manpower programs have not developed to a point where they can do much to reconcile the tension between full employment and price stability.

The British experience suggests the wisdom of encouraging reforms in industrial practices that have contributed significantly to inflation in the past. Unlike the situation in England, there is no general need in America for productivity bargaining or plant-level reorientation of collective bargaining, although there are instances, of course, where such changes would contribute to efficiency and stability. On the other hand, there are major defects in the structure of bargaining in certain industries, as noted in Chapter 8, and their elimination would make a useful contribution in seeking to mitigate wage and price pressures in these sectors in tight labor markets.

The diverse experience abroad is suggestive, but it does not provide any clear guidance to help cope with the special circumstances of the United States. Yet the opportunity is at hand to formulate new policies and new machinery for the future. There is an immense and relatively unexplored area of policy between a system of formal wage and price controls on the one hand and pure preachment and education on the other. It is possible here only to sketch the main features of a suggested approach for the decade ahead. In so doing, there is no intention to minimize the great difficulty of the problems to be resolved.

MONETARY AND FISCAL POLICY

The first essential is that monetary and fiscal policy provide an economic environment conducive to high employment and stability. Wage-price policy cannot serve as the major instrument for this task; in fact, political authorities must guard against the danger of relying too much on incomes policies in order to escape having to increase taxes, particularly in an election year. (Unhappily, inflationary pressures do not necessarily avoid even-numbered years in the calendar.) Since it is difficult to forecast expenditures correctly, and since countervailing adjustments in policies are not likely to be precise in timing or amounts, there is need to recognize that both demand and cost pressures may upset stability, just as lack of effective demand may create unemployment.

GOVERNMENT MACHINERY

Since price stability at high employment is a continuing problem in all Western societies, it is appropriate in this country to develop machinery and policies that are explicitly concerned with these issues. At least three functions need to be performed:

1) A continuing body is needed to gather facts, issue reports, and make recommendations regarding a number of troublesome sectors that contribute appreciably (and in some degree unnecessarily) to price and wage increases at high employment. In some of these sectors, there are bottlenecks in supply and inefficient use of resources—medical care and repair services are cases in point. The amount or the quality of manpower may need particular attention in other sectors, localities, or occupations. The shortages of technicians and skilled workers in many sectors provide current illustrations of manpower bottlenecks that feed inflation through rapid increases in wage rates, overtime pay, and other labor costs. In some sectors, there are defects in the structure of collective bargaining, including union rivalries and weak management organization, that contribute significantly to inflation. The construction and maritime industries and certain other branches of transportation afford illustrations. In some sectors, distribution methods and administrative procedures need review to reduce costs, as in automobile insurance. In other sectors, restrictive work practices or the failure of management to introduce technological changes would be appropriate topics for review and report. Some problem areas involve the institutions of collective bargaining, while others do not. The British National Board for Prices and Incomes offers a model to show the influence that dispassionate and competent inquiry can have. In 1968, President Johnson made a start in this direction by assigning such functions to a Cabinet Committee on Price Stability, which submitted its analysis of some structural problems and sectors in early 1969.*[41]

2) The government sector needs to organize itself to make a greater contribution to stability at high employment through such activities as the procurement of goods and construction, the use of stockpiles, the policies of regulatory agencies, and the like, at local and state levels as well as in the federal government. The government cannot expect private parties to improve their performance unless it does likewise in its business operations.

A typical illustration of the problems demanding government attention is the question of seasonality in construction. The United States is the only Western country without a significant public program to mitigate the costs of seasonality in this industry.[42] The separate decisions of isolated federal agencies, made with little regard to developments in private construction, have also had significant inflationary effects in some localities. Adjustment in the timing of construction expenditures would help to reduce wage inflation, lower costs to the government, and encourage more stable employment. Another illustration concerns the Medicare cost-reimbursement formulas, which allow medical facilities to pass on higher costs automatically instead of rewarding efficient providers of medical services. The management of government stockpiles of strategic materials can also have significant effects on prices and may dampen or exaggerate price fluctuations. More difficult political and administrative problems are posed by agricultural policy, subsidies for maritime and shipbuilding industries, and issues of rate regulation in utilities. But the effects of such policies on inflation are sufficient to provide ample opportunity for

---

* Special studies were made on the following topics: the job market and manpower policy; industrial structure and competition policy; construction; the unemployment-inflation problem.

the government to make a substantial contribution to greater wage and price stability.

3) A labor-management-public policy is needed to discuss the general problems of inflation and economic activity on a continuing basis and to develop more general perspectives for private and public decision makers. The simple lesson of the past, both here and abroad, is that no policies of direct restraint on wages and prices will operate for long, unless leaders of labor and management participate in their formation and execution. Strikes to raise wages excessively, widespread price increases by smaller enterprises, price rises on a few product lines, and failures to reduce prices after greater-than-average productivity increases pose almost insuperable problems to the regulator. To avoid them, a large measure of consent is needed. The crucial step of successful policy is not the technical details or rationalization of the policy, but rather its acceptability to the parties who must live under it.

THE ROLE OF THE LEGISLATURE

To develop public and private policies and to achieve greater stability at high employment, the legislative branch of government needs to be more deeply involved than it has been in the recent past. On some matters, the necessary participation can be achieved through consultation and hearings of the Joint Economic Committee and the respective committees which handle labor and manpower issues. On other occasions, resolutions, appropriations, and other expressions of legislative concern and policy can be of major significance in persuading private parties to modify their conduct. It is not enough to say that the guideposts enjoyed legislative approval simply because no legislation was enacted to set them aside. Labor and management will often be more deeply impressed by legislative views, hearings and enactments than by executive agencies. A greater degree of familiarity by legislators with the problems and with alternative private and public measures to induce greater stability at high employment is essential to an improved record in this country.

INTERVENTION IN COLLECTIVE BARGAINING

The wage-price policies advocated here are limited to general educational and exhortative meetings and the publication of detailed studies, including recommendations on structural problems of an industry, region, or occupation which contribute to inefficiency or inflation. The government should forswear, save in the most exceptional circumstances, the forms of government pressure and *ad hoc* intervention in specific price and wage decisions that characterized the application of the wage-price guideposts. The intervention of another executive agency in specific bargaining situations, in addition to government mediators, arbitrators or factfinders, will simply create fresh complications and engender conflict among government agencies.

It would also be unwise formally to require that mediators and arbitrators observe an incomes policy in their recommendations and decisions. To do so would surely evoke resentment from the parties, who would regard such a directive as an unwarranted piece of executive lawmaking. Moreover, such a requirement is not necessary to bring the government's policy to the attention of mediators and arbitrators, for it is conventional for one party or the other, in arbitration or fact-finding cases involving general compensation issues, to argue the application of the prevailing governmental policy to their own case.

MANPOWER PROGRAMS

The development of a more extensive manpower program to alleviate shortages of specialized skills is a major instrument for reducing the inflationary effects of high employment in some sectors. Training, education, and upgrading programs should not be confined to the disadvantaged, as they have so frequently been in recent years, but should be utilized as a policy tool to increase the amount and quality of labor in fields where there is most concern over wage and cost inflation. Manpower programs should include improved techniques of private and public projections of manpower requirements and manpower planning. A greater responsibility for business and labor in the training of technicians, skilled crafts, and even professional manpower, sometimes alone and often in closer cooperation with the community educational institutions, is essential to a growing economy with ever higher and more diversified technical requirements. The improvement of labor-market information, recruitment procedures, the attention to internal ladders of promotion and job requirements also have a contribution to make in increasing the effective labor supply.[43]

The extent of inflation at high employment can no doubt be somewhat mitigated through measures such as those just described. At present, the difficulties involved seem formidable, for the basic problem is relatively new; this country has not often in the past enjoyed sustained periods of high employment. As a nation, the United States has scarcely begun to work seriously on specific steps to make high employment more compatible with price stability. With continuing prosperity and full employment, changes may take place in attitudes and expectations that will make it somewhat easier to achieve reasonable price stability. At present, however, unions, employers, and households have been reacting in ways that have become instinctive as a result of repeated economic fluctuations in the past. Union members, armed with the increased bargaining power that high employment provides, may insist on the extra dime or quarter simply because the getting is good and may not become so again in the foreseeable future. The number of apprentices a joint labor-management committee will accept may be hedged against the risk of unemployment. A management may insist that prices be increased during conditions of prosperity and full employment, since the opportunity is unlikely to arise in slacker markets. Households seem to vacillate between spending high earnings and saving them for an uncertain and rainy day.

The conventional break-even points, profit margins, bargaining arrangements and strategies, and training programs have all been shaped by a world in which there has been significant economic fluctuation, periodic unemployment and idle capacity. An economy of continuing high employment requires—and tends to produce—adaptations in the habits of mind, expectations, and policies of all decision makers. How fast these changes develop may have much to do with the capacity of the economy to sustain a precariously high employment without substantial inflation. It should be a task of the governmental agencies proposed earlier (in Chapter 8) to encourage these adaptations in business, labor, and collective bargaining, as well as in government.

Collective Bargaining and the Public Sector

THE 1960's have witnessed the burgeoning of new employee organizations; collective negotiations and the use of economic power to influence the terms of employment have emerged in more new sectors and occupations than in any period since the 1930's. Government employment is the sector of the largest and most extensive expansion, with organizations springing up among teachers, police, social workers, garbage collectors, zoo attendants, lifeguards, and other state and local employees. Almost one half of the 2.7 million employees of the federal government (as of November 1967) were employed in jobs for which unions had achieved the sole right of representation; about one half of this total was in the Post Office, where almost 90 percent of employment was in units with exclusive recognition.[1] The extent of organization among the nine million state and local employees is very much lower but varies widely throughout the country. In New York, three quarters of the total of 950,000 state and local public employees have representation; over 360,000 of these gained recognition, mainly outside New York City, in the thirteen months following September 1, 1967, when new legislation for public employees became effective.[2] In many other states, however, the extent of unionization in the public sector is quite small.

In 1960, hardly more than a million employees were union members in public service. The bulk of them were in the federal service—mainly postal employees, craftsmen in navy yards and arsenals, and workers in the T.V.A., the Government Printing

Office, and the Panama Canal Zone. In state and local governments, the major centers of organization were firefighters, some police and sanitation workers, skilled maintenance crafts, employees in municipal transit and other industrial-type operations, and a growing number of clerical and administrative personnel in industrial states and major metropolitan areas.

An estimate of union strength in government jobs in 1968 would put membership at two million, with still another million in the civil-service associations and professional associations that might be called near-unions. A wide variety of organizations represent these public employees. Some are conventional labor unions; others are professional associations—such as the National Education Association among teachers—which have taken on representation and bargaining functions; others evolved from fraternal and lobbying organizations, as among the police; and still others were initially established as civil-service associations.[3] The recasting of public employment to accommodate various forms of employee organizations and negotiations is proceeding at a rapid pace. These developments are no less significant to public employment than the events of the mid-1930's were to the mass-production industries. The 1960's have already earned a place in labor-relations history as the decade of the public employee.[4]

Thus, in a few years, the barren organizing prospects and campaigns of an earlier period were replaced by success. Both public employees and managers, as well as political leaders, grew more receptive to organization and negotiation in the public sector. Fraternal and professional organizations of public employees modified their policies—in the direction of traditional labor organizations—to survive and prosper in the new environment. It was not new leadership, new resources, or new techniques that were to account primarily for the change in results, although these factors had a role in some instances. As in other cases of rapid growth in the American labor movement, a new set of favorable circumstances in the mid-1960's was primarily responsible for the growth of unions and near-unions in new sectors, and particularly in public employment.

President Kennedy's Executive Order 10988 in 1962 signaled a more favorable policy* toward organization and created procedures to facilitate union recognition and negotiation over matters of

---

* On October 29, 1969, President Nixon liberalized these policies further in Executive Order 11491.

"personnel policy," practices, and working conditions to the extent they were not governed by laws and regulations. The federal example was widely cited by unions and other organizations of public employees in their effort to achieve recognition in local and state governments. At the same time, the expansion of public employment was drawing new and younger groups into public service who seemed more receptive to unionization. The rapid expansion in the school-age population, coupled with more years of schooling, was to increase decisively the demand for schoolteachers, particularly in secondary schools. The median age of teachers in public schools dropped seven years in a decade and the median experience of teachers, from 13.1 to 8 years. In 1966–67, 37 percent of teachers were below age thirty. There was a substantial increase in the proportion of male teachers in secondary schools, and men are more likely to organize than women. The personnel practices of government managers, particularly as they relate to handling employees, were backward compared to those in large-scale private industry, thus creating widespread frustration among public employees. In many state and local governments, wages lagged far behind those in private industry. The relationships of mutual political support between the labor movement and municipal officials in some cities, such as New York, and the city administration, also facilitated union organization. The growth of employee organizations was no doubt also influenced by the spirit of unrest and protest reflected in the civil-rights movement, the opposition to the Vietnam war and student activism. The questioning of the established order and the greater tolerance for protest and direct action against constituted authority plainly fostered the organization of unions and near-unions among public employees previously unorganized.

Employment in state and local governments is growing far more rapidly than in the economy generally, or even in the private service industries. The increase was 3.5 million in the decade 1957–67 and another 3.3 million are anticipated by 1975, when, it is expected, government payrolls will carry almost 15 million employees.[5] The way in which collective bargaining operates in this sector will have decisive effects on government finances. Wages and salaries make up almost half of state and local government expenditures, and 15 percent of federal expenditures. A 5 percent wage and salary increase to all government employees would cost taxpayers $4 to $5 billion, exclusive of related fringe benefits. Public policies to deal with such urgent problems as welfare and public education are also likely to be affected in a number of ways where government employees are organized. The opposition of the New York City teachers' union to certain decentralization plans paralyzed the entire public-school system in the fall of 1968. Settlements in the public sector may even have major consequences on collective bargaining in industry generally. A private management has warned: "Settlement terms will rapidly become a pattern in this sector (government), and then—because the sector is highly visible—in the economy as a whole, when a certain level of expectations has been developed. Government is notoriously a 'soft' bargainer (since unions can always resort to political pressure, if they are thwarted at the bargaining table), so the tendency toward inflationary settlements is apt to be greatest in this area."[6]

The growth of public-employee unions, and the tendency of professional and fraternal groups to adopt union tactics, have engendered considerable emotion. As a result, several dubious precepts have been commonly bandied about: One cannot strike against the government; private collective-bargaining institutions can be readily transplanted to public employment; there can be no genuine bargaining without the right to strike; the United States can permit strikes of public employees, since foreign countries have done so without experiencing a catastrophe; the sovereign status of government precludes genuine collective bargaining; civil service and collective negotiations are incompatible. While no attempt is made to evaluate each of these statements, what follows here is intended to contribute to a skepticism of such conventional wisdom and an appreciation of the multitude of factors that so often defeat easy generalizations about public employment.[7]

Types of Activities of Public Employee Organizations

Public-employee organizations in the United States have pursued a variety of objectives and strategies. They have emerged at different governmental levels with distinctive procedures and sources of power, with different types of memberships, with special constraints and opportunities confronting them. The design of employee organizations and negotiations in public employment is even more heterogeneous than in private industry. Although greater uniformity in methods and forms appears to be developing in the 1960's, particularly with the introduction of written agreements, a brief sketch of three major types of activities of employee organizations reflects the wide spectrum that prevails.

LOBBYING AND POLITICAL ACTIVITY

The postal-employee unions have historically provided an illustration of organizations relying primarily on lobbying and political activities to influence wages and conditions of employment. The emergence of organizations of postal employees to lobby before Congress (which sets wages and other rules, such as those affecting promotion) led the Postmaster General and later President Theodore Roosevelt to issue a "gag order." The order forbade federal employees, on pain of dismissal, to seek legislation on their behalf "directly or indirectly; individually or through associations" except through the departments in which they were employed. This policy was reversed by the Lloyd-LaFollette Act of 1912, which guaranteed employees of the classified civil service the right to petition Congress, either individually or collectively, and to affiliate with the labor movement. The statute provided that employees could not be disciplined for such activity, provided that their organization imposed no obligation on employees to strike against the United States. The precedent of conditioning legitimacy and recognition on the renunciation of economic force was often followed thereafter by the federal government.

Postal unions over the years have made active efforts to elect members of Congress favorable to their interest, particularly members who serve on the Post Office committees. They press proposals before Congress for increases in wages, improvements in benefits and working conditions, and regulations applicable to the Post Office Department. They have shown great strength in securing pay increases through Congress, even over the opposition of the executive.[8] Following President Kennedy's Executive Order 10988, six postal organizations entered into an agreement* with the Post Office Department[9] which specified union recognition and procedures to handle appeals in cases of discipline and discharge.[10] Despite these developments, the postal-employee organizations

---

* The current agreement is between the Post Office Department and seven organizations for the period March 9, 1968, to March 8, 1970.

still rely primarily on lobbying and political activities that may be viewed as a form of political negotiations. The proposal to make the Post Office a nonprofit corporation with a greater role for negotiations has not enjoyed the support of postal unions, in part because they prefer the present methods of fixing wages.

The firemen have similarly used their organizations to induce city councils and elected public officials to meet their proposals. The International Association of Fire Fighters developed from local groups of firefighters who had often formed fraternal organizations and informal groups concerned with the long hours and working conditions at the firehouse. From its organization in 1918, and its affiliation with the AFL, this international union was opposed to the use of the strike weapon, although it changed its constitution in 1968 at its Toronto convention and deleted the strike prohibition.* [11] The supervisory officers of the fire departments have typically belonged to the same organization, and they have been helpful in approaching local governments. They have also been effective in gaining the support of business interests by appeals to their concerns over fire-insurance rates and the effects of improved service on such rates.

In recent years, the Fire Fighters have been changing the form of their relationships, in localities where the statutes and regulations permit, to incorporate their wages and conditions of work into collective-bargaining agreements rather than into city ordinances and regulations. This tendency is accelerating, and in a few states, disputes over terms of such agreements are handled by specialized impasse procedures or by those applicable to all public employees. But in the main, the Fire Fighters still rely largely on political processes—the lobby, referendum, and public appeal—to influence decisions by city governments on their wages and working conditions.

COLLECTIVE NEGOTIATIONS WITH PUBLIC MANAGEMENT

In a number of cases, particularly in local government, the negotiation of agreements has more closely resembled private collective bargaining than the type of lobbying and political

---

* In the early stages of its development in 1918 and 1919 alone, thirty strikes, mass resignations, or lockouts took place, often involving the issue of recognition as well as wages and hours. In recent years, there have been a few strikes of firefighters, as in Atlanta, Kansas City and Youngstown.[12]

activity outlined above. An industrial operation, such as a transit system, may have engaged in collective bargaining as a private facility, and many of the same tactics, procedures, habits of mind, and personnel are carried over by both sides when the operation is transformed into a public venture. The experience of the New York City transit system is illustrative. In such cases, the parties tend to disregard prevailing civil-service regulations or manage to have the governmental regulations changed to conform to the agreement. Despite the legal prohibition of the strike, the resort to economic force is often a realistic possibility in these negotiations.

Some of the new relationships in the public schools, in sanitation, and in municipal services in general, appear to be established on the same basis. There are some public authorities, such as thruways, bridges, and publicly owned utilities, which have practical responsibility for operating a service and greater freedom in affecting revenues and costs than the executive departments of government. These public managements may engage in collective negotiations with employee representatives without many of the limitations inherent in most areas of public employment.

PREVAILING WAGE POLICIES

Other groups of public employees have sought to influence their terms of employment by persuading the government to accept the principle of prevailing wage policies. Under this principle, the public sector will gear its wages to those paid by certain private managements. Approximately one quarter of the employees of the federal government are "wage board employees," largely blue-collar workers, whose wage scales are determined by periodic surveys of prevailing wage rates for similar occupations in various localities or areas in which they are employed.[13] These employees are heavily concentrated in navy yards, arsenals, air depots, and other installations, although some classifications are widely distributed among agencies. Many of these employees were union members prior to employment by the government in such occupations as machinists, electricians, and boilermakers, and these occupations are often more craft-oriented and less attached to a single employer.

During 1962–64, the principle of comparability in pay to private employment was applied to federal white-collar employment. The Federal Salary Reform Act of 1962 declared as a matter of policy that ". . . federal salary rates shall be comparable with private salary rates for the same levels of work." Procedures were established for an annual report on pay comparability.[14] According to President Kennedy, this enactment represented ". . . the most important federal employee legislation in forty years."

In a large number of local governments, prevailing wage standards are applied to public employees, particularly those engaged in mechanics' and laborers' occupations. In many instances there have been no formal agreements, simply an understanding resulting in a government order that wage rates negotiated for the occupation in the private sector will be followed in public employment. Sometimes a wage differential below outside rates is maintained in local government in recognition of the opportunity that public employment often provides for more stable and secure employment or higher pensions. On other occasions, public employees under prevailing wage approaches have been able to secure the best of both worlds—outside rates as well as government fringes. Moreover, under prevailing-wage orders in local governments, there is seldom any careful review of the content of jobs in public employment to determine how they actually compare with jobs in private industry.

The prevailing-wage technique in practice involves elements of negotiation, for determining prevailing wages is not a simple statistical undertaking devoid of discretion. The geographical area from which comparable wages are selected, the particular firms and occupations included in a survey, the comparative content of the jobs in government employment and the survey group, the data of a survey, and the methods of combining the survey data, all will influence the final decision. The results will also be affected by the weight given to internal wage differentials among job classifications in a federal establishment as compared to the wage differentials found to prevail outside the government facility. The value of fringe benefits may also need to be assessed. Thus, the determination of prevailing wages leaves ample room for a form of negotiation around the administration of this wage standard. In the federal service, wage-board determinations have provided an opportunity for labor organizations to participate in settling compensation. As for other conditions of employment, union representatives at these facilities often have become expert in administering government regulations to serve the interests of their members.

The T.V.A. represents a highly developed instance of prevailing-wage determination incorporated in a full collective-bargaining agreement. The agreement between the T.V.A. and the Tennessee Valley Trades and Labor Council, which has been in effect over thirty years, provides as follows:

> In accordance with provisions of the T.V.A. act, T.V.A. shall pay its trades and labor employees the prevailing rate of pay for work of a similar nature in the vicinity, with due regard to those rates which are established through collective bargaining by representatives of employers and employees. If there is a dispute as to what is the prevailing rate for a class of positions, the question shall be referred to the Secretary of Labor, whose decision is final.[15]

From the outset of the relationship, the unions recognized that a strike was not an appropriate instrument to resolve a dispute with the T.V.A. The agreement states that the unions ". . . will not permit their members to engage in work stoppages or to refuse to perform work of their craft as assigned, nor sanction their leaving the service," and that the T.V.A. will not change the conditions in the agreement except by methods specified in the agreement. The parties have also developed a special procedure to be used in the event any employee leaves work in violation of the agreement.[16] The agreement has operated extremely well over the years. The resort to the Secretary of Labor has been used on only a few occasions. There have been a few wildcat work stoppages by small groups, but these disputes, including the discipline of participants, have been settled by the parties as provided in the agreement.

The Major Issues

The design of collective negotiation in public employment is at a sensitive and formative stage, with great diversity in its forms.[17] The major issues involved are explored in the discussion that follows. Collective negotiations in the public sector will be largely shaped by the manner in which these key issues are resolved.

THE RIGHT TO ORGANIZE AND NEGOTIATE

Dr. Martin Luther King, Jr., was assassinated while in Memphis to support the sanitation workers of the city in a strike in which the decisive issue was the right of the union to negotiate over wages and other conditions of work. There was no machinery in the city or state government to resolve this issue. Such a situation is not uncommon. Aside from disputes over salaries and benefits, union recognition or union security is the most frequent cause of work stoppages in public employment in local and state government.[18]

The refusal of many governments to recognize unions of their employees has persisted over many decades. Forty years ago, Dr. Nicholas Murray Butler proposed that the right of government employees to organize be confined to mutual benefit societies that could not bargain collectively or strike. Some government officials offered to treat with independent unions but held that they would not recognize organizations affiliated with the labor movement. Indeed, opposition of Boston authorities to outside affiliation played a major role in precipitating the police strike of 1919.*

Today, the right of public employees to organize is recognized in almost all states. There is much less acceptance, however, of an obligation on the part of public authorities to negotiate with a union of public employees, and only in a relatively few of the more industrialized states† is there specific administrative machinery to determine whether a union represents a majority of employees, to specify the appropriate unit for representation, which may vary with the issue, to determine the range of problems subject to negotiation, and to resolve other questions associated with the establishment of a negotiating relationship.[20] Until such obligations are recognized and the necessary machinery established,

---

* Police Commissioner Curtis issued the following order on August 11, 1919, two days after the Boston police were granted an AFL charter:
No member of the force shall join or belong to any organization, club or body composed of present or past members of the force which is affiliated with or part of any organization, club or body outside the department, except that a post of the Grand Army of the Republic, the United Spanish War Veterans, and the American Legion of World War Veterans may be formed within the department.[19]

† Connecticut, Massachusetts, Michigan, New York, Rhode Island and Wisconsin have adopted comprehensive statutes. Many other states have adopted statutes covering specific segments of public employment.

disputes over recognition will remain the focal point of public-employee organizations.

In addition to the reasons that have motivated many private managers to resist the organization of their employees, public authorities have often invoked the doctrine of "sovereignty"[21]—a doctrine with roots in British law in the eighteenth century. According to Blackstone, the King can do no wrong; indeed, the King is incapable of thinking wrong. In more modern terms, the concept of sovereign immunity has been changed to hold merely that no state may be sued by an individual without its consent. As such, the doctrine need not interfere with the development of labor relations in the public sector. Although it is clear that the state cannot be *compelled* to enter involuntarily into any collective-bargaining relationship, there is no bar to legislation authorizing a government to enter into collective negotiations and an agreement with its employees.

More troublesome is the closely related problem concerning the extent to which the legislative branch of a government, charged with appropriating funds, can delegate to others the determination of compensation and other rules governing the employment relationship. While a state can agree to bargain collectively with employee organizations, ". . . the prevailing view appears to be that the state cannot in so doing irrevocably surrender to the bargaining agent of [its] employees the power to make governmental rules and regulations."[22] Under this view, the state must retain the ultimate legal power to make rules and determine conditions of employment. Even so, the government does not delegate power merely by agreeing to bargain with a union representing its employees, since the state retains ultimate power to accept or reject the union's proposals. Nor does it seem inconsistent with the traditional doctrine of separation of powers for the legislature to delegate to the executive branch the power to make agreements with unions, subject to normal budgetary limitations; executive agencies are regularly given power to enter into contracts in the discharge of their normal responsibilities.

The appeal to sovereignty in recent years has become increasingly unacceptable as a norm by which to dispose of the problems of public employees. The cloak of sovereignty has been used to justify unilateral and sometimes inequitable decisions by government administrators.[23] As one leading neutral with wide experience in the public field has said, "The division of powers employees faced with different market constraints must remain free essential to democracy, often results in the lack of focused bargaining. . . . What is needed to make collective bargaining work in government is development of government bargaining teams with authority to say 'I will' or 'I won't', rather than 'I can't.' "[24] Governments have become so complex that their personnel problems—like those of other large organizations—cannot easily be handled on a personal basis and are much more visible to the public. As business and the community have become more conditioned to the right of employees to bargain collectively, the absolutist position in government has become less tenable. The rise in wages and salaries in private industry, coupled with tight labor markets, have aggravated the practical problems of recruitment and made it more difficult for public management to conduct employee relations on a unilateral basis. The expansion of government into transit, housing, and other fields that are closely akin to private industry has made it awkward for the government to rely upon arguments of sovereignty to avoid collective bargaining. The example of the federal government makes such arguments seem weaker still.

NEGOTIATING UNITS AND THE SCOPE OF NEGOTIATION

A group of four interrelated questions vitally affects the consequences and the performance of collective negotiation in the public sector:

1) What is to be the range of job classifications, or employees, included in a single election district?

2) Are all subjects bargained between employee organizations and government bodies to be negotiated in the same unit, or should some subjects be considered in larger units than other topics?

3) What subjects are to be considered in negotiations? Are some topics more appropriately treated by consultation and exchanges of views and suggestions rather than by bargaining?

4) Are negotiations with administration officials to be considered final, or may there be subsequent lobbying with the legislative body after an agreement has been reached in collective negotiation?

1) The larger the employee units selected for representation, the fewer the number of elections, negotiations and possible rivalries among organizations to influence settlements. But the larger the units, the more likely it is that minorities within a group will feel that their special interests have not been adequately recognized and the greater the possibilities of internal friction. In addition, though fewer strikes may occur in large units, those that do take place are likely to have greater disruptive impact. Thus, aside from providing separate units of police, firefighters, and teachers—an arrangement on which there is typically widespread agreement—there are serious problems in deciding how many election districts should be established in a local government. Are white-collar workers to be separate from blue-collar? Are employees to be divided by departments of municipal management—parks, sanitation, streets and highways, inspection services, etcetera—or is a single unit to be preferred?

When negotiating relations were established in Philadelphia, except for schoolteachers, firemen, police, and transit workers, the city employees were grouped into a single unit represented exclusively by the American Federation of State, County and Municipal Employees. In New York City, the pattern of development was very different. There are now approximately nine hundred bargaining certifications of employee organizations, hundreds of which are established on the basis of job titles alone;[25] these are grouped into about two hundred different bargaining relationships with about ninety different labor organizations. The two shoemakers in the employ of New York City—one on Rikers Island, the other on Welfare Island—have joined together to be certified as a two-man unit that can negotiate a labor contract with the city.[26] It is little wonder that the Office of Collective Bargaining of New York City reports that the ". . . task of restructuring negotiating units in the City will be a difficult and time-consuming one."

In the establishment of collective-bargaining relations in the public service, there are strong reasons for creating broad units in most circumstances, much broader than are conventional in the private sector.[27] Civil-service rules and regulations have been promulgated to apply to large categories of employees, including almost all government workers in some jurisdictions. As a result, there is already a widely accepted tradition of broad uniformity. In private industry, one of the major factors making for narrow units is the competitive nature of the economy; managements and employees faced with different market constraints must remain free to consider their separate problems. But in the public sector, the public treasury uniformly governs financial capacity throughout much of a government. In the private sector, moreover, election districts have often been influenced largely by tactical consideration. Unions and managements have traditionally maneuvered for larger or smaller units to enhance their respective chances of election success. Both parties have paid far too little attention to the effects of election districts upon the subsequent functioning of collective negotiation. There is no reason to repeat this election gerrymandering in public employment.

The breadth of election districts in the public sector should also be influenced by the wage-determining principles that are likely to be applied in the negotiation to follow. If the government and its employees are genuinely committed to the principle of prevailing wages by occupation, then very narrow units, such as craft occupations, may be entirely appropriate, and few administrative problems can be expected within the groups accepting this wage criterion. The T.V.A. is an example. But if this principle is not fully understood and accepted within a group, or if it does not apply to all employees in the particular government, there are prospects of serious conflict and escalation. One unit of employees will emphasize their wage comparisons with outside industry, while other units may stress the internal wage relationships and the principle of equality of treatment among all government employees performing similar tasks. A wage increase to a small unit of government employees, such as those in a craft or specialized occupation, under the prevailing wage standard is likely to be followed by a wage increase to other units which prefer the principle of equality of compensation within public employment. The result is likely to involve serious and continuing conflict and wage escalation.

The dangers just described would be greatly reduced in a large unit represented by a single union. In federal white-collar employment, for example, Congress adopted both the principle of comparability with private enterprise and that of equal pay for substantially equal work. But the unit is so wide—effectively, the whole white-collar civil service—that tactical escalation among units is precluded.

2) It is often presumed that all terms and conditions of employment should be negotiated in the same election district. But

this is not true of the private sector, and the design of bargaining relations in public employment would do well to vary negotiators with the nature of the issue, particularly where many units have been established. Thus, where pensions are involved, a strong case can be made to require that the issue be negotiated by representatives of all employee organizations as a group.* The single negotiating group may permit lower administrative costs. It is essential, also, to secure uniform pension benefits or to secure general acceptance from all employees for any differential pension benefits to apply to specialized classes of employees. The competitive escalation of pension benefits is extremely expensive, as New York City is discovering in negotiations involving firemen, police, and transit and sanitation workers. For similar reasons, there are other conditions of employment, such as sick leave and health benefits, which may also be appropriately handled by a group representative of all employees.

At the other extreme, it is appropriate that many grievances and disputes over specialized working conditions be negotiated in relatively small units, provided that reasonable care is given to the wider implications of any agreement. While there are, no doubt, dangers of fostering union rivalry, it is even possible to find instances in which one union should negotiate wages and other broad issues for a large group of employees, while a different union, chosen by a subgroup, should handle the subgroup's working-conditions problems within the framework agreed upon in the larger unit.

3) The range of subjects negotiated between employee organizations and public managers varies a great deal among governments. A threefold division is to be made between topics determined by legislative bodies, those left exclusively to civil-service regulations and public managers, and those within the scope of negotiation and agreement. In federal employment, negotiation is narrowly limited to certain matters of personnel policy, practices, and working conditions; wages, benefits, and many major conditions of employment are fixed by Congressional legislation or by civil-service regulations. In local governments, the range of subjects for bargaining is typically much broader, although the precise limits are not drawn at the same place in all relations.

---

* This will remain true even though different retirement ages and benefits may be established for those in uniformed services (police and fire departments) in some cities under the influence of a military type of retirement policy.

Thus, the issue may arise whether the number of policemen to man a radio car should be determined by government alone, either through legislative ordinance or by decisions of public managers, or whether the matter should be a subject for collective negotiation.[28] Is the curriculum of a school and the choice of particular textbooks to be decided by public management, or are these subjects within the scope of bargaining? There is an understandable tendency for employee organizations to seek the broadest possible scope for negotiations and for public managers to narrow the limits of collective negotiation.*

In the end, the scope of bargaining will be influenced by the procedures adopted to resolve impasses in negotiations. If public employees are permitted to strike, the range of bargainable topics presumably should be closely confined. The exercise of economic pressure through disruption of public services is too haphazard a way of deciding significant issues affecting the public, such as institution of a police review board, decentralization of administrative services, and initiation or discontinuation of a specific government facility. This is especially true in the public sector, where decisions are much less restricted by competition and related market pressures. If disputes are settled by the more reasoned process of fact finding or arbitration, on the other hand, the scope of negotiation may be somewhat broader, although there will still be many important matters excluded from bargaining on the ground either that they should be within the province of management or that they seem more suited to resolution through the political process. Finally, a system that does not provide for strikes or arbitration, but reserves final power in a legislative body to settle bargaining disputes, can appropriately entrust a broad range of subjects to the bargaining process.

4) One further problem to be considered in the establishment of collective negotiation for public employees is the relationship between a negotiated settlement and subsequent lobbying by employee organizations before legislative bodies. In special cases, of course, the parties may agree to set aside certain issues to be handled through the lobbying process. In general, however, collective negotiation will not operate well if one party or the other

---

* In many relationships, the parties come to recognize that joint consultation is a significant supplement to negotiation, and many topics which are formally outside the scope of negotiation are appropriate areas for common discussion, sharing of ideas, and suggestions.

makes an agreement and then lobbies for provisions in conflict with or in addition to the settlement. Future negotiation will be frustrated by such bad faith. As a result, the executive officials and the employee organization should normally join in seeking legislative adoption of any settlement they make.

In creating a collective relationship in public employment, it is thus essential to recognize that the size of the unit, the grouping of employee representatives to consider various issues, the wage-setting principles to be applied, the scope of topics within the purview of negotiation, as compared to those left to government determination, and the relation of negotiation to subsequent lobbying activities—all these are closely related matters and should be reviewed as a whole.

CONSEQUENCES FOR EFFICIENCY

Just as Chapter 9 sought to appraise the impact of collective bargaining on efficiency in the private sector, so it is necessary to inquire into the consequences of collective negotiations on efficiency in the public sector. Among private employers, it was suggested that collective bargaining has improved efficiency by placing pressure on managements to innovate and seek cost reductions (that would not have been otherwise introduced), and by improving the quality and skill of the labor force. On the other hand, collective bargaining has sometimes impaired efficiency by introducing uneconomic work rules, particularly where management has been desultory and permissive. While there is less experience in the public sector, the same factors seem to be operating. The potential for uneconomic work rules, however, is much greater in public employment because budgetary pressures are much less direct and effective than market forces in exerting pressure for efficiency and survival. Many public authorities, moreover, are inexperienced in negotiating with employee organizations over workplace issues. As a result, they are often not alert and enterprising enough to prevent or buy out restrictive rules before they become too wasteful and deep-rooted.

To illustrate the point, a number of recent agreements with teacher organizations (both the American Federation of Teachers and affiliates of the National Education Association) have specified in agreements, for understandable and legitimate reasons, the maximum size of class that may be assigned to a teacher. Without such a limitation, a school board might try to offset a salary increase simply by enlarging the class size proportionally. But strict limitations on class size may eventually prove a major impediment to innovation in teaching. It is possible that some students should be taught in smaller groups and others in larger groups than specified, and it may be that some subjects are more effectively presented in very small groups. New teaching tools and methods may allow larger classes with improved quality of instruction. While many teacher agreements provide for exceptions for "specialized or experimental" instruction,[29] the freedom to make changes in class size may prove difficult and may have to be purchased at a considerable price.

Collective agreements with social workers provide another illustration. Such agreements may specify the case load—that is, the number of "clients" assigned to each social worker.[30] This limitation often seems innocuous at the start, since it is normally identical to, or only slightly below, the existing practice under administrative regulations. In the future, however, it may become advisable to make radical changes in the administration of welfare in a city. Welfare staff might be assigned according to type of service—medical questions, housing, and the like—or according to residence, or by size and age of family. More drastic proposals for revision in welfare have been discussed. Such changes in the organization of welfare would doubtless make obsolete the case loads specified in an agreement. But persuading the union to agree to make the necessary changes might prove expensive and might hamper efficient management.*

The lesson of collective bargaining in the private sector is surely that manning rules and restrictions in agreements become obsolete and difficult to modernize. Most unions in the private sector in the United States have been willing to leave initiative for change with management and to rely on bargaining or arbitration to resolve the adjustments in wage rates and seniority districts that are required by any innovations that take place. Public managers

---

* The same social-worker agreement has a provision which requires New York City to paint each work location at least once every five years. A provision requiring adequate working conditions is appropriate, but the specification of painting every five years would seem to have little place in an agreement without taking account of the quality of paint, the surface, and the possibilities of technological change in covering.

have seldom been notable for their capacity to innovate so that mere stringent limitations on technical, administrative, and organizational change should thus be viewed with particular concern.

NEGOTIATION AND BUDGET-MAKING

The introduction of collective negotiation into public employment raises some complex issues in the budget-making process and in the allocation of public funds. Collective negotiation ideally should be closely coordinated with the appropriate legislative and budget year so that the compensation increases that are proposed can be taken into account when the budget is drawn up for the ensuing year. If this is done, tax rates and other sources of revenue can be adjusted, the quantity and the quality of services determined, and priorities established in view of the new level of compensation. Moreover, by reviewing the results of all negotiations at the time of the budget decision, legislative officials can make systematic comparisons among different groups of public employees and then restrain wage distortions and inequities that typically accelerate wage increases in subsequent periods. The Philadelphia negotiations are directly coordinated with the budget-making process.[31] The Taylor law in New York also provided that negotiations—except for New York City—should be consummated prior to the budget submission date of the government unit.[32]

If bargaining takes place after a budget has been adopted, negotiation becomes much more difficult. An increase in compensation under a pre-established budget involves either a deficit or a drastic reordering of public priorities. In the latter event, public officials are forced to take funds from capital budgets, from agencies less able to resist cuts, from services whose recipients have least political muscle, or—for some purposes—from federal agencies. In order to avoid such an arbitrary reordering of priorities, public officials may seek to estimate probable wage increases in establishing their budgets for the ensuing year. If this procedure is followed, however, negotiation tends to involve a search for these allowances on the part of the employee organization and a race among organizations to secure a lion's share before the allowance for increases has been used up. Such problems cause increased complexity in the bargaining process and a greater tendency to resort to a strike to compel the raising of funds.

Impasse Procedures and the Strike[33]

The public discussion of collective bargaining in the government sector has been preoccupied with the strike, to the virtual exclusion of other issues. It is understandable that the dramatic events of a transit strike and a sanitation strike in New York City, and a number of teacher strikes—one of which included the whole state of Florida—should capture the headlines. But public indignation—or sympathy—has been directed to symptoms rather than to the improvement of methods to achieve equitable and peaceful settlements. In this regard, Theodore W. Kheel is surely right when he says that ". . . in improving the practice of bargaining lies our best chance to prevent strikes against the public interest."[34] Yet even with the best procedures the mind of man can design, the best human relations, and the best mediators available, a dispute may nonetheless persist. As a result, the issue of the strike in public employment cannot be avoided.

In the United States, strikes against the government—federal, state or local—have long been considered illegal. A statement of Franklin D. Roosevelt (on August 16, 1937) still reflects the dominant sentiments of the public: "A strike of public employees manifests nothing less than an intent on their part to prevent or obstruct the operations of government until their demands are satisfied. Such action looking toward the paralysis of government by those who have sworn to support it is unthinkable and intolerable."

Despite official disapproval, strikes are hardly unknown to public employment.[35] A work stoppage of several weeks took place in June 1836 at the Philadelphia Navy Yard to achieve a ten-hour day, which had become generally established elsewhere in that city. Two of the best-known stoppages in public employment in United States history were the Watertown Arsenal strike in August 1911, over the introduction of the F. W. Taylor method of time study,[36] and the strike of the Boston policemen of September 1919, which was broken by the State Guards under the direction of Calvin Coolidge, which contributed significantly to his rise to national office.[37]

In recent years, the number of strikes has increased with the growth of militancy and unionization among public employees. In

1967, there were 181 strikes by public employees involving 132,000 workers.[38] The great majority of the strikes took place at the municipal level. Only occasionally did stoppages occur in state governments and very rarely in federal employment.*

New forms of economic pressure have been increasingly evident to supplement the strike. A "ticket slowdown" by Detroit police in May–June 1967 involved the issuance of traffic tickets at a reduced rate in order to express dissatisfaction with the failure of negotiations to deal with the economic demands of the police. Soon thereafter, the city was afflicted with the "blue plague" as policemen suddenly increased their level of "sick" calls.[39] A supervisors' union on the New York subways in a contract dispute announced a "rules-book slowdown" in which it threatened to ". . . take 40 percent of the cars out of service." The union announced that the mood of the supervisors ". . . imperils the safety of the subways."[40] Airport congestion was greatly increased when the newly formed Air Traffic Controllers Organization dramatized their complaints by a determination to "live by the book" and maintain the required separation between airplanes.[41] Firefighters have also exerted pressure in their disputes by refusing to perform routine inspections. Human ingenuity knows few limits in designing methods of exerting pressure on the job. Most managers would rather confront an overt strike, since slowdowns, excessive absenteeism, early retirement, "sickness," restricted work operations, and the like are very difficult to confront and foster poor work practices that may have serious long-run effects on costs and efficiency.

Since a significant number of work stoppages in state and local governments arise over the recognition of organizations to represent public employees, the enactment of state or city legislation to provide an agency to resolve these issues is essential to the orderly development of employee organization and collective

---

* The distribution of strikes in 1967 by various types of government service was as follows:

Public schools and libraries	89
Administrative and protection services	24
Sanitation services	23
Hospitals and health services	19
Publicly owned transportation and utilities	11
Street and highway departments	5
Miscellaneous services	10

negotiation. Experience has plainly demonstrated the error of simply imposing heavy penalties for such strikes without providing for procedures to resolve them. The Condon-Wadlin law in New York provides a case in point. Such laws do not prevent strikes. Indeed, they are so one-sided against employees that officials will often not enforce violations. As a result, the legislation becomes a nullity, and it breeds a disrespect for law that endures long after the statute is repealed and better legislation is enacted in its place. Nevertheless, only a few states have laws guaranteeing recognition and providing machinery to resolve disputes over representation. The enactment of such legislation deserves the highest priority.

Once a negotiating relationship has been established, the concern shifts to the resolution of disputes over the terms of employment. The settlement of these disputes calls for the design of procedures to govern collective negotiation and to provide effective alternatives to conflict. In the first instance, it is probably wise to ask the parties involved to design their own machinery. Employee organizations differ widely in their objectives and methods: Governmental units are of varying size and confront diverse budgetary restraints and procedures. The scope of civil-service regulations and collective negotiations are far from uniform, and great differences appear in the nature of government operations and the authority of government negotiators. The influence of employee organizations and the labor movement in the community also varies sharply. It stands to reason, therefore, that no one procedure, imposed legislatively, will suit all the situations to which it would apply.

There are already a variety of procedures available in the public sector, and inventiveness in this field is at an early stage. The parties may develop some variant of the prevailing-wage approach and identify the procedures and the comparable sectors to be used in making these determinations. They may establish various study committees to operate during the term of the agreement, particularly on difficult prospective issues, with resort to fact finding and recommendations before a body of their own design and choice. They may design a system of public hearings with settlement through normal political processes. As George Meany has observed, "Perhaps the best answer in this field is some system of voluntary arbitration."[42]

In the absence of procedures agreed to by the parties to resolve disputes over provisions of an agreement, or in the event that such machinery fails, the government involved in the dispute has an obligation to provide a general procedure. There is wide agreement that provision should be made for mediation between the employee organization and the governmental unit if the parties fail to resolve the dispute by direct negotiations. But what should happen in the event that the dispute remains unresolved and the parties have reached a serious impasse?

There are three groups of major contending views on impasse procedures: 1) Government employees should be allowed to strike except when the public health or safety is in jeopardy.[43] 2) If the impasse cannot otherwise be settled, no strike of public employees is permissible and the dispute should be resolved by compulsory arbitration binding on both the governmental employer and the employee organization. 3) Recommendations should be made by a fact-finding body, and in the event further mediation around these recommendations does not resolve the dispute, the appropriate legislative body should review the dispute and enact a statute prescribing the terms and conditions of employment. The recommendations of the fact finders should have presumptive validity, but should not be binding on the legislature.[44]

Proposals to legalize strikes of public employees are advocated on the grounds that they would put collective bargaining in the public sector on the same footing as private negotiations, reduce the time-consuming process of negotiation, and eliminate intransigence on the part of some public officials who use the authority of government to resist reasonable settlements in negotiation. In general, strikes of public employees do not burden the community more than stoppages in the private sector. Moreover, public employees often perform services identical to those performed by private employees who have the right to strike. Employees in city transit systems, shipyards, and public office buildings, it can be argued, should be no less favorably situated than comparable employees in private industry.

The opposing arguments emphasize the peculiar nature of the public-employee strike. In the private sector, union demands are usually checked by the forces of competition and other market pressures. Negotiators are typically limited by such restraints as the entry of nonunion competitors, the impact of foreign goods, the substitution of capital for higher-priced labor, the shift of operations to lower-cost areas, the contracting out of high-cost operations to other enterprises, the shutdown of unprofitable plants and operations, the redesign of products to meet higher costs, and finally the managerial option to go out of business entirely. Similar limitations are either nonexistent or very much weaker in the public sector. While budgets and corresponding tax levies operate in a general way to check increases in compensation, the connection is remote and scarcely applicable to particular units or groups of strategically located public employees. Unhampered by such market restraints, a union that can exert heavy pressure through a strike may be able to obtain excessive wages and benefits.

Another distinctive feature of the public-employee strike involves the nature of the sanction imposed. Most strikes in the private sector exert pressure by hurting the employer's pocketbook. Occasionally, when the stoppage closes down an entire industry or the employer occupies a vital or unique position in supplying certain goods and services, a strike may also inconvenience the public. But inconvenience of this sort is normally a by-product of the walkout. In the public sector, however, the union can seldom hope to generate much pressure by making the government sustain economic losses. Instead, the strike succeeds, if at all, by inconveniencing the public enough to bring grass-roots pressure to bear on elected officials. In this sense, an effective strike by government employees tends inherently to be harmful to the public.

In response to these arguments, it is said that government-employee strikes would not be allowed in situations where the welfare, health, and safety of the public would be unduly jeopardized. But this concession creates problems of its own. The judicial system, which is usually designated to decide when the public welfare is endangered, is not well suited to make such determinations; any effort to balance the freedom to strike against the inconvenience to the public ultimately rests upon political considerations and value judgments of the most intractable kind. In addition, for those categories of employees prohibited from striking, all the problems of devising suitable settlement procedures remain to be solved. Furthermore, it would be most difficult, as a practical matter, to confine the strike to some public employees and refuse to grant the same rights to others in the same locality and agency. The New York City experience with the police and firefighter negotiations over salary differentials for supervisory employees in October 1968 is illustrative of the interdependence of settlements. In wartime, the government also learned that it was essential in many nondefense plants to support the no-strike no-lockout policy—even to the point of seizure—in order to avoid creating intolerable pressures in the essential industries.

Additional problems would remain for the groups of employees who would be allowed to strike. The standard of health and safety is not acceptable. Thus, a strike of teachers for three or six months or a strike of postal workers for a month might not adversely affect the health or safety of the public, strictly speaking, but such strikes could well impose much greater costs on the community than any benefits to be gained from allowing such conflict to go on. In private collective bargaining, strikes of long duration play a significant role; but there are few important public services—even among those which do not affect health or safety— that the community would allow to be shut down for many months. On the other hand, since the effectiveness of strikes in the public sector derives from the power to inconvenience the public, many employees—park attendants, zookeepers, janitors, and the like—would be so weak that they would be better off under some alternative method of resolving disputes. As one report has expressed it, "Equitable treatment among the various classes of government employees cannot be provided if those unions with the power to bring the public to its knees exert this power to secure preferred treatment for their particular members."[45]

There are many issues of public policy that are so important to the community that they should not be decided by the economic force of a particular group. School decentralization, medical care, the closing of government installations, the governance of a community college, and the status of the postal system are all pertinent illustrations.* It would also seem politically unrealistic in the country at present to expect legislative bodies to sanction strikes in public employment; this fact in itself is one measure of the community's evaluation of the competing interests of government employees and the public concern for uninterrupted services.

The alternative proposal to resolve disputes in public employ-

---

* These decisions made by public agencies are vital to the community; that is typically why they have been allocated to the public sector. The strike against public decisions would generally be more harmful than strikes against private decisions. The strike is not appropriate primarily because such decisions should be made by political processes involving all the interests affected by the decision, including the labor organizations involved acting through their lobbyists and political representatives.

ment by an advance commitment to arbitration may be appropriate in some limited circumstances. Arbitration is used in resolving grievances where the issues and the mandate of the arbitrator are clear. On contract matters, arbitration has been used where the precise question to be arbitrated and the standards to be applied by the arbitrator have been agreed to already by the employee organization and the public management. Thus, parties might well agree upon the wage standard of comparability to private employment and upon the type of private employers and job classifications to be used in the comparisons and yet leave to arbitration the factual question of the required wage change to achieve the agreed-upon standard. There may be merit in using a continuing arbitration board which develops an expert knowledge of these problems rather than a series of different arbitrators.

But there are strong arguments against requiring arbitration as a system of regularly resolving bargaining disputes in the public sector.[46] Many of the difficulties with compulsory arbitration in the private sector apply to the government as well. (See Chapter 8.) There are also serious doubts whether, as a matter of policy, a legislative body should assign to an arbitrator the decision to commit large and unknown amounts of the public funds. Increases in employee compensation or changes in working rules may require tax increases or cutbacks in other programs to provide the needed revenue. This is particularly likely where negotiating units are broad. Arbitrators are seldom equipped to weigh the interests of government employees against the full array of claims on the public treasury. Legislators are elected in a democratic society to make such evaluations of the public welfare and priorities.

The third alternative impasse procedure is fact finding with final resolution to be made, if necessary, by the legislative body. This procedure provides a role for both expert opinion of neutrals and for legislative judgment on questions beyond the province of the labor-management specialist.[47]

Where it works well, fact finding can be a useful and even a powerful device. It seems to focus public opinion and to economize on the legislators' time, while providing them with the guidance they need.[48] Fact finding is also a flexible procedure; it provides maximum opportunity for mediation, before, during, and after recommendations made privately or publicly. The exposure to hard facts also helps to deflate extreme positions; it allows neutrals to develop and "try on for size" possible accommodations, while

338   *Labor and the American Community*

permitting the parties to modify a recommendation to their mutual advantage. The uncertainty of the ultimate legislative action may stimulate a settlement, and the parties can preserve the opportunity for reaching such an agreement even after recommendations have been made.

In some instances, of course, the legislative body will unwisely reject the recommendations of a fact-finding board. Thus, critics may argue that the procedure is inherently unfair, since the employer—that is, the government—has the ultimate power to decide, even unfairly, in its own case. But what is the alternative? Some observers will suggest that the union be allowed to strike whenever the government refuses to accept the recommendations of the fact-finding body. But fact finders can make egregious errors, and surely they are not qualified to weigh the added labor costs of a settlement against tax increases and competing public programs and expenditures. Decisions of this kind may be more appropriately resolved by political processes and elected officials than by strikes or labor arbitrators. If so, the union is not without recourse, for it can bring political pressure to bear through its constituents and lobbyists. In this respect, the union occupies a very different position vis-à-vis the government than it would vis-à-vis a private employer with final power to fix the terms of employment. It is true that the union may have very little political influence and some legislative bodies may disregard its pleas for this reason. But similar drawbacks will exist in any system; if strikes were allowed, for example, many public employees would also have too little power to protect their legitimate interests. As a result, considering all the interests at stake, the wisest course may lie in letting the legislative body decide on the recommendations of a neutral panel. If the legislature disregards the recommendations too freely and too unfairly, strikes are likely to occur, regardless of the law, to bring home the interests of the employees. Short of this, the strike seems an inappropriate way to resolve the impasse.

The question arises as to the sanctions or penalties to be applied in the event of a strike in violation of law. In the past, legislation at the state and local level has often concentrated on penalties against the employee rather than the employee organization. The Condon-Wadlin law in New York, for example, provided that any employee who went on strike automatically forfeited his employment. He might be reemployed but on the conditions that his compensation did not exceed that received before the strike, that he would not receive an increase in compensation for three years, and that he would be on probation without tenure for five years. These tough penalties proved impractical, and the New York Legislature was put through the humiliating experience of excusing transit workers from these sanctions retroactively. The general view of recent reports on public employees is that penalties should be directed more to the employee organization, in the form of fines and loss of organizational status, than to individual employees, although differential disciplinary penalties under civil-service regulations are appropriate for leaders and followers involved in an illegal stoppage. Penalties for violations of court orders should be left to the courts. Reliance on imprisonment of union leaders to secure enforcement of court injunctions and orders should be abandoned as ineffective; such a step tends to produce martyrs rather than compliance, and thus encourages deliberate defiance of the courts.

The strikes that have taken place in public employment often have occurred without benefit of settlement recommendations; a few have been in protest against recommendations or as a result of governmental refusal to accept them. There have been few, if any, strikes growing out of legislative enactments derived from fact-finding recommendations. There are, however, no absolute guarantees against strikes in public employment, certainly not in a democratic society in a period when organization of employees is rapidly being introduced into new sectors of government.

The ultimate issue is not whether there will continue to be isolated strikes, but whether the system of industrial relations that is being designed and is emerging in the public sector is to utilize in its mature stage the strike as a means to settle disputed wages and conditions of employment. It is too early to predict the answer at this formative stage, although the alternative of collective negotiations without the strike weapon is presently the clear choice of public policy. To achieve a viable system of labor relations, however, will require more than orderly procedures for recognition, for the establishment of negotiating relationships, and for impasse resolution; it will also demand the development within public agencies of skilled management concerned with constructive relationships, with employee organizations, and with aggressive ideas to reduce labor costs, rather than with the rights of sovereignty. The recruitment and training of such management, with basic

changes in old bureaucracies, is an essential first step. The accompanying change in some unions—members and leaders alike—is no
less imperative.

Conclusion

Amid the controversy and change associated with the organization of public employees, what major issues of concern seem to
be emerging? In the public mind, of course, the dominant preoccupation is the threat of strikes and the disruption of important
government services. If experience is any guide, however, even in
the communities which are experiencing the most trying disputes,
the level of strikes will reach a peak and then gradually subside as
relationships become established and negotiators on either side
become more professional. This is precisely what took place in the
private sector following the rapid growth in union organization in
the middle thirties. And in certain communities, where reasonable
alternatives to the strike are provided by law and sensibly administered, even the initial period of turbulence may be avoided.

Another likely consequence of organization in the public
sector is the increased tendency of public-employee unions to
engage in political activity to secure improved compensation and
working conditions. For unions in private industry, political action
typically brings benefits to the membership that are either indirect
or distinctly secondary to those obtained at the bargaining table.
To the public-employee union, however, politics will be a matter
of much greater concern if the legislative and executive officials
who are elected play a major role in determining wages and working conditions.* As these relationships are more widely perceived
by members and leaders alike, public-employee unions may begin
to develop long-dormant capacities for registering voters, contributing funds, and mobilizing campaign workers.† What this
portends for local politics is hard to foretell. Presumably, organization will beget organization by opposing interest groups, but even
so, the result will be to intensify greatly the degree of group
activity and pressure in the local government arena.

---

* The Fire Fighters candidly state: "In public employment, absent the strike
weapon, employee unions use political, rather than economic persuasion on
the legislative body; but this is the nature of government."[49]
† The role of unions in national and state politics is explored in greater detail
in Chapter 14.

Perhaps the most troublesome problem in the growth of public-employee unions is the danger of excessive settlements and inefficient work practices. Public employees, like all segments of the American community, have large aspirations for income. The National Education Association, for instance, in the period of a single year between conventions, raised its sights for minimum teachers' salaries for the country from a scale of $8,000–$16,000 to $10,000–$21,000.[50] Although all unions tend to have large appetites, the public-employee organizations are well situated to translate their desires into concrete achievements. As previously noted, they may develop increasing political power, as well as greater negotiating skills, to achieve their ambitious objectives. The demands of government employees, moreover, are much less restrained by market forces than is the case in the private sector, and managers in the public service are probably less alert, on the whole, in detecting and avoiding inefficient work practices.

It is, no doubt, true that in many localities compensation of public employees has lagged well behind that of employees in the private sector, insofar as such comparisons are possible. Public employees have thus argued that they are "subsidizing" the public in that tax rates are lower than they should be to support a more adequate level of compensation. While many such situations remain, particularly among unorganized public employees, the situation is changing. In the federal service, the principle of comparability with private industry has actually been written into law.[51] With increasing organization and militancy, there are already instances arising in which public-employee negotiation is setting new patterns that will lead the private sector. As organization continues to grow, the problem of wages and working conditions in the public sector may not be that they lag behind the private sector but that they have crept uncomfortably ahead.

Frontiers of Substantive Bargaining

THE EARLIEST collective-bargaining agreements encompassed little more than a scale of wage rates and the standard hours of the work day. Over the years, the range of subjects in written agreements has greatly expanded. During World War II, unions made great strides in bargaining for grievance arbitration and other safeguards to protect their members against unfair decisions on the part of management. In the past twenty years, the most significant growth in the scope of bargaining has probably been in the areas of pensions, health and welfare, and insurance. More recently, there has been renewed activity in the development of programs to cushion the shock of unemployment and technological change. The question naturally arises whether substantive issues that are emerging today will carry collective bargaining into new fields.

Critics who have grown tired of unions are often pessimistic on the chances for new growth in collective bargaining. Despite an occasional slam-bang strike, these writers feel that negotiations have gotten more routine, further removed from the rank and file, and more firmly in the grip of the specialist, be he lawyer, actuary, or accountant. But is it true that collective bargaining must become more stale and routine? Can unions look forward to little more than developing greater skill in resolving the same old problems of arranging wages and working conditions? Such predictions show little appreciation of the past evolution of collective bargaining, or the changing problems of the workplace, and offer too dreary a view of the future. New opportunities for bargaining arise as new needs develop among the workers at the workplace. And there will be no lack of new needs as long as union leaders are alert to recognize them and deal with them over the bargaining table.

New needs develop for a variety of reasons. With rising wage levels, more and more workers can more readily satisfy their basic wants. As a result, union members may set less store on getting new pay increases and acquire a keener interest in greater economic security, longer vacations, better working conditions, better education and training, and the like. This tendency is mirrored in a long accumulation of survey data, suggesting that income matters relatively less to employees now than it did decades ago when the economy was closer to subsistence levels.[1]

Changes in technology are an even more fertile source of new needs. The rise of the factory spawned a whole host of new concerns growing out of noise, monotony, machine hazards, pace of work, and discipline. In recent years, automation and technological change have created their own special problems. In some plants and industries, more expensive equipment has reduced traditional skill requirements, leaving the worker with more free time and making him more dependent upon the social aspects of the job. In other instances, modern technology has demanded new and more complicated forms of training in order to equip employees for fresh responsibilities.

Today, one of the most intriguing tendencies of many employees is their desire for greater individuality, autonomy, and freedom of choice once they have achieved higher levels of education, income, and economic security. These needs can evoke two responses: The first is to enrich the employee's job or prepare him for other, more challenging positions; the second is to provide a method to enable him to participate to a greater extent in the conduct of the enterprise in which he works.

The latter alternative seems much the least promising of the two. In a period where demands for participation are heard from many quarters, one cannot wholly dismiss the possibility of expanding the influence of employees over the business that provides them jobs. Nevertheless, worker participation has a long history in other countries and, by and large, the experience holds forth little prospect of moving very far in this direction in the United States.[2]

For half a century or more, countries in Western Europe have experimented with various forms of joint management-employee councils. Originally devised, in many cases, as a means of inducing greater labor-management cooperation in time of war, the councils drew support from several disparate strands of social thought. Communists saw these organizations as a step toward eventual worker control of industry. Progressive Catholics envisioned them as instruments for achieving a more cooperative community within the firm and a corporative organization of society. Liberal critics hoped that worker-management cooperation might help to bridge the gulf that separated the proprietary and the laboring classes.

Today, several kinds of councils exist in Western Europe, established either by agreement, as in Sweden and England, or by legislation, as in France and Germany. Some of the councils meet periodically to afford an opportunity for elected worker representatives to consult with management on the financial condition of the firm and its marketing and production policies. Other councils operate the company cafeteria, the medical facility, and various social and recreational activities. In a few instances—notably in the coal and steel firms in Germany and the nationalized enterprises in France—workers actually occupy a minority of the seats on what is the rough equivalent of the company board of directors.

In general, these experiments in worker participation have not had noteworthy results. They have clearly not justified the dire fears expressed by some employers, particularly in Germany prior to instituting the codetermination machinery in the coal and steel industries. But neither have the experiments realized the hopes entertained by their sponsors. Here and there, where the employer has had a genuine desire to make participation succeed, the joint councils have maintained a lively interest among the employees, and are said to have produced new ideas and points of view that have been put to good use in the operation of the firm. In the vast majority of cases, however, the councils have come to very little. Some employers have simply ignored them; others have influenced them by controlling the information the workers' representatives receive or by diverting the discussion to innocuous subjects. As for the workers themselves, they do not seem to have had sufficient interest in participation to insist on their full rights under the law. Many studies even indicate that the majority of employees view their councils with indifference or contempt.*

---

* Workers' councils have a somewhat different role in Yugoslavia and other Eastern European countries.

If anything, the prospects for worker participation seem even more remote in America than in Europe. Much of the intellectual backing for cooperation does not exist in this country. In addition, workers' councils are not needed in America to fill a vacuum at the plant and company level for, unlike the situation in Europe, unions in the United States have established vigorous local bodies to represent employees at the workplace. The American labor movement, moreover, has been hostile to workers' councils ever since World War I, when employers sought to use such employee-representation plans as company unions to win the loyalty of their employees away from the unions. Hence, labor would doubtless oppose such consultative bodies unless they were firmly under union control. This result would in turn be anathema to employers who would fear that consultation would quickly lead to collective bargaining over the conduct of the business.

In such an unfavorable environment, there is little prospect of special bodies for worker participation,[3] unless such a development were strongly desired by large numbers of employees. Thus far, however, the American worker has given very little evidence that he cares at all about participating in the running of the business that gives him his livelihood. As a result, the growth points of collective bargaining are more likely to lie in enlarging the employee's freedom and interest in his own work.

To many critics, unions (along with other large organizations) cannot satisfy the worker's desire for greater individuality and autonomy; they inevitably swallow up their members and press them into a common mold. Other writers observe how little unions have appreciated the psychological needs of their members. As Arthur Kornhauser puts it: "American unionism concentrates its efforts on restricted economic gains for the members. The findings of our study, as well as a great deal of other evidence, show how shallowly these usual activities of the organization enter into the life patterns of workers and how very slightly they engender active involvement."[4] Perhaps these arguments are valid. Yet there are various ways by which unions can increase the opportunities for freedom and self-realization in work, and it is in these endeavors that some of the most interesting and important frontiers of bargaining can be found.

Training and Education

Programs of training and education can increase freedom by widening the types of work that the employee can perform. Such programs are likely to be the next sector of major expansion in the scope of bargaining. There are many precedents for labor and management interest in this area. From their very outset in the early decades of the nineteenth century, unions in America have been strong supporters of free public education and vocational education. Within the skilled trades, apprenticeship programs have from the earliest days provided for training future journeymen on the job and in related classroom instruction. Hammered out by agreement between unions and managements, these programs typically specify entrance qualifications, selection procedures, duration of training, and the subject matter and hours of classroom training.[5] In other instances, unions and employers have taken an interest in training because of the local, state, or federal licensing laws that govern such occupations as barbers, electricians, marine officers and seamen, airplane pilots and mechanics, railroad engineers, and the like. Professional and para-professional occupations such as nurses, teachers, and firemen have likewise been led by public regulation of entrance standards to pay attention to training.

Although the emerging breakthrough of collective bargaining into training and education may build upon these historical precedents, the current impetus is largely derived from other sources. To some degree, the rising interest in education and training can be linked to the rediscovery by economists of the significance of "human capital." The very first page of Adam Smith's *Wealth of Nations* (1776) stressed the decisive contribution to a nation of ". . . the skill, the dexterity and judgment with which its labour is generally applied." In later generations, Smith's observations were often lost amid the concern over foreign trade, capital investment, and wage levels. But in the last decade, particularly, there has been a new recognition of the impact of "investments" in education, training, and health on economic growth and development.[6] One study has even estimated that almost one quarter of the total growth in the gross national product during the years 1929–57 in the United States can be attributed to the improved quality of the labor force ". . . because its members . . . had received much more education."* ⁷ These findings have obvious relevance to current conditions in this country. Approximately eight million workers have less than eight years of schooling.⁸ Their opportunities for promotion, or for new jobs should they become unemployed, are severely restricted; their adaptability to new job requirements is low, adversely affecting both their income prospects and their cost to employers. Thus, government, management, and labor have found a mutual interest in developing programs, or administering public manpower grants, to provide basic education, skill training, or more advanced job-oriented instruction to raise skill levels or broaden job versatility.

A period of prolonged high and expanding employment, such as the nation has experienced in recent years, provides further incentives for training programs. Skilled employees become harder to find, while the needs for these skills continue to grow. Through hard experience, many employers find that systematic training programs offer a more effective or less expensive method of meeting their needs than wage increases, advertising, raiding, or extensive use of overtime. In this setting, federal manpower programs and equal-opportunity regulations have provided an example, an opportunity, and a spur to fill employment needs from the ranks of disadvantaged groups. Labor unions or managements alone, or both through collective bargaining, have begun to make provision for the recruitment and training of new personnel from the disadvantaged and for the upgrading of the least-qualified and least-skilled among present employees.

The factors just mentioned do not exhaust the list. The widespread concern over technological displacement, particularly in the early 1960's, was another influence promoting joint labor-management interest in retraining programs; the adjustment to technological change was also the major rationalization for the original Manpower Development and Training Act of 1962.⁹ Moreover, a society with high and rising levels of technology might naturally be expected to show a greater interest in further training and education. Whatever the mix of factors at work, training and

---

* The estimate of the percentage of national income growth attributed to education in the years 1955–62 is 17 percent, and the estimate of the percentage of national income per person employed attributed to education in the same period is 25 percent.

education programs are being provided for in an increasing number of collective-bargaining relationships.

The extent and variety of these programs also have increased rapidly. Some programs are confined to incumbent employees and are adopted to upgrade, to refresh, or to extend the range of skills and competence. Others are designed particularly for new employees, and a growing number of these are intended to facilitate the employment of the disadvantaged. Still others are concerned with raising the general educational and cultural level of employees and union members.* A few illustrations may help to convey an appreciation of the diversity of these programs in their objectives, content, and financing, and the relative roles of union and management.

In 1965, basic steel companies in the Chicago and Baltimore areas agreed with the United Steelworkers of America on a program to raise the educational level of existing employees, particularly in the lower labor grades, in order to make them eligible for promotions as vacancies occur. As President I. W. Abel of the Steelworkers and R. Conrad Cooper representing the industry have said, "The companies and the Union have a mutual interest in improving the basic skills of employees so that they may take advantage of training and job opportunities as they become available."[10] Under this program, classes are held close to the workplace, before or after work, to facilitate attendance. Each worker receives up to six hours of classroom instruction a week for a total of at least 150 hours, unless he finishes his course sooner.

The initial venture was financed from federal funds; the training is conducted by the Board for Fundamental Education, a nonprofit organization. In the first semester, 1,227 employees attended one or more classes; in the second semester, 1,625 workers were enrolled. There were 259 employees graduated from a basic course that included the fundamentals of reading, writing, spelling, mathematics, and English; on the average they raised their reading ability 2.6 grade levels and improved their computation skills 2.3 grade levels. Another 252 employees completed an advanced course of study that included instruction in good English usage, fractions, decimals, percents, science, and history; on the average, this group improved 3.8 grade levels in reading and 4.5 grade levels in their computation skills. The same type of instruc-

---

* The present discussion excludes programs for union officers or stewards, considered in Chapter 5, or those for management personnel.

tion program may be developed to provide employees with more education and a certificate of high-school equivalency.

A national retraining program for journeymen plumbers and steamfitters was established in 1956 by agreement between the United Association and the National Constructors Association.[11] The agreement created an "International Training Fund" financed by payments by contractors in accordance with hours worked. Jointly administered, the fund extends financial assistance to local joint training committees to provide equipment and to improve the local training programs under national standards; it also maintains a staff of training coordinators and conducts an annual program for the training of instructors in these programs and for superintendents at Purdue University. These Purdue sessions are used to provide a regular opportunity to introduce new training requirements in the light of new materials, methods, and innovations. While the same agreement and administrative arrangements are used to enrich the local training of apprentices, the journeyman training program is a separate operation. In 1956, only 32 programs of this kind existed, offering training to about 1,000 journeymen. By 1967, the number of programs had increased to 397 with an enrollment exceeding 18,000. In the period since the fund was established, over 80,000 journeymen have taken advantage of the training programs. The annual grants from the national fund for all retraining and apprenticeship have been $1.2 million in recent years; these funds have been supplemented by very much larger expenditures by the local unions and local contractors. Both union and management take pride that their privately financed programs reduce the industry's complete dependence upon public schools and eliminate the exclusive use of public funds to support training that primarily is intended to meet the needs of private enterprise.

The International Typographical Union established a training center at its headquarters in Colorado Springs. Members of the national union are eligible to attend a variety of specialized short-term courses (one to seven weeks) designed to retrain a journeyman in new technologies and innovations in the printing and publishing industry. Photocomposition and accompanying new processes employed in composing a complete type form ready for the press have increasingly replaced the conventional hot-metal methods that older journeymen learned when they served their apprenticeship and learned the trade. As a consequence, systematic courses for journeymen in the new technologies prepare the members for modern technology and thus maintain the work jurisdiction of the union. Among the more than twenty courses are those relating to Fotosetter operation and mockup (3 weeks), Teletypesetter (3 weeks), and Linofilm maintenance (9 weeks).[12] The training center is maintained and financed by the union, but in a number of localities, publishers have, by agreement, sent employees to take courses and have paid their expenses or maintained them on the payroll; in this respect managements have participated in the program.

The expansion of collective bargaining into formal training, beyond apprenticeship, may raise eyebrows on the grounds that these functions are more appropriately the province of the public-school system. But this conventional view fails to recognize the extent to which other institutions are already in the training business. Large-scale business enterprises are very much educational institutions; training of a labor force is a joint output with production and services. In enterprises with sophisticated technology this is particularly significant. IBM has a larger annual expenditure for training and education in various forms than the budget of Harvard University. The military has also become a significant training institution. Many proprietary schools have been established to train workers for such jobs as airplane mechanics, programmers, hairdressers, and clerical occupations. Moreover, new relationships between the formal educational system and both labor and management are required if educational preparation for work and programs of periodic retraining are to become more successful.[13] Managements and unions are likely henceforth to carry a larger share of responsibility for long-term employee development.[14]

Unions can bargain for programs to finance college education as well as job training. For example, the Amalgamated Clothing Workers' Chicago Joint Board has established an educational fund covering technical schools as well as colleges and universities. The fund is not merely designed for top students but is open to the children of all eligible workers no matter where they rank in the class.[15] Interest in programs of this kind is less well developed, but growing. "Bring it to the bargaining table," urges Dr. Herbert A. Levine of Rutgers. "Unions can meet the needs of their members for educational opportunity by negotiating an educational fund, similar to pension and welfare funds, to which employers contribute a portion of the wage bill."[16] Critics may again argue that support of this kind must become the responsibility of government and should not be assumed by labor and management. Yet bargaining over scholarships may make as much sense as pensions or health and welfare programs did twenty years ago. Strategically placed workers have begun to negotiate such educational benefits, and in our pluralistic society, collective bargaining in this area may, in the end, assume the same goading role that it has played in increasing public social-security benefits and inducing Medicare.

Toward Greater Self-Determination for the Employee

Most agreements specify differing benefits and levels of compensation for different groups of workers according to their job classification, department, length of service, method of wage payment, marital status, or other categories. But variations of this kind do not necessarily give much freedom of choice to the individual employee. Within the group to which the individual belongs, the terms of employment may be identical, with few if any options being left to the discretion of each worker. One wonders, therefore, whether ways can be found within collective bargaining to enlarge the area of free choice available to individuals in the same job classification or with the same length of service.

To put the issue in proper perspective, it is necessary to recognize the considerable extent to which collective-bargaining agreements already offer scope for the varying preferences of employees. Piecework and incentive-pay systems allow a worker to make a limited choice between income and effort, a choice that cannot be made under the standard wage rate. Most promotion procedures also allow the individual to choose whether to bid for the higher job, and provide that the junior will be preferred if he has displayed ability which is plainly superior to others with greater seniority. Vacation provisions ordinarily allow employees to make a limited choice of dates for their vacation subject to the operating needs of management; in some cases, there is the further choice of whether to take the paid vacation or work instead and draw vacation pay on top of regular compensation. The allocation of overtime may involve further opportunities for choice, subject to the imperative of equitable distribution of overtime among employees interested in such work (and income) and the right of the management to require enough overtime from the types of workers required to produce the added output desired. The assignment of employees among shifts also provides an occasion for some recognition of individual preference. At times, in plants with continuous operations, all employees in a department may vote to decide between working on a fixed shift or rotating periodically among shifts. The principle of seniority ordinarily is used to allow individual employees a choice among fixed shifts. Retirement plans increasingly contain individual vesting provisions, which reduce the costs of moving from one job to another and allow workers to retire at an earlier age if they wish to do so.

A range of discretion also exists in some industries, such as transportation and construction, in the choice among work assignments. In airlines, the schedule of monthly trips for pilots, stewardesses, and other flight personnel can be arranged to equalize the hours of flying, or they can be so scheduled that there is a significant variation in hours, recognizing that some employees prefer the minimum scheduled hours and pay while others are hungry for money. Throughout the transportation industry, collective bargaining has typically organized assignments to permit individual employees, according to seniority, to choose among runs according to their preferences for income, hours of work, time of day, burden of work, or some other feature.

Another way to expand the area of individual choice is to alter the requirements of the job. For example, management may provide for two individuals to work part time to cover a single position. For many sales positions in tight labor markets, this arrangement has already proved successful in appealing to the large number of persons who prefer to work part time on a regular basis. In the usual case, the two employees can make their own schedules, provided that they keep the job filled at the specified hours. They may divide the work as between mornings and afternoons, between weeks, or may exchange hourly flexibility to suit personal necessities. While the arrangement may involve higher costs by virtue of fringe benefits and administrative costs (unless part-time wage rates or salaries are set correspondingly lower), the flexibility to management in tight labor markets and to employees seeking regular part-time work is appealing, especially in sectors employing female workers. In the future, such use of part-time work may become increasingly widespread as employers seek to attract women to fill the growing number of tasks requiring persons with high levels of intelligence and education.

While the opportunities for individual choice and the exercise of options can no doubt be enlarged, there are limits to such expansion. Full individual bargaining is virtually a negation of collective negotiation; it can also eliminate bargaining's market-stabilizing function, which enables unions to protect their members by "taking wages out of competition." Nevertheless, to the extent that individual employees can exercise choices that do not harm other employees or the union, or impose higher costs on management, the effort is worth making and a clear social gain will have been achieved.

An obvious way to expand individual choice still further is to group certain fringe benefits—such as vacations, holidays, supplementary unemployment compensation, health and welfare, and pension contributions and sick leave—into a lump-sum account for each individual and permit employees to distribute the compensation involved among the various programs in accordance with their own individual preferences. Such an arrangement may permit workers and their families to adjust their contributions to their age and style of life. At certain periods, particularly in the child-rearing years, employees may be especially concerned with health and insurance; at later stages, pensions and vacations may have a higher priority. The allocation of a fixed percentage of compensation to medical insurance, vacation and pensions throughout a working life is insensitive to these shifting interests and unresponsive to changing needs of employees and union members. For added flexibility, compensation arrangements might also recognize that emergencies, prolonged illness, family problems, and the like, create periods of particular stringency, so that provision could be made for contingency reserves to be available in case of special need.

At one time these notions would have been dismissed as impractical. Today, the computer makes it feasible to administer the maze of individual choices involved. Nevertheless, the proposal has its limits. There is a legitimate concern that individuals may not make adequate provision for pensions, medical care, or some other benefit and may later become a serious charge on the community or the parties, as well as bitterly critical of both labor and management for not providing sufficient compensation. It is not a sufficient reply to extol consumer sovereignty or stress the moral responsibility of the individual employee. Experience abundantly demonstrates that individuals can repeatedly fail to make adequate provision for remote contingencies, to their eventual misfortune. As a practical matter, therefore, any plan for expanding individual choice in allocating benefits would need to specify certain minimum allocations, particularly for health and welfare insurance, disability and pensions. Another limitation concerns the extent to which risks are spread within a group of employees. If individuals who are seldom ill make no expenditures on health and welfare plans, the adverse selection will result in very much higher charges for those with illnesses. The provision of at least some minimum level of benefits again seems indispensable. Even with these limitations, however, the scope for increasing individual choice seems large indeed. And now that so many collective-bargaining relationships have matured, there should be much less reason for unions to fear that individual options will be used to divide the members and undermine the collective-bargaining relationship.

The Nature of Work

Fresh challenges for collective bargaining arise not only from new interests of workers but from the discovery of needs that have existed all along. Over the past few decades, many of the most subtle and interesting forms of satisfaction and discontent have come to light in precisely this way. In many cases, the discovery of these needs has been the work of industrial psychologists in reaction against the mechanistic theories of scientific management developed by Frederick Winslow Taylor at the turn of the century.

To Taylor, an engineer by training, maximum productivity could be achieved by designing jobs with sufficient exactness to take advantage of the most efficient sequence of motions on the part of the individual worker. Under this system, the employee was left little freedom and spontaneity. What was required was ". . . not to produce more by his own initiative but to execute punctually the orders given extending into the smallest details."[17] Various rationalizations were developed to make this system seem more palatable from the employee's standpoint. To Taylor himself, scientific management could only improve the morale of the workers since it increased output and thereby raised wages as well. To Henry Ford the new concepts would be welcomed because ". . . the average worker . . . wants a job in which he does not have to put forth much physical effort. Above all, he wants a job in which he does not have to think."

As time went on, it grew increasingly clear that Taylor's principles often went awry because they failed to take adequate account of the psychological and group reactions of employees. In silent protest against the system, workers set informal production norms far below their real potential. If only to relieve the tedium of work, they invented all manner of artful dodges to befuddle the company engineer into setting easier quotas on their jobs. They were absent too often from work; they quit too frequently for other jobs; they were involved in too many accidents and unwittingly broke too many tools. In the face of these difficulties, research teams were called in by many of the more progressive companies. As these investigators got more deeply into the problem, they began to discover a whole battery of desires and discontents that colored the attitude of workers toward their jobs.

Some of these dissatisfactions had to do with the physical environment—the design of the machine, the color of the walls, the temperature of the room. Others involved the pace of work and led to much research to trace the effects of rest periods, assembly-line speeds, and the rhythm of the job on monotony and fatigue. An entire school of thought sprang up on the subject of human relations in the workplace; studies accumulated on the techniques of supervision and the impact of informal work groups and their norms on the behavior of employees.

Still other researchers grappled with the problem of alienation in work. The specialization of tasks recommended by Taylor had narrowed many jobs to the point where they had lost meaning; the worker could not perceive the purpose of his work and how it contributed to the entire production process. At the same time, specialization also multiplied the number of interdependent jobs, and thus gave rise to more onerous forms of coordination and supervision. Out of the research directed at these problems came a series of experiments on the design of jobs. [18] These inquiries have centered on three aspects of the job: the variety of tasks to be performed; the amount of discretion given to the men in deciding how to perform the work; and the respective roles of employees and supervisors in establishing the norms and sanctions for the job. Some of the most interesting experiments have involved the creation of teams of workers. These groups are given a wide range of functions to perform—preferably all the functions that make up a natural unit or process of production. The members of the team have broad responsibility for deciding upon the organization of work, the methods to be used, the standards to be observed. Conversely, foremen and supervisors lose much of their coercive authority and assume a supportive role, giving advice and technical aid and marshaling help as needed from other parts of the company. Under such conditions, Taylor would have predicted little but anarchy and confusion. Yet many of the experiments have resulted in large improvements in quality and productivity, with marked reductions in turnover and accident rates. The very magnitude of these gains suggests a deep need on the part of many workers for more autonomy, variety, and creativity in their work.

Closely related to the experiments in job design are the inquiries of Frederick Herzberg[19] and others into the nature of satisfaction in work. Though still highly controversial, Herzberg's thesis is particularly interesting because of its obvious bearing on the role of the union. The research is built around surveys asking employees to relate those events or facets of their job that have given them satisfaction or dissatisfaction in the past. In a wide variety of occupations, employees have indicated that the factors which produce satisfaction in work are not the same as those which create dissatisfaction. Thus, wages, working conditions, and methods of supervision can cause dissatisfaction, and when corrective measures are taken, the discontent may disappear for a while. But these measures produce little positive satisfaction. Instead, such satisfaction comes primarily from other sources—notably from aspects of the job that provide recognition, responsibility, achievement, variety, and interest. Changes in the different aspects of the job also tend to have effects of varying duration on the attitudes of employees. In general, the removal of the dissatisfying factors seems to alleviate discontent for relatively short periods of time, whereas stimulating the more positive factors in the job tends to produce longer periods of satisfaction. The implications for the union are reasonably clear. By and large, union efforts in bargaining and contract administration serve to alleviate discontent temporarily. If Herzberg is correct, however, unions cannot go further and bring their members greater positive satisfaction in work unless they enlarge the scope of bargaining and grapple more directly with the ways in which jobs are organized and controlled.

These varied lines of research suggest a significant challenge for collective bargaining. To be sure, the problems to be solved are not of crisis proportions. Many workers find considerable social satisfactions in their job. Others do not seem to mind repetitive, uninteresting work. Indeed, a survey of 3,000 factory workers in 1947 revealed that a full 79 percent found their jobs to be "mostly" or "nearly always" interesting. At the same time, the 20 percent of factory workers who reported their work to be dull "all or most of the time" represent many millions of human beings. In addition, a full 59 percent of the entire sample asserted that they would choose a different trade or occupation if they were free to start over again. A number of pilot projects in motivation and job design have also had a strong enough impact on productivity and turnover to suggest great scope for enlarging the interest and attractiveness of work. Indeed, large majorities of the workers involved in these projects have much preferred the new jobs to the old. In sum, there appear to be important needs that remain unfulfilled for large numbers of workers.

Employers and unions have responded quite differently to this challenge. On the part of management, the reaction is spotty, but a number of companies have shown real interest in the subject. They have experimented in new techniques, sponsored research, and have sometimes made extensive changes in their methods of job design and supervision, ordinarily because these changes have been more profitable. Unions, on the other hand, have shown little or no interest in the psychological dimensions of work. If boredom has been a problem to their members, unions have responded by providing escapes from work; they have bargained for shorter hours, longer vacations, more frequent rest periods. But very seldom have they interested themselves in work enrichment, job design, and other ways to make the content of work more meaningful and interesting. Even the Auto Workers Union, for all the talent in its staff, has hardly scratched the surface of these problems, although many of its members have assembly-line jobs that are so repetitive and rapidly paced as to be among the most dispiriting occupations to be found in American industry.

These responses, of course, are not entirely unexpected. Although unions and managements may share a common concern over the welfare of the worker, their motivations and capabilities are critically different. Management's interest in the feelings of their employees is buttressed by the lure of achieving greater levels of efficiency. Since qualified experts report that most factory workers perform well below their capability, the alert executive can hardly fail to consider the realm of industrial psychology as a possible means for improving productivity, and perhaps lowering rates of turnover and accidents as well, in order to lower costs. And when he learns that disgruntled employees have joined a union in his competitor's factory, he is bound to examine the morale of his work force with quickened interest. Thus motivated, he finds it natural to call upon the professional, the researcher, the specialist, and set them to work upon the problem. This is the procedure he has learned in business school and the response he has relied upon in attacking questions of marketing, production, forecasting, and other problems that have arisen within his organization.

Yet one can hardly say that the businessman has done all there is to do to improve morale and satisfaction within his plant. Far from it. If morale conflicts with efficiency—as it sometimes does—the employer cannot make substantial compromises to benefit his employees without running serious competitive risks. Assembly-line jobs may be a crashing bore, but no auto company is going to manufacture cars by hand. Moreover, many of the newer concepts of job design are extremely difficult to implement, even though they are said to promise substantial productivity gains. To create autonomous work crews setting their own standards and disciplinary rules will require management's giving up part of its authority. Such innovations contradict deep-seated managerial instincts and threaten to downgrade the supervisory personnel. As a result, though many managers keep abreast of research on job design, comparatively few have tried to put the new concepts into practice. Instead, the tendency has been to search for milder—and probably less effective—palliatives ranging from bowling teams and better company newspapers to the simple grouping of petty, routine tasks in what is euphemistically referred to as "job enlargement." In view of the record thus far, one recent study has concluded that ". . . the most formidable obstacle which the creation of meaningful work encounters is management and supervisor resistance."[20] There is little reason for this situation to alter on a broad scale unless the potential gains in productivity make such changes irresistible.

These inhibitions create opportunities for the enterprising labor leader. He can insist upon bargaining over the quality of work, or at least ask that study committees be established to pursue the matter further. In highly fragmented industries, labor organizations might even be able to carry out the needed research in job design that none of the small employers could afford to undertake by themselves. Yet these opportunities are not easily seized in the union environment. Even if a union official reads an article on the discontents of work, he is unlikely to find time to pursue the subject unless it is forced upon him by pressures welling up within his organization. Such pressures did arise to move unions beyond wage bargaining to job security, fringe benefits, seniority, and other equitable safeguards. But members are much less likely to exert pressure for job enrichment, autonomous work groups, and other changes catering to subtler psychological needs. Most workers do not readily articulate these needs nor do they know much about the possible cures. In addition, employers do not seem to conceive of the union as an instrument for securing changes of this kind. The union, for its part, lacks management's familiarity with research. As a result, the labor leader does not put specialists to work on these problems or familiarize himself enough with existing literature to articulate these needs to the rank and file. Even if he did, implementation of new job designs would require local leaders of exceptional talent. Not only must they work well with management and elicit genuine cooperation from the men, they must also have a considerable grasp of the business and technological details involved in restructuring patterns of work and authority.

For these reasons, it is unlikely that unions will begin suddenly to play a major role in improving the quality of work. The task requires precisely the resources that unions find in such short supply: a capacity for research at headquarters and a corps of able local leaders to put new ideas to work in the shop and factory.

In addition, real progress along these lines would require a special type of relation between labor, management and workers—one that employers as well as union leaders might find hard to accept. Most of the research on basic changes in job design suggests that the company must embrace the new concepts wholeheartedly, and make thorough efforts to insure that every echelon of management understands and supports the innovations being tried. Without these attitudes and preparations, different parts of the company work at cross-purposes, and the employees do not have enough confidence in management's intentions to cooperate fully. As a result, it seems doubtful that much progress can be made if unions have to force their employers to introduce changes in the content and design of work. Grudging compliance is simply not enough; there must be an atmosphere of mutual trust, and this is a climate that currently exists in only a minority of labor-management relations. The fault is not all on the side of management. In union ranks, there are many leaders who prefer to operate in an atmosphere of discontent and opposition. Without discontent, members may cease to believe that unions are necessary. Without an opponent, union officials may lack a symbol to use in whipping up militancy and determination among the rank and file. To these leaders, the newer concepts of work may be distasteful because they blur the lines between workers and management and weaken the adversary spirit.

In short, the prospects for union initiative are not bright. But they are not hopeless. Many unions do work in harmony with a number of employers. And practical experience, as well as research, testify to the fact that loyalty to the union can be strong however friendly the relations with management. On the other side of the table, employers are bound to be skeptical and suspicious of union proposals to alter the methods of work. Yet many of these changes do promise to improve productivity, and considerable experience has accumulated in some firms to demonstrate these results empirically. As a result, for all the difficulties, there are also opportunities that do not exist in other areas of bargaining, where the union's gain is inevitably management's loss.

Unions could conceivably reap enormous advantages if they should begin to interest themselves in the enrichment of work. To millions of members, particularly workers of a younger generation, there is the chance of being able to have a more meaningful, enjoyable experience during the working day. To organizers, there is the opportunity to learn much more about the needs and motivations of those who will be asked to join the union. To the labor movement itself, there is the possibility of gaining the interest and recognition that comes to organizations at work on the growing edge of important social problems. In the last analysis, it is only these possibilities that create any real hope for union action along these lines. For the obstacles are large enough—and the political incentives sufficiently slight—that no union leader can be expected to make much of a commitment without a vision of great reward, to himself, to his organization, or to his membership.

13

Beyond Better Wages and Working Conditions

THROUGHOUT THE Western world, the concept of a labor movement has meant much more than organizing workers into unions and bargaining for better wages and conditions of employment. In Scandinavia, for example, the labor movement is not confined to the trade unions. Unions are only one strand in a larger network that includes a cooperative organization and a labor party. Thus conceived, the movement permeates the entire texture of the community. For example, Swedish cooperatives control 25 percent of the retail food business; they have undertaken production of many commodities, particularly when such action served to combat excessive prices of private producers; they have provided newspapers, educational facilities, and a variety of other cultural activities aimed at the workers and union members who make up the bulk of their clientele. The Social Democrats—the labor party—have likewise had an enormous influence, having remained in power for more than thirty years. Though formally independent of the unions, they receive over half their votes and more than 80 percent of their funds from union members.

In other industrial democracies, the labor movement has not developed to a comparable extent, particularly in the cooperative field. But in almost all of these nations, there are labor parties which draw their main support from union members. And it is also common to find a network of workers' organizations engaged in education and recreation activities as well as various types of cooperative and commercial endeavor.

The United States has not produced a labor movement of comparable breadth. No viable labor party has emerged except in one or two limited areas. And the cooperative movement, tiny as it is, has had little connection with the unions. Under these conditions, labor organizations in America have had to decide whether to expand their activities to fulfill some of the functions performed abroad by other working-class institutions.

Union leaders have not been of one mind on this issue. To Dave Beck, former president of the Teamsters, members ". . . join our union for only one purpose; to sell their labor for the highest price they can get. . . . This international union and its various subdivisions, its local unions—is the machinery of our people to sell that labor."[1] On the other hand, according to Walter Reuther:

> It was inevitable in the early days of unionism, since there was so much to be done in the matter of improving living and working standards, that the labor movement would be devoted almost exclusively to those things. In the next phase, these things will be deemphasized—not neglected—and the unions will take on the broader function of concern for the quality of our society as a whole. The labor movement will become less of an economic movement and more of a social movement. It will be concerned with the economic factors, of course, but also with the moral, the spiritual, the intellectual, and the social nature of our society, and all of this in terms of an ultimate objective—the fulfillment of the complete human being.[2]

Although the issue remains in dispute, unions in America have turned to activities well beyond the field of organizing and bargaining over the terms of employment. Some of these activities are designed to benefit members and their families: medical programs, recreational facilities, legal services, and the like. Others are broader in scope, as labor's political and legislative programs, which seek not only to influence labor laws but also to obtain social-welfare legislation of broad application. Still other activities involve unions in a variety of civic endeavors, such as charitable drives and antipoverty agencies.

The earliest examples of union welfare programs involved the payment of cash benefits to members in time of need. At the time when unions first began to develop in this country, the community took little or no responsibility to assist persons afflicted with illness, unemployment, injury, or widowhood. Under these circumstances, unions were a natural agency to provide protection against such losses. In fact, so many labor organizations began as benefit societies that it is hardly an exaggeration to say that trade-unionism in America arose almost as much from a desire to band together for mutual insurance as from a desire to bargain collectively.

Aside from providing cash benefits, a few unions made sporadic attempts in the last century to protect their members by founding cooperative businesses and stores. To some leaders, cooperatives were valued chiefly as a source of cheaper goods or a place of employment for union members during a strike or recession. To a few visionaries, these ventures seemed to offer a path by which the workingman could escape from capitalism and exploitation to enjoy the full fruits of his labor. In either case, cooperatives represented an ambitious undertaking for a young and precarious trade union.

Experience was not kind to the fledgling cooperatives. Union members supported them in time of strike or depression, but their interest rapidly dwindled when better times returned and jobs could be had elsewhere. Many of these ventures, moreover, were inadequately capitalized and too poorly managed to survive. Greater success might have been achieved under the more highly cartelized conditions that prevailed in Europe. But the rigors of competition in this country pushed many American cooperatives into bankruptcy.

In comparison with the cooperatives, the early benefit programs fared tolerably well, and many still survive today. With the exception of strike benefits, however, most of these programs had to be adjusted substantially to changing conditions. Some of them were cut back or abandoned entirely after the advent of workmen's compensation and other forms of social insurance. Others were redesigned to supplement the government programs and were financed increasingly by employer contributions rather than union dues.

As the older programs changed or disappeared, a new array of activities began to emerge. One of these services—which is still flourishing—is the union counseling program, developed under the auspices of the AFL–CIO. For many years, courses have been conducted in many cities and towns to train rank-and-file members in the use of community health and welfare services. Members have been taught, with the help of representatives from local agencies, to understand the operation of programs in such fields of service as public assistance, social security, workmen's compensation, unemployment insurance, recreation, health services, family and child guidance, and retirement. More recently, classes have also been instituted in consumer counseling and mental health. Since these programs began, some 70,000 unionists have been trained to go back to their locals and advise fellow members who are ignorant of public benefit programs or need referral to some appropriate community agency. The service undoubtedly suffers from the lack of any systematic effort by the Federation to determine whether the counselors are performing their functions effectively. Nevertheless, the program has succeeded in many locals in making much-needed advice available to the rank and file.

Other benefit programs have been instituted through efforts of some internationals and certain local federations. The New York City Central Labor Council, for example, has established a rehabilitation program to encourage the early identification and referral of members suffering from physical impairment, and the Auto Workers Union has developed a network of retirement programs to give preretirement counseling and provide recreation centers for elderly members. Although these examples are not uncommon, most programs have originated in local unions. As a result, the range of programs and services varies enormously among different cities and labor organizations—indeed, too widely to permit any comprehensive description. But some notion of the range of benefits can be grasped by looking at the programs offered in a single large city. The following benefits are provided by several of the larger locals in Los Angeles:

1) Credit unions to make loans to members on reasonable terms.

2) Health services, including medical clinics, convalescent homes, psychiatric counseling, dental clinics, and plans for purchasing drugs, glasses, hearing aids, and the like, at reduced cost.

3) Legal services and representation before accident commissions, unemployment compensation boards, or even help with private legal problems of all kinds.

4) Retirement facilities, including clubs, old-age homes, recreational facilities, and pensions.

5) Purchasing programs to allow members to buy consumer goods at a lower price.

In some cases, more unusual programs have developed, often reflecting the special character of the local membership. Thus, the Screen Cartoonists run an art gallery to enable members to exhibit their work. The building trades have initiated plans and obtained federal support for low-cost housing projects, in part to provide jobs for their members. And the Laundry Workers, representing employees whose work is often arduous and disagreeable, have built a large hotel outside the city limits for the rest and recreation of their members.

The very scope of these programs invites consideration of how broad a role the union of the future might play in the lives of its members. In theory, at least, the union occupies a strategic position from which to bring benefits to its dues payers. With a large membership, it can capitalize upon the advantages of mass purchasing power to make available a variety of goods and services at reduced cost. With sufficient imagination, it can work in numerous ways to enrich the lives of retired members, who are so often neglected, spiritually as well as economically, in American society. And given the vision and the will, the union might even serve as an innovator and a catalyst to engage the members in a range of cultural and educational pursuits to occupy their steadily growing leisure hours.

From the standpoint of organized labor, an expansion of benefit programs also might bring advantages not only to the membership but to the movement as a whole. Unions often encounter difficulty in expanding their membership because unorganized firms have become so adept at matching the wages and conditions that unions have won through collective bargaining. By emphasizing new benefits and services, unions might conceivably make a fresh appeal to the unorganized—an appeal that smaller employers, at least, would find hard to emulate. In addition, a variety of benefit programs might provide opportunities for involving the members more closely in the life and affairs of the union, thus giving greater meaning to union membership.

In view of these advantages, it is worth taking a careful look at benefit programs to examine their potentialities for the future. This is a subject, however, that can easily degenerate into the most utopian sort of speculation. To keep perspective, therefore, it is well to look closely at actual experience, for the record reveals many pitfalls, as well as opportunities, in the efforts of unions to establish these programs.

The Pitfalls

THE LABOR BANKING FIASCO[3]

A succession of disappointments during the last century turned most experienced labor leaders away from the idea of cooperative business ventures. At the close of the First World War, however, a fresh upsurge of interest arose over the creation of union banks. Several factors helped to account for this enthusiasm. Some spokesmen saw the labor bank as a way of meeting the special financial needs of working people. Hours of service could be adjusted to allow employees to bank after working hours, while credit could be offered to workers under reasonable terms and less onerous restrictions than those of commercial banks. Other advocates had much broader objectives in mind. They viewed the labor bank as a method of promoting such union objectives as financing cooperatives, helping unionized firms, and assisting locals in time of strikes. Doubtless, still other union officials had more dubious motives. For these leaders, a union bank might provide a "window on Wall Street" that would enhance their personal influence and enlarge the prestige of their organizations. Finally, a few visionaries had even more grandiose objectives. According to one enthusiastic writer:

> The labor banks seek on the one hand to use the money given into their care to provide steady employment, under decent conditions, at fair money wages for the workers, and on the other to increase the purchasing power of money wages by requiring maximum production and efficient distribution at reasonable margins of profit by those to whom credit is extended. . . . [The] influence of these policies upon general living and working conditions will be multiplied as the labor banks increase in numbers and resources, and enterprises financed with their funds come into increasing competition with those following the restrictive formula of profit-making.[4]

Although the AFL remained cool to these arguments, several unions moved ahead to establish banks. The Machinists led the way in 1920 with the opening of a bank in Washington, D.C. Later in the same year, the Brotherhood of Locomotive Engineers launched the first of several banking ventures. Thereafter, the Amalgamated Clothing Workers, the Brotherhood of Railway Clerks, the Order of Railroad Telegraphers, the Flint Glass Workers, and other labor unions took similar action. By 1925, the number of union-sponsored banks reached thirty-six, and their total resources rose above $115 million.

Despite these proud beginnings, the labor banking movement lay in ruins within a decade. By 1933, only four banks were still operating. In part, of course, this rapid decline resulted from the Great Crash, which took a heavy toll throughout the banking system. But other factors also were at work, for many labor banks had already disappeared before the onset of the Depression.

To begin with, union members did not flock to labor banks, as many proponents had assumed they would. In many cases, the banks were not conveniently located to serve the rank and file. And many other members seemed unexpectedly satisfied with the older, established banks and rather skeptical of the new ventures sponsored by their unions. These doubts later proved to be justified, for many of the new banks suffered greatly from poor management. Union leaders often were unable to make wise judgments in selecting personnel to run the banks. Some were inclined to offer jobs to relatives and friends; still others took personal control, although they lacked experience in banking matters. As one study pointed out: "There is much reason to believe that the degree of success attained [by labor banks] varied inversely to the extent labor directors and officers filled positions which should have been occupied by businessmen and trained bankers."[5]

As time wore on, the banks became a cat's-paw in the internal political struggles of the sponsoring unions. Incumbent leaders often used their bank to make appointments and loans favoring the prevailing faction in the union. Political rivals seized upon the banks as an election issue, arguing that they were badly run and that they diverted the leaders from the job of running the union. Under pressure of these criticisms, many examples of mismanagement were brought to light, which only added to the general lack of confidence in the new institutions.

Not all labor banks experienced these problems. The leading exceptions were the Amalgamated Clothing Workers' banks, which have enjoyed a steady, if unspectacular, growth until the present day. But even the Amalgamated banks did not fulfill the hopes of the more ambitious advocates of the movement. Special services were offered to workers in the form of more convenient hours and the successful use of "character" loans without collateral. Yet the banks did not revitalize the cooperative movement, nor did they make the strike obsolete. Instead, their successes were commercial. They resulted from the efforts of a professional management which adhered, for the most part, to accepted banking principles without undue interference from union officials.

Although the banking adventure is only a curiosity of labor history, it does illustrate several practical problems in union benefit programs. Above all, it reveals the danger of falling prey too quickly to the romantic visions put forward by those who so often urge unions to experiment along radically different lines. Labor banks also point up the problems that can arise when unions engage in complex ventures beyond their natural function of representing employees. Such tasks lie outside the normal experience of union leaders. They must be carried out within a political system that exposes the union leader to strong temptations and pressures not commonly felt by those who customarily manage business enterprises. At the very least, such programs make heavy demands on the time and energy of leaders who are typically overburdened with the normal tasks of running their union. Perhaps these problems are not insurmountable. The continued success of the Amalgamated banks suggests that they need not be. But the difficulties surely are large enough to caution against ambitious benefit programs unless they provide some service that is strongly needed by the rank and file and not readily available from another source.

THE CASE OF THE NEGLECTED SPA

If labor leaders were in error when they supposed that their members would flock to use union banks, they were not alone in failing to understand the sentiments of the members. The following example reveals how easy it is, even today, for the best-intentioned officials to misjudge the needs of their constituents.

In the late 1950's, the leaders of a large metropolitan local decided to build a health spa and recreation center for their members. From many points of view, the plan seemed ideal. Inasmuch as the members worked for very low wages under hot and disagreeable conditions, a resort facility in a country setting seemed particularly appropriate. At the same time, other features could be added to the facility to increase its value to the members. A few cottages would be set aside for retired members. For married members living in urban ghettos, a camp could be organized to which their children might go in the summer at a very low cost. Since muscular and circulatory illnesses were a great hazard in their line of work, a hydrotherapeutic pool could be installed to allow members to secure needed treatment under ideal conditions.

These ideas eventually resulted in a handsome resort on a twenty-acre site overlooking a lake only a ninety-minute drive from the city. Forty bedrooms and dining facilities were laid out in a quadrangle surrounding a swimming pool. With a game room, a playground and picnic areas, the completed facility had every appearance of a first-class resort motel—but at prices that were extremely reasonable. The project seemed to fulfill all the hopes and plans of the union leaders. Yet five years later these expectations had not been met. In the words of one of the managers of the facility, "In spite of intensive campaigns and considerable expenditure of money over the past five years, utilization by the members has been very, very low."

Disappointed by this experience, the officers of the local turned to a union-leader-turned-professor and asked him to conduct a study of the facility.[6] A survey of the membership yielded a number of revealing conclusions about the spa. In response to questions about their weekend pursuits, the members mentioned a number of activities, but few talked of taking trips, and fewer still referred to any active interest in sports. As for vacations, more than 70 percent either stayed at home or did not take a vacation at all. Of those who did travel, the great majority went to visit relatives. Very few mentioned specific recreation activities, and no one spoke of going to parks, camps, resorts, or recreational centers. These replies moved the investigator to conclude: "As a group, they do not seem attracted by resort-type facilities. The attractions that draw them from their homes seem to emanate from the place of origin or from places where their friends and relatives live—not vacation resorts."

Members also were asked why they had not visited the spa. The answers themselves do more than any statistical tabulation to reveal the anatomy of the problem:

"The work is so hard that when you get home you don't feel like going anyplace."

"There is nothing to do there but just sleep and eat. If I were sick I would go there; but for a vacation, no—besides you can't bring a bottle up there. Whoever heard of a vacation without a few drinks?"

"I can go to a beach or a park and have a good time with the family and it doesn't cost anything."

"Because the union runs it and the members don't like the union."

"The Anglos hate the Mexicans. . . . The Mexicans who have been, don't go back because of the Negroes. . . . I work with blacks but I don't want to live with them."

"People would rather stomp and jump and get 'em a bottle than spend weekends down there."

"I'd have to take two buses and then the red tape of making reservations and having to cancel them."

"I thought the spa was something for children."

The fate of this single resort by no means suggests that unions have no useful role to play in the vacation and recreation activities of their members. The Ladies' Garment Workers' Union has succeeded for many years in attracting large numbers of members and their families to its Unity House resort. If there is any moral to the story of the spa, it is to beware of deciding too quickly what the members really want and need. To quote from the conclusion of the study:

> Evident in so many of the interviews . . . is that this is a situation where something was created (the spa) according to middle-class values and middle-class tastes and made available to persons who have not yet fully adopted those values or enjoyed those tastes.

The Potentialities of Benefit Programs

Critics will be quick to point out that the fate of the recreation spa typifies the growing distance between union leaders and the rank and file. Sociologists will speak of bureaucratization and loss of solidarity in the unions—processes that learned writers associate with the onset of middle age in a social movement. Yet history does not support these diagnoses. Unions have always made mistakes of this kind. The early ventures into labor cooperatives foundered on a mistaken assumption that union members would be eager to escape their employee status and share in the ownership of business. In the twenties, leaders in the banking movement clearly overestimated the willingness of members to patronize the labor banks. And only a decade later, the more progressive unions found that courses in literature, economics, and other cultural subjects could not hold the attention of more than a tiny fraction of the membership. There is nothing strange in this. It is only natural that unions should attract a number of visionaries and idealists with ideas that outstrip the wishes of the members. Nor do their dreams and innovations always go astray. The experience of unions in the field of medical care provides a telling example of the potentialities of benefit programs that respond to deeply felt needs of the rank and file.

HEALTH PROGRAMS[7]

Union efforts to protect their members against sickness go back at least to 1877, when the Granite Cutters launched a program of sick benefits financed by union dues. By 1904, twenty-eight of the 107 national unions had followed suit. Although most of these services simply provided for cash payments, a few organizations began to establish medical facilities for the benefit of their members. The printers built a home for the sick and aged as early as 1892, and the Ladies' Garment Workers opened their first diagnostic clinic in 1913.

These early efforts were modest in scope until the close of World War II. Thereafter, interest rapidly developed in establishing collectively bargained health and welfare funds. The Mine Workers used their fund to build a network of hospitals and health facilities, especially in areas of Appalachia, where medical care was in a rather primitive state. In most cases, however, union negotiators simply bargained for health insurance to provide cash benefits for their members. By 1960, such plans gave varying amounts of medical coverage to more than 37 million employees and dependents.

Unlike the banking and recreation ventures previously described, medical programs enjoyed wide support among the rank and file. As these sentiments became clear, union leaders sought to increase the scope and adequacy of health plans. At first the efforts took the form merely of negotiating larger contributions from management. Union officials soon came to realize, however, that they could not achieve their objectives simply by bargaining with

employers. Since the nature and cost of medical benefits were
determined less by employers than by insurance companies and
the medical profession itself, unions were increasingly drawn into
negotiations with these groups as well.

The process began with union efforts to expand the scope of
health-insurance coverage. In meetings with Blue Cross and private insurance carriers, unions worked to include new groups
within their health plans, notably dependents and retired members. At the same time, unions also attempted to enlarge the range
of insured risks and services to include house calls, diagnostic
treatment, outpatient services, maternity care, and major medical
treatments involving thousands of dollars of expense. These efforts
often met with sharp resistance from managements and insurance
companies, who argued that the incidence of risk was difficult to
assess and that the costs of administration and possibilities of
abuse were unduly high for particular benefits. Bit by bit, however, labor negotiators succeeded in adding new benefits and
services to negotiated medical plans.

As time went on, unions became increasingly troubled by
the ever-rising costs of medical care. In part, the problem simply
reflected the constant increases that were experienced everywhere
in the cost of medicine. But union leaders also felt that many
doctors raised their fees once they learned that a substantial part
of the cost was being met through collectively bargained insurance
plans. Perhaps these fears were exaggerated. Nevertheless, union
after union negotiated more expensive plans only to learn that the
cash benefits fell substantially short of meeting the members'
medical bills. This problem naturally led to complaints from union
members who had expected that all, or almost all, of their medical
bills would be covered by the plan. Because of these pressures,
labor leaders began to seek ways of controlling costs so that they
could negotiate an adequate schedule of benefits. These efforts
forced many unions to look beyond the insurance company to the
medical profession itself.

The primary aim of many local unions was to establish a fixed
fee schedule that they could use as a firm basis in setting benefits
under their plans. This goal led union leaders to seek negotiations
with local medical societies. The profession proved hostile to the
idea of negotiated fee schedules; in many areas, labor could make
no headway against this opposition. Some unions, however, did
succeed in bringing considerable pressure to bear by threatening

to draw upon some other source for their health needs. In the San Francisco Bay area, for example, unions took preliminary steps first to establish their own facilities and then to turn to the Kaiser Plan, which provided medical service to individuals or groups on a prepaid basis. By these means, labor representatives managed to enter into serious negotiations with local medical societies and to establish a reasonably firm list of fees.

In many cases, what started out as a concern about medical costs developed into a concern about the quality of the medical service received. A number of independent studies had exposed a wide variety of abuses and wasteful practices on the part of certain doctors. A survey by the California Physicians Service concluded that 7 percent of the benefits paid under its plan were attributable to fraudulent billings for work not actually performed.[8] A Michigan Blue Cross report disclosed that one day in five of hospitalization was unnecessary.[9] Other studies revealed a serious problem of needless surgery; in fact, one well-known investigation concluded that more than 50 percent of a sampling of appendectomies actually were unnecessary.[10] After summarizing the available evidence, Professor Joseph W. Garbarino observed: "As a tentative conclusion, it is suggested that the abuse figure for the average plan at any point in time probably falls between 15 and 30 percent of the true medical costs that would be appropriate to the plan."[11] No plan could hope to eliminate abuses entirely. But many unions naturally felt that greater controls over quality and utilization could achieve considerable savings and perhaps improve the level of care as well.

Union efforts to control abuse have understandably provoked opposition from many doctors, who fear intrusions on their independence. Nevertheless, labor has managed to increase its influence. In many communities, unions have encouraged group-practice plans that permit greater specialization by a panel of doctors of higher competence than the individual worker might select on his own initiative. In other cases, unions have urged periodic checks and evaluation studies to maintain and improve the quality of service they receive. A few unions have established health centers in well-known hospitals, where they can draw upon the staff and facilities of acknowledged high quality. Other labor organizations have hired doctors on a salary, rather than on a fee-for-service basis, in the hope that this technique can reduce the incentive for unnecessary and extravagant care. Still others have obtained greater representation on boards of directors of medical plans in order to press more effectively for improvements in service. Perhaps the most radical developments emerged under the Mine Workers Welfare and Retirement Fund, where a determined administration established closed panels of doctors and a system of surveillance that disqualified doctors who engaged in abuses or fell below established standards of quality. In a few instances, grievance procedures have been established to insure consideration of complaints from individual members.

As yet, these efforts are still in an uncertain stage. Despite several interesting experiments, labor organizations have not developed any proven techniques for successfully controlling abuse by their members or the medical profession, or otherwise appreciably lowering the cost of medical care. Nor is it clear how much progress can be made against the opposition of the medical profession. Apart from these uncertainties, union ventures in the medical field also have been afflicted by several of the same problems already encountered in earlier benefit programs. Health plans have plainly put a great burden on union staffs because of the time and expertise required to work effectively in this complex field. It is said, too, that a few locals have used medical programs as a source of jobs for friends and relatives. And Congressional investigations have unearthed several cases involving kickbacks from insurance companies to union officials, excessive premiums, and other shady practices.

Despite these problems, there is a basic difference separating the health plans from other kinds of benefit programs. The members have unquestionably given their endorsement to union efforts to protect them against the costs of sickness and hospitalization. Without doubt, it is this grass-roots support that has enabled the union health-care movement to survive its difficulties, just as banking and cooperative businesses could not. The results have been impressive. Under pressure from the members, unions have negotiated health benefits for millions of workers. And they have likewise progressed toward a highly imaginative form of representation and bargaining. In several communities, at least, labor has managed to bargain for consumers of medical care by negotiating not merely with employers but with insurance companies and medical societies as well. The impact of these efforts on the quality of care may be problematical. Unions have clearly succeeded, however, in broadening the scope of medical plans to cover more risks and more people than would otherwise have been protected. They have initiated a number of studies and helped to focus attention on the quality of care, utilization, and costs, and by developing a group of staff specialists they have contributed to the widespread appreciation of the importance and potentialities for reform in the arrangements for the delivery of medical-care services in the United States.*

THE WELFARE-STATE LOCALS[12]

The success of health programs should make students of labor and leaders alike wonder how far unions might go in providing services and benefits for their members. It is worthwhile to examine a few local unions outstanding for their array of welfare programs: Local 770 of the Retail Clerks in Los Angeles, Local 688 of the Teamsters in St. Louis, and Local 3 of the International Brotherhood of Electrical Workers in New York City. Each of these organizations has experimented not only with health services but also with education, retirement, credit plans, and a variety of other benefits.

At the heart of the programs in all three unions is a wide array of medical benefits. For example, Local 770 of the Retail Clerks offers a basic health plan that permits each member and his family to choose between Blue Cross and the huge group-practice Kaiser Plan, with its network of hospitals and clinics. These benefits extend not only to employed members but also to those who are retired, disabled or unemployed. In addition, members and dependents are covered by a dental-care program administered by the union in its own modern clinics. Recently, Local 770 has added a program by which members and dependents can obtain comprehensive examinations in the union's preventive health center. Psychiatric offices at union headquarters provide an additional range of services, including family counseling, child and adult therapy, and premarital and teen-age counseling. Additional benefits include optical examinations, free glasses, and a drug purchase

---

* The AFL–CIO was in the forefront of the organizations which pressed successfully for the passage of Medicare in 1965. The labor movement continues to advocate a national health-insurance plan characterized by universal coverage, comprehensive benefits, adequate financing, and high quality. It is possible that the Federation may be able to play a major role in the discussions of national policy involved in the reshaping of the medical care system in the United States in the next decade.

program providing reimbursement of 90 percent of the cost of authorized prescriptions.

In the future, local president Joseph De Silva looks to an even more ambitious program that would integrate the entire range of health services within facilities administered by the union. By coordinating the various programs currently offered, the union will be able to supply complete medical information from its preventive facilities to improve the diagnosis of health problems when they occur. By operating its own health facilities, the union hopes to provide a smaller, more flexible, and more intimate brand of medical care than is currently offered by giant programs such as the Kaiser prepaid medical plan. With the addition of education programs to the facilities, the union plans to inform its members how to guard against disease and live with disabilities already contracted.

In the area of educational and cultural programs, no local in the country can surpass Local 3 of the I.B.E.W. under the leadership of Harry Van Arsdale. Some of the Local 3 programs are intensely practical, such as the five-year apprenticeship training and a variety of courses in new electrical skills and techniques. Other programs for the rank and file include labor history and trade-unionism classes taught with assistance from Cornell University. But for Van Arsdale, who himself completed only two years of high school, an education program implies much more than courses in union affairs and skill training. A special fund provides full four-year tuition scholarships to allow children of members to attend college. Over thirty grants are offered each year, and the union has awarded almost five hundred since the program began in 1949. Local 3 also provides tuition grants to every member or member's wife who wishes to take college courses for credit. Within the local itself, classes taught by union members with prior college training are offered in civics and government. Van Arsdale selects these members, called Futurians, who are trained by a retired dean of Columbia University. In addition to serving as instructors, they provide a fertile source of administrative talent for the local itself. Even more unusual are the courses in critical thinking offered to members at Bayberry, a 314-acre estate on Long Island once owned by Dwight Davis, the donor of the international tennis cup. For one week, small groups of members work from 8:30 to 5:15 on a range of subjects including public speaking, logic, semantics, and psychology. By 1968, some 13,000 members had completed this course. Although skeptics well may wonder how much progress can be made on such subjects in one short week, many members testify to the value of the classes in broadening their interests. And there are even employers who suggest that their workers have become more alert and effective after completing the course.

In recent years, Van Arsdale has pushed beyond education to introduce cultural programs. In the union's new auditorium, arts festivals consisting of exhibits, ballets, concerts, and illustrated lectures have been arranged for members. Special performances have been given of musical comedies and well-known operas and ballets. The union also arranges group travel tours, and officials of the local have been sent on expenses-paid trips abroad. (Characteristically, however, Van Arsdale has allowed only those officials to participate who have completed a specially prepared course in world affairs.)

In addition to health and education programs, the welfare-minded local may offer low-cost housing for its members. Local 688 of the Teamsters, for example, has built an apartment complex in St. Louis for its retired members. Local 770 plans a similar retirement center, complete with a wide range of recreational facilities. And Local 3 has already built an apartment development at very low rentals for 2,200 families, which has its own shopping center and meeting hall.

Beyond health, education, and housing, one or another of these unions provides a variety of additional benefits. Local 688, for example, offers extensive recreational facilities at a resort estate on Cape Girardeau, in Missouri. Local 770 administers a credit union for its members. Local 3 has established a lavish annuity program, as well as a credit facility which allows interest-free loans up to $1,000 for general purposes and $10,000 for purchase of a house or cooperative apartment. When Van Arsdale discovered that members felt they could not afford to put their names on jury rolls, he instituted a special payment of $30 per day for members serving jury duty; typically, though, he made the payment contingent on the successful completion of the union course in civics and government.

These benefit programs are largely financed through collective bargaining and are extremely costly. Members of Local 770, for example, have approximately 10 percent of their gross wages set aside for health benefits alone. The full range of Local 3's programs carries a price tag estimated at 30 percent of gross payroll. A more concrete illustration of these costs can be derived by looking at the expenditures in 1967 for the various benefits available to certain divisions of Local 3.[13]

Pensions	$1,613,245.94
Annuities	4,045,137.38
Hospitalization	356,227.25
Surgical fees	280,513.00
Other medical services	383,390.88
Dental	280,513.00
Optical	124,630.92
Bayberry program	149,590.44
Scholarship program	127,855.00
Tuition grants (members and wives)	30,442.00
Total	$7,391,543.81

The press has warmly praised benefits of this kind, perhaps too uncritically. In fact, some of the benefits raise troublesome questions. Most programs are decidedly paternalistic in the sense that the member sacrifices a substantial wage increase to support them, whether or not he wants the services in question. Moreover, although everyone must pay for the services, many members do not use them once they are provided, and some of the benefits are claimed by only a minority of the eligible employees. Members who use their own doctor, dislike ballet, or find the dental clinic too inconveniently located may well argue that they are being short-changed.

It would be superficial, however, to conclude that a union should merely seek pay increases for its members to spend as they will. By virtue of their collective purchasing power, unions can provide drugs, annuities, and other services at cheaper rates than any individual member could obtain. By developing and administering their own programs, unions also may offer more attractive or more efficient services than independent group plans. For example, Local 3 has succeeded in providing supplemental disability compensation at a much lower administrative cost than the New York State program. More important still, arguments based on allowing the worker free choice are decisive only if the individuals involved are in a position to make an informed decision. But the average worker is often at sea in trying to select a competent physician, dentist, or lawyer. As a result, a union clinic or legal service may provide the member with much more competent professional help than he could obtain if left to his own devices. In addition, many workers know little of medicine, dentistry, and psychiatric care. After instituting medical programs, unions have naturally sought to encourage full use of their facilities by educating their members to a much higher level of awareness concerning their health needs. In terms of human welfare, therefore, it is difficult to prove that union members would be better off abandoning these benefits and services for higher wages. The officials of these locals, of course, would argue strenuously that just the opposite is true, and the members appear to have given their clear support to these programs.

The Future of Benefit Programs

Whatever their merits, it is worth asking whether "welfare-state locals" represent the wave of the future—a new brand of unionism that will spread much more widely throughout the labor movement. Certainly, each of these locals has much to attract the attention of other unions. The leaders are secure, the membership is growing, and the benefit programs themselves seem to have taken firm root in the minds of the employees. Nevertheless, there are many obstacles to welfare unionism that help to explain why these locals still represent such a tiny minority.

To begin with, a broad array of benefit programs requires a large membership in order to provide an adequate financial base. It is no accident that each of the locals we have described has more than twenty thousand members. Yet there are scarcely a hundred locals in the entire country with even ten thousand members. The size barrier could be overcome if locals of several unions joined forces in a community to create a range of services. But unions have been reluctant to take this step. Some leaders fear the disagreements over policy that could emerge in an alliance of union locals. Others feel that jointly administered benefits are unattractive, because they may not strengthen the member's loyalty to his own local and thus may fail to make a significant contribution to the union as an institution. So long as these attitudes pre-

vail, the example of Local 3 or Local 770 is likely to be confined to
a minority of locals and district councils.

Further difficulties may arise in getting employers to agree to
such programs in contract negotiations. In some cases, management may resist setting aside a portion of wages for benefit funds,
either because it feels that the members do not really want the
benefits or because it dislikes establishing programs that may
enhance the power and prestige of the union. In other instances,
international unions do not give their local leaders enough flexibility in bargaining. Broad benefit programs need to be tailored to
the local membership and fitted to local conditions. This is easy
enough to accomplish where collective bargaining is local in scope.
But in industries where negotiations are national or area-wide, the
terms of agreement are fixed by international headquarters, and
local officials lack authority to divert wage gains into welfare programs. Thus, it is not surprising that each of the locals discussed
here exists in an industry in which bargaining is decentralized to
the metropolitan or county level.

Union members can create additional obstacles for elaborate
benefits. The programs work best in a union with a stable membership enjoying comfortable rates of pay. In a local composed of
young or transient employees, the members may balk at costly
fringe benefits, preferring wage increases instead. Changes in the
education and ethnic levels of the members may also require
adaptation in union programs. With the advent of large numbers
of Negro and Puerto Rican members, the Ladies' Garment Workers found it very difficult to sustain interest in the cultural and
education programs that were developed for a predominantly
Jewish membership in the twenties and thirties.

Even if none of the preceding problems arises, benefit programs may still make excessive demands on the administrative
talent within the union. To be sure, professionals can be hired
from outside to administer health facilities and manage retirement
and education programs. But if these services are to work well, the
leadership will have to devote much time to plan their development, supervise their administration, and educate the members on
the availability and value of the benefits. Complaints from members will continually arise, and these will have to be attended to
with care lest the member blame the union for getting poor dental
work, waiting for medical attention, or missing out on a scholarship for his son. These burdens can be extremely heavy for local

leaders already preoccupied with traditional union duties. Thus, it is no accident that each of the locals considered here has a leader with a nearly legendary reputation for drive and energy. Few union locals can hope to enjoy such leadership. And where the local officers are not powerful enough to escape internal political disputes or resist hostile employers, the added responsibilities of such programs will be not merely inconvenient but downright impossible.

In view of all the obstacles, what are the prospects for the spread of benefit programs? Some growth seems bound to occur. Once a few unions have pioneered, the pattern of their programs can be copied more easily elsewhere. As locals become larger and wage levels rise, energetic leaders will find added benefits and services more feasible and more attractive. Random events, such as the Supreme Court's endorsement of group legal services, may clear the way for such programs for essentially the same reasons that led to the growth of medical plans.

On the other hand, the outlook for a rapid increase in union benefits seems much more remote. In the last analysis, substantial growth can occur in three ways. The most effective stimulus will come if the members express a real desire for added services, as they did in the case of basic medical protection after World War II. But pressure of this kind has been extremely rare. Most members seem to associate unions with wages and working conditions and do not contemplate receiving off-the-job benefits. Even in Local 688, when the members were asked to list the "main things" that their union should work for, 33.7 percent mentioned higher wages, 18.4 percent referred to better conditions in the shop, and a small 9.4 percent indicated benefits outside the shop such as the union's health institute.[14] Only after the members were asked the further question of whether the union should "put more time and money into higher wages" or "more into a health plan, social and recreational activities, etcetera," was it discovered that the largest portion (38.1 percent) preferred the off-the-job benefits; 24.3 percent preferred higher wages, while 35.7 percent felt that wages and other benefits should get equal emphasis.[15]

Even without grass-roots pressure, benefit programs can spread if they are thought to strengthen the union as an institution. Thus, programs of housing, recreation, and counseling for retired members are likely to spread more rapidly if they succeed in helping union leaders mobilize elderly members for political

work or picket-line duty. Benefits and services may also be encouraged if they appear to build up rank-and-file support for the
leadership. But institutional advantages of this kind have not yet
been demonstrated. A survey of Local 688 did disclose an unusually
high rating for the performance of the union.* Yet, if it is true that
the members of Local 688 are uniquely loyal to their union, this
fact is still not widely appreciated in labor circles. Officials in all
the locals studied also are frank to admit that their benefits have
not been of great assistance in organizing new members. To be
sure, they have served to improve the union's image and bring it
favorable publicity, but this is not great recompense for the trouble
and toil required to develop the services involved.

A final stimulus to these programs would result if the labor
movement could develop extremely imaginative and dynamic leadership on a much wider scale. This alternative seems the least
likely of all. Such leadership is rare in any segment of society. It
cannot be reproduced wholesale simply by creating training programs or better methods of recruitment. On the whole, therefore,
the prognosis is for a slow, gradual development of benefit programs rather than the rapid growth associated with the medical
plans in the last two decades.

In view of all these obstacles, it is very difficult for outsiders

---

* It is impossible to provide a thoroughly reliable comparison between "welfare state" locals and other unions, because the survey data are not entirely
comparable and relate to only a few locals at particular points in time. For
what it is worth, however, we have compared survey data relating to Local
688 (Rose, *Union Solidarity*, pp. 52, 63), and data derived from sixteen local
unions in the East Bay area of California, Central Labor Council of Alameda
County and Center for Labor Research and Education, University of California
at Berkeley (Union Member Attitude Survey, pp. 12, 15).

PURPOSE	"HOW WELL ACCOMPLISHED"					
Local 688	Unusually well	Pretty well	Average	Fairly poorly	Not at all	Don't know
Get specific economic benefits (higher wages)	39.4%	41.8%	15.8%	1.7%	—	1.3%
Get job security (including seniority)	51.1	39.8	5.3	.7	.8	2.3
Get benefits off the job (recreational, medical, legal)	52.1	27.1	14.6	2.1	4.1	—

16 Locals	Highly satisfied	Satisfied	Dissatisfied	Highly dissatisfied
Wage increases	13.8%	58.4%	21.8%	6.0%
Job security	16.5	61.6	14.9	7.0
Fringe benefits	15.1	64.1	17.0	2.9

to judge whether unions should be doing more to initiate welfare programs for their members. With capable leadership already stretched thin, most labor organizations would be ill advised to launch new programs of this kind unless they fill an important need that is felt by many members and cannot be met nearly as effectively by some independent source. Perhaps group legal services will satisfy this test, since union members are often so ill equipped to choose a lawyer for themselves. Retirement programs also may provide an important opportunity, since the union is so well situated to help administer preretirement counseling and to provide, through traditional union activities, a natural outlet for many members to perform meaningful work after they have left regular employment. In the last analysis, however, unions and their membership differ enormously, and no general prescription can hope to have much validity. Under these circumstances, the best lesson for union leaders to draw from the success of the welfare locals described earlier is to consider these programs more systematically than most of them have done thus far, in order to determine whether there is not some new welfare activity that can be of real benefit to the members without overtaxing the administrative resources of the organization.

Labor in National and State Politics

POLITICAL ACTION is a major item of business for unions in the United States. In any election year, several million dollars will be spent by unions in trying to elect candidates they have endorsed. During every month that Congress is in session, more than one hundred union representatives can be found in Washington devoting all or part of their time to lobbying. In state capitals and other cities and towns throughout the country, similar efforts are constantly in progress on a smaller scale to make labor's weight felt in legislatures, municipal councils, and government offices.

These political efforts have provoked angry criticism and sharp differences of opinion from various segments of society. Among members of the general public, almost 60 percent oppose union efforts to elect preferred candidates, while 80 percent disapprove of taking up collections among union members for campaign purposes. A bare majority has even indicated that it is improper for unions to endorse favored candidates in their newspapers. Underlying these opinions is a widespread fear that organized labor may exert an undue influence over the American process of government. Several polls have revealed that unions, more than any other major interest group, are considered the most powerful political influence in the country. Yet, there are issues involved that need exploring, for liberal groups have taken quite the opposite view. Their spokesmen have repeatedly derided unions for their lack of political power and have admonished them to step up their efforts not only to advance the interests of their own organizations but also to promote the welfare of all underprivileged groups in the society.

The Evolution of Political Action in the Labor Movement

A labor movement in an industrial democracy can follow several political paths. At one extreme, it may repudiate the existing political system and seek some radical reconstruction of society by revolutionary means. Short of this, unions may accept the existing political framework but work actively to promote a labor party committed to sweeping social and economic reforms. Finally, labor may minimize political action and concentrate on strikes and negotiations to win greater benefits for its members. The latter strategy does not rule out political activity entirely, but it does imply that unions will limit this activity to lobbying for legislative goals and supporting sympathetic candidates put forward by existing political organizations.

At one point or another in American history, union leaders have made serious efforts to follow each of these paths. Even revolutionary syndicalism had its advocates in the early part of this century among the leaders of the Industrial Workers of the World. According to the preamble to the I.W.W. constitution:

> Between [the working and the capitalist] classes a struggle must go on until the workers of the world organize as a class, take possession of the earth and the machinery of production, and abolish the wage system.[1]

During its brief history, the I.W.W. was involved in several violent strikes and bloody demonstrations, and much publicity was given to the trials of several of its leaders. Nevertheless, it never gained a hold over any substantial fraction of the labor movement. By 1925, the movement had virtually expired.

Of much greater significance were the efforts to found a labor party in the United States. At the outset, these efforts took the form of uneasy combinations between unions and other social groups in support of a variety of programs that often had only a tenuous relation to the interests of working people. As early as 1828, workingmen's parties were established in a number of cities to press for free public education, lower taxes, suppression of li-

Labor and the American Community

censed monopolies, abolition of imprisonment for debtors, and a variety of local issues. Although these parties had a short life, they were followed by a series of similar ventures. The 1840's saw the birth and decline of the National Reform Association and the New England Workingmen's Association. In the 1870's came the National Reform Labor Party. During the 1880's, the Knights of Labor participated actively in the Greenback-Labor Party and, in 1892, the People's Party.

In the 1880's, socialist leaders began to work within the union movement for a labor party constructed along lines that were to become familiar in Europe. According to its advocates, such a party was to be explicitly supported by the labor movement. Its purpose was to secure legislation and welfare programs for the benefit of the working class. But it was also to work to modify the capitalist system through the eventual state ownership of railroads, telecommunications, and other key industries. In the end, none of these ventures achieved more than brief success. During the nineteenth century, working people turned to political action in periods of recession, but their enthusiasm quickly waned when prosperity returned. After 1890, the socialists pressed their views in convention after convention of the AFL, only to meet determined resistance from Samuel Gompers and most of the other established union leaders.

In contrast to the socialists and the I.W.W., Gompers and a majority of the Federation favored a third alternative: a modest political strategy that unequivocally rejected both revolution and a labor party. In essence, the Federation's programs can be summarized in three propositions.

First, the Federation assumed an independent and nonpartisan stance toward political parties. It refused to form any permanent alliance with either the Republicans or the Democrats, just as it rejected the idea of forming a labor party. And though it did not always hide its sympathies, the Federation even made it a general practice to refrain from formally endorsing Presidential candidates.

Second, the Federation gave active support to only a narrow set of legislative goals. Although it sometimes took positions on broad social issues, the Federation worked seriously to achieve only those measures that would benefit its members or strengthen its bargaining power. Thus, the major lobbying efforts of the Federation during its first thirty years were directed toward such issues as the regulation of immigration, including exclusion of the

Chinese, seamen's rights, right of petition for public employees, restriction of competition from convict labor, and, more important still, the enactment of laws to prevent federal judges from issuing injunctions against boycotts and picketing.

Third, the AFL adopted the tactics of a special interest group. A permanent lobby was established in Washington so that representatives of labor could testify on pending legislation important to the movement. In 1902, the Federation began making efforts to marshal the "labor vote" by compiling the votes of Congressmen on key issues and disseminating this information to union members. As time went on, these election efforts were widened somewhat to include publicizing labor's position on important issues and occasionally obtaining speakers to talk at public gatherings. But the Federation's efforts during political campaigns were not substantial, and they were directed almost entirely toward influencing union members.

Although every shade of political action had advocates in the American labor movement, the overwhelming majority of unions eventually gave their support to Gompers' policy of working as a pressure group for narrowly limited goals. Surprisingly enough, this result came about when labor movements in Western Europe were successfully launching political parties with broad socialist objectives. In view of this paradox, it is natural to inquire what there was in the American experience that moved the unions to pursue such a different course.

Historians can doubtless identify specific problems of tactics and leadership that helped to undermine the I.W.W., the Socialist Labor Party, and the other ill-fated political ventures of the last century. Yet the failure of *all* these movements suggests a more enduring cause. Perhaps the federal system, with its multiplicity of jurisdictions, made it more difficult for new parties to gather strength. Gompers himself made this point on occasion. Nevertheless, labor parties survived and grew in many parts of Europe under even less favorable conditions. Hence, it seems more likely that the limited political role of American labor had its roots in certain persistent attitudes on the part of the employees themselves.

Despite the rich array of political movements that tried to appeal to the American worker, his interest was never permanently engaged. It is this fragile political consciousness and the lack of class solidarity that most distinguish the American experience from that of Western Europe. Cleavages of race, religion, and language tended to divide the working people in this country, while opportunities to vote and gain a free education helped to avoid the class barriers that arose in Europe. More fundamental still, workers in the United States bore the imprint of a strong national ethos that stressed the ideas of classlessness, opportunity, and social mobility. In this atmosphere, labor-oriented parties found it very difficult to develop any broad appeal on a class basis, still less on the ground of any fundamental protest against the existing system. As Professor Gerald Grob has pointed out:

> Many workers refused to accept the permanency of their wage status and instead identified themselves with the middle class. . . . As a result, although campaign platforms sometimes included planks on government ownership of key industries, they tended even more to stress issues such as cheap money, liberalized debtor laws, producers' cooperatives and free land, which would increase the opportunity of each individual to escape the status of a wage earner. With these tendencies, the purpose of many of the new parties was confused, disunity was enhanced, and many workers understandably turned away when economic conditions improved sufficiently for them to pursue their upward goals in other nonpolitical ways.[2]

Against this background, Gompers' philosophy is not difficult to understand. After fifty years in which emerging union movements had repeatedly declined, the central problem in Gompers' mind was to develop a strong and permanent labor organization. To organize and grow strong, every effort had to be made to avoid programs that produced disunity, dissipated the energies of union leaders, or threatened the autonomy of the labor movement. With only a small membership, composed of workers with little interest in politics, the Federation did not feel prepared to launch a labor party, nor would it hazard its resources or its independence by becoming actively involved in the affairs of one of the established parties. The same reasons help to explain the limited legislative goals of the AFL. Laws to restrict immigration, regulate prison goods, or limit the issuance of labor injunctions would all strengthen unions in organizing and bargaining. Hence, the practical value of these measures was sufficiently clear, and Federation members could scarcely disagree. On the other hand, although stray planks of the Federation platform might favor government ownership of the telegraph industry, advocate free school text-books, or even disarmament, little or no effort was expended to achieve these objectives. Reforms of this kind were too radical to command strong support among the highly skilled, better-paid craftsmen who made up the bulk of AFL membership. And in the hostile climate which confronted the Federation, serious efforts for such measures would have aroused wide antagonism from the public, with little hope of producing practical results. Thus, the radical planks inserted in the AFL program were largely token gestures to satisfy political activists in the Federation conventions. And when the public mood took a more conservative turn after World War I, even these tokens disappeared from labor's platform.

Further reasons for holding narrow legislative goals are revealed in the Federation's position on social legislation. With few exceptions, the AFL consistently opposed unemployment compensation, medical insurance, minimum wages for men, and old-age pensions. Indeed, Gompers often explained this policy in language that would have done credit to many businessmen of the day:

> Sore and sad as I am by the illness, the killing, the maiming of many of my fellow workers, I would rather see that go on for years, minimized and mitigated by the organized labor movement, than give up one jot of the freedom of the workers to strike and struggle for their own emancipation through their own efforts.

> For a mess of pottage, under the pretense of compulsory social insurance, let us not voluntarily surrender the fundamental principles of liberty and freedom, the hope of the Republic of the United States, the leader and teacher to the world of the significance of this great anthem chorus of humanity, liberty.[3]

Beneath this rhetoric lay more pragmatic reasons for opposing social insurance. Many union leaders feared that their efforts to secure better bargaining contracts would be hampered if the government set minimum wages and maximum hours. Other leaders were afraid that social legislation would cause the government to compete with organized labor for the loyalty of the worker and reduce his desire to join a union. AFL Vice-President, John P. Frey, remarked in opposing social insurance:

> If you feed lions cooked meat, they are not going to roar. If you want the lions to roar you will have to hold raw meat under their noses and then they will roar. The only way to get

wage-earners interested in the trade-union movement and
make it a driving force is to convince them that . . . it is only
through the strength, the fighting strength of economic organization that you are going to get higher wages and shorter
hours.[4]

In keeping with these attitudes, social legislation was rejected by
the AFL when it threatened the key objectives of organizing and
bargaining. On the other hand, it could, and did, receive passive
support where it benefited groups outside the ambit of the Federation, such as women, children, and government employees.

The New Deal and After

As an antidote to the failures of the nineteenth century, the
"voluntarism" of Samuel Gompers proved successful. But as the
AFL consolidated its position and the twentieth century wore on,
the political attitudes of the Federation seemed increasingly in-
sular and archaic. When millions lost their jobs in the great Depression and still the AFL denounced unemployment compensation, the Federation's position could scarcely hope to continue
unchallenged.

In reality, three basic changes were taking place that would
drastically alter the groundwork for labor's political activity. To
begin with, the Depression completed a fundamental change in
political party alignment. In earlier decades, the Republican party
appealed with considerable success to all strata in the population;
now, workers, disadvantaged minorities, and poorer groups began
to turn increasingly to the Democrats. Already visible in the
campaigns of 1924 and 1928, this process assumed massive proportions by 1936. In its wake, the agenda of political issues also shifted
to focus more on differing class interests.

While the Democrats were emerging as the party of the lower
classes, the Congress of Industrial Organizations (CIO) was organizing the large mass-production industries. The vast increases in
membership, particularly among unskilled and semiskilled workers, changed the composition of the labor movement by adding
millions of members with interests closely akin to the Democratic
platform. Almost for the first time, there arose a close natural
affinity between the goals of large numbers of union members and
those of an established political party. At the same time, the

growth in union membership provided a potential source of money and votes that enabled union leaders to contemplate a major political effort.

Finally, the enactment of New Deal measures such as the Wagner Act, the social-security program, the minimum wage, and the unemployment-insurance system gave organized labor a much greater stake in the activities of government. These new programs brought a taste of the gains to be achieved through political action. They also made union members dependent upon a series of statutory safeguards and benefits and thus impelled their leaders to take steps to prevent any effort to undermine and repeal the existing legislation.

These changes began almost immediately to influence labor's political behavior, especially among CIO unions. Under the leadership of John L. Lewis, Labor's Non-Partisan League was formed in 1936 to provide support for Roosevelt's reelection. In the ensuing campaign, organized labor contributed roughly three quarters of a million dollars, a sum greater than the entire amount spent by the AFL on political campaigns during all previous years.[5] But these activities were merely the first tentative steps toward the political program that eventually was to emerge. Only with the passage of unfriendly legislation in the forties was labor propelled into giving attention to a permanent political department and staff. The enactment of antistrike legislation in 1943 led rapidly to the formation of the CIO Political Action Committee. The passage of the Taft-Hartley Act in 1947 resulted in a corresponding AFL organization—Labor's League for Political Education.

Once these organizations were created, the two federations began to develop a new course of political action that departed from the philosophy of the old AFL. While Gompers had pleaded with union leaders to keep out of political campaigns, Sidney Hillman, Philip Murray, and George Meany exhorted their constituents to get into politics with both feet. The thrust of labor's new program followed four main lines.

First, the legislative goals of organized labor were much more broadly conceived. Even the AFL discarded its old hostility toward social legislation and began to work for the expansion and liberalization of unemployment compensation, compulsory medical insurance, social security, and minimum wages. Labor unions also expressed support for reforms only indirectly related to the worker in such fields as civil rights, education, and world affairs. These positions were not merely token planks as in earlier decades. In many instances, labor made serious efforts to bring about their achievement through legislation. By the 1960's, the AFL–CIO was prepared to play a key role in passing a bill against racial discrimination in employment and was even willing to give higher priority to a Medicare program than to a change in the federal law that would guarantee in every state the right to bargain for a union shop.*

Second, the labor movement, especially the CIO, began to involve itself much more closely with the Democratic party. For example, the CIO Political Action Committee was instrumental in 1944 in blocking the nomination of James F. Byrnes for the Vice-Presidency. From 1952 on, the AFL and CIO regularly endorsed the Democratic nominee for the Presidency. At the state level, the United Automobile Workers actually undertook to revive an enfeebled Democratic party in Michigan and to assume many of the functions previously carried out by professional party workers. In many cities, the ties between local unions and Democratic party groups were strengthened and made more explicit.

Third, labor unions began to place much greater emphasis on educating their members along political lines. Under Gompers, the prevailing view was that workers could be counted on to understand where their political interests lay. Thus, the AFL thought it sufficient to publicize the voting records of legislators and rely on the membership to act appropriately at the polls. By the late forties, leaders in both federations recognized that systematic efforts were needed—through meetings, classes, and union newspapers—to educate union members on issues and candidates and encourage participation in effective political action programs.

Finally, organized labor began to pay increasing attention to influencing voters outside its own ranks. Radio and television programs were sponsored by unions. Drives were launched to register members and nonmembers. Hundreds of members and their wives were recruited and trained to canvass, address envelopes, and persuade potential voters to come to the polls.

In the intervening years, labor's political activities have hewed

---

* The priority was expressed by agreeing to have Medicare submitted to Congress at a much earlier date than the repeal of the union-shop authorization, so that the latter, rather than the former, would run a major risk of being killed by filibuster. The measure to repeal the union-shop authorization died in precisely this fashion.

quite closely to these lines, but the effort has steadily grown in scope and importance. Reported contributions from all unions for political purposes have risen from $750,000 in 1936 to more than $7 million in 1968.* Most unions of substantial size have appointed a staff director to coordinate their political programs. And while many of these officials do little more than participate in lobbying activities, a few of the largest unions have several full-time political workers, substantial numbers of members ready to work in election campaigns, and an extensive program of political seminars and conferences among active members and subordinate leaders. In addition, the merger of the AFL and the CIO has caused the political efforts of the labor movement to be reorganized and has given them greater impetus. A Committee on Political Education (COPE) has been established with a director and staff at Federation headquarters. A legislative department has been created to engage in lobbying and to coordinate the efforts of the legislative representatives of the various member unions. At the state level, an officer of the state AFL–CIO normally directs lobbying activities with the aid of a professional staff, while state COPE organizations monitor and plan labor's efforts in campaigns for statewide offices. Similar functions are carried out at the local level by county and municipal federation leaders and their COPE organizations. Hence, a structure has been created to lead and coordinate the political efforts of organized labor at all levels of government.

Diversity and Division Within the Labor Movement

Despite these efforts by the AFL–CIO, it would be wrong to assume that the Federation sits at the controls of a monolithic political machine. In making endorsements, local and international unions are free to back whatever candidates they choose. State and local federations are likewise free to make their own endorsements for state and local offices. When the choices made run counter to the wishes of higher echelons in the movement, international union officers or high Federation officials may try to persuade the local leaders to change their minds. But there is no power to order a change, and efforts at persuasion are often ineffective.

---

* In this connection, it is necessary to point out that figures on political contributions are notoriously unreliable—not merely with respect to unions, but also in the case of all manner of organizations.

In financing political activities, the individual unions are again under no obligation to contribute to COPE or to the AFL–CIO. Quotas have been established for each member union, but they are entirely voluntary and often have not been met. Even during political campaigns, unions affiliated with the AFL–CIO act quite independently in deploying campaign workers and spending campaign funds. In addition there are, outside the Federation, unions which pursue a completely independent course. The Mine Workers, the Teamsters, and the Auto Workers fall within this category. And at the state and local levels, many local unions will not affiliate with the state or local federation even though their parent unions belong to the AFL–CIO. In fact, most state federations do not include more than half of all the organized workers in the state, and in many areas some important unions pursue an independent political program which often conflicts with Federation policies.

There are many reasons for the diversity and disunity in labor's political activities. Union leaders often differ in their political philosophies, their party affiliations, and their own personal ambitions. Some unions are affected much more than others by legislation and other government policies. The result is a confusing mixture of activity and inertia, endorsement and counterendorsement, and lobbying and counterlobbying that defies any precise generalization. Nevertheless, it is possible to explain much of the diversity by isolating several different patterns of political behavior that constantly recur throughout the country. In the main, these patterns or strategies revolve around three key questions:

1) How broad a range of objectives should the union pursue through political action?

2) How closely should the union identify with an existing political party?

3) What methods of political action should the union adopt to achieve its goals?

The Range of Objectives.   Today, all the unions belonging to the AFL–CIO have formally endorsed the Federation's platform and its broad commitment to civil rights, antipoverty programs, and social and welfare legislation. In practice, however, labor organizations differ greatly in the range of objectives to which they give serious support. A few unions are strongly committed to broad legislative goals and back this commitment by devoting substantial money and time to lobbying and political campaigns. This is particularly true of the Steelworkers, the Garment Workers, and other large industrial unions. In the case of the Postal Workers, the skilled crafts, and many other organizations, however, the support is often largely nominal. The efforts of these unions are concentrated mainly on a few special goals, such as legislation providing higher wages or government subsidies, and their local unions may even remain outside the state and municipal federations in order to concentrate their energies on their particular objectives.

To some extent, the political goals of a union will depend upon the philosophy of its leader and his key lieutenants. A Walter Reuther would doubtless press for a broad legislative program regardless of the union he headed. But the character of the union's members and the nature of their needs probably exert an even greater influence. It is no accident that organized labor began to widen its goals in the thirties after its ranks had been swelled to include more semiskilled and low-wage workers, who had an obvious stake in social insurance and welfare legislation. Nor is it mere happenstance that an AFL union such as the Meat Cutters started to take a more active interest in civil rights after it began to attract many Negro and Puerto Rican workers in the food-processing industries.

Unions that lack such a membership are more likely to play a passive role in the effort to achieve civil-rights laws and social-welfare legislation. If they have an active political program at all, it will probably encompass a narrow set of objectives. If the objectives are important enough to the members, however, the union may mount a strong political effort. Public employees provide a typical example, for their very wages and working conditions depend on the decisions of legislators and other government officials. Thus, the postal unions have forged one of the most effective political-action programs in Washington, while expending little effort in behalf of the broader legislative goals of the Federation.

It is not hard to understand why certain unions restrict themselves to a narrow set of goals. Where particular government decisions are important enough to a union, its leaders may not feel that they can divert their money and staff to a wide range of objectives that are only vaguely and indirectly related to their members. Such a union may also fear that if it multiplies its goals it will run the risk of making too many demands upon lawmakers and coming into conflict with too many interest groups. Should this occur, even friendly legislators will support the union only part of the time, often on issues of secondary interest to the membership.

Many labor organizations with narrow goals seek legislation limited to the particular problems of their industry or occupation. Thus, the railroad brotherhoods have maintained a separate scheme of railway legislation covering retirement, labor relations, work injuries, and the like, instead of being lumped with other unions and industries under broad statutes such as the National Labor Relations and Social Security acts. The postal unions have favored special appropriation bills to deal with pay increases for their employees. By obtaining narrowly drafted legislation of this sort, the union can limit the number of interest groups that will oppose its policies. Such labor organizations often will concentrate on their special legislative domain to such an extent that they will ignore Federation policy in lobbying or endorsing candidates if it seems important to do so to further their interests.

Relations with Political Parties.   In some respects, the AFL–CIO still maintains the nonpartisan position toward established political parties that was developed in the era of Gompers. There are seldom any formal ties with the Democratic or Republican parties. Most union leaders would agree that a candidate of either party should be supported if he has a more satisfactory record than his opponent on issues important to labor. Thus, a few Republican candidates are endorsed in every election year by the AFL–CIO and by individual unions.

At the same time, the AFL–CIO is plainly more partisan today than it was in earlier times. The Federation has, over the past few decades, endorsed at least nine Democrats for every Republican in Congressional races, and it has favored the Democratic party with an even higher proportion of the funds expended in political campaigns.[6] Through these and other efforts, the Federation has developed a degree of influence within the Democratic party—a special stake in its long-run strength and success—that it does not have in the Republican party.

Despite this broad tendency, there are labor organizations

that do have a truly nonpartisan strategy. In a few cases, unions have followed a nonpartisan course by controlling a decisive "swing vote," which they offer to either party in return for commitments on a broad range of goals. This policy is a difficult one that can succeed only under rare conditions. The electorate must be predominately "liberal" in complexion, or the more conservative party cannot make significant concessions to labor without alienating too many of its own supporters. Moreover, to have much influence, labor must be able to swing a substantial number of votes from one party to another as the circumstances in each campaign happen to dictate. Usually this feat is hard to accomplish, for even loyal union members do not easily abandon their normal party identification. Finally, labor must be fortunate enough to avoid having to confront other groups who might also try to play a "swing" role and thereby undermine the unions' effectiveness.

These points are best illustrated in New York City, where the Ladies' Garment and Hatters' unions have played a leading role in pressing for a broadly conceived program through the efforts of the Liberal party.[7] New York offers a "progressive" climate well suited to the strategy involved. By relying on the Liberal party, which has regularly attracted the statewide support of 200,000 or more voters, these union leaders also have been able to deliver a much larger bloc of votes than would have been the case if they could give their endorsement only to the candidates of the major parties. These votes, moreover, have an obvious importance in a city where the Democrats have often failed to capture a clear majority in campaigns for major offices.

Under these circumstances, the Liberal party has undoubtedly had an influence on New York City politics by its power to nominate and support the candidates of either the Republicans or Democrats or its own separate nominees. Even so, the extent of its influence is sharply limited. The Republican party has seldom felt free to move far enough to the left to suit Liberal tastes for fear of driving its conservative supporters from the polls. Thus, the Liberal party has had to support Democratic candidates in 80–95 percent of city races over the years in New York, thereby weakening its ability to act as a decisive "swing" vote. More recently, new splinter groups have emerged, such as the reform Democrats and the Conservative party, which have worked in various ways to diminish the Liberal influence.

In view of these limitations, nonpartisan policies are much

more likely to be found among unions with narrow political objectives. Thus, it is the postal unions, the local construction trades, the Teamsters, and—in the past—the railroad brotherhoods that have been most willing to support the candidates of either party. Since an active nonpartisan strategy will often lead such a union to positions that conflict with the aims and endorsements of the Federation, an affiliated union will tend to avoid such a policy unless its special political objectives are of considerable importance to the membership. Usually, these objectives will be of such a nature as to require continuing government attention—as in the enforcement of building codes or the enactment of pay rises for government employees—for it is in these circumstances that a union is most reluctant to identify itself closely with one political organization and thus risk being cut off from the rival party when the latter comes to power.

For a union with narrow political objectives, a nonpartisan approach may be preferable, perhaps even indispensable. For a labor movement committed to a broad program of social and economic reform, the same prescription may not work so well. Since one political party is usually more liberal or more conservative than its rival, a broad labor program that advances the interests of working people is likely to strike closer to the platform of one major political party than to the others. As a result, it is almost inevitable that labor will begin to work much more closely with one party—normally the Democrats—even though union leaders may continue to talk quite sincerely in nonpartisan terms. Since the Democratic party stands for a program more closely aligned with labor's own, union leaders naturally find themselves supporting candidates of that party most of the time, developing close ties with the party's leaders, even accepting positions of leadership in the party hierarchy.

These tendencies are further strengthened by the fact that labor cannot hope to push a broad program effectively by relying merely on campaign contributions and endorsements. The broad social and welfare goals of the Federation are too controversial for labor to make much headway by these techniques alone. Therefore, union leaders must seek to build support among the voters and elect more lawmakers who are basically in sympathy with labor's goals. This task is all but impossible if unions attempt to persuade the voter to follow first the candidate of one party, then the candidate of another, depending on their position on labor's program. Normally union members are too closely identified with one of the major parties to shift around in this manner.* [8] Thus, it is much easier to attempt to strengthen the loyalty of union members toward the Democratic party and to increase the proportion of potential party supporters who actually register and vote than to reorient the party preferences of the rank and file at each election. Having adopted this course, labor is driven to work still more closely with the Democrats and to develop an even stronger stake in the long-run vitality of that party. Although such cooperation may not rule out an occasional endorsement of a candidate from a rival party, such practice will be very much the exception and may be used largely as a device to warn the favored party that it should not take labor's support too much for granted.

Although the Federation is thus driven to adopt a partisan policy, this strategy represents something of a shortcut. Labor must capitalize and build upon established Democratic habits and loyalties because it cannot reverse the typical pattern of American voting behavior by educating union members to vote for issues rather than parties. But this strategy can easily go awry. To begin with, there is always the danger that issues and candidates will emerge that will cause many union supporters to vote for another party not genuinely sympathetic to labor's goals. The candidacy of George C. Wallace is only the latest in a series of illustrations.

A second danger with any partisan strategy is that unions will be left in an exposed position when their favored party is out of power. This problem is particularly acute for unions, such as the building trades, which have vital day-to-day political interests requiring continuous access to government officials. For most other unions, however, these risks are not so formidable. Even if labor has openly supported the losing party, an administration will not normally discriminate against unions, much less cut back the social legislation that labor supports, for to do so would antagonize many neutral citizens as well as arouse the unions to make a particularly determined effort in the next election. Indeed, an opposing administration may even make efforts to accommodate the unions in order to dissipate solid labor opposition and prove that its party is not insensitive to the interests of the workingman. As a result,

---

* For example, in 1961, Harry Van Arsdale, president of the New York City Central Labor Council, started the Brotherhood party. However, only a very small percentage of union members switched their affiliation in the mayoral election that year.

many unions can tolerate the risk of putting most of their eggs in a single party basket.

Perhaps the greatest problem with any partisan strategy is that labor will often be taken for granted by the Democrats. Democratic leaders often are particularly anxious to build a solid majority by winning support from progressive businessmen and other middle-of-the-road groups who are indifferent, or even opposed, to some of labor's goals. To do so, the party may slight labor's interests in order to cater to these other groups, reckoning that labor will have no practical alternative but to continue giving its support. Rightly or wrongly, many union leaders accused the Kennedy and Johnson administrations of pursuing exactly this policy in refusing to make a major effort to enact key labor bills, such as provisions to broaden the scope of allowable picketing or to repeal federal laws permitting the states to pass right-to-work legislation. To counteract this danger, labor leaders can threaten to cut back their campaign efforts or to endorse more Republican candidates. But unless the Republicans are prepared to make real concessions in exchange for labor support, these veiled threats may not seem credible enough to induce a marked change in Democratic policies.

A labor organization that finds an established party with a program largely compatible with its own occupies the most natural position from which to adopt a partisan strategy. Essentially, this is the situation that confronted the CIO when it first began to forge a closer relationship with the Democratic party. But there are many states and municipalities in which neither party is particularly sympathetic to union interests. If this situation prevails, labor can pursue a partisan course only by somehow creating a major party worthy of its support. Two or three different methods have been employed by unions to reach this goal.

In several Southern states, the dominant Democratic party is much too conservative for union tastes. As a result, the state federations have sometimes responded by supporting archconservative Republican candidates. The theory behind this strategy is that labor will help to hasten the arrival of a genuine two-party system in the South. In the process, it is hoped that the most conservative elements in the Democratic party will defect to the Republicans, leaving an organization much more oriented toward liberal union programs.

Although ingenious, this policy has several dangers. It is likely to provoke resentment among Democratic leaders. It also may produce a certain amount of confusion among union members and sympathizers, who may not understand the motives behind labor's action. Furthermore, the strategy is likely to cause dissension within the Federation's own ranks. Some union leaders are bound to balk at a policy that will deliberately provoke the dominant party for a number of years in the hope of achieving political gains in the long run. Such reactions will be particularly common among unions who depend on continuing political contacts and among more conservative labor leaders, who are less inclined to feel that the prevailing party is "hopeless" or "reactionary." Union officials in Washington also may be embarrassed at union support of conservative Republicans. To further their national interests, Federation leaders may try to press the state and local officials to reverse their stand, thus making it easier for more conservative local unions to break ranks and create disunity. Finally, the logic behind the entire strategy is not altogether clear. If labor and liberal elements are not strong enough to prevail in a one-party state, they will not necessarily do much better merely by helping to create a powerful Republican organization. Ultimately, the key question is whether unions are ineffective because they have too little influence within the Democratic party or because the political complexion of the state itself is unfavorable. Only if the first alternative prevails can the unions hope to gain by taking a long-run gamble on recasting the party structure in the state.

A very different strategy has occasionally emerged in a few states where organized labor has confronted a disorganized or moribund Democratic party. Under such conditions, unions may seek to enter the party and make a major effort to increase its potency. A classic illustration occurred in Michigan after World War II.[9] The Michigan Democratic party had become largely ineffective, with the leadership exhibiting greater interest in dispensing federal patronage than in building an organization to win elections. In 1948, after serious misgivings, the United Auto Workers resolved to "capture" the party by allying with reform Democrats, certain other labor unions, and, more informally, with the A.D.A. and the League of Women Voters. By dint of a successful grassroots effort to elect precinct delegates, the coalition managed to gain control of the state convention and depose the Old Guard. Thereafter, the party was reorganized and refinanced, and it chose candidates and platforms corresponding much more closely to the political beliefs of the U.A.W.

There is little doubt that the Auto Workers emerged with greater influence over the party and, ultimately, in the political life of the state. By participating heavily in the reorganization and the day-to-day operations of the Democratic organization, the U.A.W. could play a greater part in selecting candidates and programs than it could have hoped to achieve by merely supplementing the work of the existing party structure. On the other hand, the experience also reveals the limits of this policy. Such a strategy can succeed only if the existing party apparatus is weak enough to be supplanted. Where the organization is strong—as in Chicago, for example—not only will the unions find it impossible to capture the party, but they also may be unable to contribute enough to election activities to obtain significant influence over party decisions. In the second place, even if such a strategy can succeed, it will cost the unions heavily, both in money and in the effort required to mobilize and train a large number of effective party workers. In short, the policy will be attractive only to powerful unions with a strong belief in the necessity for effective political action. In addition, as with all partisan strategies, unions suffer from the drawback of having to rely on party identification to mobilize the votes of their members. Hence, in the city of Detroit—where municipal elections are nonpartisan and the party label is of no use—union candidates for mayor have been regularly defeated despite a heavy concentration of U.A.W. members.* Finally, as a political minority, unions can generally revitalize a major party only by forging an alliance with other similarly oriented groups. This process inevitably requires a number of compromises on labor's part. If these compromises are not made, the alliance will either dissolve or labor's dominance will become so obvious as to provoke a strong reaction from the electorate. Thus, the U.A.W. has gone to considerable lengths to integrate other groups into its political apparatus, and has modified its original goals to take more moderate positions on a number of significant issues.

In theory at least, unions can adopt still another strategy and

---

* A study published in 1963 points out that from 1946 to 1955 nominees endorsed by the CIO Political Action Committee won 91.2 percent of all general elections for partisan offices at the state, Congressional, and county levels, but less than 38 percent of contests for municipal offices where elections are nonpartisan.[10]

create their own political party if the existing political organizations are not sufficiently responsive to labor's interests. In practice, however, this alternative has proved uniformly impractical. Less than 30 percent of union members accept the idea of a labor party,[11] and experience suggests that members will not easily break their traditional party affiliations.* Moreover, union members and their families represent only a minority of the electorate, and voters outside the labor movement are likely to react very negatively to the specter of political domination by unions. These problems are particularly severe in states where neither of the established parties is friendly to labor, for it is precisely these states where union membership is smallest and the environment most hostile. As a result, unions are likely to work toward a third party only under special circumstances, as in the case of the Liberal party in New York, where labor leaders may feel that they can create a swing vote to influence the major political organizations.

The Techniques of Political Action. A union that is seriously engaged in political action can resort to several methods to achieve its legislative goals. It can lobby, endorse candidates, contribute money to campaigns, or put its members to work in registration drives, watching at the polls, addressing envelopes, and the like. A large and strongly committed organization—like the AFL–CIO— will make extensive use of all these techniques. But many unions emphasize one or two methods at the expense of others. Although a union's choices may reflect its traditions or the style of its leaders, other factors normally contribute more to the decision.

Many labor organizations rely primarily on lobbying and endorsements and make only modest financial contributions or campaign efforts. Such unions often lack the manpower to mount an extensive grass-roots campaign, or their objectives are too narrow or of too little importance to warrant an expensive political program. In some cases, the union leader may even conclude that a strong grass-roots effort will inhibit him in pursuing a nonpartisan course for limited objectives. If the members are asked to contribute time and work to political campaigns, they may insist upon a greater voice in deciding whom to endorse and what issues to push. Once the members are involved in this way, the leaders may

---

* For example, the ill-fated Brotherhood party in New York.

Labor and the American Community

find it more difficult to work with an official of the Republican party for fear that such activity will be criticized and misunderstood. They may feel handicapped in the give-and-take of lobbying because certain concessions may expose them to attack for compromising union principles. They may find it impossible to engineer an endorsement for a conservative legislator who agreed to go along with a key bill in the last legislative session. Hence, union leaders accustomed to nonpartisan lobbying for limited goals may actually resist efforts to encourage a grass-roots organization.

Many unions supplement their lobbying by giving contributions to favored candidates. While most unions give only modest amounts, a few make political donations that seem quite extraordinary in comparison with the practice of other unions of comparable size. The majority of these unions have important political goals but lack the manpower to mount a sufficient grass-roots effort to accomplish their objectives. Thus, the members of the postal unions are willing to contribute heavily to campaign funds and testimonial banquets since their wages depend on the willingness of Congress to approve postal pay rises. In some cases, the political interests of union members are reinforced by the strong personal ambitions of their leader. Paul Hall of the Seafarers' Union has accumulated a political war chest of half a million dollars a year.[12] The Seafarers have doubtless pursued this course as a result of the union's stake in federal maritime legislation. But Hall is also known to give generous support to other causes not immediately relevant to his members, and his willingness to do so is commonly attributed to a desire to enhance his own stature and influence within the Federation. Likewise, Pipe Fitters Local 562 in St. Louis has been noted for large contributions that seem designed not merely to enhance the union's influence over building codes and prevailing wage determinations, but also to expand the political power of the local leaders.*

---

* If the members are not genuinely committed to the union's political program, large contributions will generally depend on the strong position of the leader, a position often buttressed by his control over the hiring halls. The business agent of the St. Louis Pipe Fitters exemplified this technique. Members of the union paid a "voluntary contribution" of fifty cents per day into the local's political fund. But union members were normally too few in number to fill more than half of the available jobs in the local's jurisdiction. The remaining positions were given to employees from other unions who were allowed to take these jobs—at more than seven dollars per hour—in exchange for a daily "donation" of two dollars into the political fund. Through this device, the

A very different situation prevails in unions that engage their members in a strong grass-roots effort. Generally these unions are partisan to the Democratic party and strongly committed to a broad range of political goals. Through registration and campaign work, they hope to elect the party's candidates and thus promote its social and economic platform. Without such efforts, it would be difficult for the union to make much progress, for lobbying and contributions by themselves cannot move many legislators to support a wide range of controversial programs affecting such matters as social insurance, poverty, civil rights, and labor legislation.

How Influential Are the Unions?

Critics differ widely in appraising how much influence labor wields in matters of politics and government. Unfortunately, the issue hardly permits an intelligible answer. In elections, for example, so much depends upon the issues in the campaign, the nature of the candidates, and the constituency involved that there can never be much hope of providing a single index of labor's impact, let alone its influence over the process of government as a whole. This discussion, then, will be confined to a general description of labor's influence on policy making within the several branches of the federal government, a description that will suffice to answer at least some of the more urgent questions that have been raised with respect to labor's political role.

THE JUDICIARY

The influence of the unions varies considerably from one branch of the federal government to another. Its impact is weakest, of course, on the work of the judiciary. The point is not that judges decide "legal" rather than "political" questions. On the contrary, federal judges in the United States confront many policy issues in applying the Constitution and interpreting broad regulatory statutes. But traditions of impartiality in the judiciary are strong, and these traditions are protected from political pressure, at the

---

business agent amassed a sum estimated at $400,000 to $600,000 each year which was expended in contributions to a variety of local, state, and national candidates.

federal level at least, by the fact that appointments to the bench are for life. Initial appointments, to be sure, are potentially subject to political influence, but once again there are strong moral currents running against the selection of judges for the benefit of any particular interest group. Hence, labor's influence on the judiciary is virtually nil, save perhaps for the possibility that by working to elect a Democratic administration, labor may help to bring about the appointment of a greater number of judges with somewhat more liberal views on social and economic issues.

THE EXECUTIVE BRANCH

The impact of labor on the executive branch is much harder to describe, since no two administrations are alike, and the variety of issues is so broad. Nevertheless, a few helpful observations can be made from the experience of the past twenty years. To begin with, much turns on which party is in power. Persons concerned with labor's influence in the executive branch will rarely be troubled during a Republican administration. It is Democratic administrations that give rise to concern. Since the Federation usually will have supported a Democratic President in his campaign by contributing substantial amounts of money and manpower, his administration is naturally inclined to be more sympathetic to union interests. Labor has sought to capitalize on this opportunity in several ways.

Unions have taken an active interest, first of all, in appointments to administrative posts that are related to its welfare. The building trades have been particularly concerned over the position of Solicitor in the Department of Labor, because the Solicitor has watched over the administration of the Davis-Bacon Act, which requires that prevailing wage scales be determined for federal construction projects. The building trades have also sought a voice in appointments to the Bureau of Apprenticeship so that they can keep informed of the Bureau's activities and influence changes that might adversely affect their interest in apprentice programs. Elsewhere in the Labor Department, the Federation has usually succeeded in having at least a half dozen persons with a union background appointed to key posts, and no major position in the Department has been filled without prior consultation with the AFL–CIO. More important still, although most top officials in the Department have not come from union posts, a Secretary or Assistant Secretary has seldom been able to make much headway against the determined opposition of the Federation, as Secretary Wirtz discovered when he tried to arrange the removal of the Under Secretary of Labor, a former union official supported by the AFL–CIO.

Outside the Labor Department, unions have been actively interested in appointments to the National Labor Relations Board, which interprets and administers the statutory provisions bearing on such vital matters as picketing, bargaining in good faith, and elections to determine whether a union will gain bargaining rights for groups of employees. The administration has regularly consulted the AFL–CIO on key appointments to the Board and its staff, and the Federation has usually been able to prevent a proposed appointment to which it has taken strong exception.* For similar reasons, labor has wielded influence over appointments to the National Mediation Board, which administers the statute regulating labor-management relations in the airline and railroad industries. And labor has also tried, with markedly less success, to gain representation on certain other agencies, such as the Highway Safety Commission, which affect the interests of particular unions.

In addition to appointments, organized labor has taken an interest in various administrative activities carried on within the executive branch. Through friends and appointees in various agencies, the Federation has been kept informed during Democratic administrations of developing policies within the Labor Board, the Equal Employment Opportunities Commission, the Labor Department, and other executive agencies and departments. Union representatives have regularly sought, and obtained, access to these agencies to present their point of view on policy matters important to them. Most important, unions have tried to exert some influence over the formation of legislative proposals developed in the administration for submission to Congress.

In legislative matters, union representatives normally have enjoyed easy access to all executive departments and have been consulted at an early stage in the development of proposals affecting their interests. On important issues, George Meany consulted directly with the President. Reminiscing just before leaving office, President Johnson observed that he had met with Meany on forty-nine separate occasions during his five years as Chief Executive.

---

* Typically, management organizations also have been contacted.

Apart from talking with administration officials, the Federation has
tended to rely upon the Labor Department as its advocate within
the executive branch. This is not to say that the Department is
simply a mouthpiece for union interests during a Democratic administration. The Secretary of Labor has rejected union demands
which he has considered untenable, and often he has succeeded in
moderating the Federation's position in significant respects. Nevertheless, on matters that are reasonably debatable, a Democratic
Secretary has generally supported the labor side.* This tendency is
understandable. To carry out a number of its responsibilities—for
example, that of resolving strikes—the Department must cultivate
a close working relationship with organized labor. In seeking to
maintain this relationship, the Department would find itself seriously handicapped if it took a less favorable stance toward labor's
proposals than other agencies within the administration. Moreover,
if the Department were unresponsive to labor's reasonable demands, the Federation might cause trouble when future appointments had to be made. If the Federation had a friendly voice on a
Congressional appropriations committee—as it did for many years
in representative John E. Fogarty—it could easily create difficulty
when the Department sought money for its programs. Finally,
certain key appointees in the Department have come from union
posts and—even with the most conscientious of motives—they
naturally have been more sympathetic than most outsiders toward
the legislative goals of the Federation.

Aside from its relations with the Labor Department, the
Federation normally has had an influence in a Democratic administration commensurate with the effectiveness of its lobbying and
campaign activities. The AFL–CIO contributes millions of dollars
and man-hours to help elect Democratic candidates, and this is
enough to insure that its views are given careful attention by the
executive branch, especially in an election year. In addition, if the

---

* The role of a Democratic Secretary of Labor contrasts sharply with that of
his Republican counterpart. The Republican, if he chooses, can gain respect
and gratitude from union leaders in exchange for very little, since no one has
expected him to accomplish much for organized labor under the administration he works for. The Democrat is in a much harder position. Since manpower
and employment problems will be important matters for his administration, he
naturally hopes to play a significant role through developing these programs in
the public interest. At the same time, union leaders expect him to succeed in
promoting their various interests within the executive branch. Hence, the
Secretary is under pressure not only to satisfy these expectations, but somehow
to do so without compromising his reputation for impartiality and disinterested
expertise within the administration.

Federation can mount effective opposition in Congress on a particular issue, the administration must accommodate itself to labor's position in order to avoid risking defeat. Conversely, unions have exerted influence by virtue of the assistance they have been able to provide in mustering Congressional support for administration proposals. In many cases, the executive branch and the Federation have needed each other's assistance to insure success, with the result that the administration has engaged in a bargaining process with union spokesmen in order to fashion a program commanding the active support of both.

It is important to recognize that labor's influence within Democratic administrations is not unique. Farmers, business interests, and other groups have similar methods for promoting their views. These pressures may conjure up visions of an executive branch manipulated this way and that by a series of powerful lobbies. But this is not a true picture, for there are various checks that serve to moderate the impact of labor, along with that of other interest groups.

Consider the example of the National Labor Relations Board. Unions have had a certain influence over appointments to this agency, but it is traditional during a Democratic administration that two of the five positions on the board will go to Republicans or to persons not considered undesirable in business circles. In addition, union lawyers and union officials have never been appointed to the board. These are not clearly defined traditions, but there are strong pressures to prevent a President from deviating from them sharply. One such pressure emanates from the labor-relations bar, which would be greatly disturbed over the danger of an excessively biased board. Another inhibition results from the fact that a board so susceptible to the charge of partiality would invite more stringent review by the courts and create a threat of having its decisions overruled by legislative action.

These checks against abuse are not perfect. Democratic boards do decide a number of close cases in a manner opposite to the probable decisions of a board appointed by a Republican administration. Republican boards do likewise. This tendency causes the law to vacillate in doubtful areas and thereby provokes considerable criticism and ill will among the labor-relations bar. But very rarely has the board reached decisions that could not win a measure of support among disinterested experts. Hence, by influencing appointments during Democratic administrations, unions have

only gained an advantage in doubtful cases where weighty arguments can be made on both sides, and even this influence has been
circumscribed by the right to appeal board decisions for review
by the federal courts.

Other checks are available to limit union influence over the
legislative programs of a Democratic administration. In the last
analysis, of course, labor's influence depends on what Congress
can be expected to approve, and both the Federation and the
White House must accommodate their program to these restraints. Within the administration itself, unions often count on the
Labor Department to support their positions, but the result has
been to weaken significantly the influence of the Secretary of
Labor. Realizing that the Department is often cast in the role of
labor's advocate, the White House has tended to rely on the advice of neutral agencies, such as the Budget Bureau and the
Council of Economic Advisers, in reviewing its legislative program. For example, labor advocated applying the Davis-Bacon Act
to the "model cities" program. It pressed for the inclusion of farm
workers under the National Labor Relations Act. In these cases,
and many others, the Department of Labor supported the Federation. Yet in each instance, the White House refused to accept
labor's position.*

In sum, the influence of labor over a Democratic administration does not appear to be a matter of serious public concern.
Although many Republicans may feel that the executive branch
simply follows the "union line," this impression is largely an illusion. Since the constituencies of the Federation and a Democratic
administration substantially overlap, their leaders have naturally
arrived independently at roughly similar conclusions on a large
number of policy issues. Even the influence of the Federation over
the Labor Department is not clearly undesirable. Democratic
Presidents have been content to have the Department serve as a
vehicle for receiving union demands, moderating their excesses,

---

* Even if the Department of Labor had been wholly free of union influence,
it might well have argued, for example, to include farm workers within the
N.L.R.A. And its arguments would doubtless have had greater force within the
administration. Yet the Federation has apparently concluded that the benefits
in the existing situation outweigh the costs. Thus, union leaders resisted the
efforts of the Secretary of Labor in the Kennedy-Johnson Administration to
make the Department play a more independent role. And when the proposal
was made to merge the Departments of Commerce and Labor and thus reduce
the influence of any single interest group, it was labor, above all others, that
worked to defeat this scheme in Congress.

and promoting them within the administration. Other agencies and departments perform a similar function for opposing interest groups, and the White House can easily turn to the Budget Bureau, the Council of Economic Advisers, and other neutral bodies for advice in reaching a final decision.

CONGRESS

Most commentators on labor's role in the legislative process have been preoccupied with the tactical errors that union lobbyists have committed in the past.* But the more important question is how much influence unions can exert on the content of legislation. The answer depends primarily on the context in which the lobbying takes place.

By and large, union lobbyists endanger the public most when labor joins forces with employers to obtain some common objective or when labor's goal is so narrow that it does not come to the attention of the public or arouse the active opposition of some important interest group. For example, with only a few exceptions, unions and employers can be expected to join in opposing government regulation of emergency strikes. Individual unions and employer associations may also cooperate in particular ventures such as attempts to secure tariff protection or to secure increases in rail or truck rates. Postal unions may reach a tacit agreement with commercial interests to oppose increases in third-class rates in ex-

---

* It is commonly alleged that unions are too slow to compromise and hence, too likely to be left clinging to hopeless positions instead of marshaling their forces behind some palatable and realistic alternative. This difficulty was strikingly evident during deliberations over the Taft-Hartley amendments and the Landrum-Griffin Act.[13] Labor lobbyists also seem to resort too quickly to threats and other crude devices that antagonize even their potential allies. To quote one investigator, "Whereas in no single case did any of these legislators complain about pressures from industry, there were a number of remarks describing the ineptness, boorishness, or lack of organization evident in labor pressure groups."[14] It is also said that union lobbyists make too little effort to contact Republicans, and that their lobbying efforts are commonly undercut by divisions of opinion among important segments of the labor movement. Still other criticisms have been made to the effect that the information and supporting memoranda prepared by union lobbyists often are too superficial and doctrinaire to carry weight.

These problems have cost labor dearly in the past. Nevertheless, some of the difficulties mentioned are being corrected gradually at the national level (although they still remain serious in many state legislatures).[15] Moreover, careful studies of the lobbying process reveal comparable weaknesses among industry, associations, and other lobbying groups—lack of staff, internal divisions among members of the interest group, inefficiencies of all kinds on the part of lobbyists.[16]

change for receiving a free hand in pressing for postal pay raises. Companies and unions may cooperate in promoting legislation to subsidize and protect United States ships from foreign competition. These alliances may not succeed in overcoming an aroused public opinion. But public opinion will have to be much more active and articulate than if labor and management had not made common cause—more active and articulate than one can reasonably expect in view of the nature of many of the issues involved.

These are the classic dangers of lobbying, and labor is not immune to them. At the same time, the great bulk of union lobbying efforts do not give rise to these problems. Whether the issues at stake have to do with labor legislation, civil rights, minimum wages, or social insurance, most of labor's important objectives are of such a nature as to arouse wide public interest and determined opposition from employer groups and other lobbies. Under these circumstances, the union lobbyist can do little more than find ways of gaining access to legislators and making sure that they are aware of all the information, arguments and counterarguments supporting the union's position. In short, his influence will seldom be better than the quality of the arguments he presents on the issues or the information he supplies on the sentiments of constituents back home. Since so many of labor's issues are of this type, organized labor occupies a different position from that of many industry associations, which often seek objectives that affect a relatively disorganized body of consumers in diverse ways that largely escape public notice. For this reason, as several Republican politicians have privately indicated, labor lobbyists probably are less prone to abuse their influence than many other interest groups, not because union leaders have any greater claim to virtue, but because their political goals happen to be of a sort that imposes effective checks upon their power.

In the long run, unions may make a greater impact through their efforts to influence the elections that determine the composition of Congress. It is this possibility that most disturbs many of labor's critics. Noting the millions of dollars in union dues and contributions, the eighteen million members, and the millions more who are relatives of members, one can easily conjure up the specter of organized labor's domination of the entire political life of the country.

Attempts are constantly made to measure union influence by estimating the size of the "labor vote" or by calculating the percentage of candidates endorsed by the AFL–CIO who win election to the Congress. In the main, these efforts are bound to fail, since union efforts cannot be easily disentangled from all the other forces affecting elections. The voting habits of union members vary too much according to the candidates and the issues involved in each election. The fortunes of candidates endorsed by the AFL–CIO are also heavily affected by such problems as war and peace, race, and corruption over which the unions can exert little control. Under these circumstances, it is pointless to compare labor's "box score" from one election to another. Fewer union-endorsed Democrats will be elected when an Eisenhower runs than when a Goldwater heads the ticket, regardless of how effectively or ineffectively the unions campaign.

Confronted with these problems, it is better to analyze labor's election activities in general terms, without attempting to quantify the votes or candidates it can "deliver" in any political campaign. In making such an analysis, one must look separately at several distinct types of activity, for unions may enter a campaign in various ways—by simply endorsing one of the candidates, by contributing money to his campaign, or by providing services in the form of campaign workers, free publicity, or access to a union meeting.

1) Endorsements. The effect of union endorsements cannot be measured precisely, but most professional politicians attach little significance to them. Granted, it may be embarrassing for the Democratic candidate in a lower-income district not to receive the blessing of the AFL–CIO. Conversely, a moderate Republican may profit from labor endorsements if he wishes to demonstrate to workers and liberal groups that he is not uninterested in the needs of working people. On the other hand, some union members may react to an endorsement by voting for the opposing candidate, especially where the union in question is controlled by an unpopular or autocratic leader. Others will not even be aware of the endorsement, and most who are aware do not seem to be influenced one way or the other. The same considerations apply with even greater force to voters outside the trade unions. Opinion surveys suggest that a clear majority of the public will be influenced against a candidate who receives labor's endorsement. Indeed, to quote one authority on voting behavior, "It is well known that labor's endorsement can be the kiss of death in a deeply conservative area, that a portion of the electorate, hostile to labor unions, uses the labor stand as a guide to how it ought *not* to vote."[17]

2) *Financial Contributions.* If endorsements antagonize a segment of the public, even greater suspicion is aroused when unions make substantial campaign contributions to favored candidates. Over 70 percent of the public disapproves of the practice, and various laws have been passed which have sought, ineffectually, to limit labor's right to offer support of this kind.[18] Campaign contributions raise three separate considerations. The first is the possibility that unions will be able to provide such large sums to the Democrats that the Republican party will either be swamped completely or reduced to competing with the Democrats for union favor. The second is the risk that unions may provide such a critical source of support *within the Democratic party* that Democrats will be unduly influenced by labor whenever they are in power. The third is the danger that particular legislators will be so dependent on labor support that they will have to commit themselves to support the unions on key issues instead of exercising their own independent judgment.

The first of these considerations is the least worthy of concern. According to the best information available, the Republican party has almost always received more money than the Democrats despite the help of labor unions.[19] Moreover, union contributions have never amounted to much more than 5 percent of the *total* contributions to both parties—a proportion scarcely large enough to exercise a decisive influence in any direction.[20] It is always possible, of course, that unions will step up their financial support in the future. But even if union members allow this to occur, a rise in union contributions will usually be matched by corresponding increases in the campaign chests of opposing candidates. And if this spiral should arouse concern, it should be possible to find some legislative solution to the problem, presumably by subsidizing campaign costs to such a degree that further contributions will not make a critical difference.

The effect of union contributions on the Democratic party is somewhat more serious, for it is estimated that labor has provided in the neighborhood of 10 to 20 percent of all party receipts over the past twenty years.[21] Even so, this proportion is not overpowering. Moreover, the influence of labor money is counteracted in several ways. Politicians are aware that unions have little choice in most elections but to continue giving support to Democratic candidates, even if the party has not been wholly responsive to labor's requests. For similar reasons, it is not in labor's interests to press its demands to the point of alienating significant numbers of potential Democratic votes. Under these circumstances, unions can extract few important concessions that would not have been forthcoming in any event, for union leaders will wish to avoid a Republican administration and will be forced to respect the decisions which the Democratic leadership considers necessary to retain the support of the electorate.

More troublesome is the possibility that union contributions will cause individual legislators to support labor on certain key issues. Although candidates in most constituencies can turn to several quarters for financial support, there are a few who may have to rely to a very large extent on union help. Whether or not explicit commitments are made, such a candidate, once elected, may feel obliged to favor the unions on key issues—either because he will need funds in future elections or simply out of normal instincts of gratitude.

The problem of campaign contributions is least troublesome in the case of the broad legislative programs that are the chief concern of the Federation. On issues of social legislation, labor-management regulation, civil rights, and the like, there are too many legislators to persuade, too many other interest groups to contend with, too much public attention paid to Congress to permit unions to make much headway through contributions. To be sure, the problem could conceivably become more serious if unions offered financial help to candidates *for nomination.* As Alexander Heard has pointed out in his authoritative study of political finances:

> The necessity for obtaining essential election funds has its most profound importance in the choosing of candidates. The moneys can usually be assured, and often withheld, by the relatively small corps of political specialists whose job it is to raise money. . . . Here political careers are launched or thwarted. Here persons with access to money find their greatest opportunity to influence the selection of public officials and therefore the conduct of the public's business.[22]

As yet, however, dangers of this kind have not materialized to any significant extent, for unions have seldom attempted to influence the choice of candidates, save in constituencies where the

Democrats are so strong that nomination is tantamount to election. In most instances, COPE officials are wary of attempting to enter the nominating process, fearing that to do so might raise unpleasant risks of alienating rival candidates who might ultimately be nominated, or of provoking dissension among unions having different views over which Democratic candidate should be supported.

If campaign contributions create a problem, it is in those cases in which unions have narrow legislative interests that depend on the good will of particular Congressional committees and their chairmen. To gain such favor, a union may well find it worthwhile to offer lavish campaign contributions to the few key legislators involved. Unions in such fields as the maritime industry and the postal service are said to have dispensed many thousands of dollars in this way. Of course, if the Congressmen in question are strong-minded enough, or if they have ready access to other sources of funds, or if there are opposing interest groups to take effective countermeasures, such practices may do little harm. But where these conditions are not present, the dangers to the public are all too apparent.

At the same time, it would be unwise to look upon this problem as a "labor abuse" to be corrected by regulating union contributions as such. Many other interest groups play exactly the same game. The root of the difficulty is that campaign costs have risen to the point that even excellent candidates have to seek assistance from groups with a stake in issues on which the successful candidate may eventually vote. So long as this situation prevails, it would be shortsighted to try to cure the problem by imposing restrictions on unions alone. The opportunities for abuse may well increase if there are fewer competing sources to which candidates can turn for funds. If corrective action is desired, it is far better to search for some general solution that will ease the financial burden, either by subsidizing all candidates or by effectively limiting their campaign expenditures.

3) Campaign Efforts. According to many politicians, labor has its greatest political impact, not by offering money, but by providing services: campaign workers to canvass, address envelopes, or drive reluctant voters to the polls; sound trucks and newspaper space to publicize a nominee; union halls and members to give the candidate a platform and an audience. The sheer magnitude of this effort seems impressive. In the 1960 campaign, ten million leaflets describing the voting records of Congressmen were distributed.[23] Five million circulars comparing the Kennedy and Nixon records on key labor issues were prepared.[24] Over four hundred branches of the Women's Activities Division (W.A.D.) made over one million telephone calls reminding union members and supporters to register and go to the polls.[25] In St. Louis alone, 407 union members registered 85,077 new voters in a single day.[26]

How significant are these activities? To the professional politician, they seem invaluable. Yet it is easy to exaggerate their importance in the outcome of elections, for a host of factors combine to decrease their effectiveness. Despite the impressive record in certain areas, many state and local federations have not yet made a serious attempt to mobilize and train a body of campaign workers. In other areas, the Federation's efforts are hampered by disputes among its larger members. Individual unions may support opposing candidates and thereby cancel out much of the work done by the Federation. In some districts, the local Federation does not even have a functioning COPE organization, because it lacks substantial numbers of union members or cannot manage to work harmoniously with the local Democratic organization.

Even if the local COPE organization is effective, its very success often elicits countermoves that blunt its impact. The local Democratic organization may make less of an effort, realizing that much of the necessary work is already being done by the Federation. More often, the COPE effort will simply provoke increased activity on the part of the opposing party organization. Finally, one must beware of overestimating the effect of campaign work. Although little systematic research has been done in this field, one study has sought to isolate the effect of different levels of campaign activity on the voting in various election districts possessing constituencies with comparable voting histories.[27] The results of the study indicated that even where one candidate had the benefit of an efficient campaign organization and the other did not, the effect on the total vote averaged no more than 5 percent. If these findings are reliable, labor's campaign work will not necessarily prove decisive even under the rare conditions where the unions campaign vigorously and the opposing candidates do not.

Despite these qualifications, there are important ways in which organized labor can have an impact on political campaigns. In the first place, labor can quickly close ranks and overcome its accustomed inertia when it is faced with a recognized threat to the movement. Let a right-to-work proposal go on the ballot or an archconservative run for an important office, and the unions can devote virtually unlimited amounts of time and energy to the campaign.

In the Ohio elections of 1958, for example, a right-to-work referendum served to galvanize union opposition in a state where labor's political activities had been notably unsuccessful in the past.[28] In the course of the campaign, unions and labor-front groups devoted an estimated $1,378,824 to defeating the proposal, outspending the opposition by almost two dollars to one. With the help of intensive labor efforts, registration figures reached a new high, exceeding even the totals recorded in the Presidential years of 1952 and 1956. And in the election itself, not only was the referendum beaten decisively, but Democratic candidates defeated Republican incumbents in the race for Governor and United States Senator.

Examples of this kind can easily be repeated. The result has been to alter the character of politics and government in several of the more industrialized states by making Republican politicians more reluctant to promote conservative candidates or antilabor issues that will be interpreted by the unions as a vital test of strength. Occasionally, such a candidate will run and may even be elected. But on the whole, experienced politicians agree that such a campaign is often unsuccessful, always expensive, and likely to give to labor's political machine a push that will carry over to other candidates and other campaigns.

Unions can also exert political influence because they are well situated to affect the voting habits of their members. To be sure, union members do not live in a closed society or social class; various surveys have shown that members rely more on television, daily newspapers, and national magazines than on union sources for their political information.* Nevertheless, having many means of access to their members, labor organizations can more easily communicate their political views and relate this information to the special concerns of their constituents than can many other kinds of organizations. And since many members doubtless look

---

* In the Kraft poll, sponsored by the AFL–CIO, union members were asked to identify "the most helpful source of information" on political matters. Twenty-one percent listed Walter Cronkite, CBS television commentator; 18 percent cited *Newsweek* magazine; 16 percent mentioned President Johnson; and 14 percent listed AFL–CIO president George Meany.[29]

upon their union as an organization particularly devoted to their interests and needs, they may pay special attention to the information and advice which it supplies to them.

The potency of this influence is difficult to appraise. It is well known, of course, that union members vote more heavily Democratic than other citizens of comparable education, income, and background. For example, in the 1956 Presidential election, the proportion of Democratic votes was 20.4 percent higher among union members, and 17.1 percent higher among families of union members, than among other sample groups of voters matched for similar education, income, and other conditions of life.[30] But some part of this difference must be attributed, not to union influence, but to the fact that persons choosing to join a union are more inclined to vote Democratic than those who do not join.* Until this latter factor can be isolated and measured, the degree of union influence cannot be ascertained.

Much more probing work along these lines has been carried out by the Survey Research Center at the University of Michigan.[31] In analyzing the voting habits of union members in the 1956 Presidential campaign, the Center arrived at four highly pertinent conclusions:

1) The more a member identifies with, and is interested in his union, the more likely it is that he will vote according to the union's political norms. Thus, 64 percent of the members (or their wives) who identified highly voted Democratic in 1956, compared with 36 percent of the weakly identifying group.[32]

2) The more clearly the political norms of the union are communicated to the members, the more likely they are to vote in accordance with those norms. According to the Center's calculations, 67 percent of the members voted Democratic in unions which most plainly and abundantly affirmed their support for the Democratic candidate, while the proportion fell to 44 percent in unions whose political norms were least emphasized and least clearly expressed.[33] These figures are hard to interpret, because the unions that supported the Democrats most vigorously may happen to have a membership with lower education and income levels that would be more likely to vote Democratic even without

---

* One confidential survey of employees who recently participated in N.L.R.B. elections revealed that workers voting for the union were 7 to 15 percent more favorable to the Democratic party than workers voting against the union.

union publicity. But it is significant that CIO unions—which have generally supported the Democrats more clearly and vigorously than AFL unions—yielded a significantly higher Democratic vote than AFL unions and that this disparity was maintained even after samples were adjusted to eliminate differences in income and educational levels.[34]

3) As a general rule, the longer the voter has been a union member, the more apt he is to vote Democratic.* The reverse is true of members who identify very weakly with the union.[35]

PERCENTAGES VOTING DEMOCRATIC IN 1956
BY AGE AND UNION IDENTIFICATION

	Length of membership		
	0–4 years	5–14 years	15 years or more
High identification	50%	66%	68%
Low identification	49	45	33

These figures tend to confirm the view that unions cannot carry many votes with them when they switch their support from one party to another; they exert significant influence only through a gradual process of reinforcing the loyalties of sympathetic members toward the Democratic party.

4) The tendency to follow the political norms of the union is greater among those who accept the legitimacy of union participation in politics. Thus, a composite survey of four Democratically oriented groups, including unions, revealed that 65 percent of those who strongly believed in the legitimacy of group political activity voted Democratic, while only 41 percent of those who were much less inclined to support such activity voted Democratic.[36] Once again, the identification of the member with the group plays an important role, for individuals who identified closely with their group were much more likely to affirm the legitimacy of its political activities.

These findings suggest that unions can increase their influence significantly to the extent that they can expand their membership, make clear their political objectives, persuade their members of

---

* It might appear that these figures merely suggest that older workers are more likely to vote Democratic than their younger fellows. But further analysis suggests that this is not the case, for the data revealed that older employees who had recently joined a union behaved like their younger co-workers and not like older members who had been in the union for greater lengths of time.

the need for political action, and increase their loyalty to the organization. This last point is especially important, for the findings suggest that members who do not appreciate their union or identify with it may actually react negatively to union efforts to influence their vote. As a result, the political activities of a union may be seriously blunted unless the organization can win the approval and involvement of its members in bargaining, administering grievances, and all of its other nonpolitical endeavors.

Another method by which labor can have an important impact on campaigns is by making efforts to increase the turnout of voters. Unions have gone about this task in three ways. On election days, union workers have contacted eligible voters to urge them to go to the polls and even to offer transportation or baby-sitting assistance. Prior to the election, COPE also has organized campaigns in many areas to persuade potential voters to register. Finally, union lobbyists have attempted to persuade sympathetic legislators and public officials to amend the election laws to make it easier for potential voters to register and come to the polls.

The strategy behind these efforts becomes clear upon examination of the voting statistics in past elections. Over the last twenty-five years, roughly 60 percent of all potential voters have cast a ballot in Presidential elections. (These figures contrast strikingly with those of Western Europe, where 75–90 percent of the potential electorate normally go to the polls.)[37] Looking further, one finds that nonvoting in the United States seems closely correlated with income and occupation.[38]

	PERCENTAGE NOT VOTING IN PRESIDENTIAL ELECTIONS	
	1948	1952
Occupational status		
White-collar	19%	19%
Semi-skilled	29	26
Unskilled	50	40
Income		
$5,000 and above	18%	13%
4,000–5,000	25	17
3,000–4,000	26	24
2,000–3,000	39	31
under 2,000	54	47

Those who do not vote tend to be somewhat unpredictable politically, with only a weak attachment to either of the established parties. Nevertheless, as one might expect from the income and status of most nonvoters, the majority will normally favor the Democrats, except in elections where the Republican candidate has an exceptionally broad popular appeal. As a result, labor generally stands to gain by increasing the voting turnout, especially in lower-income urban areas. Moreover, unlike many other forms of campaign activity, union efforts to increase the vote cannot easily be matched by Republican opponents, both because most nonvoters tend to be Democratic and because labor is more familiar than other organizations with the problems and techniques of reaching the poorer, working strata that are especially likely not to participate in elections.

There are no comprehensive data to measure the success of union efforts to increase the vote. Scattered statistics show that labor has made impressive attempts in certain localities. In 1960, for example, 63,214 new voters were registered with union help in Allegheny county, while 100,000 were added to the rolls in Spanish-speaking sections of California.[39] Yet, there is little indication that labor has made a large overall impact on the size of the vote. Participation rates, which averaged 55.4 percent in Presidential campaigns from 1932 to 1944, rose to only 60 percent from 1948 to 1960, when unions began to make serious efforts to increase the vote.[40] AFL–CIO officials concede that the Federation has had little success in many localities in launching registration drives. Although COPE offers to help finance such drives on a matching basis, many local federations and union leaders are either too preoccupied with other problems or too lacking in manpower and resources to undertake a serious effort along these lines.

Attempts to amend registration and voting laws have likewise met with only occasional success. In many ways, this is the critical battleground. Careful surveys have revealed that registration requirements are the major cause of nonvoting and that participation increases markedly when these laws are simplified.[41] As a result, labor would achieve its goals with much less effort if it could succeed in liberalizing these requirements. Very often, however, such efforts have met with firm opposition from public officials and party professionals, who fear the effects of adding large numbers of voters from low-income groups, because they seem to represent such an erratic and unpredictable political force.

With all these difficulties, labor may still make its greatest long-run impact by helping to enlarge the voting electorate. Union registration drives are steadily growing in size and sophistication, and each year more local labor leaders probably will cooperate in these efforts. As for voting and registration laws, urban unrest may reinforce the doubts of many politicians over the wisdom of encouraging lower-income groups to vote. Nevertheless, there has been a slow but noticeable trend since 1924 toward liberalizing these requirements, and the process seems likely to continue, if only because the nation's deepest democratic sentiments favor the extension of the vote to all adult citizens. The effect need not be to give the Democratic party a perpetual majority, even though the bulk of the nonvoters seem normally disposed toward the Democrats at the present time. Instead, the more likely result will be to shift both parties to the left toward a new equilibrium more responsive to the economic and social needs of less affluent segments of the population. As this process unfolds, the effects will doubtless be favorable to the broad social and economic platform advanced by the AFL–CIO.

Conclusion

The preceding discussion has disclosed a whole battery of restraints that confine the political power of labor much more than one might suppose on taking note of the millions of union members and the size of union treasuries. Within the ranks of labor, there are three principal limitations: the disunity of the labor organizations, whose leaders often adopt disparate political tactics and work for disparate political objectives; the unwillingness of union members to shift their habitual party allegiances; and, finally, the apathy of the members toward political action, an attitude rooted in a broad distrust of politics and in the traditional primacy of collective bargaining in the American system of industrial relations. Outside the union hall, still further obstacles intrude. Labor's power to demand special concessions from a Democratic administration is often blunted because the Federation has little choice but to support the party. Unions are also hemmed in by opposing interest groups which counter their lobbying efforts, expose their activities to publicity, and work to defeat their favored candidates. Above all, success in politics ultimately requires votes. As a result, in the highly publicized areas in which unions deal, few legislators wish to make concessions to unions that will offend broad segments of the electorate.

The limits on labor's political influence are mirrored in the work of Congress over the past thirty years. After all, the most favorable laws ever received by labor were enacted in the thirties, when unions had no campaign organizations and made no serious effort to lobby, even for such vital laws as the National Labor Relations Act. In subsequent years, as labor's political effort gathered momentum, the Taft-Hartley restrictions were enacted, followed by the Landrum-Griffin Act twelve years later. More recently still, labor has failed to eliminate right-to-work laws and other legal restraints, despite the presence of a friendly administration. In short, the record suggests that organized labor has not been able to achieve important legislative goals unless its objectives have corresponded with the sentiments of the electorate or the prevailing convictions in Congress.

Despite these limitations, it would be wrong to assume that labor's political power has been negligible. Without union efforts, workers and low-income groups would have little organized political support, and their interests would be more vulnerable to the pressure of other powerful groups. Through constant lobbying and political campaigning, unions have doubtless helped to give birth to Medicare and to enlarge social security and unemployment and workmen's compensation benefits. In addition, labor's success in registering voters and persuading them to go to the polls must have contributed something to the success of the Democratic party in maintaining control over Congress in all but two sessions since 1933, and holding the Presidency during all but three terms.

It is extremely difficult to estimate whether labor's influence in national politics will increase or decline. Much will turn on whether unions can identify themselves with political issues that really matter to their constituents. In an era when broad social legislation and collectively bargained fringe benefits are already an established fact, union members are likely to feel less strongly about labor's traditional political objectives, yet it is difficult to imagine other goals that can unite a large majority of union members. With the growing unionization of hospital workers, sanitation men, and farmworkers, on the one hand, and teachers, policemen, and federal employees, on the other, the union movement seems to be growing more heterogeneous, thus complicating the problem of finding a platform that the bulk of the membership can support with enthusiasm. If such goals cannot be found, the result will be increased apathy and greater susceptibility to the lure of other causes and candidates than those endorsed by labor's high command.

At the same time, there are still large numbers of low-income, unregistered voters, and the Federation may succeed in bringing them to the polls as its techniques become more sophisticated and better financed. To be sure, many other forces will have to combine with union efforts before the electorate can be significantly enlarged, and many groups will help determine the demands that eventuate from this new political force. But it is probably unrealistic to expect voting rates to persist indefinitely at their present level among low-income groups or to ignore the fact that a rise in these rates will almost inevitably help labor to realize many of its broad social and economic goals.

In the light of this discussion, what answer can be given to the various groups who have been so critical of labor's political role? To those who fear that unions will corrupt the political process and manipulate Congress, the conclusions should be reassuring. To many other readers, however, the answer will doubtless seem inconclusive. Those who support the "welfare state" objectives of the labor movement will applaud any progress the unions make and castigate them for not doing more. Those who dislike these objectives will keep on criticizing the unions and even cry out for legislation to curb their campaign activities. So long as labor's efforts are judged by the goals it pursues, no convincing verdict can be reached, for the goals themselves are rooted in value premises on which honest men will inevitably disagree.

There is a deeper sense, however, in which the political activities of unions can be appraised in a less controversial manner. In the last analysis, the major thrust of labor's activities has been to increase the political participation of poorer segments of society and to provide a coordinated and coherent political voice to workers who would otherwise be largely disorganized. Whatever one may think of the political platform that results from this activity, it is hard to deny the value of these endeavors in a democratic society. It is precisely because issues of policy are so often controversial that the nation has based its system of government on the vote of all interested members. Under these circumstances, one can hardly disapprove of the efforts of any organiza-

tion to broaden the participation of all interested groups in the
political process. The society has likewise witnessed the growth of
a host of organized interest groups that press whatever influence
and arguments they can muster on executive and legislative officials. Under such a system, one can scarcely oppose the effort of
labor unions to provide an organization of their own to promote
the interests of their members and of other working people.

These arguments are more than theoretical. If one examines the
field of labor and protective legislation, one will quickly discover
the effects of a lack of organization and participation in the political process. The least organized groups with the lowest levels of
voting participation include agricultural workers, domestic ser-
vants, and unskilled labor in small shops and marginal industries.
In the great majority of states, these employees are systematically
excluded from workmen's compensation systems, minimum-wage
laws, and unemployment insurance, and they are likewise deprived of any law permitting them to organize and bargain collectively without fear of retaliation. Even those who disapprove of
such measures will be hard-pressed to justify the discriminatory
treatment that denies the benefits of these laws to those who appear to need them most. Such discrimination, however, is the
natural fate of those who remain unorganized in a highly organized
political system. To the extent that unions work to correct this im-
balance, they bring a greater measure of fairness to the entire
governmental process.

Labor Unions and the City

ORGANIZED LABOR has taken an active interest in local government since the early part of the last century. In fact, labor's first venture into politics occurred when unions joined in creating local workingmen's parties in the late 1820's. From then until the First World War, union efforts were often directed toward electing their leaders as mayors and councilmen. Although these campaigns were seldom successful, labor did manage to elect mayors in San Francisco, Milwaukee, Scranton, and a number of other cities during that period.

After the First World War, unions paid much less attention to electing their leaders to office and turned more toward pressure-group activities to secure certain goals of immediate practical importance. Over the intervening years, these objectives have not changed fundamentally.

Labor seeks, among other goals, an accommodation with the police on the question of strikes. Ideally, union leaders would like to count on a tolerant attitude from policemen toward mass picketing and minor disturbances on the picket line. At the very least, labor hopes that the police will remain neutral and not harass picketers or give assistance to employer efforts to undermine a strike.

Labor leaders also desire a limited amount of patronage. In some instances, unions seek appointments that will give them a measure of influence over agencies that may affect their welfare. Thus, the Plumbers' union would like to be represented on the plumbing licensing board, the Teamsters seek a man on the traffic commission, and so forth. In other cases, a labor leader may

                   Labor and the American Community

simply want enough influence to succeed, on rare occasions, in rewarding a friend or removing a troublesome subordinate by having him placed on the public payroll.

Construction unions have a strong interest in several city programs that directly affect their wages and conditions of employment. They may wish to encourage urban renewal and other projects that will expand employment. They will certainly press to have building contracts awarded to union firms. And they will also push for a prevailing-wage policy.

Public-employee unions have even broader and more obvious interests in the policies of the city administration. Their initial concern is that the city encourage—or at least not oppose—union efforts to organize municipal workers. As these employees become organized, their unions will have an evident interest in having the city grant generous wages and working conditions. And in some departments, at least, it is extremely important that city administrators avoid contracting out work that could be performed by union members.

These concrete, job-oriented goals still predominate in every large city. Here and there, of course, labor has interested itself in broader ends—public housing in Los Angeles, fair employment practices in St. Paul, progressive tax rates in Boston. In St. Louis, Local 688 of the Teamsters even organized a network of political stewards who gathered complaints from members against city officials and mobilized support for rat-control ordinances, charter revisions, and antismog controls. But these examples are uncommon. In the main, organized labor has not actively worked for nearly as broad a range of goals in the city as it has at the state and national levels.

There are several reasons for this narrow urban focus. In many cities, the building trades have heavy representation and, to an increasing extent, so do public-employee organizations. Some of these unions have traditionally been disinterested in broad social and political goals; all of them have direct, immediate city-government interests that can easily crowd out any latent concern over a wider range of urban issues. To become involved in broader urban issues may alienate members and complicate the achievement of more immediate objectives vital to the organization.

One might expect a different response from the large industrial unions, whose leaders have so often supported broad political programs. But these unions are in a distinct minority in many cities. Hence, industrial unions have often geared their political efforts to these higher levels of government and have been less concerned with metropolitan affairs except in the occasional case where the union headquarters is located in a city other than Washington, D.C.

The issues that dominate urban politics also help to narrow labor's goals. At the state and national levels, union leaders can capitalize on issues of social legislation, such as unemployment insurance or Medicare, and receive enough rank-and-file support to allow them to take liberal positions on other domestic questions where the members are less concerned and united. At the city level, however, such issues of social legislation are less likely to arise; the pressing questions have to do with problems of race, poverty, education, transportation, and taxation. Members are sharply divided on the latter issues even in the industrial unions. In many Southern cities, labor organizations cannot afford to take strong positions in matters involving race. And in Detroit, although the U.A.W. predominates, labor has lost several mayoralty campaigns because union members would not follow their leaders in support of candidates with liberal records on race and poverty issues. As a result, even industrial unions have had to moderate their aims in order to achieve greater unity and accommodate the feelings of their members.

The success of labor in achieving its goals varies enormously from one city to another.[1] In Dallas and Birmingham, unions have little or no political impact. In St. Paul, on the other hand, almost any attractive Democrat can count on being elected if he has strong labor support, and few Democrats will be nominated over the opposition of the AFL–CIO Trades and Labor Assembly. Most cities fall somewhere between these extremes.

To a large extent, labor's success depends on the character of the union movement in the city in question. Where union members make up less than 30 percent of the working population, as in Atlanta and Los Angeles, their influence is likely to be slight. Where the percentage rises toward 50 percent, as in Detroit or Minneapolis-St. Paul, the opportunity for influence is obviously much greater. But numerical strength is not enough to insure success. For reasons already described, such unions as the Auto Workers, Carpenters, and State, County and Municipal Employees have sharply differing objectives at the urban level. Where organized labor is divided among unions of this type, it is seldom

able to achieve the unity possible in a city like Detroit, where the
Auto Workers are such a dominant factor in the movement. The
character of union leadership can also play a decisive role. Here
and there, a hyperactive and effective leader succeeds in welding
different unions together and cajoling them into devoting substantial time and effort to political action. In most instances, however, union officials at the urban level turn out to be surprisingly
apathetic in political matters. For example, in more than a few
cities, leaders in the construction trades have not even been alert
enough to lobby for urban renewal programs despite the enormous
potential in creating new jobs for the members.

The political environment in the city can also play a decisive
role in shaping the impact of union political action. In many
Southern cities, political influence is still heavily concentrated in
the hands of business leaders who are suspicious of labor and
hostile to many of its aims. In these communities, unions can do
little except to work for a liberal coalition which eventually may
challenge the existing leadership. Even in cities where liberal
Democrats with working-class support control the government, the
nature of the party structure can have a profound effect upon the
strength of labor influence. In Boston, for example, the Democrats
are firmly entrenched, but the party has been splintered among a
series of ethnic and local leaders. These divisions, in turn, have
helped to fragment the loyalties of union leaders and thus dilute
labor's strength. In Chicago, on the other hand, the party is highly
unified and remains in the control of a strong machine. The
machine has its own corps of precinct captains and political
workers and need not rely heavily on the unions to win at the polls.
As a result, labor's influence within the machine has not been particularly large, and unions have been badly beaten when they have
tried to buck the organization by running their own candidates.

In a few cities, labor is numerically strong, reasonably unified,
and willing to engage actively in grass-roots campaigning in
cooperation with the Democratic party. Even where these conditions prevail, however, there are nuances and variations in strategy
that can significantly affect labor's influence. In this respect, the
situation in St. Paul and Minneapolis offers a telling illustration.[2]

By 1950, labor was heavily organized in both of the Twin
Cities, with union members accounting for roughly 50 percent of
the work force. In each city, labor was reasonably unified; the
Minneapolis movement was dominated by the older AFL unions,

while AFL and CIO leaders had achieved considerable rapport and mutual respect in St. Paul. Both central labor bodies were allied with the dominant Democratic-Farmer-Labor party (D.F.L.), and both were accustomed to contributing substantial money and manpower to political campaigns. With this foundation, labor enjoyed substantial power in each community. Good relations with the police were assured. City construction contracts were regularly awarded to unionized firms at prevailing wage scales. Public employees were heavily organized and enjoyed wages and fringe benefits that equaled or exceeded those in the private sector. Nevertheless, the behavior of the two labor bodies differed in subtle ways that eventually led to a stinging defeat for one and continued prosperity for the other.

In St. Paul, the Trades and Labor Assembly had gone much further than in Minneapolis to integrate itself within the D.F.L. The party clubs were populated largely by union members and their relatives. Union activists were frequently found serving as precinct captains and ward leaders. Moreover, labor did not try to compete with the D.F.L. If the two disagreed on an endorsement, the unions simply withheld their own approval; they did not run a rival candidate or seek to undermine the D.F.L. nominee. The Trades and Labor Assembly had also succeeded in building a strong reputation throughout the city. Union representatives took an active part in a broad range of civic and charitable endeavors. No hint of scandal touched the unions. Above all, organized labor pursued a policy of tact and moderation in city politics. It worked, by and large, to promote good candidates and not merely men who were friendly to unions. And though it was powerful enough to dominate the City Council, at least in the short run, it chose not to do so; generally it endorsed only three of the candidates seeking election to the six positions on the council. This practice reflected a general policy not to seek power for its own sake but to become actively involved only where issues important to labor were at stake. As a result of these tactics, the Trades and Labor Assembly entered the sixties as perhaps the most influential political group in the entire city.

In Minneapolis, on the other hand, the central labor body was less closely allied to the D.F.L. Party clubs were dominated by issue-oriented liberals and intellectuals, and efforts to interest unionists in this activity were unsuccessful. Labor had undoubted influence because of its numerical strength and grass-roots campaign work, but it was widely alleged that the leader of the central body tended to "throw his weight around" and flaunt the unions' power. Labor irritated many politicians by insisting that all D.F.L.-endorsed candidates for municipal office agree to vote as a unit on issues affecting appointments and government organization. Labor was also said to press, on occasion, for candidates with little qualification beyond their demonstrated friendship for union causes. In 1957, the central labor body finally overreached itself when it tried to guarantee favorable treatment to unionized employees in the school system by electing a clear majority of union representatives to the school board—an issue which served to crystallize an opposition that had been latent for some time. Citizens' groups of both conservative and liberal complexions sprang up to combat "labor bossism" on the school board. After an acrimonious campaign, all of labor's candidates for the school board, as well as its candidates for the mayoralty and three aldermanic positions, were defeated.

It is a rare community where all of the obstacles impeding organized labor in attaining substantial political influence can be overcome. In some cities, union membership is too small. In most, unions are sharply divided—craft unions, for example, differing with public-employee organizations—and these cleavages are crisscrossed in turn by individual leaders with their own political ambitions. Apart from these divisions, many union officers simply lack the time, the energy, or the skill to work at creating an active political force of their organizations. Even if all these pitfalls are avoided, the general public is suspicious of a politically active union movement and is quick to unite in opposition to labor if its leaders assert their power too visibly.

It is difficult to tell whether this picture will undergo substantial change in the future. Labor's objectives have not altered significantly in several decades, and there is little evidence that unions are devoting greater efforts to grass-roots campaigning in municipal elections. Nevertheless, three trends are beginning to emerge that seem bound to leave a mark on labor's influence in the cities.

To begin with, the rapid growth of municipal-employee unions is very likely to affect the thrust and intensity of labor's political effort in the city. Unlike union members in the private sector, public employees have a vital stake in the city administra-

tion, which fixes their wages and establishes their working conditions. The size of the stake depends in large measure on the
procedures used to determine the terms of employment. If wages
and conditions are established by a quasi-judicial tribunal of
acknowledged authority, the need for political action seems less
acute. On the other hand, if employment terms are ultimately left
to the mayor's discretion, municipal unions are bound to be increasingly caught up in the political process. Union officials will
gain an influence at City Hall commensurate with their ability to
assist the mayor in preventing strikes. At the same time it will
become even more important for municipal union leaders to help
elect city officials who will not use strict measures to put down the
strikes that do occur. These points take on added significance in
the modern city with the demise of the old-line political machine.
No longer armed with a loyal band of precinct workers and block
captains, many mayors will find it increasingly hard to mobilize
the human energy that is needed to run an effective campaign.
Municipal unions, on the other hand, may have a large enough
political stake that they will fill this gap by developing their own
machine for the benefit of friendly candidates. If so, their influence
is bound to grow proportionately.

A second important trend is the dwindling number of union
members living in the central city. From 1959 to 1965, the total
proportion of the population living in the twelve largest central
cities rose from 13.3 percent to 13.7 percent. During the same
period, the proportion of union members in the same central cities
declined from 21.3 percent to 17.1 percent.[3] These fluctuations
reveal the lure of the suburbs to an increasingly affluent union
membership. In fact, a private poll of the AFL–CIO revealed in
1967 that almost half of all members now reside in the suburbs.[4]
The significance of these figures seems reasonably clear. Perhaps
municipal-employee unions will grow more influential as they
intensify their campaign efforts in recognition of their obvious
stake in city government. But unless the labor movement as a
whole finds some reason to intensify its political efforts, its influence in the cities seems bound to diminish as its proportion of the
urban population continues to dwindle.

The final, and most problematical, trend affecting organized
labor is the growth of Negro power in urban politics. Blacks already outnumber whites in Newark and Washington, D.C. If
present trends continue, they will have a clear majority by the turn

of the century in nine of the largest cities, including Chicago, Philadelphia, Detroit and St. Louis.[5] The influence of the Negro in city politics will doubtless grow apace. But what this will mean for organized labor is still obscure. If the teachers' unions and construction crafts continue to be seen as a symbol of opposition, and if local unions are still dominated by white leaders and suburban dwellers, the prospects for conflict loom large. On the other hand, it is at least conceivable that unions could create a working alliance with Negro politicians and through it ultimately enhance their influence.

Service in the Community

Although labor has seldom tried hard in city politics to press for broad community objectives, it has contributed to these ends through other channels. For several decades, unions have been devoting substantial time and money to a variety of charitable and civic causes. The Federation has long cooperated in collecting money for the United Fund, the Red Cross, the Community Chest, and other local charities. Labor leaders have actively aided blood-donation campaigns and have helped to organize and support the CARE program to ship food abroad. In addition, individual locals have often backed particular causes that have appealed to their leaders and members. Several unions—particularly those with very liberal leaders or high proportions of nonwhites in their membership—have regularly contributed to civil-rights and civil-liberties organizations. Other locals have sponsored scout troops, youth centers, Little League teams, and charity bazaars.

Through these efforts, organized labor has had an impact on many community activities, an impact that greatly exceeds the relative strength of its membership. In recent years, approximately one third of all United Fund and Community Chest collections have come from plants represented by AFL–CIO unions.[6] Roughly one third of all Red Cross blood donations have been given by union members,[7] and approximately one quarter of all Boy Scout leaders are AFL–CIO members.[8]

Apart from contributing time and money, labor has also sought a greater voice in the civic and welfare activities of the community. To this end, the AFL–CIO has established a community services program under the general guidance of a staff director in Washington. A major purpose of this program has been to encourage participation by labor representatives on the boards and councils of welfare organizations of all kinds. According to the director:

> The AFL–CIO Community Services program is a reflection . . . of the firm belief of the American labor movement in the process of integration as opposed to a policy of isolation. The active participation of AFL–CIO affiliates and trade union members in the affairs of their communities is the tangible expression of labor's cooperative effort. . . . It is in labor's community-services work, perhaps more than in any other area, that the class struggle is most visibly rejected.[9]

What lies behind this deliberate effort to place union leaders on community boards and agencies? Leaders give different answers. To some, the program is simply part of labor's civic responsibility, a natural outgrowth of its broad commitment to social and humanitarian ends. To others, participation is equally valued as a means of raising labor's status and polishing its image as a constructive force in the community. Still others see greater participation as a way of counteracting the domination by business and professional groups in order to insure that community services will be responsive to all elements in the society.

These are all brave goals. But what progress has actually been made toward achieving them? In terms of numbers, the success has been striking. At the close of World War II, when labor was just beginning to interest itself in community services, only a few hundred union members could be found on the boards of civic and welfare agencies. By 1950, the number had grown to an estimated 10,000.[10] Today, the Community Services Department claims more than 75,000 representatives currently serving in these positions.[11]

Yet numbers give only a faint indication of success. The key question is whether representation has produced any tangible impact on the community or on organized labor itself. By this measure the picture is much less impressive.

Studies carried out in a variety of cities and towns reveal that civic leaders generally perceive union officials as wielding far less influence in community affairs than business and professional people.[12] And local union leaders regularly agree with this assessment. To be sure, these surveys are imprecise, for the influence of any group varies significantly depending upon the nature of the issue involved. But other studies have investigated the impact of different groups on a variety of community decisions, and these studies also suggest that labor spokesmen have had very little impact.[13] In general, union leaders are likely to have an influence only on issues where they command some special leverage. For obvious reasons, they often have an effect on community efforts to attract new companies or prevent existing firms from leaving. And they may also exert some influence on charity boards because of the help they can give in raising money from employees. Yet even in these instances, union leaders are normally asked to participate because of their power, and not because their advice is valued for its own sake. More often than not, they are simply asked to help carry out community programs without having had an important voice in planning the program or deciding whether to put it into effect. When they do participate, they are commonly regarded as representatives of an interest group, and their opinions are treated with skepticism for that reason. In short, they have not succeeded, as many businessmen have done, in being looked upon as public-spirited individuals rather than labor spokesmen when they take their place on community boards and agencies.

There are evident reasons for these attitudes. Business executives and professional men have had a much longer time to establish themselves as disinterested civic leaders. Many of them will instinctively regard the union leader with a suspicion carried over from the adversary process of strikes and bargaining. In the respectable milieu of the established community agency, education and background can easily put a distance between labor leaders and the other community leaders with whom they try to work.

Yet these observations do not tell the whole story. A few dedicated union leaders have clearly succeeded in leaving a mark on their communities. If others have not had comparable success, one suspects that part of the responsibility must be laid on the union representatives themselves. All too often, union leaders have accepted civic posts without devoting the time and effort required to make a substantial contribution. In many cases, the leaders involved have not even bothered to attend meetings with any regularity. At the national level, to be sure, the AFL–CIO has made some effort to formulate general principles to guide their representatives in certain areas of community work. In the field of hospital construction, for example, the Executive Council has prepared a statement outlining several common deficiencies and urging labor representatives to insist upon careful planning before constructing new facilities, to press for consumer representation on hospital boards, and to oppose racially discriminatory practices affecting patients or staff. The effect of these statements on union spokesmen in the community, however, is problematical. All studies of labor's community programs seem to support the judgment of Professor James B. McKee:

> Apparently, [labor leaders] have no need for a greater voice, for they have not brought to the decision-making process a new set of interests, a new program, a new ideology. They do not have a specific labor program, but they have accepted the community welfare program at face value.[14]

In sum, union participation in community activities has had, at best, only a mixed success. It has probably done something to integrate labor more closely into the society around it. Here and there, union officials have also succeeded in gaining greater confidence and rapport with members of the community "establishment." But one suspects that many labor leaders are too quick to assume that respect and understanding can be easily gained by simply mixing convivially with community leaders on neutral ground. Union officials have not clearly faced up to the fact that enduring respect is normally won only in proportion to the effort and imagination that they bring to their civic tasks. Many leaders would reply that they are simply too burdened with other tasks to devote themselves wholeheartedly to community projects. If this is true, however, one wonders whether labor has not been overly anxious to gain representation. As matters now stand, union officials too often find themselves in the uncomfortable position of taking enough time for civic activities to divert them from their regular work without investing enough effort to make a discernible contribution to the community.

The results of this dilemma show up most clearly in examining labor's record in carrying out its proclaimed intention to make community services more responsive to all elements in the society. In the field of health care, unions have served the interest of lower-income groups by working to broaden the coverage of medical insurance and to encourage the growth of prepaid plans. But in other areas of community service, the picture is much less bright. During the past few years, public concern over poverty has exposed the inadequacy of many social services in meeting the needs of the poor. Had union representatives really been alert in promoting the interests of the entire community, they might have led the way in uncovering these deficiencies and developing proposals for their cure. Such was not the case. Organized labor joined the fight against poverty once the issues were drawn and the battle lines laid down. Despite all its representatives on civic agencies, however, labor did little in local areas to dramatize the issue of poverty for the public or to plot the programs by which the problem could be alleviated.

Organized Labor and the Urban Crisis

In the past five years, America's perception of the city and its problems has changed markedly. Today urban problems seem sufficiently urgent that many people are no longer gratified by occasional displays of civic responsibility; they consider it imperative for all established institutions to cooperate actively in helping to resolve the city's problems. This change in attitude creates a novel challenge for unions along with other private organizations.

The familiar difficulties that beset the modern city involve a broad spectrum of issues touching on unemployment, crime, substandard housing, decaying schools, racial discrimination, traffic congestion, and inadequate health facilities. It may be true, as some thoughtful critics point out, that many of these problems are no worse, and may be even less acute than they were several decades ago. But certainly our frustrations and impatience with the problems have grown—so much so that it is common to speak of an urban crisis in America.

Organized labor has not been unaware of these problems. In September 1967, the Executive Council of the AFL–CIO issued a statement that laid down a broad "urban platform" for the Federation.[15] In essence, the statement consisted of a set of proposals for devoting many billions of government dollars to a range of urban programs: public housing, urban renewal, mass transit, public facilities (hospitals, water supplies, sewage systems, etcetera), projects for job creation and training, better education, and so forth. Coupled with these proposals were several other reforms, such as open-housing legislation, economic planning for urban needs, and a restructuring of the welfare program.

Although the policy statement is necessarily cast in rather general terms, certain points emerge quite clearly. The Federation is plainly committed, on the legislative level, to attacking urban problems on a large scale. Judging from experience, this commitment is more than nominal; the Federation will lobby actively for large-scale urban programs and work hard to secure the election of legislators who share these aims.

At the same time, the policy statement leaves certain gaps that are often apparent in labor's approach to broad issues of national policy. To begin with, the statement does not contain any new thinking about urban problems. Instead, the proposals are little more than a compilation of familiar steps that have long been advocated by other groups concerned with the urban predicament. In addition, the statement nowhere faces up to the hard problem of raising the billions of dollars required to put its programs into operation. By what devices will the money be raised? What priorities should be attached to the Federation proposals and to other related programs if all of the funds are not available? Finally, there is scarcely a word about what the unions themselves will do to help resolve urban problems. Most competent observers have become convinced that necessary progress cannot be made by simply relying upon the government. And surely there are ways by which unions themselves could make contributions, yet not a word of these matters appears in the statement.

It is not fair, of course, to judge labor's efforts in the urban field on the basis of a single statement from the AFL–CIO. In fact, unions have made concrete efforts in the urban field, particularly in the area of poverty. The work of unions in this field is particularly interesting because two differing approaches have been tried. One is a program flowing out of the mainstream of the American labor movement that builds upon the traditional methods of the AFL–CIO. The other, a project for "organizing the poor," is a more radical experiment conceived by a group of intellectuals whose basic ties are to the United Auto Workers. By analyzing the results under both of these approaches, one may learn much about labor's capacities and limitations in helping to confront the urban crisis.

The AFL–CIO has worked along a number of fronts to assist the war against poverty.[16] The Federation has given full support to the legislation establishing the Poverty Program. This backing has not been nominal; it has engaged the active attention of union lobbyists, and this support has continued during recent efforts to

cut back the program. The AFL–CIO has also tried to inform
subordinate union leaders about the antipoverty program and to
persuade them to give it full support. To this end, 10,000 manuals
were distributed to local leaders explaining the antipoverty legislation and suggesting ways for labor to assist in implementing the
program. Over 100,000 shorter pamphlets on the same subjects
were distributed throughout the Federation. An entire issue of the
monthly journal was devoted to labor participation in the war
against poverty, and other articles have been included in other
issues on the same subject. Staff representatives from Washington
have also organized conferences to discuss problems of poverty
with fifteen hundred local leaders. Similar discussions were included on the agenda of innumerable conventions, meetings, and
union summer schools. Union representatives, moreover, have
been encouraged to seek representation on local poverty boards
and community-action organizations. By 1967, over five hundred
union officials were serving in such capacities. In addition, regional
programs have been organized with federal support to train local
union leaders to work in poverty programs in their communities.
In the first of these efforts, over one hundred leaders from Appalachia were given four weeks' training by the staff of West Virginia
University. According to the university's evaluation, most of the
participants worked actively in poverty projects on returning to
their communities, and their involvement was markedly greater
than in other communities which had not contributed trainees to
the program.

Unions have also cooperated in retraining low-skilled workers,
largely under programs supported through the Manpower Development and Training Act (M.D.T.A.). By the end of June 1966,
twelve thousand workers were involved in M.D.T.A. projects in
which unions were actively engaged in the training process. Additional programs were also being sponsored by individual unions
under the Job Corps and Neighborhood Youth Corps programs.

The net effect of these endeavors is thus far decidedly mixed.
The Federation has made its greatest contribution to the war
against poverty through its work at the national level. It has clearly
been a major force in supporting legislation to combat poverty and
in working to elect candidates who favor large government programs in this field. At the grass-roots level, however, little progress
has been made. Here and there one finds a dedicated leader involved in the poverty program or a local union with a vigorous

training program. But union leaders have not displayed much initiative in most communities. Some labor officials have actually blocked efforts to place the graduates of government training programs because of fear that the jobs and wages of union members would somehow be impaired. Although other unions have helped sponsor training programs, these efforts are still very modest in scope. And most of the programs sponsored by unions have been directed more at upgrading their own members than reaching the hard-core unemployed outside their ranks.

In order to attack the problem of poverty at the grass roots, a very different approach has been advocated by the Industrial Union Department of the AFL–CIO, headed until recently by Walter Reuther. This program has been described most articulately by one of its major architects, Jack Conway:

> The labor movement must be an instrument for social change. One of its major functions is to dissent, to express dissatisfaction, to create restlessness, and out of this dissent, dissatisfaction, and restlessness to fashion an economic and social order better than the existing one.
>
> Naturally, in our attempts to carry this out, we turn first to our union organizations and our own union experience. . . . As we try to transfer this experience into the area of general social change, we consider the possibility of using prototypes of union forms and structures to attack the problems of poverty. Why not, for example, experiment with the concept of a "neighborhood union" or "community union"? We believe that just as the auto worker and the steel worker and other industrial employees gained self-respect and dignity through organization, so, too, can the poor gain self-respect and dignity by the same methods.
>
> The community union is a new concept, a new form of institution, but it is well within the best traditions of the trade-union movement. A community union could mesh traditional trade-union functions with modern community-center functions. It could, for example, bring tenants together to bargain collectively with slum lords. It could have its own grievance procedure and steward system so that the complaints of a neighborhood could be voiced effectively. It could institute educational programs and retraining programs. It could raise the political awareness and political effectiveness of long-neglected people.[17]

Without doubt, the idea of a community union is one of the most imaginative ideas to emerge from organized labor in the postwar period. But how has the idea fared in actual practice? To answer this question, one must turn to the three major communities in which the idea has been tried: Chicago, Newark, and Watts.

CHICAGO

The initial experiment in community unions took place on Chicago's West Side. The *dramatis personae* were by no means confined to the Industrial Union Department. The prime catalyst in the early stages was Gilbert Cornfield, a lawyer with close union connections and a deep concern over developing a broader social conscience within the labor movement. Another key participant was Martin Luther King, Jr., whose Southern Christian Leadership Conference (S.C.L.C.) was actively represented in Chicago by one of King's lieutenants, James Bevel. Still another key figure was Al Raby, head of the Coordinating Council of Community Organizations (C.C.C.O.), a group of 36 Negro and civil-rights groups. Finally, the I.U.D. itself was represented by its regional director Charles Chiakulas.

In the fall of 1965, Cornfield initiated a series of discussions that were to last almost six months. Out of these talks emerged a plan to create a community union in the Woodlawn district that would provide representation for local residents on a broad series of community issues. The organization was to be built along traditional union lines with a regular dues-paying membership. But the necessary staff would be contributed equally by civil-rights groups and the I.U.D. with each of these organizations contributing a fair share of the subsidy required to cover operating expenses.

The first undertaking of the fledgling community union was to organize hospital workers on the West Side. This effort seemed a natural one since the hospitals employed substantial numbers of low-paid workers who lived nearby in the huge, black ghettos. In the end, however, the project was to terminate in total failure. The reasons for its demise expose a number of the problems involved in efforts to organize the poor.

From the beginning, the community union project was largely dominated by the I.U.D. This tendency was not entirely due to the efforts of Chiakulas and his co-workers; the civil-rights organizations left a vacuum that was inevitably filled by the I.U.D. In part, the gap resulted from a reluctance on the part of civil-rights groups to engage in the slow, frustrating task of building a permanent grass-roots membership. These groups were never enthusiastic about the drive, and their representatives could not match the organizing know-how of the I.U.D. staff. The energies of the civil-rights organizations were sapped still more by a widening rift between Bevel of the S.C.L.C. and Raby of the C.C.C.O. By 1966, the two men were scarcely on speaking terms. To complicate matters, differences of opinion sprang up between the labor and civil-rights leaders over the purposes of the community-union venture. From the I.U.D. came a request to divert the staff into a registration effort to strengthen the campaign to reelect Senator Paul Douglas. On the part of Dr. King, attempts were made to involve the organization in efforts to support open housing and overcome racial discrimination in unions. Union leaders, fearful of antagonizing their members, were no more receptive to the S.C.L.C.'s proposals than was Dr. King to go along with Chiakulas' desire to involve the organization in partisan politics.

As the I.U.D. began to play an increasingly dominant role, the weaknesses in its staff became apparent. Though more experienced than the civil-rights workers, the I.U.D. organizers were "outsiders" to the local community and without a "feel" for its people and their problems. At the same time, the representatives of civil-rights groups who were selected to assist in organizing proved increasingly undependable. As the Negro leaders grew more wary of Chiakulas and his objectives, the efforts of the civil-rights representatives became still less effective. The *coup de grâce* to the entire campaign occurred late in 1966 when representatives of the Teamsters and the Building Service Employees arrived at the hospitals claiming jurisdiction over the employees. At this point, the S.C.L.C. and C.C.C.O. withdrew entirely from the community union, and the organizing drive ground to a halt.

Thereafter, the community union engaged in a number of projects that further demonstrated its basic weaknesses. For a time, it joined forces with the Latin American Defense Organization (L.A.D.O.)—a group led by Obed Lopez, a militant organizer of Mexican extraction. Once again, however, the I.U.D. began to dominate the organization. It insisted that the I.U.D., rather than L.A.D.O., have its name inscribed on the headquarters' window. It pressed hard for the development of a dues-paying membership, and it eventually made demands that the staff contribute time to Senator Douglas' registration campaign. The entire undertaking eventually collapsed after the I.U.D. locked Lopez out of the office.

The community union then turned to helping in the organization of tenant unions, which had begun to spring up in Chicago. In several apartment buildings, tenants had been organized to picket and withhold rent in order to obtain agreements from their landlords guaranteeing repairs, stable rents, and even grievance procedures. The I.U.D. actively sought to enter into these activities by lending organizers, training building stewards, and helping to staff negotiating committees. But the I.U.D. again encountered resistance from its would-be allies. To civil-rights groups, labor seemed bent on magnifying its own importance. Negro leaders bridled at union publicity, such as the following U.A.W. editorial on the tenant fight against the Condor and Costalis buildings in the East Garfield district:

> Displaying the determination of Flint auto workers 30 years ago, the tenants vowed that no one would pay rent to Condor and Costalis. . . . The real estate firm sought an injunction and, as in the early days of auto organizing, the court upheld property rights over human rights. Only when the I.U.D. filed a brief in support of the tenants did Condor and Costalis come to terms and the tenants have an agreement and a union.[18]

Further difficulties were encountered during the I.U.D.-sponsored drive to organize tenants in buildings operated by the Schavin Corporation. Using traditional union methods, outside organizers worked for many weeks to obtain 500 membership cards from Schavin tenants and then demanded that the company negotiate. When the company refused, the organization sought to mobilize its members, only to discover that many tenants had forgotten about the cards and had lost interest in the union. In this respect, the experience with Schavin contrasted vividly with the success of the Condor-Costalis drive, in which the necessary organization was carried out much more swiftly and effectively by local residents under the leadership of a Woodlawn minister.

In addition to these setbacks, basic problems began to emerge that cast a shadow over the very concept of tenant unions. Even if residents could have been organized quickly for a showdown with the landlord, interest soon flagged, and rapid turnover magnified the problem of creating viable, permanent organizations. Moreover, the economic potential of the tenants' union proved considerably smaller than its supporters had anticipated. In the more prosperous buildings, bargaining might divert resources from the landlord into lower rents and better maintenance. But in the poorer tenements, landlords often lacked the profits that would be needed to improve the position of the residents. For these buildings, only rent supplements and other forms of government assistance could better the condition of the tenants.

In the face of these problems, the community union steadily declined. While continuing to offer assistance to tenant organizations, it had failed to achieve real leadership or success in the tenant movement. Its campaigns in other areas had proved abortive, its alliances with civil-rights groups had broken down and it had no support from local unions in the area. By the summer of 1968, the organization had dwindled to a single representative and a secretary.

NEWARK

One of the I.U.D. representatives in the Chicago venture was Norman Hill, a Negro who had come to the Department's legislative branch in Washington after several years at the Congress of Racial Equality. Hill joined the I.U.D. out of a conviction that labor and civil-rights groups should forge a close alliance in order to further their own mutual interests. Although the Chicago experience was a sharp disappointment to him, he left determined to start afresh and avoid the mistakes that had been made in that initial venture. With Jack Conway's backing, he moved to northern New Jersey where the established unions seemed prepared to support the community-union concept to a degree that the Chicago unions had not.

In planning this new venture, Hill decided against cooperating closely with civil-rights organizations, because of his conviction, growing out of his earlier years with CORE, that these groups were not prepared to give sustained assistance to the slow task of organizing ghetto residents. As a result, Hill looked for his staff to an entirely new source—the interns of the Rutgers Labor Education Program, which was training antipoverty and union organizers with the support of Office of Economic Opportunity (O.E.O.) funds. With the help of these interns, Hill planned to concentrate on organizing small factories and retail stores in ghetto areas. Since the established unions were not interested in these targets, Hill hoped that his organization could avoid the jurisdictional battles that helped to jettison the hospital drive in Chicago. And once the employees in these stores and factories were signed up, the organization could then develop into a community union by expanding its functions beyond negotiating for better wages and working conditions. In particular, Hill planned to bargain with retail owners over their sales and credit practices in the ghetto and ultimately to represent the union members in their relationships with landlords, police, and government officials.

In the end, these plans were never implemented. The entire project was badly disrupted by the Newark riots in the summer of 1967. By the following fall, Norman Hill had left to join the A. Philip Randolph Institute in New York City. The organizers from Rutgers never materialized. And with the growing rift between the AFL–CIO and the Auto Workers, control over the project passed from the I.U.D. to the Citizens' Crusade Against Poverty, a private organization partly financed by the U.A.W.

Hill's departure brought about a marked change in the role and purpose of the community union. The new organization turned away from organizing and bargaining toward an effort to sponsor training programs for the hard-core unemployed. With the help of a $250,000 grant from the Labor Department, a project was initiated to supervise the training of eighty black youths and their placement with six home-improvement companies. At the same time, efforts were under way to renovate an abandoned brewery as a social and recreation center and to organize basic education courses for ghetto residents. These developments, of course, signaled a clear shift in philosophy. The decision to administer training programs for the poor with the help of government money was a decision to work "within the system" for the betterment of ghetto residents, instead of bringing pressure from without as a militant community union. In short, the community union had shifted its tactics to a point much more closely aligned with the programs of the AFL–CIO.

WATTS

The experience in Watts began, not as a U.A.W. project, but as a coalition of twelve different unions, with encouragement and support from the Institute of Industrial Relations at U.C.L.A. From preliminary meetings between these organizations emerged

the concept of a Watts Community Labor Action Committee
(W.C.L.A.C.) built around a core of union members living in
Watts. As originally conceived, this committee would not be aimed
primarily at bargaining with landlords but would provide representation in dealing with all public and private interests that
affected the welfare of Watts residents.

A number of months were to pass before someone could be
found with the talents and energies required to take charge of the
committee. And almost immediately the Watts riot of 1965
erupted, forcing the committee to divert its energies into finding
food and lodging for those whose homes were burned and destroyed. Eventually, however, the committee was ready to return
to its original course under the leadership of an extremely energetic and resourceful U.A.W. steward in Watts, Ted Watkins.

In the early stages of its history, the committee was presented
with an issue that provided full scope for representing the interests
of community residents. A clear need existed to construct a new
hospital in Watts. To build the hospital, however, it was considered necessary for the voters of Los Angeles County to approve a
bond issue. Through the efforts of the committee, the bond issue
was placed on the ballot and two hundred volunteers were organized to canvass in support of the measure. As events turned out,
the issue failed by a narrow margin to obtain the needed two
thirds majority. But further lobbying by the committee resulted in
a decision by the County Board of Supervisors to approve alternative financing for the project.

The success of the hospital drive seemed to augur well for the
committee as an effective pressure group for local interests. As
events turned out, however, a series of forces deflected the committee from its original course and pointed it toward an entirely
different role in the community.

As in Chicago, the task of building a solid pressure-group
organization in Watts was extremely difficult. The union members,
who were conceived as the core of the organization, were actually
something of an elite set apart from the community. The poorer
elements in the city were totally unused to the idea of group action.
They were extremely skeptical of schemes and plans from any
group, white or black, and were inclined to believe that any
proposal would ultimately be used to exploit them. In this atmosphere, pressure quickly developed to take actions yielding immediate, dramatic results.

In the face of these pressures, a number of tempting opportunities arose. The Office of Economic Opportunity expressed a
willingness to make funds available for training and community
programs. City officials seemed interested in assisting various
types of constructive projects. These opportunities were not
ignored. With O.E.O. funds, a program was established for giving
remedial training, recreation, and neighborhood work to several
hundred teen-agers. An Army camp agreed to lend its facilities for
a summer camp for two thousand children. A transit company
made land available near its tracks to facilitate vegetable farming.
A check-cashing service was created to eliminate the fee commonly
required to cash welfare checks. A service station was acquired to
be run both to raise money and as a training facility. Additional
training programs were established to allow residents to fill a
variety of jobs in the new hospital.

As each new program developed, a burst of favorable publicity followed, first in local newspapers and later in national
magazines. Mayor Sam Yorty inspected committee projects on
several occasions, along with many other well-known visitors.
Federal support soon grew to substantial proportions. By the
summer of 1967 a total of $1,175,000 in federal money had been
promised for projects in the following year.

As time went on, it became clear that the committee was
moving further and further away from its original conception as a
militant citizens' organization to bargain with the "power structure." No organizing drive had been conducted. No broad-based
membership had been assembled. No dues were being collected.
Far from bargaining abrasively with city officials, the committee
was working more and more closely with them. By 1968, Chairman
Watkins even endorsed the incumbent county supervisor against a
rival Negro politician.

As the committee prospered, the interest of the participating
unions waned. From a public-relations standpoint, the committee
provided them with excellent publicity, and they continued as
official sponsors. But with so much money coming in from outside
sources, several of them lagged in their financial contributions, so
that union support was increasingly supplied out of U.A.W. funds.

These developments did not pass unnoticed. In 1967, a meeting was held among the representatives of the sponsoring unions.
To the meeting came Jack Conway of the I.U.D. with a proposal
to begin organizing a permanent dues-paying membership and to

construct a genuine community union. As expected, this suggestion was endorsed by Paul Schrade, Director of U.A.W. Region 6.
But the other unions took a much more negative attitude. A
militant community union with a dues-paying membership could
cause trouble for them in several ways. The evolution of the committee seemed to suggest that a strong community union would
develop into an appendage of the U.A.W.—a result that many of
the other unions viewed with some suspicion. As members of the
organization took jobs in nonunion plants, they would presumably
retain their community-union membership. Eventually, therefore,
the organization could easily emerge as the traditional *bête noire*
of the American labor movement, a rival union. Apart from this
danger, there was the obvious threat that a full-grown community
organization would begin to put pressure on the established
unions to relax seniority provisions of their agreements and provide preferential employment to Negro and Mexican-American
workers. In addition, political struggles with the city could result
in embarrassing relations between the sponsoring unions and local
officials. Thus it became clear that several sponsoring unions might
withdraw their support entirely if Conway's proposal were
adopted.

As for the committee itself, no clear indication was given of
where it stood on the proposal. But there was reason to question
how sympathetic it might be to any basic transformation in its
structure. Though vastly successful in developing programs and
mobilizing community support, Ted Watkins gave little sign of
strong militancy. Working with friendly public agencies seemed
more congenial to him. Moreover, as events had developed, Watkins *was* the Labor Action Committee. The work of the committee
was primarily an outgrowth of his ideas, his work, and his organizing capacities. Indeed, it was probably inevitable that a strong
personality of this kind should emerge if the project was ever to
get off the ground. Some observers of the committee were inclined
to doubt that Watkins could easily abandon a structure where he
functioned so well in favor of a grass-roots organization, where
greater power and participation would shift to the hands of the
community residents themselves.

In the face of these pressures, the Watts Community Labor
Action Committee had not changed course by mid-1968. Without
doubt, it had proved far more durable and successful than the
I.U.D. experiments in Newark and Chicago. But in its own way, it

fell equally short of becoming the militant community union
originally envisioned by Conway and his associates in the I.U.D.

The Community Union in Perspective

The community-union movement is still in an experimental
stage. But the picture that emerges is obviously more clouded than
the vision first painted by Jack Conway.

The experience to date suggests that the outlook for a community union will be bleak unless an indigenous leader can be
found with unusual energy and charisma. For surely this quality
of leadership does much to distinguish the failures in Newark and
Chicago from the limited success achieved by a Watkins in
Watts.* This point can prove troublesome to a labor leader who
wishes to organize the poor. It is always difficult for a union, or
any other organization, to produce a charismatic figure. The problem is compounded when the leader must be found in a poor
community with which the union has few direct ties.

Even if such a leader emerges, there is little assurance that a
viable community union will result. The problem is not that the
poor are impossible to organize. Successful campaigns among farm
laborers, hospital workers, and garbage collectors reveal that the
job is not beyond reach. But these campaigns did not result in
community unions in the true sense, for the organizations involved
were built upon as an occupational base. The community union,
on the other hand, rests upon residence rather than jobs, and this
organizing principle runs headlong into several difficulties. It leads
to competition with a variety of other community organizations,
many of which are internally divided and jealous of their own
prerogatives. It gives rise to all manner of suspicions and potential
conflicts with established unions organized along traditional occupational lines. And it requires a sensitivity to local issues and a
special organizing skill that the average union does not possess in
abundance. In the face of these obstacles, the temptations are
great to abandon the idea of a militant, dues-paying membership
altogether and become another community agency for administering government money to alleviate the heavy burden of ghetto
problems.

---

* Leadership also does much to explain the success of Cesar Chavez in the
somewhat similar task of organizing farm workers in California.

An Agenda for the Future

The Federation has made substantial efforts to support legislation to combat urban difficulties and to arouse interest in these issues throughout the union movement; the local unions have been much less interested in accepting like responsibilities in their own communities. Can unions do more to confront urban problems at the grass roots? This is a significant question not only for the welfare of the community but also for the union movement itself. This point is not always perceived by progressive labor leaders, who often conceive of their community efforts purely in humanitarian terms. Laudable as these motives may be, they endanger any meaningful commitment to social causes. If union programs are considered simply as a form of civic virtue, they are bound to be slighted in time and money in favor of other problems that seem more pressing to the organization.

A part of labor's stake in community problems has to do with the manner in which unions are viewed by the public, and particularly by its more influential and thoughtful members. As survey data presented in Chapter 1 bear out, labor leaders are generally regarded as spokesmen for narrow, partisan interests. They are respected less than any other important group for their views and policies on matters of wider community importance. This low opinion is clearly harmful to labor, both in attracting able, imaginative people to the movement and in gaining an attentive audience for its point of view.

To counteract this impression, the Federation has spent hundreds of thousands of dollars each year on radio and television programs and other public-relations ventures. This effort is largely misconceived. Such programs carry little credibility and even less interest; they are swallowed up in the swirl of public information on labor problems and other issues.

In the last analysis, fundamental changes in public attitudes toward social institutions rarely come about solely by conventional methods of public relations. Instead, they are much more likely to develop from a visible effort by a group or institution to grapple with important social problems. After the disillusionment of the thirties, attitudes toward business improved dramatically when so many companies appeared to make a vital contribution to the defense effort during World War II. And big-city mayors, who once were a symbol of corruption and degrading politics, took on new stature when, in an encouraging number of instances, they became a vital force in the battle against urban decay.

A large commitment to urban problems could have an effect on union growth. As we have indicated much earlier in the study, union membership is disproportionately small among the lowest-income workers. If this situation is to improve, labor must gain support from local leaders of these disadvantaged groups. At present, however, most leaders at the community level ignore or distrust the unions. Melvin King, of the Boston Urban League, is not atypical of black leaders in many big cities when he declares that ". . . those in power in the labor movement are the enemy."[19] These attitudes will not be overcome by television programs or even by lobbying for worthy causes in a distant national legislature. Real support is likely to grow only when labor begins to make visible efforts at the community level to represent the disadvantaged or work in other ways to improve their economic condition. Thus, union efforts to organize sanitation workers in Memphis, hospital workers in South Carolina and Baltimore, and farm workers in the South and West have brought assistance from civil-rights and religious leaders, and even student groups. And this support, in turn, has concededly been of great help to the unions in making progress in their organizing efforts.

Unions may also gain greater political influence if they become more heavily involved in social and community problems. The policies of the Federation have gained support for labor among national civil-rights leaders. Once again, however, relations are often much more strained at the community level. In the long run, this situation could have a growing significance for the union movement. The poor and disadvantaged are likely to develop greater political power in the cities as a variety of groups work at building higher levels of organization and political involvement in ghetto communities. At the same time, unions will have a more vital concern in city government as municipal employees become unionized and urban programs grow larger and more important as a source of jobs. These trends will inevitably increase labor's interest in maintaining good relations with poorer segments of the urban community and in developing political ties with the representatives of these groups.

Despite these considerations, many local union leaders are

likely to neglect community problems on the ground that unions are not visibly suffering under the existing state of affairs. These leaders are shortsighted, however, if they assume that their position in the city will remain in its present form without further effort on their part. It is conceivable that in time municipal-employee unions will be viewed increasingly as the source of irritating work stoppages, unjustified wage demands, and eventual tax increases; that organized labor will be considered an enemy by increasingly powerful local black communities; that local unions will act as political spokesmen for lower-middle-class whites who will be more and more angered by concessions made to Negroes and the poor. In short, the issue is not simply whether unions enlarge their constructive role in solving urban problems; there is also a danger that the present situation will deteriorate, leaving unions increasingly isolated and reviled as a bastion of narrow self-interest.

If the union movement faces up to its growing stake in community problems, it must reckon with the web of restraints alluded to in earlier chapters: the shortage of capable leaders and staff, particularly at the local level; the indifference—and even hostility —of many members toward less fortunate groups; rivalries and suspicions among different unions. To avoid these obstacles, a heavy burden will have to fall upon the AFL–CIO. Only the Federation is far enough removed from the rank and file to escape opposition from some elements of the membership. Only the Federation is in a position to mediate interunion rivalries and assemble a capable staff that can work on community problems without being drawn off into more traditional union pursuits. But if the AFL–CIO is to increase its efforts, it will not be able to act exclusively through its Washington office. Local federations are much better situated to cope with the infinitely varied problems and opportunities of different urban communities. As a result, it will be necessary for the AFL–CIO not only to devote larger resources to community service but also to gain greater influence over subordinate bodies in order to spur them to greater activity. To make a greater contribution to community problems, the Federation must also become a source of new programs and ideas instead of merely repeating the nostrums of the New Deal and lobbying for the programs of Democratic administrations. In Washington and, much more, at the local level, labor must try to achieve a reputation as a center of initiative and ideas by developing the capacity to identify emerging community needs, publicize their existence, and suggest new programs for meeting them.

Turning from policy to practice, unions must shape their community efforts to reflect their special talents and strengths. An obvious starting point is to build on labor's ability to influence the process of employment of the hard-core unemployed.* While employers enjoy a natural advantage through their preponderant control over the hiring process, unions could do more to sponsor federally assisted training projects. By enlisting cooperation from unions which include substantial membership from minority groups, local federations might also stimulate greater efforts to persuade employers to create employment opportunities—both within and outside the bargaining unit—for Negroes and hard-core unemployed.

Another special advantage of the union movement is its experience in organizing groups of lower-income people and its capacity to find within its ranks individuals from every income and occupational group with experience in leadership and organization. With these resources, it would be advisable for unions to continue experimenting in the development of community organizations. The problems involved are doubtless large, perhaps even insurmountable, but unless labor is prepared at least to explore this field, it could easily find itself preempted entirely by other community organizations. Perhaps unions could do no more than establish organizations along the lines of the Watts Labor Action Committee. Perhaps other groups can be established to bring together neighborhood leaders with union representatives in the same community to plan joint projects and establish goals which the local federation could support. Even these efforts would at least attract a measure of good will in addition to providing more effective vehicles for putting outside resources to work in ways that reflect the needs of the local community.

A final asset over which unions have some influence is the many billions of dollars contained in collectively bargained pension funds. In some industries, the funds are jointly administered by unions and management trustees. In others, management administers the funds unilaterally or purchases policies from insur-

---

* The Federation has recently added fifty staff persons under a Department of Labor contract to work with the National Alliance of Businessmen in the employment and training of the disadvantaged.

ance companies, but unions might influence these policies to some degree at the bargaining table.

It would be naïve to suggest that unions should take steps to divert large amounts of these funds into socially useful instruments in the ghetto. Legal restrictions would bar such action, and managements might well be opposed. In addition, however valuable such projects might be, the vast majority of union members would presumably reject the idea of giving up higher pensions to finance high-risk, low-yield investments in the central city. Nevertheless, certain uses of these funds might make a great contribution to community problems without significant impairment of the interests of the union members. Trustees of pension funds, for instance, could invest in mortgages for low-income or aged groups protected by government insurance and guarantees, as the new Urban Affairs Department of the AFL–CIO has been advocating.

The difficulty of all these endeavors should not be underestimated. They would require a major commitment by the AFL–CIO and its member unions to influence and energize a host of local federations and, through these bodies, to enlist support from local unions that are willing to become more involved in the problems of their community. How much can be done along these lines remains uncertain. But the obstacles are large enough to rule out hope of significant progress unless the union movement comes to recognize its strong self-interest in pushing forward along these lines.

Conclusion

Perceptions of the Labor Movement

This study began with a sketch of the opinions held by the public and several major subgroups on the subject of unions. After examining these opinions in the light of the available facts, one must conclude that unions are among the least understood of our social institutions. Interestingly enough, in contrast with opinions on most other subjects, views about unions often seem to stray furthest from the facts the higher one moves up the scale of income and education.

The public as a whole seems most troubled over the problems of corruption and strikes. This concern is not without foundation. Collective bargaining in America is beset by strikes to a much larger extent than in other industrial democracies, although it is fruitless to speculate whether unions or management are primarily responsible. As for corruption, the public doubtless overestimates its prevalence in the union movement, but organized labor in the United States seems to have suffered much more from this disease than its counterparts in other economically developed nations.*

The majority of businessmen, however, go on to emphasize an added list of complaints which seem either exaggerated or largely unsupported by known facts. In business circles,† for example,

---

* Since the Labor-Management Reporting and Disclosure Act of 1959, union government in the United States has been subject to extensive public regulation of a sort virtually unknown abroad.

† Business opinion, of course, is not uniform, and the views of industrial-relations specialists often diverge from those described. Nonetheless, the opinions reported in the text are those often expressed by leading business spokesmen and by periodicals representing organized business.

unions are often said to be a major cause of inefficiency. In fact, the impact of unions on efficiency is much more mixed and uncertain than that of other factors, such as protective tariffs, import quotas, or the Interstate Commerce Commission's regulation of minimum rates. At present, it is even impossible to determine whether the net effect of unions on productivity is positive or negative. In certain industries, to be sure, unions have fought to maintain restrictive work practices. Although such practices are often undesirable, many of them are actually defensible compromises between efficiency and leisure, or safety, or job security or other legitimate values. In other instances, responsibility for the practices must be shared by management for its laxity in agreeing to, or even initiating, the rules in question, or by the government for its lack of policies cushioning the shock to the workers that would result upon the abandonment of the practices.

Another frequent business complaint—that unions are a major cause of inflation—stands on equally shaky footing. Unions force up wages and prices somewhat in certain industries where employers are sheltered from outside competition or weakened by internal divisions. But once again, there is no reliable way of determining the overall impact of unions on rising prices, and most economists who will hazard a rough estimate have concluded that unions are only a minor factor in inflation.

Businessmen are also on dubious ground when they claim that unions are the most powerful political interest group in the country. This assertion may help a trade association to rally its members to support a larger lobby in Washington; it may even represent an understandable reaction to the thought of millions of union voters and hundreds of labor officials working in election campaigns. But the evidence does not show that unions have been particularly successful in electing its favored candidates, nor do labor's mounting political expenditures seem to have succeeded in persuading larger proportions of the membership to back union candidates. In the legislatures, labor's greatest triumphs came in the thirties, before it had mobilized for political action; since then, Congress has acted on several occasions to regulate unions and restrict their activities. All in all, labor may well have less affirmative political influence than other interest groups, because so many of its major goals encounter opposition from other powerful groups. Unlike many business organizations, labor does not deal primarily with narrow political objectives that can be won without rousing important adversaries or attracting wide attention from the public.

In certain respects, the views of liberal intellectuals are more interesting than those of businessmen, because they provoke a careful look at the internal dynamics of the union movement. The liberal criticisms are captured with particular vividness in the following editorial from *The New Republic*.

> As the delegates [to the AFL–CIO Convention] examine the state of their unions, they are bound to confront the fact that dedicated youngsters, who in the thirties would have been on labor's picket line, are marching to a different drummer. They are fighting elsewhere, for civil rights, peace, or better garbage collection in a slum. To them, the AFL–CIO is just another protective association, speaking for the possessors and not the dispossessed. The unions, they say, care more about repealing a section of the Taft-Hartley Act than about the poor, and more concerned with security and seniority for themselves than with a better life for all. Such criticism is too sweeping to be just. But there's no doubt about it, the drama has gone out of the labor game, and it cannot be put back by public relations.[1]

These comments are typical of many statements from intellectual quarters that once produced the unions' stanchest allies. Yet the portrait that emerges seems grossly oversimplified. At the very least, a clear distinction must be drawn between the role of labor in national politics and Congressional legislation, and the activities of the local and international unions in their own communities. At the national level, the AFL–CIO has been a major political force in support of liberal domestic policies. The Federation has supplied the bulk of the lobbying effort to extend and improve social and welfare legislation and to initiate new programs such as Medicare. It has been the principal administration supporter in enacting and defending antipoverty legislation. It has consistently worked for civil-rights legislation; in fact, it initiated and insisted upon the provisions of the Civil Rights Act of 1964 outlawing discrimination by unions as well as by employers. It has openly supported large-scale programs to renew cities and rehabilitate slums.

Organized labor can perhaps be faulted for its failure to come forward with new ideas and new programs to combat important domestic problems. In the main, labor has been content to favor proposals put forward by the Democratic administration. But having backed these programs, the Federation has clearly been generous in its efforts to elect sympathetic candidates, lobby the administration's bills through Congress, and persuade its member bodies through a steady stream of conferences, articles, and education programs to support these goals.

At the grass-roots level, the record has been markedly different. It is here that local unions can be found still persisting in discriminatory practices against Negro workers. In other fields of activity, the problem is one of indifference and inertia. Unions have hardly been involved at all in community efforts to grapple with urban problems. Although a few training programs have been instituted for the unemployed and several hundred union representatives have sat on community boards, labor's involvement in the war against poverty has been modest. The one innovative program for the poor has been the I.U.D. experiment in community unions, and even this venture has thus far been a failure. Only in the medical field has labor played a significant role in attacking a major domestic problem at the grass-roots level, and there, labor's efforts have been confined almost entirely to the protection of its own members and their families.

Why has labor failed to do more in furthering social causes? In the view of liberal critics, the problem reflects, above all, a failure of leadership. According to C. Wright Mills:

> This is where labor stands: there are labor leaders who are running labor unions, most of them along the main [i.e., conventional] drift; there are left intellectuals who are not running labor unions, but who think they know how to run them against the main drift; and there are wage workers who are disgruntled and ready to do what must be done.

> It is the task of the labor leaders to allow and to initiate a union of the power and the intellect. They are the only ones who can do it; that is why they are now the strategic elite in American society. Never has so much depended upon men who are so ill-prepared and so little inclined to assume the responsibility.[2]

Implicit in this view is the assumption that union members stand ready to join in a major effort to combat poverty, discrimination, urban squalor, and other social ills if their leaders will only take the initiative. As A. H. Raskin observes, ". . . the conquest of want, illiteracy, intolerance; the building up of both health and decent housing; the realization of the scientific Golden Age . . . would be vastly more inspiriting, to union membership and leadership alike, than the present ever more routine function in the policing of day-to-day plant grievances and the writing of mechanized contracts."[3]

Unfortunately, the evidence is not kind to this thesis. Union members seem no more willing than the rest of the population to make large commitments to such causes as combating poverty and other urban problems. Particularly revealing are the priorities attached by union members to major contemporary government programs. When a 1968 Harris poll asked union members which programs they most wanted to retain, the respondents were most in favor of financing the war in Vietnam (23 percent), aid to education (20 percent), and anticrime and law-enforcement efforts (17 percent). Poverty (8 percent) and welfare programs (5 percent) lagged far behind, while aid to the cities (3 percent) ranked next to last on the list.*

Apart from existing government programs, most union members are also opposed to a variety of new measures for alleviating domestic problems. A majority would reject a $32 billion program to rebuild the cities, and the opposition rises to 62 percent when the program is coupled with a $35 per capita increase in taxes. Fifty-eight percent of union members oppose a negative income tax to subsidize the poor. And 68 percent believe that Negroes are already trying to move too fast toward racial equality.

Union leaders, on the other hand, do not appear to be more conservative than their members. On the contrary, several studies reveal that leaders are more sympathetic than the rank and file toward liberal programs. These tendencies are graphically illustrated in the following unpublished surveys in 1965 of a major industrial union.

Do you feel desegregation of schools, housing, and job opportunities for American Negroes has recently proceeded too fast, not fast enough, or as fast as it should?

(White respondents only)

	Too fast	About right	Too slow	Don't know
International staff	0%	28.1%	69.2%	1.8%
Convention delegates	21.2	37.7	35.1	5.1
Local officers	36.5	28.7	25.2	8.7
Rank and file	31.6	31.2	20.9	16.3

---

* These polls and those described in the following paragraph were specially prepared for the authors by Louis Harris Associates.

*We are sending economic aid to some underdeveloped coun-
tries like India, Nigeria, and Tunisia which have not joined
us as allies and which, in a number of cases, have sought aid
from Communist countries as well. Do you think we should
increase, keep about the same, decrease somewhat, cut sharply,
or stop economic aid to such neutralist countries?*

	In-crease	Stay the same	Cut some-what	Cut sharply	Stop	Don't know
International staff	54.5%	23.6%	3.6%	9.1%	5.5%	3.7%
Convention delegates	32.4	30.2	11.9	9.1	11.2	4.1
Local officers	20.5	28.8	12.1	16.7	17.4	4.5
Rank and file	20.3	26.8	14.6	15.3	17.6	5.4

Such findings cast a dark shadow on the entire liberal thesis
with respect to labor unions. On the one hand, critics on the left
repeatedly attack the unions for their failure to achieve higher
levels of democracy, greater involvement of the rank and file, and
closer rapport between leaders and members. On the other hand,
the same critics also castigate union leaders for not making much
greater efforts to campaign against a variety of social ills. Yet the
data suggest that these two views are hard to reconcile. Because of
the indifference and opposition of union members, grass-roots
democracy threatens to hamper, rather than promote, union programs for social reform. Indeed, the disinterest and hostility of the
members undoubtedly help to explain why union efforts to combat
poverty, racial discrimination, and other domestic problems have
almost invariably been more impressive at the Federation level
than in the local communities.

Most union critics do not even recognize this dilemma, let
alone try to deal with it in detail. Among those who do see the
problem, two major arguments are made. Some see the solution in
inspired leadership. According to Sidney Lens:

> Throughout history crusaders have given electrifying impulses
> to tens of millions of people, have welded them together in
> a way which solid, stable institutions could never do. The
> texture of life is made up of dreams of tomorrow. The crusader
> gives reality to that dream.[4]

Other writers suggest that education programs may unite the
members under the banner of reform. As C. Wright Mills pointed
out:

Insofar as the union is responsible, the reason for this apathy and lack of understanding began with the organizing slogans by which members were cajoled to join; they talked only about bread and butter. And there is no workers' education program adequate to remedy the bad beginnings.[5]

Neither of these views seems particularly realistic. In any society, very few people have the capacity to give "electrifying impulses" to millions of others. Those who have succeeded generally do so by awakening their followers with the promise of gain or glory or by arousing their sense of having been unfairly treated. Much rarer are those who can persuade the multitude to make real efforts to ease the deprivations and exploitation of others. Inspirational leaders cannot be produced ready-made, nor is it fair to criticize an institution for failing to develop enough individuals with these qualities.

Education programs may appear more promising. Despite the efforts already made by a few unions, there is much that could still be done to inform the members on the issues of poverty, international affairs, social legislation, and the like. The result of these efforts would doubtless help to win some added support from members for union efforts to combat social problems. But survey data do not suggest that education programs will have very large effects upon rank-and-file attitudes, nor does the length of membership in a union significantly affect attitudes on economic assistance or other issues of foreign affairs.

A battery of problems blunt the edge of worker education. To develop real understanding and sympathy for problems of race and poverty, a union must find some means of treating these issues intensively in courses, meetings, or other face-to-face relationships. But how is this to be done? Unlike their counterparts in Scandinavia, American workers have never responded in large numbers to education programs, regardless of the agency presenting them. The small minority that do attend union courses tend to be active members who are already more inclined to accept the values of the leadership. Union meetings provide another forum for discussion, but meetings, too, are poorly attended; they are crowded with more immediate business and populated, once again, by the more active union sympathizers. In the end, therefore, the union must probably fall back upon its regular publications to reach a broad spectrum of the membership. But the union newspaper is hardly an adequate vehicle for affecting attitudes on broad domestic issues. The pertinent articles will often go unread. The written word rarely has the impact of a meeting or a discussion. And the union paper will be only one of a stream of periodicals and broadcasts shaping the attitudes of the members. In short, if the union has a contribution to make in educating its members, it is not a uniquely powerful one. The job of informing members about social issues is a burden that must fall upon the entire culture; it cannot be discharged by any single institution.

These problems help to explain the sense of estrangement that separate labor leaders from the intellectual critics with whom they were once allied. Intellectuals look to the bright rhetoric of the union movement and are disappointed at what they see accomplished. In a country where so many social problems remain unsolved, one can readily sympathize with this view. Yet, in the eyes of the labor leader, intellectuals seem content to impose their romantic visions on issues and events without taking care to investigate the facts. Intellectuals, to labor, seem willing to applaud every effort of young activists and radical groups without bothering to ask whether these activities have any lasting effect in alleviating poverty or eradicating injustice. They overlook the difficult, undramatic efforts of the Federation to elect the candidates and enlist the support that are necessary to bring about enduring legislative reforms and the taxes to support new programs. They are forever willing to expose instances of corruption and racial discrimination and to criticize the inactivity of so many labor organizations in attacking social problems. For these defects, they usually blame the union leader, while overlooking all the rank-and-file pressures that push the leader away from social involvement into a constant preoccupation with contract negotiations and administration.

Are Unions Worth Having?

The severe criticisms of labor can be traced in part to the fact that businessmen, liberal intellectuals, and the public at large all have special reasons to look upon unions with a jaundiced eye for reasons already discussed at length in the opening chapter of this study. At the same time, the social functions that unions serve are not so clearly appreciated as they were in an earlier era. Of all major institutions in America, there is none whose value to society is so widely questioned as the labor organization. Thirty years ago, the vast majority of the public assumed that unions were needed to secure higher and fairer wages for working people. Fewer people believe it today. Economists question its accuracy. And higher wages, in any event, seem less important—and indeed, of more dubious value—during an era in which most union members enjoy living standards well above the subsistence level and the economy is plagued with persistent inflation.

Nevertheless, unions today do serve several purposes of continuing importance to American society.

1) Even if unions do not have a strong, direct impact upon the real income of their members, their presence helps to gain general acceptance for the rates of pay and working conditions that prevail, even in unorganized plants. In the last analysis, no one can be sure of the wages and other terms that would exist if workers were wholly unorganized. Under these circumstances, the existence of unions, the opportunity to join such organizations, the ability to compare one's wages with the union scale—all these things help to persuade the worker that the conditions under which he labors are tolerably fair. Without unions, this assurance could not be given and workers might easily demand government regulation as the only practical alternative to protect their interests. Our experience with wage controls in World War II and in the Korean conflict suggests that this alternative would exact a heavy price in red tape and in a loss of flexibility for our firms and labor markets.

2) If unions have not greatly influenced the amount of compensation, they have certainly altered the form in which it has been given. In particular, they have taken the initiative in channeling a major portion of the workers' pay checks into health and welfare benefits, old-age pensions, and unemployment and severance compensation. Some critics may argue that it would be better to bargain for higher wages and let each worker decide for himself how to spend his money. But most would agree that pension and welfare benefits provide a badly needed device to guard against the natural inclination to be shortsighted and careless about distant but important contingencies. And few would not agree that unions have performed a useful service insofar as they have provided these benefits at a lower cost than their members could obtain by themselves while educating the rank and file in the value of such protection and the importance of taking full advantage of collectively bargained health facilities.

3) Unions have made what is perhaps their greatest contribution in securing fairer treatment for their members at the workplace. In particular, they have made enormous strides to eliminate error, malice, favoritism, and other human failings in the dismissal, discipline, promotion, and preferment of employees. By doing so, they have also encouraged countless nonunion firms to make comparable reforms in order to counter the threat of organization. In theory, of course, some of these benefits could conceivably be established by other means. For example, several European countries have established labor courts to pass upon the reasonableness of disciplinary action. But, in the United States at least, it seems unrealistic to assume that effective legislation would be enacted if workers were unorganized, and experience in connection with other statutes suggests that statutory safeguards would have little effect if there were no unions to provide the money, the confidence, and the legal talent to use the laws to good advantage. In addition, few knowledgeable observers would suppose that government tribunals would match the flexibility and competence already achieved through the system of private arbitration established by collective bargaining.

4) Unions are the most potent organized body to represent the political interests of workers and, to a lesser extent, of the poor and disadvantaged. One has only to look at the unrepresented segments of our society to see the consequences of remaining unorganized. Consider the legislative accomplishments of veterans, who are well organized, and compare them with the plight of the unorganized draftee, who receives compensation below the federal minimum wage and suffers needlessly in searching for jobs and pursuing his education because of the uncertainties of the selective-service system. Examine the coverage of our minimum-wage laws, our employment insurance, our workmen's-compensation statutes. The millions of low-paid employees who are excluded from these programs are almost invariably unorganized, and the AFL–CIO has been the major political force seeking to extend the laws to cover these disadvantaged groups. Perhaps a union is not the only way to protect the political interests of such workers. But unions have in fact performed this function for millions who would otherwise have remained unrepresented.

Challenges for the Next Decade

The sum of these contributions is substantial. Yet there are major challenges that the union movement must meet in the next decade in order to grow and prosper.

HOW TO AVOID EXCESSIVE GOVERNMENT CONTROL OF COLLECTIVE BARGAINING

Unions in the private sector will undoubtedly face a continuing threat of controls imposed to curb inflationary wage increases and prevent disruptive strikes. Employers and unions will also face a growing need to reconcile the results of a decentralized bargaining system with emerging goals of national legislation and planning—for such objectives as the production of a specified number of homes, the provision of high quality medical care, and the achievement of price stability. In the public sector, labor will likewise encounter serious risks of close government control over bargaining and sweeping prohibitions on the strike. These problems will be hard to deal with in a labor movement composed of many autonomous national unions, each under strong pressure to guard its independence and fight for immediate economic objectives. To escape unwelcome government pressure, unions will need to cooperate much more effectively with government officials in overhauling outmoded bargaining procedures, curbing troublesome union rivalries, and establishing sensible national priorities and objectives. To ignore these needs will expose unions to the danger that their power and freedom of action will diminish and that they will find themselves locked into regulatory systems overrun with the harassments of bureaucracy and red tape.

HOW TO MAINTAIN AND INCREASE THE IMPORTANCE OF THE UNION TO ITS MEMBERS

The 1960's have brought a new generation of union members, who do not remember the hardships of the Depression and do not appreciate the value of a union in such circumstances. The influx of these young workers underscores the need to refresh and enrich the contributions that labor organizations bring to their members. Higher wages, better fringe benefits, more job security, and new social legislation will all continue to have their place. But these goals cannot have the same importance that they once had, for the new members will be more affluent, better protected by government programs, and more likely to be able to fend for themselves in a full employment economy. New activities and new benefits seem in order. Just what these new services should be is hard to foretell, and the answer will probably vary from one union to another. Some unions would do well to develop collectively bargained schemes that will give individual members greater freedom to choose how to distribute added compensation among a variety of fringe benefit programs to fit their personal needs. Other labor organizations—especially those in fields of employment marked by dull, repetitive tasks—will be well advised to press for new forms of organizing work to give their members greater variety and more responsibility in performing their jobs. Other unions may seize upon education and training programs; still others on creating legal services, retirement opportunities, and other programs to improve and enrich the lives of their members away from work. But some fresh response is required, or unions are likely to experience increasing apathy from their members, diminished political influence, greater difficulty in attracting able men to union office, and continuing problems in trying to win new members.

HOW TO COME TO TERMS WITH THE
PERVASIVE PROBLEM OF RACE

Unions must exercise leadership and initiative in the workplace and the community in helping society come to terms with the problem of race. This issue affects not only employment and promotion but also political strategy, community service programs, organizing campaigns, and the selection of leaders within the organization. Unions have made considerable progress along these lines in recent years. But the challenge that faces them has grown still more rapidly with the rising impatience and militancy in the black community juxtaposed against an ever-present danger of resentment and hostility among the white membership. The unions' stake in racial matters is again clear. The need to avoid harassing legal entanglements, to build political alliances, to pre-

vent the dilution of craft skills and craft jurisdiction, and to escape
serious schisms within the union—all call for a strong effort to
promote racial understanding and equal treatment.

HOW TO DEVELOP GREATER RESPECT FOR UNIONS
IN THE SOCIETY AS A WHOLE

A union movement that has grown to major proportions only
in the last thirty years is bound to encounter considerable skepticism and even hostility. The changes involved are too sweeping,
the conflicts too numerous, and the differences of opinion too deep
for unions to escape this legacy. In the next generation, however,
these attitudes will not necessarily remain fixed. Organized labor
may simply be tolerated grudgingly as an inevitable force that
must be listened to only by virtue of its size and power. But it may
also come to be fully accepted as a valued institution—criticized
by some, but genuinely appreciated by the great majority. Union
movements abroad have moved in both of these directions, and it
is by no means clear which path will be traveled in the United
States.

Unions will go far toward attracting genuine respect if they
succeed in meeting the challenges of race, new benefits and
services for members, and escaping more controls by moderating
strikes and exorbitant settlements. But in the next generation, especially, the price of respect is likely to include a substantial, visible
contribution to the general effort to overcome poverty, unemployment, urban decay, and other major domestic ills. Unions have
already made substantial contributions in the legislative sphere by
supporting large-scale public programs to cope with these problems. But organized labor has not yet made much of an effort at
the grass-roots level to work with other groups in resolving community problems. New attempts in this direction are important,
but they are also hazardous, for unions—with a harassed, lower-
middle-class, predominantly white membership, and a steadily
growing representation among government workers—could easily
become a symbol of bigotry, reactionary politics, disruption
(through strikes in public services), and narrow self-interest.
Should unions fall into this posture, they will find themselves
caught between the normal opposition of powerful conservative
interests and the indignation of liberals, intellectuals, and minority
groups. Under these circumstances, unions would have to contend

with a climate of opinion that could hamper their political efforts, limit their ability to attract able people to their staffs, and sap the morale of their leaders.

HOW TO DEVELOP THE KNOWLEDGE AND TALENT
TO MEET THE CHALLENGES AHEAD

Within the typical union, talented leadership is thinly spread and adequate information is often lacking to deal with the problems at hand. As a result, unions do not plan effectively, nor do they budget carefully or allocate their resources systematically to achieve optimum results. These limitations will become much more critical in the future, and especially so if labor makes a serious attack upon the added problems listed here. Society has already entered a world in which common sense and general intelligence are no longer sufficient to solve most problems facing large, complex organizations. Such talents may still be needed, and not least at the highest levels of leadership. Nevertheless, unions also must have full recourse to specialized knowledge, and their top officials must be able to appreciate the need for such information and understand its import. Otherwise, unions will find themselves at a growing disadvantage in dealing with organizations that operate with increasingly sophisticated techniques in an environment that is steadily becoming more intricate and complex.

Unions face a special problem in this respect. They cannot attract the personnel to fill these needs by merely hiring technical specialists or highly trained university men with social dedication. Such individuals are too often frustrated, isolated, and unable to cope with the practical necessities of working within an organization of workingmen run by political processes. What is needed in the unions is a peculiar blend of advanced knowledge and training and a heavy dose of pragmatism and political shrewdness. Men possessing this combination of qualities are particularly hard to come by in the labor movement. Unions must continue to recruit their leaders from the ranks in order that they can understand the problems of the membership and discharge their political functions, in the best sense of the term. Yet leaders who rise from the shop floor, in many industries at least, often are neither highly trained nor readily disposed to master the technical side of their responsibilities. To be sure, union leaders can lean on professional staff and outside consultants. But neither the leaders nor the pro-

fessionals can discharge their responsibilities with distinction unless each has the qualities to understand and appreciate the work
of the other.

HOW TO DEVELOP AN ORGANIZATIONAL STRUCTURE
TO MEET THESE CHALLENGES

In a period when collective bargaining was the paramount
activity of the labor movement, a decentralized network of local
and national unions was ideally suited to the size and diversity of
the American economy. To meet the challenges of the next decade,
however, greater centralization is in order. Within the international union, top officials must have the vision and the authority to
obtain sufficient information from their locals to plan effectively,
allocate their personnel and financial resources intelligently, and
make sound appointments to their staff. In the movement as a
whole, if unions are to avoid sweeping regulatory controls and
gain an important voice in the emerging process of national
economic planning, a stronger central body will be needed to
speak for labor's interests and influence the behavior of individual
unions to accord with common objectives. If unions are to perceive
fully their stake in constructive racial policies and active urban
involvement, and if they are to give due weight to other long-term
interests, the guidance and counsel of a central body will be indispensable. If the labor movement is to attract greater talent and
bring it to bear on such problems as union administration and the
development of new services and new needs among union members, a central body will again play a key role. Only the Federation
enjoys the distance from immediate grass-roots pressure, the vantage point in national politics, the size and specialization of staff to
be able to perform these functions well. This is not to imply that
the AFL–CIO must be granted coercive powers over the behavior
of its member unions. What is required is that the Federation
perceive its role clearly, that it be given greater authority over its
subordinate federations at the state and local level, and that, by
common understanding, it gain a greater measure of influence in
persuading its member unions to cooperate in meeting common
goals. In addition, the Federation needs to establish effective working relations with the near unions and other groups of unaffiliated
employees.

It is encouraging that for all these challenges, labor's long-run interests coincide in large part with those of the public. Clearly, this is so with respect to the need to resolve racial inequalities, to develop greater knowledge and more highly trained leaders, to create new benefits for the members, and to win new respect from society at large. Perhaps the interests of the two groups seem to diverge when unions seek to avoid regulation over wage increases and strikes. But society will benefit if the threat of legislation causes union leaders to pay closer attention to preventing unnecessary strikes and excessive wage increases. And the public also stands to gain from avoiding legal controls, so long as the cost is not too great. In their separate ways, liberals as well as conservatives are recognizing the advantage of slowing the growth of government bureaucracy and encouraging the virtues of flexibility, dispersed initiative, and wider participation. All these values will be promoted if wages and working conditions can continue to be established through collective bargaining without exacting an intolerable cost in inflation and disruptive strikes.

The Determinants of Union Behavior

It is far from clear that unions will be able to meet these challenges, and the prospects are much more complex than critics are wont to perceive. At present, most commentators seem to assume that the future of the labor movement rests mainly in the hands of its leaders. This point of view is reflected in the constant criticism of labor leaders, and it is buttressed by a mass of opinion data to the effect that unions are run pretty much as the top officials see fit. Yet one must beware of such opinions, for each of the groups that most influence the public view of organized labor has its special reasons for misconceiving the role of the union leader and exaggerating his influence.

The businessman, for example, is accustomed to organizations where the leader enjoys considerable power (though not so much as the outsider tends to suppose). As a result, many executives assume instinctively that the union leader enjoys comparable authority; they overlook the fact that union officials must win office by election. Businessmen may also exaggerate the role of the union leader as a result of their natural tendency to assume a "harmony of interests" between themselves and their employees. This assumption has suffused the literature of business for decades and

stems, once again, from understandable motives. Few managements wish to harbor the thought that they are pursuing their own
interests at the expense of their employees. It would be most disagreeable to concede that wages are kept unfairly low or that the
quest for efficiency has led to harsh supervision or uncomfortable
working conditions. As a result, when employees organize or
protest or strike, many employers assume that harmonious relations within their plants have been disrupted by some opportunis-
tic union leader who has succeeded in leading the workers astray.
This reaction, once again, is not a simple matter of tactics; it
springs naturally from a network of beliefs that help many executives to justify their behavior as businessmen and human beings.

Intellectuals also have their reasons for ascribing great influence to the union leader. As Bertrand Russell has pointed out, the
liberal critic has traditionally been sentimental toward the underdog. He has been unable to champion the cause of the poor and
the disadvantaged without idealizing them as well. As a result—
until recently, at any rate—these critics could seldom bring themselves to blame union shortcomings on the members; instead, they
concluded that the leaders must somehow be responsible.

Other forces also helped to reinforce this bias. After the rush
of organizing in the thirties, union members seemed to have
become representative of the entire working class. Under these
circumstances, it would have been most awkward to fault the
members for labor's failure to press for social reform. How could
the liberal justify his programs if the beneficiaries themselves were
indifferent to them? Unless the rank and file were on his side, how
could he urge the unions to reform and still keep true to his
democratic principles? Above all, how could he harbor any opti-
mism at all if the entire working class had to be persuaded to
support his programs? With all these difficulties, it was far easier
to assume that unions were made up of willing members who were
held back by the stubbornness and selfishness of powerful leaders.
These beliefs could begin to weaken only when union members
were no longer seen as representative of the lower classes and unions
were no longer the only organized force for social reform. Thus, it
is no accident that intellectuals did not acknowledge the lack of
liberal, reformist sentiments among the members until the 1960's,
when students, black militants, and other groups had already begun
to offer organized support for fundamental social reforms. (Characteristically enough, now that the pendulum has begun to swing,

it has swung very far indeed in the minds of many critics. Union members are now viewed not only as apathetic and undisposed to social reform; they are erroneously perceived as a highly conservative force in the society.)

Because of these tendencies to exaggerate the influence of the labor leader, one must take pains to construct a more realistic picture of how union policy is actually made. Otherwise, society will often misdirect its energies by flailing away at union officials for actions that are not really within their power to change. In the process, deeper forces may be overlooked, forces that actually determine union behavior and must ultimately be changed if the conduct of unions is to change.

In the end, union behavior is the product of four broad influences that are constantly interacting upon one another: the desires of the members, the nature and abilities of the leadership, the capacities and opinions of subordinates, and the pressures of the environment. This book has been a series of illustrations showing how these forces interact in the most important areas of union activity. In the brief space remaining, it is possible only to distill these illustrations into a more succinct, more general statement.

Starting first with the rank and file, a mass of data suggests that the members are primarily interested in their union as an agent for negotiating with the employer and administering the collective-bargaining agreement. Where these functions are involved, the members exert influences through many different channels to impose certain restraints upon their leaders. Sometimes the demands of the members are very high, even impossibly so; sometimes they can be modified by the leaders through education and persuasion. Once formed, however, these demands can be ignored only at the risk of decertification, election defeat, refusals to ratify contracts, wildcat strikes, or other forms of withholding cooperation.

The members expect little and ordinarily demand even less in other areas of union activity, such as organizing, political action, or community service. Their main interest is simply that these programs not require too large an expenditure of dues, or demand too much time and attention from union officials. To enforce this interest, members exert pressure either by refusing dues increases and special levies to pay for the programs, or by withholding their cooperation or participation, which is often essential if the programs are to succeed.

Throughout the entire range of union programs, the members tend to impose closer restraints upon local leaders than upon national officials, especially if the local organizations are small. At the national level, it is much more difficult to marshal an effective protest or to oust the incumbent officials, since opposition must be mounted in many widely scattered groups of members. But in the national as well as in the local union, the influence of the member expresses itself more insistently and through many more channels than most observers have been prepared to concede. On the whole, moreover, the influence has been much less salutary than critics of unions like to acknowledge. A candid appraisal compels the conclusion that the rank and file has contributed to most of the widely condemned union shortcomings:* racial discrimination, excessive wage demands, featherbedding, and—in many instances —irresponsible strikes.†

The union leader is also limited by his subordinates. In many cases, of course, the subordinate is simply a vehicle for pressures arising from the membership. Thus, local officials will resist advice or commands which, if carried out, would threaten defeat at the next local election. But subordinates can limit their superiors in ways quite independent of any rank-and-file sentiments. Local leaders may develop personal ambitions that can be furthered by resisting the international. Staff personnel may have views and priorities that conflict with those of the union leaders they serve. Local officials or staff can simply lack the ability to carry out orders effectively. In theory, of course, the higher official may have formal authority to order his subordinates about. In practice, however, the situation is not so simple. The leader must normally obtain genuine cooperation and even enthusiasm from his subordinates, and this cannot often be achieved if the leader does not accommodate himself, to some extent at least, to the abilities and desires of those whom he commands.

The environment presses in upon the union from many directions: through the policies of employers; the market pressures

---

* Corruption, of course, is one form of union misbehavior that cannot be attributed significantly to the membership.

† Critics may often respond to the above mentioned arguments by asserting that autocratic unions can also indulge in featherbedding, racial discrimination, etc. This is undoubtedly correct, but one reason may be that democratic elections are only one way by which the views of the members are impressed upon the leader; there are other highly effective conduits for transmitting membership demands and values, even in seemingly autocratic unions.

affecting the firm, the industry and the entire economy; the attitudes of the public; the provisions of the law. With all its endless variety, the environment affects the union in three essential ways.

To begin with, the environment acts upon the members and shapes their outlook, their expectations, and their preferences. For example, the openness of the society and the lack of class divisions have had much to do with the unwillingness of union members to support a labor party. The educational system and the gradual evolution of community values have produced large changes in the attitudes of union members toward the Negro. The restless disaffection of the young pervades the unions as it does so many other institutions. Advertising and the widespread emphasis on material success inflate the demands that members make in collective negotiations. As a general rule, influences of this sort play their most vital role in helping to determine union goals.

The environment also affects the methods unions can use to achieve their goals and the degree of success that they will achieve. Thus, the creation of vast conglomerate firms has impelled many different unions to join in "coalition bargaining" to increase their bargaining power. In turn, the effectiveness of this strategy will be conditioned by the financial health and competitive position of the firm and its separate units, as well as by conditions in the economy as a whole. In similar fashion, labor's success in organizing mass-production industries in the thirties (after repeated failures in the past) was greatly helped by such factors as the impact of the Depression, the personnel policies of the firms involved, and the newly enacted federal law to protect union organization. Conversely, the inability of many of the same labor officials to organize the South ten years later was due to another set of social and community pressures that hampered the organizer and dulled the incentive of employees to join a union.

The environment affects the union movement in still another way by helping to shape the quality of labor leadership. The political traditions and the laws of this country insure that union leaders will be chosen by the members. This policy in turn implies that the leaders will be chosen from the ranks and will be generally representative of the membership. At the same time, the educational system, the programs of scholarships and student aid, the emphasis on social mobility, and the willingness to recognize talent whenever it appears, all create opportunities through which promising individuals can escape the shop floor and the assembly line from which tomorrow's labor leaders must be drawn. The low prestige that society accords to union leaders also helps to insure that many employees will take advantage of these opportunities instead of seeking a union post. In this way, environmental forces diminish the pool of talent available for union office.

What freedom of action remains to the union leader caught between the pressures of the environment and the demands of the rank and file? To begin with, he can experiment and innovate, at least on a modest scale. He may not always be able to launch new programs costing large sums nor will he be quick to experiment at the risk of failing to meet the critical demands imposed by his members. Moreover, his innovations will eventually have to win acceptance by the rank and file in order to survive and flourish. Nevertheless, the activities and achievements of the union will ultimately reflect the capacity of its officials to offer up new goals, new programs, and new benefits for the members to consider.

Union leaders can also do something to alter the opinions of the members and affect their attitudes toward the goals and policies of the organization. On specific trade-union issues—to accept or reject the contract; to strike or not to strike—the leader may have great influence, especially if he is popular and without vocal opposition. On more general matters of value, social attitude, and political choice, his opportunities for exerting influence may be sufficient to deserve attention, but they are not large. Where these issues are concerned, it is normally too difficult to reach the members, too hard to engage their attention seriously, too arduous to overcome all the competing messages reaching them through other media and other sources.

Finally, and perhaps most important, the leader can have the imagination to conceive of new strategies and new opportunities in the environment to help the union make fresh progress toward its goals. This capacity is partly a matter of knowing the environment well, but it is ultimately dependent on the intuition, the judgment, and the imagination of the leader. It is this type of influence and power that John L. Lewis demonstrated so tellingly in perceiving that the time was ripe for massive organizing in the thirties.

It is very hard to guess how much an able, imaginative leader could accomplish to make progress toward union goals. Nevertheless, it is safe to say that the process of selecting union officials— while admirably suited for certain purposes—is not likely to produce an unusual number of leaders with exceptional vision or imagination. Indeed, one would frankly expect less talent of this sort in unions than in most other major institutions. In addition, many of the forces that press upon the labor leader are strong indeed and leave him with much less freedom of action than many critics seem to recognize. For example, those who exhort the unions to exercise wage restraint, eliminate featherbedding, or refrain from strikes seem greatly to underestimate the pressures from the members. Although most union leaders have a degree of influence over the policies of their organizations, few would stay in office very long if they slighted their members' concern for safeguards against the loss of work or ignored their desire to seek pay raises—and go on strike if need be—to keep pace with wage and price increases they see occurring all around them.

One can readily sympathize with the visions of other critics who deplore the failure of union leaders to seize opportunities to turn their talents to new fields: organizing the poor, mobilizing the members to fight for consumer protection, and taking the lead in searching for a more meaningful life for workers caught between their television set and the tedium of a semiskilled, repetitive job. In one sense, unions seem naturally suited to such tasks in view of their experience in organizing mass movements, their large memberships, and their commitment to high social purposes. Yet, critics invariably overlook the enormous difficulties involved: the members' lack of interest in undertaking ventures outside the traditional union domain, their unwillingness to see their dues expended for such purposes, the shortages of talented leadership in labor's ranks, and the pressures on existing leaders, whose time and energy are already stretched thin attending to conventional union tasks. In the face of such limitations, even a leader as gifted and energetic as Walter Reuther has been unable to make noteworthy progress in organizing the poor, expanding union membership, altering Detroit politics, or expanding the skilled job opportunities for Negro members. By underestimating these problems, liberal critics have succeeded—after two decades of biting prose—in accomplishing virtually nothing except to antagonize the union leadership.

This sketch of union behavior has clear implications for the critic's role in assessing social institutions. In reality, union members, leaders, subordinates, and environmental forces interact in such an intimate way that it is treacherous to single out one set of actors in the drama and heap responsibility upon them. Union behavior must be seen as the product of a complex, interrelated process. In order to be effective and fair, the critic must seek to identify the various centers of initiative throughout this process and suggest the actions that can be taken by each of these groups to make it easier for unions to progress toward desirable goals.

Meeting Labor's Challenges

In terms of progress to occur over the next decade, union members, local leaders, businessmen, and the public as a whole seem far too numerous and too dispersed to respond to the suggestions of critics. Instead, one must look to high union officials (at the Federation and international-union level), the government, the universities, and the foundations, and ask what each can be realistically asked to do to exert a beneficial effect upon union behavior.

Among national and Federation leaders, it is probably wiser to emphasize different goals from those that are commonly stressed by labor's critics. However important it may be to improve racial practices or avoid strikes and inflationary settlements, these are not the areas where national leaders are likely to undertake much more than they are doing already. The basic problem in the racial field lies at the grass-roots level, and local leaders, who have most to say in these matters, cannot be expected to get very far in front of the members who elect them to office. National leaders can persuade and cajole and even pressure their subordinates to some extent. But they cannot force many local leaders to take unpopular stands without endangering both their own position and the morale and unity of their organization. In the end, therefore, progress in this field will depend primarily on such external factors as government policy, employment conditions, and the broad currents of public opinion that largely shape the views of union members toward the racial question.* As for strikes and wage demands, much the same is true. Leaders are hard pressed by the demands of their members, and the expectations of the members are determined not so much by their leaders as by advertising, rising costs of living, and news of substantial wage gains by other

---

* The continuing educational program of the Federation and its technical assistance to international unions and local bodies are likely to show greater results in the future, since many programs have been initiated only in recent years.

workers. Here and there, of course, a national leader is free to exercise restraint or improve the bargaining procedures in his industry with the help of employers. An active federation may occasionally lessen the risk of unnecessary strikes by encouraging mergers between rival unions. In the end, however, it is likely that other institutions can contribute more to moderating strikes and wage trends than the union leaders themselves.

A more realistic agenda for union leaders would emphasize very different items: a much expanded and upgraded program of staff training, a new emphasis on research and more effective administration, a continuous program of experimentation to find new programs to meet new needs of their members, and more imaginative, more carefully planned community programs (coupled with a restructuring of the local federations to give greater influence to the AFL–CIO). These steps may not seem as dramatic to some critics as new programs to minimize strikes and overcome racial restrictions, but they are steps which top labor leaders are much freer to undertake. Not that progress will be easy to achieve. Union officials will have to display greater flexibility of mind, less sensitivity to constructive criticism, a willingness to reach out to universities, an effort to overcome old dogmas and old prejudices toward intellectuals. Even more serious obstacles are created by the pervasive shortage of capable staff and the chronically tight budgets of most labor organizations. Yet, all these problems are soluble. They do not require impossible amounts of money nor will they run headlong against the feelings and desires of the members.

As for the role of government, the country has long relied heavily on regulatory laws to influence union behavior. At the moment, however, this prescription does not seem particularly useful. In the public sector, it is true, legislation will have to be developed to cope with the right to organize and the behavior of large, restive unions of government workers. But outside this sphere, the major opportunities for government intervention lie elsewhere.

Federal and state governments can exercise their most important influence upon the labor movement by creating an economic environment that makes it easier for union leaders to adopt constructive policies. A major opportunity lies in the rapid development of labor market policies—the amalgam of programs that seek to train the labor force for new jobs, facilitate the movement of workers from one area to another, and give economic security to those who are displaced from one job and are searching for another. Although these programs are designed to alleviate personal hardship and improve productivity, they can also have an impact upon the behavior of unions. An effective labor market policy helps to remove the employment bottlenecks and shortages of key skills, both factors that allow certain unions to win exceptional wage increases. As a result, such a policy, coupled with sound fiscal and monetary practices, can do much more than union leadership to avoid undue inflation. Moreover, vigorous labor-market policies allow lower levels of unemployment to be reached without intolerable price increases, in addition to cushioning the shock of losing a job. By alleviating unemployment in these ways, the government makes it easier for labor leaders to gain acceptance among the members for technological change. In much the same way, these labor-market conditions help to quiet the fear of unemployment that so often lies behind the pressure to exclude the Negro and the trainee seeking to escape from hard-core unemployment.

Another opportunity for government lies in action of a much more informal kind. In various ways, the government can encourage union leaders to meet with public and employer representatives and consider important long-run issues. These efforts must have a concrete purpose that matters to the labor leader. Busy men grow weary of meetings and conferences, and union officials are no exception to this tendency. But Congress can give the necessary impetus by requiring unions and employers in strike-prone industries to consider their bargaining structure and report back within a stipulated period. The executive branch can establish tripartite committees to consider legislation on fair employment practices or laws to govern public employees. In both these cases, the inchoate threat of legislation should spur union leaders to give serious thought to the matters at issue. Cynics may dismiss these suggestions, asserting that the short-term interests of unions, management, and the public are too far apart and that mutual suspicions are too deep-rooted to offer a realistic chance of success. There is plainly something to this argument, and it would be foolish not to expect a number of failures along the way. On balance, however, these risks are relatively harmless and are overshadowed by several potential gains. At a minimum, the government should succeed in causing union leaders to pay attention to long-range problems that would otherwise be ignored. In rare instances, labor and management may succeed in agreeing on proposed legislation or some change in their bargaining procedures. On these occasions, the changes are almost certain to work more effectively, because both parties have shared the responsibility for bringing them about. And even without such tangible success, serious meetings between labor and management on broad problems of concern to the public must be counted as worthwhile, simply because they may add something, however intangible, to the slow process of improving communication and enhancing the awareness of common long-term interests.

A third possibility for governmental activity is the area of subsidy. This technique has already been used on a large scale to encourage manpower training programs. On occasion, government bodies have also made grants to community unions, notably in Watts, to finance various programs for the poor. The possibilities for such assistance are extremely varied, and not all involve the granting of funds. To take only one illustration, much can be done to provide research that will help unions to overcome troublesome problems or to appreciate new areas for constructive action. The potentialities are suggested by the unions' own investigation into the futility of raiding, which helped persuade labor leaders to adopt the no-raiding pact in the 1950's. Labor Department research on hours of work in the longshore industry also did much to help resolve the negotiations of 1965. But considerably more could be done. For example, little effort has been made to exploit the vast accumulation of reports and data that unions are required to submit under the Labor Management Reporting and Disclosure Act. As a result, opportunities are lost for helping unions to perceive ways of improving their internal structure and procedures. And since the information is so little used, a vast amount of union record keeping goes for naught, while the government remains unaware of many serious defects in the quality of its basic data.

Much more controversial is the possibility of subsidizing training programs for union leaders and staff. At present, the obstacles seem insuperable. Some argue that unions should pay for their own training, since they will ultimately be the beneficiaries. Others assert that the government should not assist one powerful interest group engaged in doing battle with another. Although these arguments seem persuasive, they overlook essential points. Even if the principle of neutrality were apt in theory, it falls down in

practice, for state and federal governments have already subsidized in countless ways the education of businessmen. In the long
run, moreover, business, labor, and society as a whole are all likely
to benefit from a more highly trained union leadership. If unions
are chronically unable to provide enough funds for these purposes,
some sort of subsidy may be necessary to bring about the desired
result.

Colleges and universities too have a role to play in the labor
field that up to now has been largely neglected. The void is most
noticeable at the level of the Federation and the national unions.
Occasionally, top union leaders may attend a conference where
academicians speak or participate. Less frequently, they may call
upon a professor as a consultant. Now and then, they may discuss
a problem informally with an educator who has gained a certain
confidence through prior work as an arbitrator or mediator in some
national labor dispute. Overall, however, the volume of communication is insignificant. At the local level, the extent of cooperation
is greater. In a few localities, university staff can be found running
classes for local officials, performing an occasional piece of research for more progressive leaders or research directors, even
actively advising on training programs or community service projects. Even these examples, however, are limited to a few areas
containing universities with established centers of labor relations.

These meager contacts seem particularly striking when they
are compared with the interchange that goes on regularly between
the universities and the business community. From commercial
and accounting classes for undergraduates to advanced management programs for middle-aged executives, a full range of courses
for management is conducted by colleges and business schools.
The professors who teach these courses turn out a stream of books
and articles on the techniques of management, and many of them
are researched with the active cooperation of business firms. The
universities also allow, and even encourage, a constant flow of
consulting whereby professors help to investigate and recommend
solutions for a host of practical problems confronting their corporate clients. Although the results of this interchange are obviously
hard to assess, many observers put great stress upon them. For
example, in J. J. Servan-Schreiber's celebrated account of American
business influence in Europe, the author joins with former Secretary of Defense Robert S. McNamara in giving major credit to

management education for the success of American enterprise abroad.

The lack of contact between unions and the universities results in part from the traditional distrust by the labor leader of intellectuals, a feeling augmented in recent years by the broadsides delivered by several intellectual critics against the union movement. Another contributing factor may be the absence of any leading university in Washington, where the bulk of the unions have their headquarters. But both of these causes are secondary. Much more important is the fact that college training is not a recognized path to a union career. Only a handful of universities feel a need to offer any programs specially designed for would-be labor leaders. Even Cornell, with its established school of labor and industrial relations, finds that very few of its graduates move on to positions in the unions. Without students, there is little incentive to establish institutions comparable to business schools. Without these institutions, there is no occasion to assemble a faculty to prepare classes and provide research and consulting on a wide range of problems confronting the union leader. Nor is there a steady stream of graduates who retain throughout their careers a ready contact with the university and an understanding of its capabilities.

At present, few top union leaders seem at all concerned over the state of their relations with the universities. Such indifference is regrettable, for there are already too many points at which unions suffer from a lack of adequate knowledge and trained leadership. It is essential, therefore, that organized labor take the initiative in searching within higher education for methods of cooperation and points of contact that can offer to unions the same useful interchange that has benefited business, government, and charitable institutions in the United States. This will not be an easy task. Much of the research and advice from the universities will turn out to have little value; this has always been the case in most fields. Hence, there will inevitably be frustrations and disappointments that can be accepted only if leaders within the labor movement are firmly persuaded of the long-term value of closer relations.

If cooperation develops, it will presumably occur at two different levels. To the Federation and the international union, universities can offer professors capable of consulting and inter-

ested in performing research on problems affecting unions. In
addition, the universities can help in setting up unionwide training
programs either for promising younger leaders or for key staff
personnel, such as research directors and heads of organizations.
No less important, however, is the cooperation that can take place
at the local level, not merely with universities but also with the
burgeoning community colleges. The model for such interchange
already exists in a few areas, where active training, consulting, and
even research are carried on in cooperation between university
staff and a few progressive unions. The problem is to enlarge the
number of areas and colleges that are involved in these relations
and to increase the number of local unions that take advantage of
them. To accomplish this will require the good will and understanding of the educational institutions involved. Boards of
trustees will have to recognize that the community has an important, long-run stake in helping unions develop better-trained, more-
knowledgeable union leaders. Even more critical is the initiative
that must flow from the labor movement itself. In particular, the
local federation must step forward to encourage the locals in its
area to take advantage of the help that colleges and universities
can offer. In this regard, the AFL–CIO headquarters in Washington will have an important role to play in trying to impress upon
its local bodies the importance of moving on with this task.

Another institution that might have beneficial effects upon
union behavior is the charitable foundation. At present, of course,
foundations have next to no connection with organized labor. Quite
possibly, unions are considered self-sufficient, so that helping them
would seem just as unnecessary as the awarding of grants to corporations. To offer such assistance might also appear to be taking
sides in the great adversary scramble between labor and management. Yet neither of these explanations offers a complete answer.
By making grants to business schools, foundations have spent millions of dollars to educate executives to become more proficient at
their trade and more responsive to the broader needs of society. If
foundations are serious in pursuing these aims, they would do well
to consider giving assistance to similar endeavors within the labor
movement.

Given a will to do so, foundations could serve at least three
purposes in working with labor unions. They could provide funds
to launch experimental programs which are too long range in their
effect or too unrelated to rank-and-file interests to be financed

completely by union funds. They could also exert a much-needed check to insure that such projects are not poorly conceived or inadequately staffed. And finally, foundations might provide a source of new ideas to enrich the programs proposed by union leaders or even suggest new lines of action to pursue. The climate within most unions is not conducive to innovation, nor have many unions followed the lead of other institutions by purposefully building a capacity for generating new ideas within their organizations. A foundation could conceivably play a role of some significance in helping to overcome these deficiencies.

Foundations could also offer many other types of help to unions. A logical candidate for assistance is the AFL–CIO Labor Training Center or some other program of high-level training that could be sponsored by universities in conjunction with established labor organizations. Another area needing encouragement is the development of new services for members in such fields as old-age facilities, legal services, and health programs. Even more congenial to foundation interests are community projects wherein associations of unionists in poor communities take the initiative in developing education or recreation programs, or other services needed in the area. Perhaps, the most intriguing possibility is the creation of a research institute under the cosponsorship of the AFL–CIO and one or more foundations. An undertaking of this kind might accomplish much more than the channeling of added funds into research. By creating a board of trustees with representatives from within and outside the unions, the sponsors could help to ensure research that would be responsive to union needs yet better conceived and broader in scope than what typically passes for research in most unions today. The staff of the institute might also serve as a training ground for future union research directors and labor-relations professors alike. And more important still, such a body could serve an indispensable role in building a much-needed bridge between the labor movement and the universities.

The need for building bridges underscores the special isolation of the union movement in American society. It is special because there is no traditional class division, no basic separation over matters of value and matters of ideology. Unions in America have been unswerving in their affirmation of private property, the capitalist system, and the prevailing system of government. The isolation is of a more tangible kind. It manifests itself in the estrangement of the unions from the universities; the paucity of union officials in high government positions; the lack of any contact between the world of labor and the world of foundations; the absence of regular interchange between labor and business leaders (save for bargaining across the table over new contracts or grievances).

Under certain conditions, this isolation might have real value by shielding the unions from being co-opted and permitting them to stand apart from the "establishment" to act as its critic and its conscience. But unions are not alone today in speaking out for the poor and the disadvantaged. Indeed, educational institutions and foundations—the very groups with which the unions most need to cooperate—are among the most active in their social criticism. As a result, there is little danger that closer integration with these institutions will still the voice of dissent.

The dangers for the labor movement lie in very different fields. Unions face evident risks that they will be taken more and more for granted by their members, that they will function at a growing disadvantage in dealing with institutions possessing greater knowledge and superior techniques, and that their social role will be preempted increasingly by other groups. Should these risks materialize, the prospects are that unions will become progressively duller bureaucracies, more fractious at times to arouse an indifferent membership, but largely ignored in the major developments of the society and rather widely disliked as a necessary evil and a source of periodic inconvenience.

These dangers can be mitigated if unions draw closer to neighboring institutions for knowledge and fresh ideas. With the help of these institutions, union leaders may find it somewhat easier to move toward long-range goals that are as beneficial to organized labor as they are to the public as a whole. In the end, however, basic changes in the labor movement will depend upon the members themselves and on the society of which they are a part. Through many different channels, formal and informal, union behavior is heavily influenced by the wishes, the prejudices, and the aspirations of the rank and file, and these attitudes in turn are largely a reflection of sentiments that are widely held in the society. Thus, our labor organizations exhibit the same inventiveness, pragmatism, and diversity that characterize the nation as a whole. At the same time, in a society where prejudice and corruption are found in so many walks of life, it is not surprising that unions often suffer from similar defects. In a country that has tolerated higher rates of unemployment than other industrialized states, it is hardly strange that workers fight to protect their jobs. And in a nation where individual initiative and material success are highly valued, one should not wonder that unions resort easily to strikes and hard bargaining or fail to do all that they might at the grass roots to help those less fortunately situated. These conclusions are hard to accept, not only because they make the prospects for progress seem glacial, but also because they remind us that we must all have a share in the imperfections in our institutions. Yet how could one expect otherwise in a closely integrated society like our own? It is surely naïve to look to one part of society for salvation or to assume that one set of institutions is especially burdened with evil. In the end, the problems of the unions are problems for all of us and, in our varying ways, we must surmount them together or not at all.

Notes

Chapter 1

1. An extensive literature has developed on the methodology, reliability, and limitations of opinion polls. For a recent contribution, see Leo Bogart, "No Opinion, Don't Know, and Maybe No Answer," *Public Opinion Quarterly,* Fall 1967, pp. 331–45. For a discussion of these problems in the context of polls relating to labor questions, see Neil W. Chamberlain, *Social Responsibility and Strikes* (New York: Harper and Brothers, 1953). For a debate on the fairness of polls in the labor field, see Arthur Kornhauser, "Are Public Opinion Polls Fair to Organized Labor?" *Public Opinion Quarterly,* Winter 1946–47, pp. 484–500; Henry C. Link and Albert D. Freibert, John H. Platten, Jr., and Kenneth E. Clark, "Is Dr. Kornhauser Fair to Organized Pollsters?" *Public Opinion Quarterly,* Summer 1947, pp. 198–212.
2. These polls are collected in Chamberlain, *op. cit.*
3. *Report on Union Member Attitude Survey,* Joint Project of the Central Labor Council of Alameda County and the Center for Labor Research and Education (Berkeley: University of California, 1964).
4. See Arnold S. Tannenbaum and Robert L. Kahn, *Participation in Union Locals* (Evanston, Illinois: Row, Peterson, 1958).
5. Robert W. Miller, Frederick A. Zeller, and Glenn W. Miller, *The Practice of Local Union Leadership, A Study of Five Local Unions* (Columbus, Ohio: Ohio State University Press, 1965), pp. 171–72. Similar findings are recorded in a study of two other Columbus locals affiliated with internationals well-known for active concern with a broad range of community and social issues. Richard Evans Dawson, "The Local Union and Political Behavior" (unpublished Ph.D. thesis, Northwestern University, 1963), p. 220. Also see Tannenbaum and Kahn, *op. cit.,* pp. 121–23.

6. John Kirby, Jr., *The Disadvantages of Labor Unionism,* An Address Delivered before the Young Men's Hebrew Association, New York City, November 7, 1909, National Association of Manufacturers, p. 4.

7. Lemuel R. Boulware, *Statesmanship in Industrial Relations* (New York: Industrial Relations Division, National Association of Manufacturers, 1964), p. 6. Also see Clarence B. Randall, *A Creed for Free Enterprise* (Boston: Little, Brown, 1952), pp. 28–45.

8. Among the documents consulted are National Association of Manufacturers, *Monopoly Power as Exercised by Labor Unions* (1957); N.A.M., *Economic Implications of Union Power* (1962); Chamber of Commerce of the United States, *Inflation, Unions and Wage Policy* (1960); Chamber of Commerce of the United States, *Industrial Relations Policies* (1965).

9. William K. Jackson, *The Strike Menace* (Washington, D.C.: Chamber of Commerce of the United States, 1946), p. 10.

10. Chamber of Commerce of the United States, *Inflation, Unions and Wage Policy* (Washington, D.C.: Chamber of Commerce of the United States, 1960), p. 5.

11. Guy J. Puysegur, "Employers' Associations in Europe and North America," *International Labour Review,* May 1951, pp. 507–36.

12. Cola G. Parker, "The Growing Shadow of Labor in Public Affairs," *Spotlight on Union Activities,* Excerpts of Proceedings at 62nd Congress on American Industry (New York: National Association of Manufacturers, Industrial Relations Division, 1958), pp. 27–28.

13. Daniel Bell, *The End of Ideology* (Glencoe: The Free Press, 1960), p. 218.

14. James O'Gara, "On the Labor Front," editorial, *Commonweal,* March 29, 1963, p. 43. For an earlier comment on similar views, see John T. Dunlop, "The Public Interest in Internal Affairs of Unions," in *Government Regulation of Internal Union Affairs Affecting the Rights of Members,* Selected Readings Prepared for the Subcommittee on Labor and Public Welfare, United States Senate, 85th Congress, 2nd Session, 1958, pp. 8–16.

15. Bill Kovach, "Liberal Democrats Open Party Drive," *The New York Times,* November 8, 1968, p. 20.

16. Editorial, *The Nation,* May 13, 1936, p. 598.

17. A. H. Raskin, "The Obsolescent Unions," *Commentary,* July 1963, p. 18.

18. Elizabeth Brandeis, "Organized Labor and Protective Legislation," in *Labor and the New Deal,* Milton Derber and Edwin Young, eds. (Madison: University of Wisconsin Press, 1957), pp. 193–238.

19. See James Doak, *The Lobbyists* (Washington, D.C.: Public Affairs Press, 1966), pp. 135–53.
20. Martin Perline, "A Comparative Analysis of the Trade Union Press" (unpublished Ph.D. thesis, Ohio State University, 1965).

Chapter 2

1. This chapter utilizes unpublished statistical data tabulated particularly for the present study. The University of Michigan, Survey Research Center, in connection with its Survey of Consumers in 1959 and in 1966 asked the question, "Do you belong to a labor union?" The statistical data contained in these surveys of households permitted tabulations, which had not previously been prepared, to show the characteristics of heads of households who were union members compared to those who were not union members. There were 2,799 households in the 1959 sample and 2,417 in the 1965 sample. The tabulations which show the characteristics of households in which the head of the household reported being a union member, compared to all other households, were prepared for this study under the supervision of Professor Leo Troy of Rutgers University.

   It is to be regretted that similar information is not available on an annual basis from the special supplemental information collected each April in the Current Population Survey. An additional question or two on union membership is long overdue. It is hoped that the rich information here reported from the two households studies of the University of Michigan, Survey Research Center will help to persuade the Bureau of the Census and the Bureau of Labor Statistics of the significance of reporting annually such data with the larger sample of C.P.S.

2. U.S. Department of Labor, Bureau of Labor Statistics, *Directory of National and International Labor Unions in the United States, 1967*, Bulletin No. 1596 (Washington, D.C.: 1968), p. 55; Leo Troy, *Trade Union Membership, 1897–1962*, Occasional Paper 92 (New York: National Bureau of Economic Research, 1965). Also see Arthur B. Shostak, *America's Forgotten Labor Organization, A Survey of the Role of the Single-Firm Independent Union in American Industry* (Princeton: Industrial Relations Section, Princeton University, 1962).

3. The following sources are particularly relevant to this section: Ruth Kornhauser, "Some Social Determinants and Consequences of Union Membership," *Labor History*, Winter 1961, pp. 30–61; Gladys L. Palmer, *Labor Mobility in Six Cities* (New York: Social

Science Research Council, 1954); Angus Campbell, Gerald Gurin, and Warren Miller, *The Voter Decides* (New York: Row, Peterson, 1954), p. 6.

4. Selig Perlman, *A Theory of the Labor Movement* (New York: Macmillan, 1928).

5. U.S. Department of Labor, *op. cit.*, p. 64; Ray Marshall, *Labor in the South* (Cambridge: Harvard University Press, 1967).

6. Kornhauser, *op. cit.*, p. 40. These results appear to be confirmed by the Michigan Survey Research Center results.

7. Robert W. Smuts, *European Impressions of the American Worker* (New York: King's Crown Press, 1953), p. 2. Also see E. Levasseur, *The American Workman* (Baltimore: Johns Hopkins Press, 1900), pp. 444–45.

8. C. Wright Mills, *The New Men of Power, America's Labor Leaders* (New York: Harcourt, Brace, 1948), p. 291. Also see William Z. Foster, *Misleaders of Labor* (New York: Trade Union Educational League, 1927); the Communist Party analysis saw in the semiskilled and the unskilled the prospects of radical change—"Among them the spirit of class solidarity burns brightest, and that of class antagonism runs strongest." (p. 315).

9. Reinhard Bendix, *Nation-Building and Citizenship* (New York: John Wiley and Sons, 1964), p. 73.

10. See Daniel L. Horowitz, *The Italian Labor Movement* (Cambridge: Harvard University Press, 1963); Val R. Lorwin, *The French Labor Movement* (Cambridge: Harvard University Press, 1954); Henry W. Ehrmann, *Organized Business in France* (Princeton: Princeton University Press, 1957); George Lichtheim, *Marxism in Modern France* (New York: Columbia University Press, 1966).

11. Statistics compiled from U.S. Department of Labor, *op. cit.*, p. 56; *Directory of Labor Organizations: Europe*, May 1965, pp. xii–xiii; *Directory of Labor Organizations: Asia and Australia*, March 1963, pp. x–xi; and International Labour Office, *Yearbook of Labour Statistics, 1967*, Table 3, pp. 276–95.

12. See T. L. Johnson, *Collective Bargaining in Sweden* (Cambridge: Harvard University Press, 1962), pp. 23–91; Walter Galenson, *The Danish System of Labor Relations* (Cambridge: Harvard University Press, 1952), pp. 7–93.

13. These estimates were prepared by Professor Leo Troy from special tabulations prepared for this study from the financial reports filed annually by labor organizations with the Department of Labor as required by the Labor-Management Reporting and Disclosure Act of 1959.

14. Adolf Sturmthal, *Workers Councils, A Study of Workplace*

    Organization on Both Sides of the Iron Curtain (Cambridge: Harvard University Press, 1964).

15. Mills, *op. cit.*, p. 68.
16. *Ibid.*, p. 73.

Chapter 3

1. Robert F. Hoxie, *Trade Unionism in the United States* (New York: D. Appleton, 1921), pp. 50–51.
2. Joseph A. Loftus, "Meany Is Shocked by Rackets' Scope," *The York Times*, November 2, 1957, pp. 1, 9.
3. For a popular summary, see Robert F. Kennedy, *The Enemy Within* (New York: Harper and Brothers, 1960).
4. U.S. Department of Labor, *Compliance, Enforcement and Reporting in 1968 Under the Labor-Management Reporting and Disclosure Act*, p. 21.
5. *Ibid.*, p. 12.
6. *Ibid.*, p. 14.
7. U.S. Department of Labor, *1965 Summary of Operations, Labor-Management Reporting and Disclosure Act*, Appendix B, pp. 33 et seq.
8. *Task Force Report, Crime and Its Impact—An Assessment* (Washington, D.C.: President's Commission on Law Enforcement and Administration of Justice, 1967), p. 47.
9. *Ibid.*
10. Walter Galenson, *Trade Union Democracy in Western Europe* (Berkeley: University of California Press, 1961).
11. Hoxie, *op. cit.*, p. 147.
12. John Hutchinson, "The Anatomy of Corruption in Trade Unions," *Industrial Relations*, February 1969, p. 144.
13. Frederic Meyers, *Ownership of Jobs: A Comparative Study* (Los Angeles: Institute of Industrial Relations, University of California, 1964), p. 28; Hugh A. Clegg, "The Rights of British Trade-Union Members," in *Labor in a Free Society*, Michael Harrington and Paul Jacobs, eds. (Berkeley: University of California Press, 1959), pp. 119–38. Also see *Royal Commission on Trade Unions and Employers' Associations 1965–68* (London: Her Majesty's Stationery Office, June 1968), Chapter XI, "Safeguards for Individuals in Relations to Trade Unions," pp. 160–95.
14. Val R. Lorwin, *The French Labor Movement* (Cambridge: Harvard University Press, 1954), p. 164.

15.   Quoted in William M. Leiserson, *American Trade Union Democracy* (New York: Columbia University Press, 1959), p. 244.

16.   Carleton H. Parker, *The Casual Laborer and Other Essays* (New York: Harcourt, Brace and Howe, 1920), p. 76.

17.   William E. Simkin, "Refusals to Ratify Contracts," *Industrial and Labor Relations Review*, July 1968, p. 520.

18.   Martin Estey, *The Unions, Structure, Development and Management* (New York: Harcourt, Brace and World, 1967), p. 70. Edward R. Curtin, *Union Initiation Fees, Dues and Per Capita Tax, National Union Strike Benefits* (New York: National Industrial Conference Board, Inc., 1968). Table 5 provides a table of minimum local dues fixed by 81 national and international unions and Table 6 shows monthly per capita tax rates for 117 unions.

19.   See Angus Campbell and others, *The American Voter* (New York: John Wiley and Sons, 1960), p. 302.

20.   The most detailed survey on this point was conducted by John F. Kraft, Inc., for the AFL–CIO. The results are summarized in David R. Jones, "Poll Finds that Most Members Support Labor Policies," *The New York Times*, July 16, 1967, p. 17.

21.   *Ibid.*

22.   For a detailed study of the union, see Seymour Martin Lipset, Martin Trow, and James Coleman, *Union Democracy, The Internal Politics of the International Typographical Union* (Glencoe: The Free Press, 1956). Also see Benson Soffer, "The Role of Union Foremen in the Evolution of the International Typographical Union," *Labor History*, Winter 1961, pp. 62–81.

23.   Lipset, Trow, and Coleman, *op. cit.*, p. 300.

24.   A. H. Raskin, "The Government Role When Bargaining Breaks Down," *The Reporter*, January 31, 1963, p. 28.

25.   Lloyd Ulman, *The Rise of the National Trade Union* (Cambridge: Harvard University Press, 1955), p. 299.

Chapter 4

1.   For a detailed discussion of the N.L.R.B.'s unit determination policies see: "The Board and Section 9 (c) (5): Multi-Location and Single Location Bargaining Units in the Insurance and Retail Industries," *Harvard Law Review*, February 1966, pp. 811–40.

2.   See Paul E. Sultan, *Right-to-Work Laws: A Study in Conflict* (Los Angeles: Institute of Industrial Relations, University of California, 1958); and Joseph R. Grodin and Duane B. Beeson, "State Right-to-Work Laws and Federal Labor Policy," *California Law Review*, March 1964, pp. 95–114.

3. Frederic Meyers, "Effects of 'Right-to-Work' Laws: A Study of the Texas Act," *Industrial and Labor Relations Review,* October 1955, pp. 77–84.

4. 54 Stat. 767 (1940). Joseph Tanennhaus, "Organized Labor's Political Spending: The Law and Its Consequences," *Journal of Politics,* August 1954, pp. 441–71; and John F. Lane, "Analysis of the Federal Law Governing Political Expenditures by Labor Unions," *Labor Law Journal,* October 1958, pp. 725–44.

5. 367 U.S. 740 (1961).

6. See Archibald Cox, "Rights Under a Labor Agreement," *Harvard Law Review,* February 1956, pp. 601–57.

7. See *Vaca v. Sipes,* 386 U.S. 171 (1967).

8. Clyde W. Summers, "Individual Rights in Collective Agreements and Arbitration," *N.Y.U. Law Review,* May 1962, pp. 362–410.

9. This is discussed in detail by Professor Summers, *op. cit.,* p. 362.

10. For a further discussion, see R. W. Fleming, *The Labor Arbitration Process* (Urbana: University of Illinois Press, 1965), pp. 107–33; 214–15.

11. E. Robert Livernash, "Special and Local Negotiations," in *Frontiers of Collective Bargaining,* John T. Dunlop and Neil W. Chamberlain, eds. (New York: Harper and Row, 1967), pp. 27–49.

12. Henry C. Simons, *Economic Policy for a Free Society* (Chicago: University of Chicago Press, 1948), pp. 121–59.

13. Quoted in Thomas O'Hanlon, "The Case Against the Unions," *Fortune,* January 1968, p. 170. Also cited in A. H. Raskin, "Why New York is 'Strike City,'" *The New York Times Magazine,* December 22, 1968, p. 9.

14. Dodge Revolutionary Union Movement, *DRUM,* Vol. 1, No. 2, August 1968, Editorial Page.

15. Arthur M. Ross and Herbert Hill, eds., *Employment, Race and Poverty* (New York: Harcourt, Brace and World, 1967), p. 397.

16. "John Herling's Labor Letter," *Washington Daily News,* November 30, 1968, p. 4.

17. Peter T. Schoemann, "United Association and Affirmative Action" (Extension of Remarks Delivered at the Luncheon for U.A. Delegates Attending the 13th National Legislative Conference of the Building and Construction Trades Department, Washington-Hilton Hotel, Washington, D.C., March 27, 1968).

18. See Ray Marshall, *The Negro Worker* (New York: Random House, 1967), Selected Bibliography, pp. 171–74; Herbert R. Northrup, *Organized Labor and the Negro* (New York: Harper and Brothers, 1944); Sterling D. Spero and A. L. Harris, *The Black Worker* (New York: Columbia University Press, 1931); Philip Taft, *Organized Labor in American History* (New York:

Harper and Row, 1964), pp. 664–81; Herbert Hill, "Has Organized Labor Failed the Negro?" *Negro Digest,* May 1962; Arthur J. Goldberg, *AFL–CIO Labor United* (New York: Mc-Graw-Hill, 1956), pp. 195–202; Ross and Hill, *op. cit.,* pp. 365–431; Herman D. Bloch, *The Circle of Discrimination, An Economic and Social Study of the Black Man in New York* (New York: New York University Press, 1969), pp. 79–151.

19. *Report of the Proceedings of the Tenth Annual Convention of the American Federation of Labor, 1890,* p. 31.

20. Mark Perlman, *The Machinists, A New Study in American Trade Unionism* (Cambridge: Harvard University Press, 1961), p. 3.

21. *Ibid.,* p. 6.

22. *Ibid.,* p. 16.

23. *Report of the Proceedings of the Twentieth Annual Convention of the American Federation of Labor, 1900,* p. 112.

24. Marshall, *op. cit.,* pp. 165–66. Also see speeches delivered at the testimonial dinner honoring A. Philip Randolph on his 80th birthday, AFL–CIO release, May 6, 1969.

25. Taft, *op. cit.,* pp. 674–75.

26. American Federation of Labor and Congress of Industrial Organizations Constitution, Article II, Section 4.

27. Goldberg, *op. cit.,* p. 202.

28. See Michael I. Sovern, *Legal Restraints on Racial Discrimination in Employment* (New York: Twentieth Century Fund, 1966); Benjamin Aaron, "The Unions' Duty of Fair Representation Under the Railway Labor and National Labor Relations Act," *Journal of Air Law and Commerce,* Spring 1968, pp. 167–207; Paul H. Norgren and Samuel E. Hill, *Toward Fair Employment* (New York: Columbia University Press, 1964), pp. 40–55.

29. 323 U.S. 192 (1944).

30. Miranda Fuel Company, 140 N.L.R.B. 181 (1962) (*enforcement denied*), 325 F. 2d 172 (2d Cir. 1963).

31. Alfred W. Blumrosen, "The Duty of Fair Recruitment Under the Civil Rights Act of 1964," *Rutgers Law Review,* Spring 1968, pp. 465–536.

32. *Statement Presented by William Green on the Ives-Chavez Anti-Discrimination Bill, 5.984 Before the Senate Committee on Labor and Public Welfare,* June 20, 1947.

33. Marshall, *op. cit.,* pp. 40–41.

34. U.S. Department of Labor, Bureau of Labor Statistics, *The Negroes in the United States, Their Economic and Social Situation,* June 1966, Bulletin No. 1511, p. 110; U.S. Department of Labor and U.S. Department of Commerce, *Recent Trends in Social and Economic Conditions of Negroes in the United States,* July 1968, Current Population Reports, Series P-23, No. 26; U.S. Department

of Labor, Bureau of Labor Statistics, Report No. 347, p. 16; Claire C. Hodge, "The Negro Job Situation: Has It Improved?" *Monthly Labor Review,* January 1969, pp. 20–28.

35. Ross and Hill, *op. cit.,* p. 46.

36. James Tobin, "On Improving the Economic Status of the Negro," in *The American Negro,* Talcott Parsons and Kenneth B. Clark, eds. (Boston: Beacon Press, 1965), pp. 452–53.

37. Equal Employment Opportunity Commission, Office of Research and Reports, *Negro Underemployment in American Industry,* Research Report 1967-22, October 1967, pp. 16–18. The data are from EEO-1. For construction these data apply to the regular work force.

38. See Herbert R. Northrup, *The Negro in the Automobile Industry* (Philadelphia: Industrial Research Unit, University of Pennsylvania, 1968), p. 36; Herbert R. Northrup, *The Negro in the Aerospace Industry* (Philadelphia: Industrial Research Unit, University of Pennsylvania, 1968), p. 37; Richard L. Rowan, *The Negro in the Steel Industry* (Philadelphia: Industrial Research Unit, University of Pennsylvania, 1968), p. 59.

39. U.S. Civil Service Commission, *Study of Minority Group Employment in the Federal Government,* 1967, Washington, D.C., p. 3. Also see *For All the People . . . By All the People, A Report on Equal Opportunity in State and Local Government Employment,* A Report of the United States Commission on Civil Rights, Washington, D.C., 1969.

40. For a careful analysis, see F. Ray Marshall and Vernon M. Briggs, Jr., *The Negro and Apprenticeship* (Baltimore: Johns Hopkins Press, 1967).

41. See F. Ray Marshall and Vernon M. Briggs, Jr., *Equal Apprenticeship Opportunities; the Nature of the Issue and the New York Experience,* Policy Papers in Human Resources and Industrial Relations, No. 10 (Ann Arbor: Institute of Labor and Industrial Relations, University of Michigan; Detroit: Wayne State University; Washington, D.C.: National Manpower Policy Task Force, November 1968).

42. U.S. Department of Labor, Manpower Administration, release, October 30, 1968; "Federally Supported Manpower Programs in Building and Construction, October 1969" (unpublished).

43. Bureau of National Affairs, *Construction Labor Report,* December 4, 1968, No. 689, C-3.

44. See Peter B. Doeringer, ed., *Programs for the Disadvantaged* (Englewood Cliffs, New Jersey: Prentice-Hall, 1969).

45. See the statement of policy of the Building and Construction Trades Department, July 16, 1968, Washington, D.C.

46. James P. Gannon, "Militant Negroes Press for a Stronger Voice in the Labor Movement," *Wall Street Journal,* November 29, 1968, pp. 1, 16.

47. See Paul B. Sheatsley, "White Attitudes Toward the Negro" in "The American Negro - 2," *Daedalus,* Winter 1966, pp. 217–38.

48. For a number of strong statements in this vein see the monthly editorials by Peter T. Schoemann in the United Association *Journal.*

Chapter 5

1. James B. McKee, "Status and Power in the Industrial Community: A Comment on Drucker's Thesis," *American Journal of Sociology,* January 1953, p. 369.

2. Amitai Etzioni, *Modern Organizations* (Englewood Cliffs, New Jersey: Prentice-Hall, 1964), p. 31.

3. Figures taken from Abraham Friedman, "Characteristics of National and International Union Leaders" (unpublished manuscript, October 1967).

4. See Leonard R. Sayles and George Strauss, *The Local Union, Its Place in the Industrial Plant* (New York: Harper and Brothers, 1953), p. 234.

5. Arnold S. Tannenbaum and Robert L. Kahn, *Participation in Union Locals* (Evanston, Illinois: Row, Peterson, 1958), p. 234.

6. Harold L. Wilensky, *Intellectuals in Labor Unions* (Glencoe: The Free Press, 1956), pp. 129–30, 142, 146, 147, 226–28.

7. John H. Stamm, *The Second-Generation Union, A Study of the Unionization of Union Representatives,* D.B.A. Thesis, Harvard Graduate School of Business Administration, 1969.

8. Friedman, *op. cit.*

9. Benjamin Haskel, "Education for Union Loyalty," *Workers Education Bureau News Letter,* January 1949, p. 7.

10. Harry R. Blaine and Frederick A. Zeller, "Union Attitudes Towards University Participation in Labor Education: An Examination and Assessment," *Labor Law Journal,* April 1965, p. 237.

11. Thomas E. Linton, *An Historical Examination of the Purposes and Practices of the Education Program of the United Automobile Workers of America—1936–1959,* 1965, p. 118.

12. Russell Allen, "The Professional in Unions and His Educational Preparation," *Industrial and Labor Relations Review,* October 1962, pp. 16, 29.

13. "Jobs and Occupations: A Popular Evaluation," *Opinion News,* September 1, 1947, p. 4.

14. *Ibid.*

Chapter 6

1. U.S. Department of Labor, Manpower Administration, release, October 30, 1968.

2. Solomon Barkin, *The Decline of the Labor Movement, and What Can Be Done About It* (Santa Barbara, California: Center for the Study of Democratic Institutions, 1961).

3. AFL–CIO Executive Council Report on the Disaffiliation of the U.A.W., *To Clear the Record,* Washington, D.C., 1969, p. 56.

4. A. H. Raskin, "AFL–CIO: A Confederation or Federation? Which Road for the Future?" *Annals of the American Academy of Political and Social Science,* November 1963, p. 43.

5. U.A.W., Joint Resolutions Constitution Committee, Report No. 2, Special Convention, U.A.W., April 20–22, 1967.

Chapter 7

1. The literature on the theoretical analysis of collective bargaining includes the following: Sidney and Beatrice Webb, *Industrial Democracy* (London: Longmans, Green, 1914); Sumner H. Slichter, *Union Policies and Industrial Management* (Washington, D.C.: Brookings Institution, 1941); Neil W. Chamberlain, *Collective Bargaining* (New York: McGraw-Hill, 1951); Allan Flanders, *Industrial Relations: What Is Wrong with the System?* (London: Faber and Faber, 1965); Sumner H. Slichter, James J. Healy, and E. Robert Livernash, *The Impact of Collective Bargaining on Management* (Washington, D.C.: Brookings Institution, 1960); John T. Dunlop, *Industrial Relations Systems* (New York: Henry Holt, 1958).

2. Webb, *op. cit.,* p. 173, n. 1. The reference to the writing of Mrs. Webb, Beatrice Potter, is *The Cooperative Movement in Great Britain* (London, 1891), p. 217.

3. Webb, *op. cit.,* p. 173.

4. See *Royal Commission on Trade Unions and Employers' Associations,* Minutes of Evidence 2 and 3, Ministry of Labour (London, Her Majesty's Stationery Office, 1966), "We have to face that in many areas we have effectively two tiers of negotiation at the present time, the national bargaining and the bargaining on the factory floor on bonuses and piece rates," p. 47.

5. For a discussion of some other Western industrial-relations arrangements, see *Royal Commission on Trade Unions and Employers' Associations, 1965–1968* (London: Her Majesty's Stationery Office,

1968); Val R. Lorwin, *The French Labor Movement* (Cambridge: Harvard University Press, 1954); J. E. Issac and G. W. Ford, eds., *Australian Labour Relations Readings* (Melbourne: Sun Books, 1966); Adolf Sturmthal, ed., *White-Collar Trade Unions, Contemporary Developments in Industrialized Societies* (Urbana: University of Illinois Press, 1966); *The Trade Union Situation in Sweden*, Report of a Mission from the International Labour Office (Geneva: International Labour Office, 1961); Walter Galenson, *Trade Union Democracy in Western Europe* (Berkeley: University of California Press, 1964).

6.   Labor-Management Relations Act, 1947, Section 9 (a).

7.   See D. J. Robertson, *Factory Wage Structures and National Agreements* (Cambridge, England: University Press, 1960).

8.   See Adolf Sturmthal, *Workers Councils, A Study of Workplace Organization on Both Sides of the Iron Curtain* (Cambridge: Harvard University Press, 1964).

9.   See Robben W. Fleming, "The Obligation to Bargain in Good Faith," in *Public Policy and Collective Bargaining*, Joseph Shister, Benjamin Aaron, and Clyde W. Summers, eds. (New York: Harper and Row, 1962), pp. 60–87.

10. E. Robert Livernash, "Special and Local Negotiations," in *Frontiers of Collective Bargaining*, John T. Dunlop and Neil W. Chamberlain, eds. (New York: Harper and Row, 1967), pp. 27–49.

11. See A. H. Raskin, "The Great Manhattan Newspaper Duel," *Saturday Review*, May 8, 1965, p. 8.

12. See John T. Dunlop, "The Function of the Strike," in *Frontiers of Collective Bargaining, op. cit.*, pp. 103–21.

13. *The Public Interest in National Labor Policy* (New York: Committee for Economic Development, 1961), p. 32.

14. H. A. Clegg and T. E. Chester, "Joint Consultation," in *The System of Industrial Relations in Great Britain*, Allan Flanders and H. A. Clegg, eds. (Oxford, England: Basil Blackwell, 1954), pp. 323–64; James J. Healy, ed., *Creative Collective Bargaining: Meeting Today's Challenges to Labor-Management Relations* (Englewood Cliffs, New Jersey: Prentice-Hall, 1965); William Gomberg, "Special Study Committees," in *Frontiers of Collective Bargaining, op. cit.*, pp. 235–51.

15. See *The Princeton Symposium on The American System of Social Insurance* (New York: McGraw-Hill, 1968).

16. "The Public Interest: Variations on an Old Theme," *Proceedings of the Eighteenth Annual Meeting of the National Academy of Arbitrators, 1965* (Washington, D.C.: B.N.A. Incorporated, 1965), p. 195.

17. W. Willard Wirtz, *Labor and the Public Interest* (New York: Harper and Row, 1964), p. 49.

Chapter 8

1. Philip Taft, "Violence in American Labor," *The Annals of the American Academy of Political and Social Science,* March 1966, pp. 127–40.
2. See *Hearings before the Subcommittee on Improvements in Judicial Machinery of the Committee on the Judiciary, U.S. Senate, 90th Congress, 1st session on S. 176 Providing for the Establishment of a United States Court of Labor-Management Relations,* October 17, 1967, Washington, D.C., 1968. Cited as Hearings, U.S. Labor Court.
3. See James J. Healy, ed., *Creative Collective Bargaining: Meeting Today's Challenges to Labor-Management Relations* (Englewood Cliffs, New Jersey: Prentice-Hall, 1965).
4. Theodore W. Kheel, letter to the editor, *The New York Times,* September 4, 1967, p. 20.
5. A. H. Raskin, "Collision Course on the Labor Front," *Saturday Review,* February 25, 1967, pp. 32–33.
6. Leland Hazard, "Strikes and People: A Proposal," *The Atlantic Monthly,* December 1966, pp. 116–18; New York City Transit Authority, *The Effect of the 1966 New York City Transit Strike on the Travel Behavior of Regular Transit Users.*
7. See *Hearings Before the Subcommittee on Labor of the Committee on Labor and Public Welfare, U.S. Senate, 90th Congress, 1st session on S. J. Res. 18, 1967.* Cited as Hearings, Railroad Shopcraft Dispute.
8. Murray Schumach, "Union Chief Irate; Says that 'Judge Can Drop Dead in his Black Robes,'" *The New York Times,* January 5, 1966, p. 1.
9. Damon Stetson, "Union Image Hurt by Transit Strike," *The New York Times,* March 8, 1966, p. 23.
10. *Royal Commission on Trade Unions and Employers' Associations,* Written Evidence of the Ministry of Labour (London: Her Majesty's Stationery Office, 1965), p. 69. For a discussion of international comparisons of strikes and lockouts, see Arthur M. Ross and Paul T. Hartman, *Changing Patterns of Industrial Conflict* (New York: John Wiley and Sons, 1960).
11. Lionel Robbins, *The Theory of Economic Policy in English Classical Political Economy* (London: Macmillan, 1953), p. 105.
12. A. H. Raskin, "Labor Day: Who Divides and Who Conquers?" *The New York Times,* September 4, 1967, p. 21.

13. *Hearings, U.S. Labor Court,* p. 15.

14. Public Law 88–108, August 28, 1963; Public Law 90–54, July 17, 1967.

15. National Association of Manufacturers, Subcommittee on Emergency Disputes Industrial Relations Committee, *Big Labor and Big Strikes: Analysis and Recommendations,* New York; *Hearings, U.S. Labor Court,* p. 99 and *Hearings, Railroad Shopcraft Dispute,* p. 295.

16. *Hearings, U.S. Labor Court,* p. 95.

17. For an early reference to this procedure, see George W. Taylor, *Government Regulation of Industrial Relations* (New York: Prentice-Hall, 1948), pp. 358–61.

18. See William Gomberg, "Special Study Committees," in *Frontiers of Collective Bargaining,* John T. Dunlop and Neil W. Chamberlain, eds. (New York: Harper and Row, 1967), pp. 235–51.

19. See Irving Bernstein, *Arbitration of Wages* (Berkeley and Los Angeles: University of California Press, 1954); Richard Ulric Miller, "Arbitration of New Contract Wage Disputes," *Industrial and Labor Relations Review,* January 1967, pp. 250–64.

20. Federal Mediation and Conciliation Service, *20th Anniversary Report, 1947–67* (Washington, D.C., 1968), p. 31.

21. *Ibid.,* p. 36.

22. United Steelworkers of America, AFL–CIO–CLC, *News from the USWA,* September 3, 1967.

23. Clyde W. Summers, "Ratification of Agreements," in *Frontiers of Collective Bargaining, op. cit.,* pp. 75–102.

24. William E. Simkin, "Refusals to Ratify Contracts," *Industrial and Labor Relations Review,* July 1968, pp. 518–40.

25. It is to be recalled that at the request of Secretary of Labor James P. Mitchell, E. Robert Livernash directed a study of basic steel following the 116-day strike of 1959–60. See *Collective Bargaining in the Basic Steel Industry,* U.S. Department of Labor, January 1961. In 1967–68 the Canadian Construction Association initiated a major study of labor-management relations and the economics of the construction industry with a labor-management steering committee, H. Carl Goldenberg and John H. G. Crispo, eds., *Construction Labour Relations* (Canadian Construction Association, 1968).

26. See *Royal Commission on Trade Unions and Employers' Associations, 1965–68* (London: Her Majesty's Stationery Office, 1968); *Canadian Industrial Relations,* Task Force on Labour Relations, Privy Council Office, Canada, 1969.

27. Donald B. Straus, *The Development of a Policy for Industrial Peace in Atomic Energy* (Washington, D.C.: National Planning Association, 1950); *Report of the Secretary of Labor's Advisory*

Committee on Labor Management Relations in Atomic Energy Installations (Washington, D.C., 1957); Wayne E. Howard, *The Missile Sites Labor Commission, 1961 through 1967* (Washington, D.C.: Federal Mediation and Conciliation Service, 1969).

28. See *Collective Bargaining*, A Report by the President's Advisory Committee on Labor-Management Policy, May 1, 1962.

29. Despite criticism to the contrary, such boards are not illegal or extra-legal. See Herbert R. Northrup, letter to the editor, *The New York Times*, March 26, 1968, p. 44.

30. See Benjamin Aaron, "Emergency Dispute Settlement," *Labor Law Development* (New York: Matthew Bender, 1967), pp. 185–208, and "Public-Interest Disputes and Their Settlement: Observations on the United States Experience," *Labor Law Journal*, August 1963, pp. 746–52.

31. Aaron, *op. cit.*, p. 200.

32. George H. Hildebrand, "Cloudy Future for Coalition Bargaining," *Harvard Business Review*, November–December 1968, pp. 114–28.

33. See for instance the arbitration on incentives growing out of the July 30, 1968 settlement in the basic steel industry. In the Matter of Incentive Arbitration Between Coordinating Committee, Steel Companies and United Steelworkers of America, August 1, 1969.

34. Constitution of the Pacific Coast Metal Trades District Council, adopted March 15, 1967, amended May 8, 1969, Article VII, "Negotiations, Strike Action and Contract Ratification."

Chapter 9

1. Francis A. Walker, *The Wage Question, A Treatise on Wages and the Wage Class* (New York: Henry Holt, 1886), p. 408.

2. Alfred Marshall, *Elements of Economics of Industry* (London: Macmillan, 1893), p. 401.

3. Charles E. Lindblom, *Unions and Capitalism* (New Haven: Yale University Press, 1949), p. 156. Also see Edward H. Chamberlin, *Labor Unions and Public Policy* (Washington, D.C.: American Enterprise Association, 1958), pp. 1–46.

4. Sumner H. Slichter, "The American System of Industrial Relations: Some Contrasts with Foreign Systems," in *Potentials of the American Economy, Selected Essays by Sumner H. Slichter* (Cambridge: Harvard University Press, 1961), p. 277.

5. Sumner H. Slichter, *Union Policies and Industrial Management* (Washington, D.C.: Brookings Institution, 1941), p. 205.

6. *Cigar Makers' Official Journal*, October 1923, p. 4.

7. This is a form of all-or-nothing bargaining for both price and quantity. See Wassily Leontief, "The Pure Theory of the Guaranteed Annual Wage," *Journal of Political Economy*, February 1946, pp. 76–169. For a discussion of types of provisions of agreements, see the Report of Emergency Board No. 151, December 31, 1962, pp. 22–36.

8. Norman J. Simler, "The Economics of Featherbedding," *Industrial and Labor Relations Review*, October 1962, p. 121. Also see Paul A. Weinstein, ed., *Featherbedding and Technological Change* (Boston: D.C. Heath, 1965).

9. For the classic discussion, see Slichter, *Union Policies and Industrial Management, op. cit.*, Chapters VIII and IX.

10. Dorothea DeSchweinitz, *Labor and Management in a Common Enterprise* (Cambridge: Harvard University Press, 1949).

11. Sumner H. Slichter, James J. Healy, and E. Robert Livernash, *The Impact of Collective Bargaining on Management* (Washington, D.C.: Brookings Institution, 1960), p. 951.

12. Benjamin Aaron, "Government Restraints on Featherbedding," *Stanford Law Review*, July 1953, p. 680.

13. Frederick Winslow Taylor, *Scientific Management, Comprising Shop Management, The Principles of Scientific Management, Testimony Before the Special House Committee* (New York: Harper and Brothers, 1947), p. 33. (The handbook was first published in 1903.)

14. See S. B. Mathewson, *Restriction of Output among Unorganized Workers* (New York: Viking Press, 1931); and Donald Ray cited in William Foote Whyte, *Money and Motivation* (New York: Harper and Brothers, 1955), p. 15.

15. F. J. Roethlesberger and W. J. Dickson, *Management and the Worker* (Cambridge: Harvard University Press, 1939); and William Foote Whyte, *Men at Work* (Homewood, Illinois: Richard D. Irwin, 1961).

16. John M. Baitsell, *Airline Industrial Relations, Pilots and Flight Engineers* (Cambridge: Graduate School of Business Administration, Harvard University, 1966).

17. Slichter, Healy, and Livernash, *op. cit.*, p. 317.

18. See *Report of the Presidential Railroad Labor Commission*, Washington, D.C., February 1962, Chapter 4, and supporting exhibits and transcripts of hearings.

19. Public Law 88–108, 88th Congress, S.J. 102, August 28, 1963.

20. See Charles C. Killingsworth, "The Modernization of West Coast Longshore Work Rules," *Industrial and Labor Relations Review*, April 1962, pp. 295–306; *Men and Machines*, International Longshoremen's and Warehousemen's Union and Pacific Maritime Association, 1963.

21. Paul T. Hartman, "Union Work Rules: A Brief Theoretical Analysis and Some Empirical Results," *Industrial Relations Research Association, Proceedings of the Nineteenth Annual Winter Meeting,* December 28–29, 1966, pp. 333–42.
22. Slichter, Healy, and Livernash, *op. cit.,* pp. 333–34.
23. *Ibid.,* p. 947.
24. See Herbert R. Northrup and Gordon R. Stockholm, *Restrictive Labor Practices in the Supermarket Industry* (Philadelphia: University of Pennsylvania Press, 1967).
25. Wayne T. Brooks, "The Customer's Stake in Construction Industry Bargaining," Remarks before the A.G.C. National Labor Conference, May 20–21, 1968.
26. See Benjamin Aaron, *op. cit.,* pp. 687–721; Notes and Comments, "Drafting Problems and the Regulation of Featherbedding—An Imagined Dilemma," *Yale Law Journal,* April 1964, pp. 812–49.
27. 312 U.S. 219 (1941).
28. 93 *Congressional Record,* 6441 (1947).
29. Aaron, *loc. cit.* See *N.L.R.B. v. Gamble Enterprises, Inc.,* 73 Sup. Ct. 560 (1953) and *American Newspaper Publishers Association v. N.L.R.B.,* 73 Sup. Ct. 552 (1953).
30. "Excerpts from Summary of Urban Panel's Report," *The New York Times,* December 15, 1968, p. 70. See also *Report, The National Commission on Urban Problems,* December 1968 (mimeographed). Also see *National Conference on Construction Problems, Task Force Report,* July 1969, Washington, D.C., Chamber of Commerce of the United States.

Chapter 10

1. Roger M. Blough, "The Folklore of Inflation," Speech to Business School Alumni Association, Emory University, Atlanta, Georgia, November 6, 1967.
2. Statement by the AFL–CIO Executive Council on "The National Economy," Chicago, Illinois, August 23, 1966.
3. Milton Friedman, "The Inflationary Fed," *Newsweek,* January 20, 1969, p. 78.
4. For the source of these data, see U.S. Department of Commerce, Bureau of the Census, *Long Term Economic Growth, 1860–1965,* October 1966, pp. 149–50, 202. Also see Albert Rees, *New Measures of Wage-Earner Compensation in Manufacturing, 1914–57* (New York: National Bureau of Economic Research, Occasional Paper 75, 1960).
5. See "Creeping Inflation, A Debate between Sumner H. Slichter and Dr. Heinz Luedicke," *Journal of Commerce,* 1957.

6. Gottfried Haberler, "Wage Policy and Inflation," in *The Public Stake in Union Power*, Philip D. Bradley, ed. (Charlottesville: University of Virginia Press, 1959), p. 65.

7. Milton Friedman, "Some Comments on the Significance of Labor Unions for Economic Policy," in *The Impact of the Labor Union*, David McCord Wright, ed. (New York: Harcourt, Brace, 1951), pp. 168–87.

8. H. G. Lewis, *Unionism and Relative Wages in the United States, An Empirical Inquiry* (Chicago: University of Chicago Press, 1963).

9. John T. Dunlop, "Comments," *Aspects of Labor Economics* (Princeton: National Bureau of Economic Research, 1962), pp. 341–44.

10. Sir John Hicks, "Economic Foundations of Wage Policy," *Economic Journal*, September 1955, p. 391.

11. Paul H. Douglas, *Real Wages in the United States, 1890–1926* (Boston: Houghton Mifflin, 1930), p. 562.

12. Joseph W. Garbarino, *Wage Policy and Long-Term Contracts* (Washington, D.C.: Brookings Institution, 1962).

13. See Harold M. Levinson, *Determining Forces in Collective Wage Bargaining* (New York: John Wiley and Sons, 1966), pp. 133–214, 260.

14. "The Urban Crisis: An Analysis, an Answer," *The American Federationist*, October 1967, pp. 1–8.

15. Arthur M. Okun, "Perspective on Business in 1969," Council of Economic Advisers, September 18, 1968.

16. Warren L. Smith, "The Inflation Problem in Perspective," Council of Economic Advisers, September 19, 1968.

17. David C. Smith, "Incomes Policy," in *Britain's Economic Prospects*, Richard E. Caves, ed. (Washington, D.C.: Brookings Institution, 1968), p. 104; H. A. Turner and H. Zoeteweij, *Prices, Wages and Incomes Policy in Industrialized Market Economies* (Geneva: International Labour Office, 1966); Murray Edelman and R. W. Fleming, *The Politics of Wage-Price Decisions, A Four-Country Analysis* (Urbana: University of Illinois Press, 1965); *Government of Canada, Policies for Price Stability* (Ottawa, Canada: Roger Duhamel, Queen's Printer and Controller of Stationery, 1968); Kingsley Laffer, "Whither Arbitration? Problems of Incomes Policies in Australia and Overseas," *The Journal of Industrial Relations*, November 1968, pp. 206–21.

18. See Herbert Stein, "Unemployment, Inflation and Economic Stability," in *Agenda for America*, Kermit Gordon, ed. (Washington, D.C.: Brookings Institution, 1968), pp. 277–300.

19. "Report of the Vice-President's Task Force on Inflation," Otto Eckstein, Chairman, October 1968 (mimeographed).

20. John T. Dunlop, "American Wage Determination, The Trend and Its Significance," in *Wage Determination and the Economics of Liberalism*, Chamber of Commerce of the United States, January 11, 1947, p. 15.

21. John T. Dunlop, "Productivity and the Wage Structure," in *Income, Employment and Public Policy, Essays in Honor of Alvin H. Hansen* (New York: W. W. Norton, 1948), p. 341.

22. *Economic Report of the President, 1950*, p. 101.

23. *Economic Report of the President, 1960*, p. 91.

24. *Economic Report of the President, 1962*, p. 189. For a restatement of the guideposts by the Council, see *Economic Report of the President, 1966*, pp. 89–90; *Economic Report of the President, 1967*, pp. 119–34.

25. *Economic Report of the President, 1966*, p. 91.

26. See John T. Dunlop, "Guideposts, Wages and Collective Bargaining," in *Guidelines, Informal Controls and the Market Place*, George R. Shultz and Robert Z. Aliber, eds. (Chicago: University of Chicago Press, 1966), pp. 82–85.

27. *Economic Report of the President, 1966*, p. 92; Robert M. Solow, "The Case Against the Case Against the Guideposts," in *Guidelines, Informal Controls and the Market Place, op. cit.*, p. 53. Also see Edward F. Denison, *Guideposts for Wages and Prices: Criteria and Consistency* (Ann Arbor, Michigan: Institute of Public Policy Studies and Department of Economics, 1968).

28. Walter Heller, *New Dimensions of Political Economy* (New York: W. W. Norton, 1967), p. 43.

29. John Sheahan, *The Wage-Price Guideposts* (Washington, D.C.: Brookings Institution, 1967), p. 96.

30. David C. Smith, *Incomes Policies, Some Foreign Experiences and Their Relevance for Canada*, Prepared for the Economic Council of Canada (Ottawa, Canada: Roger Duhamel, Queen's Printer and Controller of Stationery, 1966), pp. 129–49.

31. J. Pen, "The Strange Adventures of Dutch Wage Policy," *British Journal of Industrial Relations*, October 1963, pp. 318–30.

32. David C. Smith, "Incomes Policy," in *Britain's Economic Prospects, op. cit.*, pp. 120–26; Derek Robinson, "Implementing an Incomes Policy," *Industrial Relations*, October 1968, pp. 73–90.

33. "Symposium on Productivity Bargaining," *British Journal of Industrial Relations*, March 1967, pp. 1–62.

34. Allan Flanders, "The Case for the 'Package Deal,'" *The Times* (London), July 9, 1968, p. 23.

35. *Royal Commission on Trade Unions and Employers' Associations, 1965–1968* (London: Her Majesty's Stationery Office, 1968), pp. 12–53; Lloyd Ulman, "Collective Bargaining and Industrial Efficiency," in *Britain's Economic Prospects, op. cit.*, pp. 324–80.

36. Swedish Ministry of Finance, Secretariat of Economic Planning, "Inflation and Economic Development," July 1965.

37. Assar Lindbeck, "Theories and Problems in Swedish Economic Policy in the Post-War Period," *Survey of National Economic Policy Issues and Policy Research, American Economic Review*, Supplement, June 1968, p. 20; Bertil Olsson, "Labor-Market Policy in Modern Society," in *Toward a Manpower Policy*, Robert A. Gordon, ed. (New York: John Wiley and Sons, 1967), pp. 249–83.

38. O.E.C.D., Reviews of Manpower and Social Policies, *Labor Market Policy in Sweden*, O.E.C.D., Paris, 1963.

39. Rudolf Meidner, "The Employment Problems of Individuals and Groups," *International Conference on Automation, Full Employment and a Balanced Economy*, American Foundation on Automation and Employment, Inc., 1967.

40. Ulman, *op. cit.*, p. 379.

41. *Economic Report of the President, 1968*, pp. 126–28; see *Studies by the Staff of the Cabinet Committee on Price Stability*, Superintendent of Documents, Washington, D.C., January 1969.

42. Jan Wittrock, *Reducing Seasonal Unemployment in the Construction Industry*, O.E.C.D., Paris, 1967.

43. O.E.C.D., Reviews of Manpower and Social Policies, *Manpower Policy and Programmers in the United States*, O.E.C.D., Paris, 1964; Frank H. Cassell, *The Public Employment Service: Organization in Change* (Ann Arbor, Michigan: Academic Publications, 1968); Bureau of the Budget, *Special Analyses, Budget of the United States*, "Federal Manpower Programs," Special Analyses K, Washington, D.C., 1969, pp. 134–47; *Manpower Report of the President*, Washington, D.C., January 1969.

Chapter 11

1. U.S. Civil Service Commission, "Union Recognition in the Federal Government, August 1966 and November 1967," February 26, 1968.

2. *Interim Report*, State of New York, Governor's Committee on Public Employee Relations, June 1968, Appendix A; State of New York, Excerpts of Remarks of Governor Rockefeller, October 15, 1968.

3. Joseph Krislov, "The Independent Public Employee Association: Characteristics and Functions," *Industrial and Labor Relations Review*, July 1962, pp. 510–20.

4. Jack Stieber, "A New Approach to Strikes in Public Employment," *MSU Business Topics*, Graduate School of Business Administration, Michigan State University, Autumn 1967, p. 68.

5. *Report of the National Commission on Technology, Automation and Economic Progress,* Volume 1, February 1966, p. 29.

6. General Electric, Personnel and Industrial Relations, "Our Future Environment," April 1968, p. 8.

7. See Milton Derber, "Labor-Management Policy for Public Employees in Illinois: The Experience of the Governor's Commission, 1966–67," *Industrial and Labor Relations Review,* July 1968, p. 558.

8. Wilson R. Hart, *Collective Bargaining in the Federal Civil Service* (New York: Harper and Brothers, 1961), p. 250.

9. See P.O.D. Publication 53.

10. Harry R. Blaine, Eugene C. Hagburg, and Frederick A Zeller, "Discipline and Discharge in the United States Postal Service: Adverse Action and Appeal," *Industrial and Labor Relations Review,* October 1965, pp. 92–98.

11. *Report and Recommendations of the International Association of Fire Fighters,* Fact Finding and Review Commission, February 5, 1968; see "Firemen Remove No-strike Clause," *The New York Times,* August 21, 1968, p. 42.

12. J. Joseph Lowenberg, "Labor Relations for Policemen and Fire Fighters," *Monthly Labor Review,* May 1968, pp. 38–39.

13. See Toivo P. Kanninen, "Rate Setting by the Army–Air Force Wage Board," *Monthly Labor Review,* October 1958, pp. 1107–12; *The Wage Board System,* Subcommittee on Manpower of the Committee on Post Office and Civil Service, House of Representatives, 89th Congress, 2nd Session, March 1966.

14. H. M. Douty, "Fair Comparison: The Case of the United States White-Collar Civil Service," *Economica,* November 1965, pp. 375–92; United States Civil Service Commission, *Federal Personnel Manual System,* December 1, 1967; United States Civil Service Commission, *Pay Structure of the Federal Civil Service,* June 30, 1967.

15. *General Agreement between the Tennessee Valley Authority and the Tennessee Valley Trades and Labor Council Governing Hourly Employment.* Revised through August 1, 1966, Article VIII (1).

16. *Ibid.,* see Article II and Supplementary Schedule H-XXIII.

17. *Final Report,* State of New York, Governor's Committee on Public Employee Relations, March 31, 1966, pp. 55–63.

18. James T. Hall, Jr., "Work Stoppages in Government," *Monthly Labor Review,* July 1968, p. 53. The data refer to 1967.

19. Sterling D. Spero, *Government as Employer* (New York: Remsen Press, 1948), p. 258.

20. Jean T. McKelvey, "The Role of State Agencies in Public Em-

ployee Labor Relations," *Industrial and Labor Relations Review*, January 1967, pp. 179–97.

21. See Hart, *op. cit.*, pp. 38–54 for a good discussion.

22. *Ibid.*, p. 51.

23. *Final Report*, State of New York, Governor's Committee on Public Employee Relations, March 31, 1966, p. 17.

24. Arvid Anderson, "The U.S. Experience in Collective Bargaining in Public Employment," Annual Conference, Public Personnel Association, Toronto, Canada, August 22, 1966 (mimeographed), p. 20.

25. *Interim Report*, State of New York, Governor's Committee on Public Employee Relations, June 1968, Appendix B, p. 52.

26. Peter Millones, "Now City Will Have to Cope with a 2-Man Union," *The New York Times*, July 30, 1968, p. 35.

27. See New York State, Public Employment Relations Board, release, August 29, 1968, for announcement of six negotiating units for 150,000 state employees.

28. *In the Matter of the Arbitration between the City of New York and Patrolmen's Benevolent Association of the City of New York, Inc. and Uniformed Firemen's Association, Local No. 94*, October 9, 1966, Peter Seitz, Arbitrator, Office of Collective Bargaining, Board of Collective Bargaining. *In the Matter of the City of New York and Social Service Employees Unions*, Decision No. B-11-68, January 9, 1969.

29. See for example *Agreement Between the Board of Education of the City of New York and United Federation of Teachers, Local 2, American Federation of Teachers, AFL-CIO, Covering Day School Classroom Teachers and Per Session Teachers, July 1, 1967–September 7, 1969*, p. 18.

30. *First Bargaining Contract between the City of New York and the Social Service Employees Union*, August 1965, Article V. Also see *Second Bargaining Contract*, October 1967, Article VII.

31. George H. Hildebrand, "The Public Sector," in *Frontiers of Collective Bargaining*, John T. Dunlop and Neil W. Chamberlain, eds. (New York: Harper and Row, 1967), pp. 134–35.

32. *Public Employee's Fair Employment Law, Article 14 of the Civil Service Law*, Chapter 392 of the Laws of 1967, Section 209. New York City was specifically exempted from this provision in Section 212.

33. Reference may be made to a number of reports to state governments dealing with impasse procedures and other issues in public employment: *Report of the Interim Commission to Study Collective Bargaining by Municipalities, State of Connecticut*, February 1965; *Report of the Tripartite Panel on Collective Bargaining Procedures in Public Employment*, New York City, March 31, 1966;

Final Report, State of New York, Governor's Committee on Public Employee Relations, March 31, 1966; *Report to Governor George Romney,* Advisory Committee on Public Employee Relations, State of Michigan, February 15, 1967; *Report and Recommendations,* Governor's Advisory Commission on Labor-Management Policy for Public Employees, State of Illinois, March 1967; *Report and Recommendations,* Governor's Commission to Revise the Public Employee Law of Pennsylvania, June 1968. Also see *An Employee Relations Ordinance for Los Angeles County, Report and Recommendations of the Consultants' Committee,* July 25, 1968; *Report on Collective Bargaining and County Public Aid Employees,* Cook County Commissioners Fact Finding Board, October 12, 1966; *Statement of Public Members of Tripartite Panel to Improve Municipal Collective Bargaining Procedures,* New York City, March 31, 1966; The City of New York, *OCB, The Beginning . . . 1968,* Annual Report, Office of Collective Bargaining, 1969. Also see *Report of Task Force on State and Local Government Labor Relations,* Executive Committee, National Governors' Conference, 1967, Chicago Public Personnel Association, 1967; *California Public Employee Relations,* An Analysis of the Meyers-Milias-Brown Act of 1968, Institute of Industrial Relations, University of California, Berkeley, California, 1969.

34. Theodore W. Kheel, *Report to Speaker Anthony J. Travia on the Taylor Law,* February 21, 1968.

35. David Ziskind, *One Thousand Strikes of Government Employees* (New York: Columbia University Press, 1940). Actually, the volume records 1,116 strikes.

36. Hugh G. J. Aitken, *Taylorism at Watertown Arsenal, Scientific Management in Action, 1906–1915* (Cambridge: Harvard University Press, 1960).

37. Spero, *op. cit.,* 252–84.

38. James T. Hall, Jr., "Work Stoppages in Government," *Monthly Labor Review,* July 1968, p. 53.

39. *Findings and Recommendations on Unresolved "Economic and Other Issues" Detroit Police Dispute Panel, Detroit Police Officers Association and City of Detroit, February 27, 1968,* p. 13.

40. Emanuel Perlmutter, "Subway Supervisors Map Plans for a Rules-Book Slowdown," *The New York Times,* August 14, 1968, p. 30.

41. "Airlines Try a Race Against Time," *Business Week,* August 3, 1968, p. 100.

42. David R. Jones, "Arbitration Plan Backed by Meany," *The New York Times,* February 20, 1968, pp. 1, 37.

43. *Report and Recommendations,* Governor's Commission to Revise the Public Employee Law of Pennsylvania, June 1968, p. 13;

Jack Stieber, *op. cit.*, p. 71; Theodore W. Kheel, *Report to Speaker Anthony J. Travia on the Taylor Law*, February 21, 1968, and "Points for Consideration by the Governor's Conference on Public Employment Relations," B.N.A., *Government Employment Relations Report*, October 21, 1968, No. 267, H-1; Donald H. Wollett, "The Taylor Law and the Strike Ban" (mimeographed), August 20, 1968.

44.   *Final Report*, State of New York, Governor's Committee on Public Employment Relations, March 31, 1966; Frederick R. Livingston and Donald H. Wollett, *Statement before the Public and School Employees Grievance Procedure Study Commission*, Trenton, New Jersey, April 6, 1967; *Report and Recommendations of the Consultants' Committee, an Employee Relations Ordinance for Los Angeles County*, July 25, 1968; *Report and Recommendations, Governor's Advisory Commission on Labor-Management for Public Employees*, Illinois, March 1967, pp. 26, 30, 31; *Report of the Interim Commission to Study Collective Bargaining by Municipalities, State of Connecticut*, Advisory Committee on Public Employee Relations, February 15, 1967, pp. 10–13; Anderson, *op. cit.*, pp. 10–15. Also see *Faculty Participation in Academic Governance*, Report of the A.A.H.T.E. Task Force on Faculty Representation and Academic Negotiations, Campus Governance Program (Washington, D.C.: American Association for Higher Education, 1967).

45.   *Interim Report*, State of New York, Governor's Committee on Public Employee Relations, June 1968, p. 10.

46.   Hildebrand, *op. cit.*, pp. 144–46.

47.   See George W. Taylor, "Impasse Procedures—The Finality Question," *Government Employee Relations Report, op. cit.*, G-1.

48.   Hildebrand, *op. cit.*, p. 147.

49.   William A. Lang, *The Development and Techniques of Collective Bargaining in the Municipal Service*, International Association of Fire Fighters, AFL-CIO, April 1966, p. 20.

50.   M. A. Farber, "New Leader Calls on Teachers to Assert Rights," *The New York Times*, July 7, 1968, p. 42. Also see Leon H. Keyserling, *Goals in Teachers' Salaries in Our Public Schools*, Conference on Economic Progress, December 1967.

51.   Public Law 87–793, Section 502. See Douty, *op. cit.*, pp. 375–92.

Chapter 12

1.   See Victor H. Vroom, *Work and Motivation* (New York: John Wiley and Sons, 1964).

2.   See Adolf Sturmthal, *Workers Councils, A Study of Workplace*

Organization on Both Sides of the Iron Curtain (Cambridge: Harvard University Press, 1964); H. A. Clegg, *A New Approach to Industrial Democracy* (Oxford: Basil Blackwell, 1960); Herbert J. Spiro, *The Politics of German Codetermination* (Cambridge: Harvard University Press, 1958).

3. Sumner H. Slichter, James J. Healy, and E. Robert Livernash, *The Impact of Collective Bargaining on Management* (Washington, D.C.: Brookings Institution, 1960), pp. 918–45; Frederick G. Lesieur, *The Scanlon Plan, A Frontier in Labor-Management Cooperation* (New York: John Wiley and Sons, 1958). For an illuminating discussion of the historical experience, see William Gomberg, "Special Study Committees," in *Frontiers of Collective Bargaining*, John T. Dunlop and Neil W. Chamberlain, eds. (New York: Harper and Row, 1967), pp. 235–51.

4. Arthur W. Kornhauser, *Mental Health of the Industrial Worker, A Detroit Study* (New York: John Wiley and Sons, 1965), p. 291.

5. See for instance *National Steamfitter Pipefitter Apprenticeship Standards*, Mechanical Contractors Association of America and the United Association of Journeymen and Apprentices of the Plumbing and Pipe Fitting Industry of the United States and Canada, 1966.

6. See for instance Theodore W. Schultz, *The Economic Value of Education* (New York: Columbia University Press, 1963).

7. Edward F. Denison, *The Sources of Economic Growth in the United States and the Alternatives Before Us*, Supplementary Paper No. 13, published by the Committee for Economic Development, January 1962, p. 267. Also see Edward F. Denison, *Why Growth Rates Differ, Postwar Experience in Nine Western Countries* (Washington, D.C.: Brookings Institution, 1967), pp. 296–345.

8. Denis F. Johnston, "Education of Adult Workers in 1975," *Monthly Labor Review*, April 1968, p. 12.

9. Garth Mangum, *MDTA Foundation of Federal Manpower Policy* (Baltimore: Johns Hopkins Press, 1968), pp. 9–10.

10. U.S. Department of Labor, "Pilot Program Opens New Opportunities for Steelworkers," release, May 23, 1967.

11. United Association of Journeymen and Apprentices of Plumbing and Pipe Fitting Industry of the United States and Canada and the National Constructors Association, *International Training Fund, Facing the Craft Challenges of Tomorrow*, 1968.

12. International Typographical Union, *Know-How as to Modern Printing*, Colorado Springs, Colorado.

   Fotosetter operation and mockup—For linecasting machine operators only, since time does not permit keyboard training. Course includes Fotosetter operation and markup of copy; darkroom procedure; handling of correction devices; maintenance. One week devoted to training in basic paste makeup.

Teletypesetter—Students taking this course must already have touch typing and have a speed of 40 words per minute. Course includes instruction on the proper keyboard manipulation, setting up of the TTS for various operations and practice on the different styles of typesetting required for newspaper and book and job work.

Linofilm maintenance—Students taking this advanced course must have completed the basic I.T.U. course in electricity and electronics in their local, or must have electronic knowledge sufficient to pass a Training Center exam. This course covers all phases of testing, repair, and maintenance of the Linofilm, switching logic, and electronic circuitry as applied to digital computations. Also see *Annual Reports of Officers and Proceedings of 109th Convention of the International Typographical Union* (Colorado Springs: September 2–8, 1967), pp. 9s–10s.

13. Garth L. Mangum, *Reorientating Vocational Education* (Washington, D.C.: National Manpower Policy Task Force, May 1968).

14. For a discussion see Neil W. Chamberlain, "Manpower Planning," in *Frontiers of Collective Bargaining, op. cit.,* pp. 211–32.

15. "Scholarship Plan Offered by Union," *The New York Times,* December 24, 1965, pp. 1, 18.

16. Stanley Levy, "Push for Aid in Education, Unions Urged," *Pittsburgh Press,* November 27, 1967, p. 16.

17. The quotations in this paragraph are from Georges Friedmann in *Industrial Society, The Emergence of the Human Problems of Automation,* Harold L. Sheppard, ed. (Glencoe: The Free Press, 1955), pp. 153, 365.

18. See Louis E. Davis, "The Design of Jobs," *Industrial Relations, A Journal of Economy and Society,* October 1966, pp. 21–45.

19. Frederick I. Herzberg and others, *The Motivation to Work* (New York: John Wiley and Sons, 1959); Herzberg, *Work and the Nature of Man* (Cleveland: World Publishing, 1966).

20. Fred K. Foulkes, "Meaningful Work: A Study of Company Programs" (unpublished Ph.D. thesis, Graduate School of Business Administration, Harvard University, 1967).

Chapter 13

1. Dave Beck, Address at the Closing Session of the First Annual Meeting, Central States Conference of Teamsters, Chicago, Illinois, April 26, 1954.

2. Walter Reuther, *The Corporation and the Union,* one of a series of

interviews on the American character (Santa Barbara: Center for the Study of Democratic Institutions, 1962).

3. See generally James B. Kennedy, *Beneficiary Features of American Trade Unions* (Baltimore: Johns Hopkins Press, 1908).

4. See generally Richard H. Boeckel, *Labor's Money* (New York: Harcourt, Brace, 1923).

5. Industrial Relations Section, Department of Economic and Social Institutions, Princeton University, *The Labor Banking Movement in the United States* (Princeton: Princeton University Press, 1929), p. 262.

6. Fred Schmidt, "Recreational Indifference: An Inquiry into the Failure of Workers to Utilize Negotiated Recreational Facilities" (Institute of Industrial Relations, University of California at Los Angeles, 1965) (unpublished).

7. See generally Joseph W. Garbarino, *Health Plans and Collective Bargaining* (Berkeley: University of California Press, 1960); Raymond Munts, *Bargaining for Health* (Madison: University of Wisconsin Press, 1967); and Ray E. Trussell, *The Quantity, Quality and Costs of Medical and Hospital Care Secured by a Sample of Teamster Families in the New York Area* (New York: School of Public Health and Administrative Medicine, Columbia University, 1962); and *Report of the Governor's Committee on Hospital Costs*, State of New York, Marion B. Folsom, Chairman, 1966.

8. Garbarino, *op. cit.*, p. 62.

9. *Ibid.*, p. 57.

10. Munts, *op. cit.*, pp. 43–44.

11. Garbarino, *op. cit.*, p. 84.

12. See generally A. H. Raskin, "Labor's Welfare State: The New York Electrical Workers," *Atlantic Monthly*, April 1963, pp. 37 *et seq.*; and Arnold M. Rose, *Union Solidarity, the Internal Cohesion of a Labor Union* (Minneapolis: University of Minnesota Press, 1952).

13. Joint Industry Board of the Electrical Industry, *Annual Report*, 1967.

14. Rose, *op. cit.*, p. 142.

15. *Ibid.*, pp. 52–53.

Chapter 14

1. Paul F. Brissenden, *The I.W.W., A Study of American Syndicalism* (New York: Columbia University Press, 1920), p. 351.

2. Gerald Grob, *Workers and Utopia* (Evanston: Northwestern University Press, 1961), p. 79.

3. Samuel Gompers, "Voluntary Social Insurance vs. Compulsory," *American Federationist*, May 1916, p. 333.

4. John P. Frey, statement recorded in *AFL Convention Proceedings*, Washington, D.C., 1932, p. 342.

5. Louise Overacker, "Labor's Political Contributions," *Political Science Quarterly*, March 1939, p. 58.

6. Harry M. Scoble, "Organized Labor in Electoral Politics: Some Questions for the Discipline," *Western Political Quarterly*, September 1963, pp. 676–77, 679–80, 684.

7. Houston I. Flournoy, "The Liberal Party in New York State" (unpublished Ph.D. thesis, Columbia University, 1956).

8. On party identification among voters generally, see Angus Campbell, Philip E. Converse, Warren E. Miller, and Donald E. Stokes, *The American Voter* (New York: John Wiley and Sons, 1960), p. 148, where the authors report that a majority of voters have never crossed party lines in Presidential elections.

9. Fay Calkins, *The CIO and the Democratic Party* (Chicago: University of Chicago Press, 1952), pp. 112–46.

10. Edward Banfield and James Q. Wilson, *City Politics* (Cambridge: Harvard University Press and M.I.T. Press, 1963), p. 287.

11. Opinion Research Corporation 12th Annual Survey, March 9, 1956.

12. For an account of Hall's political program, see Jerry Landauer, "Seafarers' Union Builds Fund Aimed at Winning Friends in Congress," *Wall Street Journal*, December 29, 1967, pp. 1, 8.

13. Sar Levitan, "Union Lobbyists' Contributions to Tough Labor Legislation," *Labor Law Journal*, October 1959, pp. 677–78; and Alan K. McAdams, *Power and Politics in Labor Legislation* (New York: Columbia University Press, 1964).

14. Frank Bonilla, "When is Petition 'Pressure'?" *Public Opinion Quarterly*, Spring 1956, pp. 39, 46.

15. Melvin A. Kahn, "Labor and the Law-Making Process: The Case of Indiana" (unpublished Ph.D. thesis, Indiana University, 1964).

16. Raymond A. Bauer, Ithiel de Sola Pool, and Lewis Anthony Dexter, *American Business and Public Policy* (New York: Atherton Press, 1963), p. 324. Typical of the findings of these authors is the statement that ". . . lobbies were on the whole poorly financed, ill-managed, and out of contact with Congress and at best only marginally effective in supporting tendencies and measures which already had behind them considerable Congressional impetus from other sources."

17. Donald E. Stokes, "Voting Research and the Labor Vote," in *Labor and American Politics*, Charles M. Rehmus and Doris B.

McLaughlin, eds. (Ann Arbor: The University of Michigan Press, 1967), p. 389.

18. A 1966 poll of the Opinion Research Corporation (see above, Chapter 1); and John F. Lane, "Analysis of the Federal Law Governing Political Contributions by Labor Unions," *Labor Law Journal*, October 1958, p. 728.

19. See generally Alexander Heard, *The Costs of Democracy* (Chapel Hill: University of North Carolina Press, 1962), especially pp. 20 *et seq.*

20. *Ibid.*

21. Scoble, *op. cit.*, p. 675.

22. Heard, *op. cit.*, p. 35.

23. Nicholas A. Masters, "The Organized Labor Bureaucracy as a Base of Support for the Democratic Party," *Law and Contemporary Problems*, Spring 1962, p. 259.

24. *Ibid.*

25. Mary Goddard Zon, "Labor in Politics," *Law and Contemporary Problems*, Spring 1962, p. 249.

26. Masters, *loc. cit.*

27. Daniel Katz and Samuel J. Eldersveld, "The Impact of Local Party Activity upon the Electorate," *Public Opinion Quarterly*, Spring 1961, p. 11.

28. Glenn W. Miller and Stephen B. Ware, "Organized Labor in the Political Process: A Case Study of the Right-to-Work Campaign in Ohio," in *Labor and American Politics, op. cit.*, pp. 317–28.

29. David R. Jones, "Poll Finds Most Members Support Labor Policies," *The New York Times*, July 16, 1967, p. 17.

30. Campbell, Converse, Miller, and Stokes, *op. cit.*, p. 306.

31. *Ibid.*, pp. 219–332.

32. *Ibid.*, pp. 306–08.

33. *Ibid.*, pp. 313–16.

34. *Ibid.*, p. 312.

35. *Ibid.*, pp. 324–25.

36. *Ibid.*, pp. 321–22.

37. Seymour M. Lipset, *Political Man: The Social Bases of Politics* (Garden City: Anchor Books, 1963), pp. 183–230.

38. John F. Lane, *Political Life: Why People Get Involved in Politics* (Glencoe: The Free Press, 1959), pp. 48–49.

39. Masters, *op. cit.*, p. 259.

40. Richard M. Scammon, "Electoral Participation," *The Annals of the American Academy of Political and Social Science*, May 1967, p. 60. Also see "Gallup Finds 15 Million Sat Out Election," *The New York Times*, December 11, 1968, p. 29.

41. Stanley Kelley, Jr., Richard E. Ayres, and William G. Bowen,

"Registration and Voting: Putting First Things First," *American Political Science Review,* June 1967, p. 359.

Chapter 15

1. See generally Kenneth E. Gray and J. David Greenstone, "Organized Labor in City Politics," in *Urban Government,* Edward C. Banfield, ed. (Glencoe: The Free Press, 1961), pp. 368–78; J. David Greenstone, *Labor in American Politics* (New York: Alfred A. Knopf, 1969).
2. Alan Altshuler, *A Report on City Politics in St. Paul; A Report on Politics in Minneapolis* (Cambridge: Joint Center for Urban Studies, 1959) (mimeographed).
3. These figures were derived with the help of Professor Leo Troy from national surveys undertaken by the Survey Research Center at the University of Michigan.
4. See "John Herling's Labor Letter," *Washington Daily News,* July 15, 1967.
5. *Report of the National Advisory Commission on Civil Disorders* (New York: Bantam Books, 1968), Chapter 16, "The Future of Cities."
6. Letter of November 19, 1968, from George A. Shea, Director, Labor Participation Department, United Community Funds and Councils of America Incorporated, to J. G. Dustan.
7. Telephone conversation between Kenneth Kramer, National Headquarters, American Red Cross, and J. G. Dustan on December 19, 1968.
8. Letter of November 15, 1968, from George C. Freeman, Director, Local Council Finance, Boy Scouts of America, to J. G. Dustan.
9. Telephone conversation between Leo Perlis, Director, Community Services Department, American Federation of Labor and Congress of Industrial Organizations, and J. G. Dustan on November 14, 1968.
10. Leo Perlis, "Union and Community Services," in *The House of Labor,* J. B. S. Hardman and Maurice F. Neufeld, eds. (New York: Prentice-Hall, 1951), p. 334.
11. Letter of October 7, 1968, from Leo Perlis, Director, Community Services Department, American Federation of Labor and Congress of Industrial Organizations, to J. G. Dustan.
12. William H. Form and Warren L. Sauer, "Labor and Community Influentials: A Comparative Study of Partnership in Imagery," *Industrial and Labor Relations Review,* October 1963, pp. 3–19.

13. James R. Hudson, "Power with Low Prestige: A Study of Unions in a Dependent Community" (unpublished Ph.D. thesis, University of Michigan, 1965); and Donald E. Wray, "The Community and Labor-Management Relations," in *Labor Management Relations in Illini City,* Vol. I, Milton Derber, coordinator (Urbana: Institute of Labor and Industrial Relations, University of Illinois, 1953).
14. James B. McKee, "Status and Power in the Industrial Community: A Comment on Drucker's Thesis," *American Journal of Sociology,* January 1953, p. 369.
15. "The Urban Crisis: An Analysis, an Answer," *The American Federationist,* October 1967, pp. 1–8.
16. See Julius F. Rothman, "A Look at the War on Poverty," *The American Federationist,* November 1967, pp. 1–8.
17. "Community Unions, A Talk with Jack Conway," *Center Diary #18* (Santa Barbara: Center for the Study of Democratic Institutions, May 6, 1967), pp. 20–24.
18. Editorial, *Solidarity,* August 1967.
19. Melvin King, quoted in Alan H. Sheehan, "Labor Criticized on Black Poor," *Boston Globe,* June 17, 1968, p. 8.

Chapter 16

1. Editorial, "Organized Labor's Ten Years Together," *The New Republic,* December 11, 1965, pp. 7–8.
2. C. Wright Mills, *The New Men of Power—America's Labor Leaders* (New York: Harcourt, Brace, 1948), p. 291.
3. A. H. Raskin, "The Obsolescent Unions," *Commentary,* July 1963, pp. 18, 25.
4. Sidney Lens, *The Crisis of American Labor* (New York: Sagamore Press, 1959), p. 280.
5. Mills, *op. cit.,* p. 236.

Index

ABOUT THE AUTHORS

DEREK C. BOK, President of Harvard University, has been Dean of the Harvard Law School and an arbitrator and consultant to the Department of Labor. He is the author of *Labor Law* (with Archibald Cox) and several reports to the President's Committee on Labor-Management Policy.

JOHN T. DUNLOP is a professor of law at the Harvard Law School. A member of the American Academy of Arts and Sciences, he has written *Wage Determination Under Trade Unions* and *Cost Behavior and Price Policy;* co-authored *Collective Bargaining: Principles and Cases* and *Labor Productivity;* and edited *Economic Growth in the United States* and *Potentials of the American Economy.*